PHILOSOPHY COMES TO DINNER

Everyone is talking about food. Chefs are celebrities. "Locavore" and "freegan" have earned spots in the dictionary. Popular books and films about food production and consumption are exposing the unintended consequences of the standard American diet. Questions about the principles and values that ought to guide decisions about dinner have become urgent for moral, ecological, and health-related reasons. In *Philosophy Comes to Dinner*, eighteen philosophers—some leading voices, some inspiring new ones—join the conversation, and consider issues ranging from the sustainability of modern agriculture, to consumer complicity in animal exploitation, to the pros and cons of alternative diets.

Andrew Chignell is associate professor of philosophy at Cornell University. His research and teaching is focused mainly on Kant and other early modern philosophers. He is also co-instructor of "The Ethics of Eating," a massive online open course (MOOC) at edX.org.

Terence Cuneo is the Marsh Professor of Intellectual and Moral Philosophy at the University of Vermont. He is the author of *The Normative Web* (2007), *Speech and Morality* (2014), and *Ritualized Faith* (2016).

Matthew C. Halteman is associate professor of philosophy at Calvin College and a fellow in the Oxford Centre for Animal Ethics. He is the author of *Compassionate Eating as Care of Creation* (2008).

PHILOSOPHY COMES TO DINNER

Arguments about the Ethics of Eating

*Edited by Andrew Chignell, Terence Cuneo,
and Matthew C. Halteman*

Routledge
Taylor & Francis Group

NEW YORK AND LONDON

First published 2016
by Routledge
711 Third Avenue, New York, NY 10017

and by Routledge
2 Park Square, Milton Park, Abingdon, Oxon, OX14 4RN

Routledge is an imprint of the Taylor & Francis Group, an informa business

Library of Congress Cataloging-in-Publication Data
Philosophy comes to dinner : arguments on the ethics of eating / edited
    by Andrew Chignell, Terence Cuneo, and Matthew C. Halteman.
        pages cm
    1. Food—Moral and ethical aspects.   2. Food habits.   3. Food
preferences.   4. Dinners and dining—Moral and ethical aspects.
I. Chignell, Andrew, 1973– editor.
    TX357.P525 2015
    394.1'2—dc23
    2015017814

ISBN: 978-0-415-80682-4 (hbk)
ISBN: 978-0-415-80683-1 (pbk)
ISBN: 978-0-203-15441-0 (ebk)

Typeset in Bembo
by Apex CoVantage, LLC

We dedicate this volume to Gus Halteman, bulldog and Michigan native, now going twelve years and strong on a diet of vegan kibble and carrots. In addition to being loved for his stout efforts to best Terence at tug-of-war, and his proclivity for invading Andrew's personal space on road trips, he is the dog who first invited Matt to see animals as unique individuals. As such, he is the one who got the ball rolling on these issues for all three of us. Without him, this book may not have come to be.

Photo by Emily Schreur

CONTENTS

ABOUT THE CONTRIBUTORS

Anne Barnhill is assistant professor of medical ethics and health policy at the University of Pennsylvania. She is a philosopher and bioethicist who writes about food ethics, public health ethics, the ethics of influence, and the ethics of obesity prevention, among other topics.

Mark Bryant Budolfson is assistant professor of philosophy at the University of Vermont. He often works at the interface of ethics and public policy, especially on collective action problems such as climate change and other dilemmas that arise in connection with common resources and public goods.

Andrew Chignell is associate professor of philosophy at Cornell University. His research and teaching is focused mainly on Kant and other early modern philosophers. He is also co-instructor of "The Ethics of Eating," a massive online open course (MOOC) at edX.org.

Terence Cuneo is the Marsh Professor of Intellectual and Moral Philosophy at the University of Vermont. He is the author of *The Normative Web* (2007), *Speech and Morality* (2014), and *Ritualized Faith* (2016).

Tyler Doggett is associate professor of philosophy at the University of Vermont. He is co-editor of the *Oxford Handbook of Food Ethics*.

Andy Egan is professor of philosophy at Rutgers University.

Matthew C. Halteman is associate professor of philosophy at Calvin College and a fellow at the Oxford Centre for Animal Ethics. He is the author of *Compassionate Eating as Care of Creation*.

Elizabeth Harman is associate professor of philosophy and human values at Princeton University.

Dan Hooley is a doctoral candidate in philosophy at the University of Toronto and an associate fellow at the Oxford Centre for Animal Ethics. His research centers on the political status of nonhuman animals and their place in our legal and political institutions.

David M. Kaplan is associate professor in the Department of Philosophy and Religion at the University of North Texas. He is editor of *The Philosophy of Food* (2012) and co-editor with Paul B. Thompson of the *Encyclopedia of Food and Agricultural Ethics* (2014).

Benjamin J. Bruxvoort Lipscomb lives in rural western New York, where he and his family keep a small flock of chickens and keep trying to raise eggplants. He teaches philosophy (specializing in ethics and the history of the modern era) at Houghton College.

Adrienne M. Martin is the Akshata Murty '02 and Rishi Sunak Professor of Philosophy, Politics, and Economics and George R. Roberts Fellow at Claremont McKenna College. She teaches and publishes on a range of subjects in philosophical ethics and moral psychology.

Jeff McMahan is White's Professor of Moral Philosophy at the University of Oxford. He is the author of *The Ethics of Killing: Problems at the Margins of Life* (2002) and *Killing in War* (2009).

Tristram McPherson teaches at The Ohio State University. His work focuses on ethics and its methodological, semantic, and metaphysical foundations.

Nathan Nobis teaches philosophy at Morehouse College in Atlanta, Georgia. His interests include practical ethics, especially bioethics, as well as philosophical perspectives on psychotherapy and family law.

Christina Van Dyke is professor of philosophy at Calvin College and specializes in medieval philosophy and the philosophy of gender. She teaches and writes about Thomas Aquinas, mysticism, perfect happiness in the afterlife, and the ethics of eating.

Ted A. Warfield is professor of philosophy at the University of Notre Dame. He works in a variety of areas, including epistemology, philosophy of action, and philosophy of mind.

Megan Halteman Zwart is assistant professor of philosophy at Saint Mary's College, Notre Dame, Indiana. Her teaching and research interests include the ethics of eating, Hellenistic philosophy, and contemporary approaches to philosophy as a way of life.

INTRODUCTION

Matthew C. Halteman, Terence Cuneo,
and Andrew Chignell

Setting the Table

Everyone is talking about food. Chefs and food critics have become celebrities. "Locavore" has earned a spot in the dictionary. Ex-presidents, daytime talk-show icons, and pop music moguls are experimenting with veganism. Restaurants and grocery stores peddle a bewildering array of new foodstuffs touted as organic, farm-to-table, humane-certified, and cruelty-free. To say that food production and consumption are increasingly in the public eye is to understate the point.

At the same time, an explosion of popular books,[1] documentary films,[2] and development and government reports[3] has raised public consciousness about the less savory consequences of our industrial food system and the dietary habits to which it has given rise. Although it is by no means the only problem, these critics often target industrial *animal* production as particularly troublesome. Feeding the roughly fifty billion land animals consumed every year requires huge amounts of oil, land, and water to grow grain, and the subsidization of this process threatens subsistence farming in the Global South and thus food security for billions.[4] Raising these animals in confinement systems (or CAFOs: concentrated animal feeding operations) confronts us with unprecedented concentrations of ecologically threatening liquid manure and greenhouse gasses, the specter of epidemic disease such as swine and bird flu, environmentally compromised and economically depressed rural communities, and degraded animal welfare.[5] Processing this many animals at a profit means dangerous and often exploitative working conditions for a disproportionately minority workforce.[6] And eating this many animals is strongly correlated with the onset of preventable diseases that are estimated to cost $314 billion a year for interventional medicine.[7] To add insult (and irony) to injury, these so-called diseases of affluence disproportionately affect economically disadvantaged people, especially people of color. Communities of color, for instance, often lack open access to nutritious foods, both in rural areas where many farmers of color have been driven out of business by decades of governmental loan discrimination favoring industrialized farms, and in urban areas where highly processed foods are cheap and abundant but fresh produce is often scarce, particularly in poor neighborhoods.[8]

These and other negative consequences of the way we produce our food, unintended though they may be, have become so serious on so many fronts that they are now virtually impossible to ignore. Places where one could previously count on enjoying blissful unawareness of these problems, such as university cafeterias in Texas[9] and buffets in Las Vegas casinos,[10] are turning over a new leaf. Key leaders in conservative Christian circles—people one might expect to be deeply skeptical of animal advocacy—are spearheading efforts to galvanize evangelicals against animal exploitation in farming.[11] Even the dietary advice guidelines emanating from the US Office of Disease Prevention and Health Promotion—guidelines that have a long history of being shaped by the influence of the agriculture industry over government[12]—are shifting dramatically away from endorsing the animal-based standard American diet toward a more plant-based approach.[13]

That our food system is compromised in a wide variety of morally and practically significant ways is thus increasingly taken for granted by experts and the general public alike, even in some of the quarters that one might think would be among the most resistant to disrupting the food status quo. But if there is now broad agreement that our eating habits and the industrial food system that supports them require serious overhaul, there is far less agreement about exactly what our food future should look like. The question of which principles ought to guide our decisions about how to produce, purchase, consume, and dispose of food has become urgent—for moral, ecological, cultural, economic, and health-related reasons.

Philosophy Comes to Dinner?

It should go without saying that a set of problems as complex and multifaceted as those set before us by the food we eat cannot be solved from the philosopher's armchair. Indeed, a glance at the breathtaking disciplinary diversity of the faculty profiles at any cutting-edge food studies program[14] underscores both the insufficiency of any single discipline's expertise to address these issues satisfactorily and the necessity of working together, not just in education, but across all institutional sectors that have a stake in addressing these problems (e.g., agriculture, business, government, nonprofit, and religion).[15]

We are acutely aware of this fact, and we chose our title—*Philosophy Comes to Dinner: Arguments about the Ethics of Eating*—with an awareness of our discipline's humble standing with respect to these huge problems. The image of philosophy "coming to dinner" is meant to highlight the fact that our discipline is, figuratively, just one guest around a very crowded table of accomplished and insightful others, many of whom will play a larger role than we can hope to play in transforming our food system. The subtitle—*Arguments about the Ethics of Eating*—indicates that our contribution to the conversation aims, for the most part, to offer subtle, careful, and hopefully charitable efforts to clarify some of the main ethical issues raised by the way we eat, and to arrive at some conclusions (tentative as they may be).

People who aren't professional philosophers (and even some who are) might wonder about our credentials for this job. After all, though the standard repertoire of topics that philosophers address is diverse (including everything from the existence of God to the nature of material objects), it has not, until recently, included the topic of food.[16] And when a topic lies at the edges of the historical and contemporary philosophical discussion, it is tempting to conclude that it is philosophically unimportant or uninteresting.

One aim of this book is to show, on the contrary, that arguments about food are of great philosophical interest, and that the conclusions of these arguments will matter to many of us. For example: In contemplating how we should respond to the food system crisis described above, many of us will wonder whether it makes sense to eat mostly organic as opposed to nonorganic produce, whether we should eat locally produced food as opposed to food produced thousands of miles away, and whether the lack of fresh fruits and vegetables in our children's school cafeterias should be a matter of serious concern. There are also, as mentioned earlier, pressing practical questions about whether we should eat animals and animal products. Some readers of this book may be or have tried to be vegetarian or vegan. They will be keenly aware of how convictions about the ethical propriety of eating animals affect eating, shopping, restaurant-going habits, and even the character of their relationships with family and friends.

Many of the issues that interest us regarding food, then, are ethical, and thus philosophical. The chapters in this volume are motivated by three main convictions about these issues:

(1) The first is that they deserve careful and sustained reflection, not just from philosophers, but from almost everyone who enjoys food autonomy—the freedom to make choices about how and what to eat.[17] We need to be aware that there are ethical dimensions of food production and consumption; we also need to think hard and well about how food is produced, whether certain foods should be purchased or eaten, and how we should assess our own eating practices (and those of others).

(2) The second conviction is that philosophers can aid us in thinking carefully about these ethical issues, and help us to avoid mistaken ways of characterizing them. By bringing to bear different ethical views on these issues, we should be able both to see the range of positions available and to judge which of these positions are most defensible. Moreover, as David Fraser

points out, philosophers (and humanists generally) are typically not stake-holders in these debates—they don't stand to gain or lose, get elected, hired or fired, depending on the perspective they take on the ethics of eating. In Fraser's words,

> academic moral philosophers could be the trustworthy sources of information and analysis that are needed to guide the public through the rhetorical claims and counterclaims of the advocacy writers. Philosophers are . . . educated in ethics, mandated to conduct and publish research, free from the short deadlines of commercial journalism, and free from the industry-funded research contracts that put many scientists into conflicts of interest when they are asked to comment on industry practices.[18]

(3) The third conviction is that what philosophers say about these things some-times needs to be addressed and accessible to a wide audience. Unlike, say, conversations regarding the nature of material objects or the refutation of external-world skepticism, which are hardly of widespread interest, ethical issues regarding food are (or should be). Some philosophical writing about food should be sensitive to this fact if philosophy aspires to make a concrete contribution to the change it hopes to see in the world.

In light of these three convictions, our hope is that the audience for this book will include just about anyone who has an interest in these topics. Maybe you're a food ethicist or a food studies researcher; we hope that experts like you find the book engaging. But maybe you're a student in an ethics class, or a foodie with an appetite for intellectual stimulation, or an activist seeking strategies of persua-sion. Maybe you're a chef or restaurateur looking for insight into the motivations of a new generation of food consumers, or a professional philosopher who cares about the ethics of eating but hasn't yet had the occasion to delve seriously into the topic. Whoever you are, we are glad that you picked up this book and hope that our efforts to balance rigor with accessibility provide you with a challeng-ing, edifying read.

One advantage of producing a volume whose topic lies outside the philo-sophical mainstream is that there is less pressure to cover the core themes and the main figures and then try to say new things about them. Instead, there is the liberty to raise new questions, to address standing questions from fresh angles, and more generally to take up issues that seem particularly relevant or important. You will find, then, that this book does not aspire to be encyclopedic or to cover the full range of issues that one might expect a book on the ethics of eating to address. Instead, the strategy that we have taken as editors has been to approach a diverse group of philosophers—the vast majority of whom has interests in food ethics but has not published in this area—and ask them to write on themes that they find intriguing. The fact that a good number of our authors are not applied ethicists by trade—or ethicists of any sort—is a feature of the book that excites us. We hope that, as these urgent issues become increasingly important in mainstream discussion, more and more philosophers—regardless of their areas of specialization—will turn their time and talents to teaching and writing on the ethics of eating.

Our editorial approach, then, has been more like inviting a bunch of great cooks to a potluck in anticipation of tasting some delicious surprises than like attempting to orchestrate an all-inclusive smorgasbord. But we are nonetheless pleased with the breadth of coverage that our authors brought to the table. Professors looking to provide students with examples of how to apply deontological (chapters 1 and 14), virtue ethical (chapters 2 and 7), consequentialist (chapters 8, 9, 10, 11, and 14), and feminist (chapter 2) perspectives to pressing contemporary problems have plenty of options. Foodies attempting to discern whether to pack hoop-raised pork or jack-fruit into their wicker picnic hampers have options too; there are multiple slants on conscientious omnivorism (chapters 1–3 and 9) that give herbivores plenty to chew on, and a couple defenses of veganism to give flesh-eaters pause (chapters 4 and 5). There is advice to help you imagine your way into new dietary ideals and motivate you to live up to them (chapter 7), and there is advice to help you fail better when falling short of your ideals is inevitable (chapter 6).

As you'll see from the table of contents, we've served up this varied fare in two main courses. The chapters in part I focus on dietary ideals: they either articulate and defend a specific ideal (e.g., agrarianism, conscientious omnivorism, veganism) or provide practical instruction on how to live out such ideals. The chapters in part II focus on some of the puzzling questions raised by reflection on the ethics of eating, and either criticize popular answers from a fresh perspective ("Is veganism really always best in a system this empirically complex?") or clarify key concepts or problems that figure into our ethical decision-making about food ("What is consumer complicity in a commercial industry's wrongdoing and under what conditions does it obtain?"). A few central themes emerge: We have already mentioned "the animal question" above, but there is also a related question, discussed by many of our authors, about whether ethical objections to industrial animal agriculture, say, can underwrite the conclusion that we ought not to consume the products of that system (chapters 1, 4–6, and 8–11). Other topics range from the pros and cons of "eating local" (chapter 13) and consuming artificial ingredients (chapter 14), to the question of whether the moral reasons that motivate vegetarianism could also motivate our reducing or ultimately eliminating predation in the wild, insofar as that were to become practicable (chapter 15).

We have briefly articulated some reasons for believing that it is important to think philosophically about food and what, very broadly, you can expect from the chapters that follow. We have also gestured at why these chapters might be interesting to academic and general audiences alike, and how they might frame these issues in ways that that you would probably not find in an op-ed page of the *New York Times*. At this point in the typical collection of academic papers, it would fall upon the editors to summarize the contents of the chapters that follow. We decided to take a different approach, one that is in the spirit of this volume and meshes nicely with its title. The approach is to let the authors speak for themselves, offering a brief, informal summary of their chapters and some insight into why they wrote on the topic they chose.

So, picture yourself at a dinner party with a group of philosophers. And suppose that you are intrigued enough by the table banter to ask about what they're up to in their latest work. If the contributors to this book happened to be at the table, here are the answers you would receive.

THE MENU

Part I: Dietary Ideals

Chapter 1: Conscientious Omnivorism

Terence Cuneo

Where I live (in Vermont), it is common to find local farmers selling beef, chicken, pork, and lamb at farmers' markets. The farmers raise these animals in free-range conditions without pumping them full of antibiotics. These farmers clearly believe that their products are a more ethical alternative to the factory-farmed meat that is sold at the local grocery market. My chapter, "Conscientious Omnivorism," is an attempt to puzzle through the position that these farmers and their patrons seem to endorse, namely, that: (1) being a consumer of factory-farmed meat is ethically wrong; and (2) being a consumer of so-called family-farmed meat is ethically permissible. This position I call "conscientious omnivorism." I'm interested in knowing whether it is defensible.

In my chapter, I offer an argument for the conclusion that being a consumer of factory-farmed meat is morally problematic. This argument develops the idea that being a consumer of such meat has considerable symbolic ethical disvalue. I doubt this is the only reason why being a consumer of factory-farmed meat is morally problematic, but I think it is one that deserves development. I then explore the issue of whether the reasons I offer for holding that being a consumer of factory-farmed meat is morally problematic generalize to the case of being a consumer of family-farmed meat. I offer an argument that these reasons do not generalize. I contend that while there are strong reasons not to be a consumer of any sort of meat, there is also reason to hold that being a consumer of family-farmed meat is ethically permissible. I offer this argument in an exploratory spirit. I am not sure that it is correct.

Chapter 2: Manly Meat and Gendered Eating: Correcting Imbalance and Seeking Virtue

Christina Van Dyke

Eating is a gendered act. Men are portrayed as constantly hungry and ready to eat, women as having small appetites that are satisfied with fruits, vegetables, and diet drinks. Furthermore, while men are encouraged to indulge and even take pride in their appetites (for food, sex, and power), women are taught to tightly repress their hunger, focusing instead on satisfying the appetites of others. Food is also gendered, with meat, in particular, construed as "male" food. So strong is the connection of meat with men and male power that some feminist theorists argue that rejecting the consumption of animals and animal products constitutes a vital step in overcoming patriarchal structures and their linked environmental injustices.

I agree that meat consumption is tied to the systematic objectification of women and nonhuman animals. Nevertheless, I worry that presenting veganism as "the" moral ideal might reinforce rather than alleviate the current patterns of gendered eating. In this chapter, I advocate a feminist account of ethical eating that treats dietary choices as moral choices insofar as they form a vital part of our relationships to ourselves and to others. I argue that we should think of such choices in Aristotelian terms as a mean *relative to us*—falling on a continuum between the wrong of doing injustice to ourselves and the wrong of doing injustice to others. What is moral for individuals to eat is not a fixed ideal, but rather depends on particulars of their physiological, psychological, economic, cultural, and relational situations.

Chapter 3: "Eat Responsibly": Agrarianism and Meat

Benjamin J. Bruxvoort Lipscomb

We have two major food movements in contemporary Western society: vegetarianism/veganism and agrarianism/locavorism. Their concerns overlap, but they haven't had much to say about one another. I ask what contemporary agrarians might or ought to say about animal agriculture and meat eating, drawing especially on the work of Wendell Berry. Berry notes that we only live by using, even consuming, other creatures. The question, then, is how to use responsibly—how to use in a way that doesn't degrade or exhaust what we use. Berry offers two necessary conditions for responsible use: intimacy of acquaintance with what you're using, and mutual dependency (recognized on your part) between you and what you're using. The first condition, limiting the scale at which you operate, enables you to know what you're doing; the second—which at its best involves affection—motivates you to act responsibly.

I spend half my chapter elaborating this, and the other half applying it to animal agriculture. I argue that it is possible, applying Berry's conditions, to defend raising animals for meat. It depends, though, on the species we're talking about, and the characteristic shape and potentialities of the animals' lives. Moreover, responsible animal agriculture needs to be radically different from most animal agriculture in the contemporary West: limited in scale, in symbiosis with plant agriculture, and producing meat that is an enhancement to people's diets, not the heart of it. I suggest in closing that the most important challenge from agrarians to vegetarians and vegans stems from agrarianism's more ecological vision.

Chapter 4: Why I Am a Vegan (and You Should Be One Too)

Tristram McPherson

Many people become vegan after coming to understand the horrifying suffering inflicted on animals by the industry that provides us with meat and other animal products. I argue that these people show ethical insight: because of the way animals are treated, we *should* become vegan.

My chapter starts by arguing that it is wrong to make animals suffer. You might think: Even if this is true, it's got to be *worse* to make a person suffer. I agree. I argue that the way that suffering feels explains why inflicting suffering is wrong, but facts about our distinctive capacities explain why it is generally worse to inflict suffering on us than on animals. I then argue that it is wrong to kill an animal when doing so deprives the animal of a worthwhile future. Again, I grant that it is usually worse to kill a person, both because we typically have richer futures than animals and for independent reasons. Because killing animals and causing them to suffer is wrong, the animal industry is engaged in wrongdoing on a massive scale.

But, you might wonder, why does this mean that *you* should not eat meat? After all, when you order the veal cutlet, the calf is already dead, and ordering the veggie burger instead won't bring it back! I argue that it is wrong to cooperate with wrongdoers in order to enjoy the fruits of their wrongful labor. Because animal industries are wrongdoers on a massive scale, this principle entails that consuming animal products is usually wrong.

Chapter 5: A Moral Argument for Veganism

Dan Hooley and Nathan Nobis

We offer a relatively simple and straightforward argument that each of us ought to be vegan. We don't defend this position by appealing to "animal rights" or the view that animals and humans are "moral equals." Rather, we argue that animal agriculture causes serious harms to other animals (such as pain, suffering and death) and these harms are *morally unjustified* or caused *for no good reason*. This is true for both "factory farming" and smaller, so-called humane farms. We argue that attempts to justify these harms don't succeed, and conclude that raising and killing animals for food is wrong.

In the second part of our chapter we explain how this argument relates to the choices of individuals to buy and consume animal products. Since most people don't raise and kill animals themselves, the argument above doesn't *directly* address most individuals' daily choices. To address this concern, we offer a plausible, general moral principle that describes when consumers should not purchase or consume a product: Most simply, we should not support those who act wrongly by seriously harming others, provided we can safely and easily avoid doing so. Since, for most people, it *is* safe and relatively easy not to support those who do wrong by raising and killing animals for food, we should not buy or consume animal products.

After making our case that we ought to be vegan, we respond to some of the more challenging objections to our argument. We argue that these objections don't succeed and so, given our previous argument, nearly everyone is morally obligated to eat a vegan diet.

Chapter 6: Non-Ideal Food Choices

Tyler Doggett and Andy Egan

Most of us fall off the wagon sometimes. Some of us never quite get on the wagon. Some of us bounce off it and on it. Some of us pick the wrong wagon, or pick the right wagon and get on the wrong way. There are better and worse ways of doing all these things. You might be a vegan who accidentally eats some chicken. Or you might be a parent who, in a weak moment, binges on his kids' Halloween candy. Our chapter examines some other, more interesting cases. It examines a case in which you become vegetarian even though the argument that moves you gives no support to vegetarianism and, in fact, is just as amenable to omnivorism. It examines a case where you become vegetarian even though your argument supports veganism. It examines a case in which you adopt an eating policy that is much less restrictive than what your own argument supports. And it examines a case in which you adopt an eating policy that is much more restrictive than what your own argument supports.

Chapter 7: Philosophy as Therapy for Recovering (Unrestrained) Omnivores

Matthew C. Halteman and Megan Halteman Zwart

Most of us have had our interest piqued by an argument that suggests we should change something about our behavior: how we act, speak, eat, drive, or purchase. However, even when we suspect that such an argument should persuade us to modify our way of thinking or acting in the world, we may find ourselves unable to undertake the changes required. This is especially true when the arguments in question concern food, because our eating habits are usually supported both by uninvestigated beliefs we don't even realize that we hold, and by deeply entrenched habits we may not know how to break.

In this chapter, we identify two obstacles to concrete moral progress on dietary modifications: a *malaise of imagination*, in which a person has difficulty taking an argument seriously because she can't imagine how it pertains to her; and a *malaise of will*, in which a person who has been convinced by an argument lacks the will to act on his new convictions. We then propose two modes of philosophical inquiry that can provide a kind of therapy for these malaises of imagination and will. In the case of the malaise of imagination, we draw on resources from philosophical hermeneutics (Gadamer) to help individuals excavate, test, and modify hidden assumptions by pursuing new experiences that help broaden the imagination. In the case of the malaise of will, we turn to philosophy as care of the self (Hadot) to help individuals identify habits of thought and action that prevent progress towards new dietary goals, and replace these habits with transformed behaviors.

Part II: Puzzling Questions

Chapter 8: Eating Dead Animals: Meat Eating, Meat Purchasing, and Proving Too Much

Ted A. Warfield

My chapter is a critical discussion of some serious attempts to argue from the general claim that industrial meat processing is morally unacceptable to the specific claim that one or more individual behaviors (meat eating, meat purchasing) is morally wrong. Why would these individual behaviors be wrong? One commonly given answer is that by engaging in these behaviors, one supports industrial meat processing with one's dollars. A persistent concern about these arguments is that they overgeneralize. Suppose, for example, I pay my telephone bill. I know that in doing so I am paying someone who pays someone who pays someone who pays someone who is paid by someone . . . who pays someone to torture chickens. Should I stop paying my telephone bill? It seems not. Or suppose I know that by purchasing chicken meat, I might make a difference to the production of such meat. After all, my behavior might determine whether a threshold or tipping point of sales is reached, which prompts a reduction in the production of chicken meat. Should I stop buying chicken meat for this reason? Not obviously, since the probability that my purchase makes a difference might be vanishingly low. My conclusion is that those who offer arguments that move from the general claim that industrial meat processing is morally unacceptable to the specific claim that meat eating or meat purchasing is morally wrong have more work to do.

Chapter 9: Consumer Ethics, Harm Footprints, and the Empirical Dimensions of Food Choices

Mark Bryant Budolfson

If we want to make the world a better place, including the natural environment, what should we do within the domain of food? Should we adopt vegetarian diets and promote organic and local agriculture? What about our goal of feeding the entire world—is that consistent with a move to organics? I argue that the answers to these questions are more complicated than they initially appear, and I aim to identify and illuminate the most important empirical considerations based on recent research. Among other things, I explain why an "altruistic omnivore" who eats carefully chosen conventional foods, including meats, can have a smaller harm footprint than a typical vegetarian who follows a philosopher like Peter Singer's advice. This raises problems for familiar arguments for vegetarianism, as well as more general arguments in consumer ethics.

Chapter 10: Can We Really Vote with Our Forks? Opportunism and the Threshold Chicken

Andrew Chignell

It seems pretty obvious that at least some aspects of our current industrial food system are morally problematic. Just go on YouTube and do a bit of searching: You'll find videos from inside animal "factory farms" as well as vegetable, fruit, and nut facilities that depict serious mistreatment of the animals and workers involved.

When you see that kind of thing, it's natural to think that purchasing the products of the system that generated them is also morally problematic. That's presumably why activists and reform groups encourage us to boycott the products of objectionable companies or systems. But here's an important empirical fact to consider: The industrial food system is massive, opaque, and full of waste and buffers at almost every stage. As a result, it is deeply insensitive to slight changes in demand. And this, in turn, suggests that your individual decision to purchase its products occasionally (or not to purchase them) will almost certainly have *no* effect on the lives of any of the people or animals involved.

An "opportunist," as I'll use the term here, is someone who cites these facts about the insensitivity of the global food system as reason to think that purchasing its products is *not*—at least not always—morally wrong. In my chapter I take a look at some arguments in favor of such "opportunistic purchasing" and suggest that they are harder to resist than we might expect. In the last section I briefly consider whether an appeal to concepts like "symbolic value" and "collective obligation" can come to the rescue.

Chapter 11: Factory Farming and Consumer Complicity

Adrienne M. Martin

Many people believe there is something bad about purchasing products produced through wrongful means, such as factory-farmed meat. This chapter aims to solve the following puzzle: The individual consumer isn't the person stuffing the animals in the cages or setting corporate policy regarding stocking density. Indeed, given the great demand for inexpensive meat, the individual's choice to refrain from buying a package of chicken breasts appears to make *no difference at all* to whether factory farming continues.

So why is there anything bad about buying it? One might think that, since the individual consumer isn't herself a factory farmer, and since her purchases make no difference to whether other people factory farm, there is nothing bad at all about buying factory-farmed meat. Thus one might think the wrongness of factory farming means that we should work to oppose the system by, for example, developing and pushing legislation to reduce factory farming, but not that there is anything bad about buying factory-farmed meat. Here the puzzle reasserts itself, because many people have the sense that there would be something *hypocritical* about simultaneously working to reduce factory farming through legislation and buying factory-farmed meat.

My main thesis in this chapter is that this sense is right, because even if buying factory-farmed meat makes no difference to whether other people continue factory farming, it nevertheless makes the consumer *complicit* in animal suffering. I develop a theory of consumer complicity that focuses on the role the consumer plays in a group that has the function of signaling demand to producers.

Chapter 12: Eating Meat as a Morally Permissible Moral Mistake

Elizabeth Harman

Many people who are vegetarians for moral reasons nevertheless accommodate the buying and eating of meat in many ways. They go to certain restaurants in deference to their friends' meat-eating preferences; they split restaurant checks, subsidizing the purchase of meat; and they allow money they share with their spouses to be spent on meat. This behavior is puzzling. If someone is a moral vegetarian—that is, a vegetarian for moral reasons—then it seems that she must believe that buying and eating meat is morally wrong. But if someone believes that a practice is morally wrong, it seems she should also believe that accommo-dating and supporting that practice is morally wrong; many moral vegetarians seem not to believe this.

In this chapter, I will offer a solution to this puzzle; I will offer a possible explanation of why people who are vegetarians for moral reasons nevertheless do accommodate the buying and eating of meat. I will offer an explanation of this accommodation behavior on which it is reasonable and makes sense. I will argue that moral vegetarians may see the buying and eating of meat as a *morally permissible moral mistake*. They may see the practice as one that one should not engage in, for moral reasons, but that is not morally wrong. Thus, they may see their accommodation of the practice as accommodation of behavior that is not morally wrong, while it is still the case that they are *moral* vegetarians who see themselves as *required* to be vegetarians.

Chapter 13: Does Locavorism Keep It Too Simple?

Anne Barnhill

Buying locally grown food may seem like a positive thing to do and an impor-tant way in which individuals can help reduce the carbon footprint of their food consumption. After all, much of the food we eat has travelled hundreds or thou-sands of miles from the place it was grown before it arrives in our grocery stores, and the trucks, trains, and boats that transport it use energy. But scholars and activists are increasingly critical of locavorism as an overly simplistic approach to making the food system more environmentally sustainable. The energy used to transport food is only a fraction of the energy used in the food system, and locally grown food is not necessarily grown in an environmentally friendly way. In addition, encouraging people to "buy local" as a way to reduce agriculture's environmental impact may give them the false impression that the food system's environmental problems will be solved if only consumers purchase the "right" foods, when in fact much bigger changes in agricultural and food policy are also necessary. Another criticism of the local and organic food movement is that it mostly ignores the needs of low-income people, who cannot reliably afford enough food or healthy food, much less afford to shop at farmers' markets and buy higher-priced local and organic food.

So, buying locally grown food is an overly simplistic and incomplete approach to improving the food system. Given this, what should we think of locavores, those who embrace buying locally grown food? Is it fair to criticize them for adopting an overly simplistic approach? And what about those locavores who buy local not just because they care about the environment, but also because buying locally is a trendy thing that "people like them" do? Is it fair to criticize them? Should we doubt their sincerity?

Chapter 14: What's Wrong with Artificial Ingredients?

David M. Kaplan

This chapter analyzes the moral arguments for and against artificial ingredients—anything added to food to maintain or improve freshness and safety, nutritional value, taste, texture, and appearance. Artificial ingredients include sweeteners, thickeners, stabilizers, colors, nutrients, and preservatives. Most would agree that there is something intuitively wrong about eating foods with long lists of artificial ingredients. But what exactly is it? Granted, some artificial colors and preservatives should be avoided for health reasons. But what about additives that pose no health risks, such as ascorbyl palmitate and polysorbate 60—or more familiar ones, such as vitamin C and baking powder? Should they be avoided as well? Is it always better to choose foods with no artificial ingredients? Are there other reasons to avoid artificial ingredients that have nothing to do with health?

The most common arguments in defense of artificial ingredients are consequentialist and deontological. The most common arguments against them are also consequentialist and deontological, in addition to those that appeal to their inherent unnaturalness and to their effects on the quality of life. After sorting through the merits and shortcomings of each class of argument, this chapter argues that an analysis of the moral dimensions of artificial ingredients must examine (1) which ingredients are in question, (2) how often something is consumed, (3) if it is consumed with knowledge, and (4) if the food manufacturer is one that deserves to be supported. Answers to these questions should help us get a clearer picture of what we should produce, purchase, serve, and eat.

Chapter 15: The Moral Problem of Predation

Jeff McMahan

If, as I believe, there are strong moral reasons to be vegetarian, because the practice of eating animals causes them to suffer and to lose life that would be worth living, then there must also be moral reasons to reduce and ultimately to eliminate predation in the wild, which also causes animals to suffer and to lose life that would be worth living. We should not, of course, attempt to reduce predation if doing so would cause overpopulation among herbivores, leading to even greater suffering and premature death through starvation and disease. But eventually it should be possible to reduce or eliminate predation in a way that would not have these effects.

I present arguments for the claim that the prevention of animal suffering matters greatly; I then argue further that the importance of reducing suffering among animals can override the impersonal value of preserving predatory species. I also argue that human intervention in the natural world is, in principle, neither presumptuous nor objectionably paternalistic. My conclusion is that we ought to begin to develop humane means by which predator populations can be reduced in size without ecological disruption.

Notes

1. The literature is voluminous and ever expanding, but some good examples of this proliferation are Bittman 2013, Freston 2011, Kingsolver 2007, McWilliams 2009, Pachirat 2013, Pollan 2006, and Safran Foer 2009.
2. On the industrial food system as a whole, see *Food Inc.* (Robert Kenner, Magnolia Pictures, United States, 2008). For some admittedly controversial claims about the health costs of the standard American diet and the benefits of transitioning to plant-based eating, see *Forks Over Knives* (Lee Fulkerson, Virgil Films, United States, 2011). On the environmental costs of industrial animal agriculture, see *Cowspiracy* (Kip Andersen and Keegan Kuhn, A.U.M. Films/Spark Media, United States, 2014). On the philosophical and scientific sources of discontent with the present food system, see *Speciesism: The Movie* (Mark Devries, Mark Devries Productions, United States, 2014).
3. Three particularly prominent examples are Food and Agriculture Organization of the United Nations (FAO) 2006, Pew Commission on Industrial Farm Animal Production (PCIFAP) 2009, and Dietary Guidelines Advisory Committee 2015.
4. FAO 2006.
5. PCIFAP 2009.
6. Pachirat 2013.
7. Simon 2013.
8. Olopade 2009. See also Terry 2014.
9. Mean Greens at the University of North Texas in Denton is the first fully plant-based university cafeteria in the United States. http://www.dining.unt.edu/meangreens, as accessed on April 30, 2015.
10. One could do worse than to bet on "Las Vegas: Vegans, Get Ready for a Feast" in a contest for Most Unlikely Headline in the *Los Angeles Times*. See at http://articles.latimes.com/2012/mar/04/travel/la-tr-lasvegans-20120304, as accessed on April 30, 2015.
11. Read all about it in another article with a decidedly unlikely headline, this time from the *Washington Post*: "Inside the Evangelical Push to Rally around Animal Ethics." See at http://www.washingtonpost.com/news/acts-of-faith/wp/2015/04/10/inside-the-evangelical-push-to-rally-around-animal-ethics, as accessed on April 30, 2015.
12. See Nestle 2002, especially parts 1 ("Undermining Dietary Advice," 29–92) and 2 ("Working the System," 93–171).
13. One of the conclusions reached by the 2015 Dietary Guidelines Advice Committee is that

    > in general, a dietary pattern that is higher in plant-based foods, such as vegetables, fruits, whole grains, legumes, nuts, and seeds, and lower in animal-based foods is more health promoting and is associated with lesser environmental impact (GHG emissions and energy, land, and water use) than is the current average U.S. diet. (Dietary Guidelines Advisory Committee 2015, part D, chapter 5, section 4)

    See at http://www.health.gov/dietaryguidelines/2015%2Dscientific%2Dreport/10-chapter-5/d5-3.asp, as accessed on April 27, 2015.
14. For instance, the seventy scholars and scientists who compose the Food Systems faculty at the University of Vermont—home to one member of our editorial team and

an additional two members of our authorship—come from disciplines as diverse as animal science, anthropology, biology, chemistry, continuing and distance learning, economics, engineering, English, forestry, geology, horticulture, medicine, nano-technology, nutrition science, philosophy, and political science.

15. The question of how to work together across these disciplinary and institutional boundaries toward holistic, sustainable solutions to multifaceted food systems problems is a research program in its own right. For examples of interdisciplinary food systems literature, see Ackerman-Leist 2013, Hesterman 2011, and Winne 2008.

16. In noting that food has not traditionally been a canonical subject of discussion in philosophy, we don't mean to suggest that philosophical ethics has been silent on these matters. Far from it. In the historical tradition, assuming one is looking for them, one can find any number of philosophers who discussed food directly, including Plato, Seneca, Plutarch, Montaigne, Voltaire, Schopenhauer, and Bentham, among others. For an overview of these and other historical philosophers' outlooks on the ethics of eating, see Williams 2003.

    More recently, some of the pioneering figures since the mid-1970s in the modern movement to rethink our eating habits (especially as they concern the interests of other animals) are practitioners of philosophical ethics—people such as Carol J. Adams, Andrew Linzey, Tom Regan, and Peter Singer. We are, of course, well aware of, inspired by, and indebted to their groundbreaking and influential contributions (such as, among many others, Adams 1975 and 1990; Linzey 1976 and 2009; Regan 1983 and 2004; and Singer 1975 and 2015). We also take inspiration from the growing philosophical literature in the philosophy of food and animal ethics, especially two previous anthologies of philosophical essays (Kaplan 2012 and Sapontzis 2004) that were particularly helpful to us in discerning how to frame our contribution.

17. We recognize that food autonomy is not something that everyone enjoys. In some cases, that's perfectly appropriate; most children lack food autonomy, insofar as parents or guardians make the key decisions about how and what they will eat. In other cases, it's lamentable; many people lack food autonomy because of poverty, lack of education, or structural injustice of some kind. We also recognize that food autonomy comes in degrees. Gainfully employed adults tend to have more of it, other things being equal, than college students (who are often beholden to meal plans in cafeterias, etc.).

18. Fraser 2012, p. 198.

References

Ackerman-Leist, Philip. *Rebuilding the Foodshed: How to Create Local, Sustainable, and Secure Food Systems.* White River Junction, VT: Chelsea Green, 2013.

Adams, Carol J. "The Oedible Complex: Feminism and Vegetarianism." In *The Lesbian Reader,* edited by Gina Covina and Laurel Galana. Oakland, CA: Amazon Press, 1975.

———. *The Sexual Politics of Meat.* New York: Continuum, 1990.

Bittman, Mark. *VB6: Eat Vegan before Six to Lose Weight and Restore Your Health . . . for Good.* New York: Clarkson Potter, 2013.

Dietary Guidelines Advisory Committee. *Scientific Report of the 2015 Dietary Guidelines Advisory Committee,* 2015. http://www.health.gov/dietaryguidelines/2015-scientific-report, as accessed on April 21, 2015.

Food and Agriculture Organization of the United Nations. *Livestock's Long Shadow: Environmental Issues and Options.* Rome, 2006. http://www.fao.org/docrep/010/a0701e/a0701e00.htm, as accessed on April 21, 2015.

Fraser, David. "Animal Ethics and Food Production in the 21st Century." In *The Philosophy of Food,* edited by David M. Kaplan. Berkeley: University of California Press, 2012.

Freston, Kathy. *Veganist: Lose Weight, Get Healthy, Change the World.* New York: Weinstein Books, 2011.

Hesterman, Oran B. *Fair Food: Growing a Healthy, Sustainable Food System for All.* New York: Public Affairs, 2011.

Kaplan, David M., ed. *The Philosophy of Food.* Berkeley: University of California Press, 2012.

Kingsolver, Barbara. *Animal, Vegetable, Miracle: A Year of Food Life.* New York: Harper Perennial, 2007.

Linzey, Andrew. *Animal Rights: A Christian Perspective.* London: SCM Press, 1976.

————. *Why Animal Suffering Matters: Philosophy, Theology, and Practical Ethics.* Oxford: Oxford University Press, 2009.

McWilliams, James. *Just Food: Where Locavores Get It Wrong and How We Can Truly Eat Responsibly.* New York: Little, Brown, 2009.

Nestle, Marion. *Food Politics: How the Food Industry Influences Nutrition and Health.* Berkeley: University of California Press, 2002.

Olopade, Dayo. "Black Folks, Green Thumbs: How the Urban Farming Movement Is Repairing the Relationships between Blacks and the Earth." *Root,* April 22, 2009. http://www.theroot.com/articles/culture/2009/04/black_folks_green_thumbs.html, as accessed on April 23, 2015.

Pachirat, Timothy. *Every Twelve Seconds: Industrialized Slaughter and the Politics of Sight.* New Haven, CT: Yale University Press, 2013.

Pew Commission on Industrial Farm Animal Production. *Putting Meat on the Table: Industrial Farm Animal Production in America,* 2009. http://www.ncifap.org, as accessed on April 21, 2015.

Pollan, Michael. *The Omnivore's Dilemma.* New York: Turtleback, 2006.

Regan, Tom. *The Case for Animal Rights.* Berkeley: University of California Press, 1983.

————. *Empty Cages: Facing the Challenge of Animal Rights.* Lanham, MD: Rowman and Littlefield, 2004.

Rossi, John and Samual A. Garner. "Industrial Farm Animal Production: A Comprehensive Moral Critique." *Journal of Agricultural and Environmental Ethics* 27, no. 3 (2014): 479–522.

Safran Foer, Jonathan. *Eating Animals.* New York: Little, Brown, 2009.

Sapontzis, Steve F., ed. *Food for Thought: The Debate over Eating Meat.* Amherst, NY: Prometheus, 2004.

Simon, David Robinson. *Meatonomics: How the Rigged Economics of Meat and Dairy Make You Consume Too Much, How to Eat Better, Live Longer, and Spend Smarter.* San Francisco: Conari Press, 2013.

Singer, Peter. *Animal Liberation.* New York: Harper, 1975.

————. *The Most Good You Can Do: How Effective Altruism Is Changing Ideas about Living Ethically.* New Haven, CT: Yale University Press, 2015.

Terry, Bryant. *Afro-Vegan: Farm-Fresh African, Caribbean, and Southern Flavors Remixed.* San Francisco: Ten Speed Press, 2014.

Williams, Howard. *The Ethics of Diet: A Catena of Authorities Deprecatory of the Practice of Flesh-Eating.* Champaign-Urbana: University of Illinois Press, 2003.

Winne, Mark. *Closing the Food Gap: Resetting the Table in the Land of Plenty.* Boston: Beacon, 2008.

PART I
Dietary Ideals

1

CONSCIENTIOUS OMNIVORISM

Terence Cuneo

Is it morally permissible for people like us—denizens of the affluent Western world—to purchase or eat meat? Conscientious omnivores believe so, provided that the meat is not factory farmed (or otherwise produced by treating animals cruelly). Moral vegetarians take a more hard-line approach, maintaining that people like us in our circumstances ought not to purchase or eat meat at all because doing so would be wrong. I find myself conflicted about which of these positions to accept. I believe that, at the very least, we should be conscientious omnivores. But I am unsure whether, having accepted conscientious omnivorism, there are principled reasons not to take the further step of embracing moral vegetarianism full stop. My project in this chapter is to explore this issue.[1]

I should warn you that my discussion does not aim to be ethically neutral, as I will be working with a broadly deontological view of what makes acts right. According to this view, when an act is right, it is not because it brings about the best consequences or maximizes value. Rather, ordinarily, when an act is right, it is determined by the rights and obligations that agents have against one another, which they possess in virtue of the worth that they have. I will work with this position not only because doing so will help to focus our discussion, but also because it seems to me true.

A Standard Deontological Argument

Most of us believe that the Native Americans who lived in the United States one hundred fifty years ago did nothing wrong when they killed animals for food. Given their conditions, they needed to do so to survive and flourish. But it is different for us. We occupy conditions in which food is ordinarily plentiful and there is no need to hunt. Although meat is typically both easily available and affordable, most of us can lead extremely healthy and satisfying lives without eating animals at all.

Many philosophers believe that, since we occupy conditions such as these, we ought to be moral vegetarians. A prominent type of argument for this conclusion, due in its essentials to Tom Regan, rests on two concepts: *being the subject of a life* and *having a basic welfare right*. Let's take a moment to unpack these concepts.[2]

A subject of a life is a creature that can flourish or fail to flourish, has strong interests in its own flourishing, and can be aware of its own flourishing or failure to flourish.[3] For present purposes, think of flourishing along broadly Aristotelian lines: Beings flourish inasmuch as they, to some sufficient degree, use and enjoy the use of their senses, have and enjoy having adequate health, have and enjoy having bonds of kinship or friendship, engage and enjoy engaging in play, and so forth. Thus understood, rocks, plants, insects, and mollusks cannot be the subjects of a life. Animals of many kinds, however, are. In ordinary conditions, both human and nonhuman animals, such as chickens, sheep, cows, and pigs, are keenly interested in using their senses, establishing and maintaining bonds of kinship, and engaging in play. (By saying this, I do not mean to elide important differences between animals of these kinds. For immediate purposes, however, these differences will not matter.) Human and nonhuman animals have at least this much in common.

It is because (in part) subjects of a life can engage in activities such as establishing, maintaining, and enjoying bonds of kinship that they have noninstrumental or inherent worth. This worth matters morally, for it is in virtue of possessing such worth that we can wrong subjects of a life. It is because a dog possesses worth of this sort, for example, that I can wrong it by intentionally crippling it. When we wrong the subject of a life, it is entitled to better treatment.[4] That, however, is more or less a different way of saying that subjects of a life have rights of various sorts, such as what I've called the basic welfare rights. At a first approximation, let's say that if an agent A has a basic welfare right against an agent B, then B morally ought not intentionally to frustrate or destroy A's flourishing by doing such things as preventing it from using its senses, destroying its capacity to form bonds of kinship, maiming its body so it cannot engage in movement or play, and so forth.

Later in our discussion, I will have more to say about these rights. For now, let me make several preliminary points about them. First, these rights are *defeasible*; they can be trumped by other countervailing moral considerations. For example, you might have a basic welfare right against me that I not maim or kill you. But if you attack me, then (all else being equal) it is morally permissible for me to maim or kill you in self-defense. Second, the basic welfare rights are *kind relative*. They are rights that a thing has against only those agents that are of such a kind that they can recognize them. If ordinary farm animals such as cows have the basic welfare rights, for example, then they do not have them against other animals such as coyotes but only against creatures like us. For, unlike coyotes, we are the sorts of beings that can recognize and honor these rights. Finally, many of these rights are *context dependent*. If I am a child, I may have a right against my parents that they provide me with adequate water and food; were I to die of thirst, they would have wronged me. But in a season of terrible drought, I have no such right. There is no water that they can provide me. If this is so, rights are ordinarily indexed to situations. The right that a child has against his parents is the right to provide him with food and water in conditions in which water is available.

Having made these observations about subjects of a life and rights, we are now in a position to formulate:

The Standard Deontological Argument

(1) If something is a subject of a life, then it has the basic welfare rights.
(2) Farm animals are the subjects of a life.
(3) So, farm animals have the basic welfare rights.
(4) In conditions such as ours, purchasing or eating the meat of farm animals violates their basic welfare rights.
(5) We ought not to violate the basic welfare rights of others.
(6) So, in conditions such as ours, we ought not to purchase or eat the meat of farm animals.

Let me offer both a comment about and a criticism of this argument. The comment is that this argument has some intuitive pull. After all, if a creature is such that it can flourish and its own flourishing matters to it, then that creates a strong moral reason not to do such things as maim or kill it. Still—and this is the criticism—the argument is not persuasive. The fundamental problem is that premise (4) appears to be false. When we purchase or eat meat, the animal whose meat we've purchased or eaten is dead. And we cannot violate the basic welfare rights of the dead. In saying this, I do not wish to deny that the dead have rights. Perhaps, for example, if you were intentionally to bad-mouth your dead grandmother at her funeral, you would wrong her. Even so, you would not violate her basic welfare rights, since she has none.

It is natural to wonder whether the Standard Deontological Argument can be repaired. Surely—it might be said—by purchasing or buying meat we can support or be complicit in activities, such as the slaughtering of animals, which violate the basic welfare rights of these animals. And, all else being equal, we ought not to do this. As will become evident in a moment, I believe that there is something to this thought. But I also believe that it is difficult to formulate a satisfactory argument for moral vegetarianism that relies on it, at least if we understand "supporting" and "being complicit" in terms of *causally supporting* an institution by, say, enabling it to stay afloat. In their chapters in this volume, Mark Bryant

Budolfson and Ted Warfield explain why. If Budolfson, Warfield, and I are right about this, then it is worth exploring different reasons for why it might be wrong to eat or purchase meat. That is my concern in the next section.

Cruelty and Symbolic Value

Call a person who purchases or uses some good a *consumer* of that good (by a "good," I mean a commodity). The argument I wish to present in this section relies on an abstract ethical principle that I will call:

> **The Support Principle**: Suppose an essentially cruel practice provides some good G. All else being equal, one morally ought not to support that practice by being a consumer of G if an alternative to G is readily available, which is comparable in cost and quality and is not the product of an essentially cruel practice, since being a consumer of G has considerable symbolic disvalue.

The Support Principle introduces the ideas of an essentially cruel practice and that of symbolic disvalue. Let me try to give you a better feel for these ideas and how they relate to one another by sketching an imaginary scenario.

Imagine that ESPN and the US government strike a deal: To reduce the population in the nation's overcrowded prisons and to provide entertainment for the ordinary person, ESPN will—for a modest fee—televise events in which prisoners fight to the death employing a variety of techniques, including those used by the ancient gladiators. At first, this arrangement proves highly controversial, since (among other things) these prisoners are coerced into fighting. But people see immediately the arrangement's impressive benefits. The population of prisons is in fact reduced dramatically. Moreover, the televised events generate huge amounts of money, which allows the government to slash taxes and reduce poverty. With time, the televised killings become wildly popular, at least among a certain segment of the population. Of course they are not the only type of game shown on ESPN. The network still televises games of baseball, basketball, football, hockey, and soccer on a regular basis.

There are, I believe, two things to say about this arrangement between ESPN and the government. First, it is morally beyond the pale. In conditions such as ours, there is no way in which manipulating human beings to kill each other for the viewing pleasure of others could be morally justified. Like forced slavery or waterboarding, gladiatorial killing is an essentially cruel practice.

The second thing to say is that because these new games are an essentially cruel practice, you have strong moral reason not to pay for or watch them. Admittedly, in your more sober moments, you might realize that, given their momentum and popularity, there is probably little that you can do to stop these games. If you and your friends neither pay for nor watch them, this will probably have little effect. Indeed, if you were to watch these events, you wouldn't thereby violate the basic welfare rights of those who are killed in them, for by merely watching these games, you wouldn't be depriving these prisoners of their right not to be maimed or killed for sport.

Even so, you have strong moral reason not to be a consumer of these games. Why is that? The answer, it seems to me, is that the moral life is about not only how to act well, but also how to *live* well. And to live well is to be for the good and against what is evil. Being for the good, however, is not simply a matter of producing or protecting what is good. Sometimes it is to engage in actions whose primary value is symbolic in which we *stand for* the good. While I have no definition of what it is to stand for the good by engaging in actions that have symbolic value (or refusing to engage in actions that have symbolic disvalue), we can readily recognize examples of the phenomenon. For example, sometimes being for the good consists in refusing to engage in actions that have symbolic disvalue, such as bowing to a cruel emperor. In other cases, it consists in actively engaging in actions that have symbolic value, such as holding vigil in remembrance of the dead. Indeed, in situations in which we are more or less helpless to change what is evil—either because that evil is so pervasive or because we must answer to other demands—engaging in activities of these sorts is often the best we can do. Since we often do find ourselves in such situations, awareness of the symbolic dimensions of our everyday activity is an important way in which we can be for the good.[5]

In principle, there are many types of actions that can have symbolic value or disvalue. Being a consumer of goods of certain types, I assume, is among them. Paying to watch ESPN's gladiatorial games is, for example, an action that has considerable symbolic disvalue, while protesting them is one that has considerable symbolic value. The former is a way of symbolically supporting or being for a practice that is cruel, while the latter is a way of standing against it. To which I should add that symbolic value or disvalue can attach to actions even when we fail to recognize it. Even if I pay no attention whatsoever to the moral dimensions of the gladiatorial games, being solely concerned with their economic aspects, being a consumer of them has considerable symbolic disvalue. Moreover, even if I deeply dislike a given practice that is essentially cruel, but continue to consume the goods it produces, my actions can have symbolic disvalue. If this is right, the symbolic disvalue of my being a consumer of a good needn't walk in lockstep with the attitudes I have toward being a consumer of that good.

There is much more to say about the notions of an essentially cruel practice and symbolic value. For the purposes of our discussion, I am going to assume that we have a satisfactory understanding of them, since we can identify instances of each, such as those offered in the examples above. The point I am interested in making is that the Support Principle yields the verdict that, all else being equal, you ought not to be a consumer of ESPN's gladiatorial games. Not only does being a consumer of the games have considerable symbolic disvalue, you also have alternatives available. You can, for example, watch a game of football or a wrestling match if you especially enjoy watching sports during your free time.

An Improved Argument

Let us now turn from sporting events to animals (by which I mean nonhuman animals). In doing so, I am going to help myself to a broadly empirical assumption for which I am not going to argue in any detail, which is that factory farming is an essentially cruel practice. This last claim has been widely argued for, so I will limit myself simply to quoting from a pamphlet recently published by the Humane Society that details its characteristics:

> How, then, are the billions of animals raised and slaughtered annually in industrial agriculture generally treated? Before their lives even begin, bioengineering often stacks the deck against them by putting optimum market value ahead of their bodily integrity. Because a higher ratio of meat to bone than occurs in nature is economically advantageous, animals are engineered to have more body mass than their skeletal structures and organ systems can feasibly support, leaving them vulnerable to increased risk of broken bones, chronic respiratory difficulty, and organ failure. Once born, these animals are debeaked, tail-docked, dehorned, branded, and castrated without anesthetic. They live predominantly indoors in crowded conditions that deny them the ability to exercise their most basic instincts, including maintaining hygiene, caring for their young, establishing natural social orders, or even having full range of movement, much less the freedom to graze or forage for food in a natural setting. To optimize weight gain, they are given heavily supplemented grain feed that their bodies are not equipped to digest, often resulting in perpetual discomfort and unnatural obesity for the duration of their lives.
>
> For transport to slaughter, they are packed into trucks where over-crowding and exposure to extreme weather conditions usually claim some of them en route. Upon arrival at the slaughterhouse, the animals too sick to move of their own volition are deposited onto "downer piles" where they may remain for hours or even days before they die. Those fit for slaughter are then routed to the killing floor, where, depending on their species, they may be shackled upside down by the legs or channeled into metal "knocking chutes" that restrict their ability to resist their captors. There, surrounded by the sights, sounds, and smells of their fellow creatures dying, they are killed, perhaps by "captive bolt" to the brainstem, perhaps by a blade to the throat. Due to the speed at which these processes are carried out and the varying levels of skill among the workers, it is not uncommon for animals to survive their attempted slaughter, only to meet their fate farther down the processing line. Fully conscious chickens, for

example, may be scalded to death in defeathering tanks, while cows and pigs may be dismembered alive.[6]

As I say, this is only a very brief description of the practice of factory farming. Much more graphic and detailed descriptions are available. Still, the description offered is enough for us to formulate the following argument for conscientious omnivorism:

An Improved Deontological Argument

(1) Factory farming is an essentially cruel practice.
(2) By being a consumer of factory farmed meat one thereby supports, if only symbolically, an essentially cruel practice. All else being equal, such support has considerable symbolic disvalue.
(3) **The Support Principle**: Suppose an essentially cruel practice provides some good G. All else being equal, one morally ought not to support that practice by being a consumer of G if an alternative to G is readily available, which is comparable in cost and quality and is not the product of an essentially cruel practice, since being a consumer of G has considerable symbolic disvalue.
(4) There are readily available alternatives to the meat produced by factory farms, which are comparable in cost and quality and not the product of an essentially cruel practice.
(5) So, all else being equal, one ought to be (at least) a conscientious omnivore.

I think this is a good argument. Look at its premises. Premise (1) seems true, as the empirical evidence in its favor is difficult to dispute. Premise (2) also looks true. Given the nature of factory farming, being a consumer of factory farmed meat appears to have considerable symbolic disvalue. The meat is, as it were, a relic of creatures that have been deeply wronged by the treatment they received. Of course this itself does not imply that you ought not to be a consumer of such meat. If the Support Principle is true, it implies this only when there are viable alternatives. However, most of us have available alternatives that are comparable in cost and quality to factory farmed meat, which are not the products of essentially cruel practices. One could consume only "family farmed" meat, for example—meat that is produced by small farms in which animals live good if shorter than normal lives.[7] Or one could be vegetarian or vegan, eating primarily (or only) plant-based foods. (I will return to the question of the sense in which dairy and plant-based foods are comparable in quality to meat in the next section.)

If this is so, premises (1), (2), and (4) of the improved argument look plausible. The real issue, then, is whether we should accept the Support Principle. While not beyond controversy, the Support Principle has at least the following going for it. For one thing, it seems to yield the right result in a large array of cases for the right reasons. Suppose you are wondering whether to be a consumer of the ESPN gladiatorial games. The Support Principle tells you that, all else being equal, you should not be if there are viable alternatives. This seems like the correct verdict. Or suppose you are wondering whether to be a consumer of blue jeans that are produced in Central American sweatshops. The Support Principle tells you that, all else being equal, you should not if there are viable alternatives. This also seems like the correct verdict. Or suppose you are wondering whether to be a consumer of avant-garde art that is composed of the body parts of slaughtered Sudanese refugees. The Support Principle tells you that, all else being equal, you should not if there are viable available alternatives. This also seems true. The Support Principle yields these correct results, moreover, without committing itself to controversial claims that being a consumer of these goods would somehow causally contribute to or enable the survival of the practices that produce these goods. Whether or not being a consumer of these goods has these consequences, the Support Principle instructs us to avoid being a consumer of them—all else being equal, of course.

What is more, the Support Principle is not overly demanding, an expression of an overly idealistic ethical code. It allows that there might be cases in which being a consumer of a good has considerable symbolic disvalue but there are reasons that permit consuming it nonetheless. For example, suppose that failing to be a consumer of such a good would (in some very difficult-to-imagine way) probably trigger the collapse of our economic system. The Support Principle is compatible with there being sufficient reason to be a consumer of that good.

These seem like welcome implications of the Support Principle. Still, one might harbor the suspicion that the Support Principle is without teeth, permitting all manner of ethically suspect actions. Here is one way to articulate this suspicion: Imagine that you have accepted an invitation to a barbeque with full knowledge that it will be a factory farmed meat-fest, with no alternatives available. You either eat the sausage, chicken, and beef served or go hungry. Since you have excellent reasons not to go hungry, you enjoy a full meat-laden meal. The Support Principle, it seems, allows you to be a consumer in such a case, which seems overly permissive.

The concern is ungrounded. The reason is that the Support Principle simply articulates a sufficient condition for when we ought not to be a consumer of a good. It tells us that, all else being equal, if being a consumer of a good has considerable symbolic disvalue and there are viable alternatives available, then one ought not to be a consumer of that good. It has no implications whatsoever for cases in which an action has considerable symbolic disvalue but there are no viable alternatives. In those sorts of cases, we will have to appeal to other ethical principles. In the case of the barbeque, for example, we might appeal to a principle that requires one, in the formation of one's plans, to be reasonably conscientious about the empirical and ethical dimensions of situations that one is likely to face when enacting them. Let me hasten to add that there might be other cases to which the

Support Principle applies that are extraordinarily difficult to assess morally. These cases might be such that acting in a certain way has both considerable symbolic value and disvalue. That there are such cases, however, does not impugn the Support Principle. It might be that the best we can expect of most moral principles is that they yield discernible ethical verdicts in only a wide range of cases.

Going a Step Further

I have argued for two main claims. The first is that a standard type of deontological argument for moral vegetarianism fails. The second is that there is a good argument for conscientious omnivorism that hinges on the concept of symbolic value. This last argument might, however, raise as many questions as it answers. For one might suspect that conscientious omnivorism is an unstable position, the reason being that, if the argument offered in the last section were sound, it is difficult to see why we wouldn't also have decisive reason to accept moral vegetarianism full stop.

To see why, suppose it is true that being a consumer of factory farmed meat has considerable symbolic disvalue. If it does, then it also seems true that being a consumer of family farmed meat has considerable symbolic disvalue. This meat is, after all, the product of a practice dedicated to raising animals for the purpose of killing them for food. It is what we might call an essentially *life-depriving* practice, one that systematically frustrates the flourishing of animals by killing them. (By "a life-depriving practice," I mean a practice that deprives only *subjects of a life* of their lives.) Raising an animal humanely for the purpose of (and actually) killing it, admittedly, is not nearly as bad as treating it cruelly and then killing it. Even so, inflicting death on the subject of a life is typically a considerable evil in the life of the creature on which it is inflicted. There have to be strong enough reasons, it would appear, to justify it.

Let's see if we can articulate this concern more precisely by formulating an argument for moral vegetarianism that is parallel to the one offered for conscientious omnivorism. This parallel argument hinges on a close relative to the Support Principle, which we can call:

> **The Modified Support Principle**: Suppose an essentially life-depriving practice provides some good G. All else being equal, one morally ought not to support that practice by being a consumer of G if an alternative to G is readily available, which is comparable in cost and quality and is not the product of an essentially life-depriving (or cruel) practice, since being a consumer of G has considerable symbolic disvalue.[8]

When explaining why its counterpart, the Support Principle, is plausible, I appealed to a scenario involving gladiatorial practices, noting that they are essentially cruel. Let me try to articulate why the Modified Support Principle seems plausible by returning to themes that we discussed earlier when considering the Standard Deontological Argument.

Recall that that argument appealed to a pair of concepts. We said, first, that something is a subject of a life if and only if it is a creature of such a kind that it can flourish or fail to flourish, has strong interests in its own flourishing, and can be aware of its own flourishing or failure to flourish. It is (in part) because subjects of a life have capacities of this sort that they have worth. This worth is of such a kind, we saw, that it renders subjects of a life the sort of thing that we can wrong. Or to employ the other key concept introduced earlier, having worth of this sort implies that subjects of a life have the basic welfare rights. Earlier I offered a provisional characterization of the basic welfare rights. I said that if A has a basic welfare right against an agent B, then B morally ought not intentionally to frustrate or destroy A's flourishing by doing such things as preventing it from using its senses, destroying its capacity to form bonds of kinship, maiming its body so it cannot engage in movement or play, and so forth. It will be helpful, however, if we go beyond this abstract characterization to identify more specific examples of these rights. When we do so, we can see that the basic welfare rights include the right not to be treated cruelly and the right not to be killed just for kicks.

We are now better situated to see why being a conscientious omnivore might not be enough. The way to do so is by formulating what I shall call:

A More Stringent Deontological Argument

(1) Family farming is an essentially life-depriving practice.
(2) By being a consumer of family farmed meat one thereby supports, if only symbolically, an essentially life-depriving practice. All else being equal, such support has considerable symbolic disvalue.
(3) **The Modified Support Principle**: Suppose an essentially life-depriving practice provides some good G. All else being equal, one morally ought not to support that practice by being a consumer of G if an alternative to G is readily available, which is comparable in cost and quality and is not the product of an essentially life-depriving (or cruel) practice, since being a consumer of G has considerable symbolic disvalue.
(4) There are readily available alternatives to the meat produced by family farms, which are comparable in cost and quality and not the product of an essentially life-depriving (or cruel) practice.
(5) So, all else being equal, one ought to be (at least) a moral vegetarian.

Let's take a closer look at this argument. Premise (1) is certainly true. Family farming, no less than factory farming, is essentially a life-depriving practice; its primary aim is to raise animals for the purpose of eating them. Premise (2) also looks plausible. While it is true that by being a consumer of family farmed meat one does not thereby violate the basic welfare rights of the animals that are slaughtered, one does nevertheless lend symbolic support to a practice that raises and slaughters these animals. Moreover, this support does appear to have considerable symbolic disvalue. For, like factory farming, family farming seems to wrong the animals that are slaughtered.

Perhaps the best way to make this last point is to recall the sorts of basic welfare rights that farm animals have. Although animals may not have a basic welfare right not to be killed, they do appear to have the right against us:

not to be killed just for the pleasure derived from killing them.

But now think of why family farmed animals are slaughtered. The primary reason is that there is a demand for their meat. And that demand, it seems, is rooted primarily in the pleasure of eating it. But it is difficult to see how it could be that these animals have a right not to be killed just for the pleasure derived from killing them but lack the right:

not to be killed just for the pleasure derived from eating them.

In short, it appears that if farm animals have the former sort of right, then they must also have the latter sort of right—at least in conditions such as ours. If so, supporting a practice that systematically violates this last right would appear to have considerable symbolic disvalue.

Granted, the mere fact that being a consumer of family farmed meat has considerable symbolic disvalue does not itself imply that we morally ought not to be consumers of it. If the Modified Support Principle is true, it implies this only when there are viable alternatives. There do, however, appear to be viable alternatives to consuming family farmed meat. Moreover, the main alternatives— which are dairy or plant-based foods—are comparable in cost and nutritional quality to family farmed meat. In fact, many would say that many types of plant-based foods are (for most of us) superior in nutritional quality.

It should be admitted that most dairy and plant-based foods lack some of the properties of meat that so many enjoy. These foods are not, for example, closely comparable in texture and taste to meat. So for premise (4) to be plausible, we must understand it broadly. "Quality" must refer to both nutritional and gustatory quality—the last being the disposition of a food to produce enjoyment when eaten. To say, then, that dairy and plant-based products are comparable in quality is not to claim that these foods produce gustatory sensations of the very same types as meat. Rather, it is to claim, first, that there are dairy and plant-based foods that are comparable in nutritional quality to meat and, second, that when eaten, produce gustatory pleasure of a type and degree comparable to that of meat; eating them is highly enjoyable. I write this with full knowledge that major changes in our food options are probably right over the horizon. The vanguard of food technologies has, apparently, produced plant-based products that are, even to experts, indistinguishable in taste and texture from meat. If this is so, then there will soon be widely available plant-based alternatives that are very close in taste and texture to meat. If one is inclined to interpret "comparable in quality" to include gustatory qualities such as *being very close in taste and texture to meat*, then one can interpret premise (4) in such a way that, while not true now, it will be true in the near future.

We have considered premises (1), (2), and (4) of the More Stringent Deontological Argument. They all seem plausible. This leaves the Modified Support Principle, which has the following to recommend it.

For one thing, it seems to issue the correct verdicts in a large range of cases. Suppose, for example, you are deliberating about whether to buy a winter coat. One option is a fur-lined parka that is produced by a life-depriving practice. The Modified Support Principle tells you that, all else being equal, you should not purchase the parka if there is a viable alternative. This seems correct. Or suppose you are going to buy some mascara. One option is a product that is tested on animals which are killed during or after the testing process. The Modified Support Principle tells you that, all else being equal, you should not buy this product if there is a viable alternative. That also seems right. Or suppose you need to replace the tuners on your vintage guitar. One option is to buy some new ivory tuners that are similar to those that came with your guitar. The Modified Support Principle tells you that, all else being equal, you should not buy these tuners if there is a viable alternative. That also seems right.

What is more, the Modified Support Principle is not morally idealistic in the pejorative sense. It allows that there might be cases in which being a consumer of a good has considerable symbolic disvalue but there are reasons that permit consuming it nonetheless. Suppose, for example, that you need a medical remedy that can only be produced by a practice that deprives animals of their lives. The Modified Support Principle does not imply that you ought not to be a consumer of the remedy.

The challenge that conscientious omnivores face should now be clear. It is to specify why, given that being a consumer of both factory farmed and family farmed meat has considerable symbolic disvalue, it is impermissible to be a consumer of the former but not the latter. Is there a good response to this challenge?

The Conscientious Omnivore's Response

I am not sure. But let me present what seems to me the best response available to conscientious omnivores. Begin with points of agreement between conscientious omnivores, on the one hand, and moral vegetarians, on the other. Proponents of both views agree that killing family farmed animals for food has considerable disvalue. By killing these animals, after all, we typically inflict a substantial evil on them. Proponents of both positions agree, then, that there is reason not to kill these animals for food. Although it is notoriously difficult to arrive at wholesale

comparative evaluative judgments, both conscientious omnivores and moral vegetarians might also agree that it would be *better* on the whole if we did not raise
and kill these animals for food, even if these animals do owe their existence to
those who raise them for food. (In this sense, family farming is a *life-giving* practice.) Finally, advocates of both positions might be prepared to say that the badness
of killing these animals is offset to some degree since they tend to have very good
(if relatively short) lives, which they wouldn't have were they not being raised
for food. To what degree this badness is offset by the fact that these animals have
good lives is a good question. But proponents of both views would agree, I think,
that their having lives of this sort does not neutralize the badness of killing them.

Where, then, do the two views part company? They differ in this important
respect: Conscientious omnivores believe that, while we may have moral reasons
not to kill these animals for food, we would not *wrong* these animals were we
to kill them for food. The disvalue that attaches to the life-depriving practice of
raising animals to eat them, say conscientious omnivores, is not a *rights-violating*
disvalue. In this respect, family farming is crucially different from factory farming, as the disvalue that attaches to the latter is of the rights-violating sort. Why,
though, is the disvalue that attaches to family farming not of a rights-violating
sort? The answer, according to conscientious omnivores, is that by giving these
animals good (if short) lives, we do not thereby humiliate or degrade them. Nor
do we treat them with under-respect, treating them as if their lives and well-
being do not matter (or have only instrumental worth).

To see how conscientious omnivores are thinking, let's begin by considering
what they would say in response to the charge that family farming is a rights-
violating practice. Earlier we considered an argument that family farming is a
rights-depriving practice that went as follows. Suppose it is true that farm animals have the right:

  not to be killed just for the pleasure derived from killing them.

If they do, we said, it is very difficult to see how they could lack the right:

  not to be killed just for the pleasure derived from eating them.

Since everyone should admit that these animals have the former right, they
should also agree that they have the latter right. And since family farming violates the latter right, it is a rights-violating practice, the support of which has
considerable symbolic disvalue.

Conscientious omnivores maintain that the argument just offered distorts their
view. The practice of family farming, as they see things, has a considerably more
complex aim than that of providing meat that people enjoy eating. This complex
aim includes, in the first place, providing animals with good lives—lives that are
typically, on the whole, much better than those they would have were they to

live in the wild. Indeed, as I understand what it is to family farm, providing such lives is an essential aspect of the practice; one could not competently engage in it without having this as a goal. The aim of family farming also includes providing food that sustains and nourishes us, which is (for many) very pleasurable to eat. This food, in turn, sustains a variety of rich social practices that many value a great deal, including those of animal husbandry, cookery, holiday celebrations, and shared meals. Finally, these farms represent an attempt to provide a viable alternative to factory farms, which treat farm animals with considerable cruelty. In this respect, the activity of family farming has symbolic value.

Once we see this, we can see that the agreement between conscientious omnivores and moral vegetarians is more extensive than we initially supposed. Advocates of both views agree not only that there is reason not to kill animals, but also that farm animals have many rights, including the rights:

> not to be treated with cruelty;
> not to be killed just for the pleasure derived from killing them;

And:

> not to be killed just for the pleasure derived from eating them.

For, proponents of these views maintain, to violate these rights would be to treat animals as if their lives and well-being do not matter.

Conscientious omnivores face the charge that family farming is a rights-violating practice. So far, we have explored how conscientious omnivores might respond to this charge. It remains to be seen, however, why these people believe that raising animals for food on family farms does not treat them with under-respect. How would we determinate that? According to conscientious omnivores, the way to do so is to identify a right such that by violating it, those who engage in family farming would treat their animals with under-respect, thereby wronging them. What right would that be?

It would be a right not to be killed in order to achieve the complex aim of family farming. To better understand the nature of this right, consider those conditions in which animals are given excellent lives on family farms. The question to ask is whether these animals have the right against those who provide these lives:

> not to be killed for the purpose of providing nourishing food, which provides gustatory pleasure, sustains valued social practices, and provides a viable alternative to factory farming.

For ease of reference, let us call this the *right to a full life*, since it is a right that animals have against those who care for them not to cut their lives short to achieve the complex aim of family farming. Conscientious omnivores must deny that animals have such a right. They can, I believe, say two things in defense of this denial.

First, if animals have the right to a full life, this will not be a direct implication of their having the other basic welfare rights mentioned above, since having the basic welfare rights does not imply having the right to a full life. We cannot, for example, derive the right to a full life from an animal's rights not to be treated with cruelty or not to be killed just for the pleasure derived from eating it. To establish that animals do have the right to a full life, we will need to see a new line of argument. It might be worth adding that were animals to lack the right to a full life, they could also have considerable inherent worth, as conscientious omnivores believe. That inherent worth, in fact, could ground the basic welfare rights such as the right not to be killed just for the pleasure of the killing. But it would not obviously imply that it would be impermissible to kill animals that are family farmed for the complex end at which family farms aim.

The second thing to say is that there are reasons for doubting that animals have the right to a full life. Toward the beginning of our discussion, I mentioned that few of us believe that the Native Americans who lived in the US one hundred fifty years ago acted in a morally impermissible way by killing animals for food and clothing. They needed to if they were to survive and flourish. Imagine, however, that these people were offered the following choice (perhaps by others of their tribe): You may either continue your way of life or stop killing animals and become farmers or merchants. Since being a farmer or merchant will be fairly lucrative, you will be able to buy clothing made from not animal skins but fabrics such as cotton and wool, which will be highly functional.

If these people were to take the former option, I take it that their justification for doing so would be very similar to that offered by conscientious omnivores when asked to justify their position. By killing animals, the Native Americans would say, they thereby provide their people with nourishing and delicious food—these activities being at the center of a deeply entrenched and valued way of life. The question to ask is whether they would be wronging the animals they kill if they were to take the first option.

It is not apparent that they would. For it is not apparent that rabbits, buffalo, deer, elk, and the like have the right not to be killed for the purpose of providing nourishing food and sustaining the natives' way of life—even when an alternative way of life that does not involve this killing is available and viable. But if these animals do not have this right—conscientious omnivores will claim—then it should also be permissible both to engage in family farming and to be consumers of family farmed meat. Admittedly, it may be that both the Native Americans in our example and conscientious omnivores have strong reasons to be consumers of less meat than they might otherwise think allowable. For it may be that to be adequately nourished and to sustain the crucial elements of their ways of life, they need only consume meat in rather limited quantities. But that is as it should be. Conscientious omnivorism does not imply that there are no good moral reasons to restrict the frequency with which one would eat family farmed meat.

The case of the natives is instructive. For if it establishes that the natives do not wrong the animals they kill, it follows that whether animals have a right to a full life does not hinge on whether killing them is necessary to survive or flourish. Nor does it hang on whether there are no alternatives to killing them for foods that are both available and viable.

I do not believe that what I have said on behalf of conscientious omnivorism vindicates the view. The answer I have offered on its behalf is controversial. Moreover, it would be helpful if the view could tell us *why* animals have the basic welfare rights but not the right to a full life. Nonetheless, I think we now have a better idea of what conscientious omnivores and moral vegetarians disagree about. Moreover, it also seems to me that what conscientious omnivores say goes some distance toward blocking the argument that we were considering; namely, if we adopt conscientious omnivorism, then we should also accept moral vegetarianism full stop. If this inference is cogent, we will need fresh reasons to accept it or reasons to believe that the attempt by conscientious omnivores to block it is flawed.

Let me close by considering a likely response to what I have said in defense of conscientious omnivorism. This response—which I call the *Twilight Zone Objection* since it is borrowed in its essentials from an episode of the TV series *The Twilight Zone*—asks us to imagine a scenario in which very intelligent and powerful aliens occupy Earth. Since they are nourished by and greatly enjoy the experience of eating human flesh, they "family farm" human beings—this practice of theirs being part of a long-standing and valued way of life that includes having done similar things to other rational beings on other planets. Under this arrangement, human beings live very good but relatively short lives, as many are slaughtered for food before the age of twenty. (Assume, for the moment, that the aliens have effective ways of eliminating the anxiety regarding being slaughtered.) Is this a morally permissible arrangement?

Well, note that the justification offered for it by the aliens is very close to that offered by conscientious omnivores for their view. This justification appeals to the fact that eating human flesh is nourishing, delicious, part of long-standing practices that the aliens value, and so forth. But if this justification fails in the case of the aliens—as most of us believe—then it should also fail in the case of conscientious omnivores. It would follow that conscientious omnivorism cannot be justified by the sorts of considerations adduced above.

The way to defuse the Twilight Zone Objection is to note that the conditions under which it is permissible for a human person to kill another human person for the purpose of eating him appear to be very narrow. Only in emergency situations in which some group will starve to death if they do not kill another human does such killing appear to be permissible. And in these conditions it may be permissible only when the person to be killed grants others the permission to kill him. By contrast, the conditions under which it is permissible to kill nonhuman animals for food seem much wider. At the very least, they include not only emergency conditions such as that just described, but also conditions in which other viable food options are not readily available, such as the conditions occupied by the Native Americans or our agrarian ancestors. But if there is this discrepancy, then it is not permissible for the aliens to "family farm" human persons. After all, the conditions under which it is permissible to kill other human persons for food are very narrow and there is no morally relevant respect in which the aliens differ from other human persons. (The fact that they are powerful enough to subject humans to family farming is morally irrelevant.) If so, the fact that the justification that the aliens offer for killing humans resembles that offered by conscientious omnivores for killing animals is neither here nor there.

I need to emphasize that this response is not supposed to justify conscientious omnivorism. It is only supposed to defuse a type of objection to the view.[9] I should also stress that this response does not identify what it is about human persons that makes it permissible to kill them for food in only the narrowest range of conditions or what it is about animals that renders it permissible to kill them for food in a much wider set of conditions. These are very difficult questions to answer well. The response I have offered simply appeals to the fact that there is this difference between humans and the other animals. Finally, it should be stressed that even if everything I have said on behalf of conscientious omnivorism is true, it does not follow that it is morally permissible to be a consumer of family farmed meat. For even if it is true that killing animals to achieve the end of family farming does not wrong them, there might be other reasons that it is wrong, as not every wrong action is a case of wronging something. I will not, however, hazard a guess as to what those reasons might be.[10]

Notes

1. In order to keep this discussion manageable, I have chosen not to engage moral veganism, which would counsel that we not purchase or consume animal products (including dairy products) at all. It may be that the arguments I consider here would apply to these views too. In their contributions to this volume, Hooley and Nobis, and McPherson defend veganism.
2. See Tom Regan, "The Case for Animal Rights," in *In Defense of Animals*, ed. Peter Singer (Oxford: Blackwell, 1985), 13–26. I have modified what Regan says to suit my purposes here.
3. It's a live question in what sense animals can have interests, desires, or the like. For present purposes, I'll assume that they can, although their character may differ in important ways from the types of interests and desires that ordinary humans have. Alasdair MacIntyre, *Dependent Rational Animals* (Chicago: Open Court, 1999), discusses the issue in chapters 3 and 4.
4. Here I am unpacking the ethical framework within which Regan is operating. Nicholas Wolterstorff, *Justice: Rights and Wrongs* (Princeton, NJ: Princeton University Press, 2008), offers an elaboration and defense of this ethical framework.
5. I am drawing upon Robert M. Adams's trenchant discussion of the category of symbolic value in his *Finite and Infinite Goods* (Oxford: Oxford University Press, 1999),

chap. 9. See also Thomas Hill, "Symbolic Protest and Calculated Silence," *Philosophy and Public Affairs* 9 (1979): 83–102.

6. Matthew C. Halteman, *Compassionate Eating as Care of Creation*, 2nd ed. (Washington, DC: Humane Society of the United States, 2010), 29–30.

7. Two points: First, there are other alternatives to being a consumer of factory farmed meat, including being a consumer of meat that is produced by hunting. For the sake of simplicity, I will set this possibility to the side, although I will touch upon the matter later. Second, I realize that not all animals raised on small family farms are treated well. When I speak of family farmed meat, then, I will have an idealization in mind. Family farmed meat is the meat of animals that have been free to graze, form bonds of kinship, fed antibiotics only when necessary, and so forth.

8. Michael Pollan appeals to a similar principle in *The Omnivore's Dilemma* (New York: Penguin, 2006).

9. There are other ways to formulate *The Twilight Zone* example that appeal to the parallels not between factory farming animals and farming human persons but between factory farming animals and farming human beings that are not persons or are on the margins of personhood, such as babies and the severely disabled. Adequately addressing cases such as these, I am afraid, would plunge us into deeply contested issues beyond what I can address here. But it may be that conscientious omnivores should be most concerned about cases such as these.

10. Audiences at Calvin College, the University of Notre Dame, the University of Vermont, Wake Forest University, and the American Academy of Religion offered feedback on an ancestor of this chapter. Mark Bryant Budolfson, Andrew Chignell, Tyler Doggett, Matt Halteman, and Travis Timmerman also commented on an earlier version of this chapter. They all have my thanks.

2

MANLY MEAT AND GENDERED EATING

Correcting Imbalance and Seeking Virtue

Christina Van Dyke

Eating is a gendered act. In Western cultural mythology, men have rapacious appetites that cannot be easily satisfied; they require 'substantial' foods (like meat and potatoes) to keep up their strength and satisfy their hunger.[1] Hearty consumption demonstrates a man's virility and reinforces his masculinity. Women, on the other hand, have appetites that can easily be satisfied with low-calorie, low-fat foods (like fruits, vegetables, and diet drinks); according to popular cultural myths, they live in constant danger of weight gain and loss of attractiveness if they indulge these minimal appetites. Furthermore, while men are encouraged to indulge and take pride in their appetites—whether it be for food, sex, or power—women are taught to tightly repress their hunger, focusing instead on satisfying the appetites of others.[2]

Food is also frequently gendered.[3] Meat, in particular, is construed as 'male' food, with nonfat yogurt, meatless salads, and other 'light' fare cast as 'female.'[4] So strong is the connection of meat with men and male power, in fact, that feminist theorist Carol Adams calls meat *the* symbol of the patriarchy and argues that the struggle to overcome male oppression must include moving away from eating meat. "How [can] we overthrow patriarchal power while eating its symbol?" she asks. "Autonomous, antipatriarchal being is clearly vegetarian. To destabilize patriarchal consumption we must interrupt patriarchal meals of meat" (200).[5] Adams is hardly alone in taking this stance: Other prominent feminists such as Greta Gaard, Lori Gruen, Marti Kheel, and Catharine MacKinnon also argue that rejecting the consumption of animals and animal products is an important step in overcoming patriarchal structures and consequent environmental injustices.[6]

The ecofeminist argument for veganism is powerful. Meat consumption is a deeply gendered act that is closely tied to the systematic objectification of women and nonhuman animals. Nevertheless, I have concerns about advocating veganism that involve its effectiveness in destabilizing patriarchal injustices. In particular, I am concerned that presenting veganism as *the* moral ideal might reinforce rather than alleviate the disordered status quo in gendered eating—that it might actually further disadvantage women in existing power structures. In this chapter, I explain these concerns, and I advocate a feminist account of ethical eating that treats dietary choices as moral choices insofar as they constitute an integral part of our relationships to ourselves and to others.[7] I argue that we should think of dietary choices in Aristotelian moral terms as a mean *relative to us*, falling on a continuum between the vice of doing injustice to ourselves, on the one hand, and the vice of doing injustice to others, on the other. On this view, what it is moral to eat for individuals is not a fixed ideal, but rather depends on particulars of our physiological, psychological, economic, cultural, and relational situations.

Objectification and Linked Oppressions

The claim that women are consistently objectified in a morally problematic way is perhaps more widely accepted in feminist writing than any other single claim.[8] This objectification is often linked to a dualist framework that opposes, for example, rational to emotional, active to passive, subject to object, culture to nature, mind to body. As political theorist Carol Cohn observes,

> in this symbolic system, human characteristics are dichotomized, divided into pairs of polar opposites that are supposedly mutually exclusive. . . . In each case, the first term of the "opposites" is associated with male, the second with female. And in each case, our society values the first over the second. (364)[9]

The negative consequences of perceiving woman as Other and Object have been seen as encompassing everything from sexual violence to eating disorders to persistent economic, legal, and political inequality.[10]

As numerous theorists have gone on to point out, moreover, women are alone neither in being objectified nor in being oppressed by that objectification. Adams, for instance, grounds her feminist-vegetarian critical theory on the observation that "women and animals are similarly positioned in a patriarchal world, as objects rather than subjects" (180).[11] Indeed, the processes of learning to ignore the subjective presence of someone and to make use of a 'someone' as a 'some*thing*' are disturbingly parallel in the cases of women and animals. As Catharine MacKinnon describes this process,

> women in male-dominated society are identified as nature, animalistic, and thereby denigrated, a maneuver that also defines animals' relatively

lower rank in human society. Both are seen to lack properties that elevate men, those qualities by which men value themselves and define their status as human by distinction. (264)[12]

Men have been consistently advantaged in ways that allowed them to identify as, say, rational and active, and to code those qualities as the 'positive' qualities in an oppositional dualistic framework. In a position to ignore and/or subvert the self-identification and subjective experience of other groups, men came to view themselves as agents acting on and over the rest of the world. Over time, the stability of male domination has led to the systematic objectification of women, nonhuman animals, and the environment.[13]

One of the most stable features in this patriarchal system (across cultures and over time) is meat consumption as a sign of male power. But the issue does not involve merely the consumption of dead animal bodies. The use of animals for their products can also be seen as an act of male domination—especially dairy products and eggs, which must come from female bodies. As Adams puts it, "A corollary and prelude to animalized protein is *feminized protein*: milk and eggs . . . Female animals become oppressed by their femaleness . . . [Then] when their productiveness ends, they are butchered and become animalized protein" (91). The consumption not just of animals but also of their products thus appears to reinforce patterns of male oppression.

In this context, veganism has sometimes been promoted as an important act of protest. In particular, theorists who adopt a 'linked oppressions' model argue that sexism and speciesism are related in such a way that refraining from the consumption of animals and their products is a vital step in undercutting patterns of patriarchal power and benefitting women and nonhuman animals.[14] Rather than being treated as "independent, discrete forms of oppression," the systemic disadvantaging of women and animals should be treated as a "bundled political problem" (Wyckoff 2). According to this view, advocated by Adams, Gaard, Gruen, Kheel, and MacKinnon, among others, ignoring the interconnections between the oppression of women and nonhuman animals can lead to people advocating policies and behaviors that inadvertently exacerbate rather than alleviate the problem. Recognizing the link between these forms of oppression, on the other hand, allows us to advocate for positive change that affects everyone. As Jason Wyckoff writes,

> whenever two forms of oppression A and B are linked, it is *at least* likely, if not necessary, that the liberation of those who are oppressed through A will be accompanied by the liberation of those who are oppressed through B. (4)

In Adams's words, "feminist-vegetarian activity declares that an alternative worldview exists, one which celebrates life rather than consuming death" (197).

Idealism, Agency, and Eating

The valorization of the vegan lifestyle as a means of destabilizing patriarchal values often connects such a lifestyle with knowledge, life, and peace—and a meat-eating lifestyle with ignorance, death, and war. Adams, for instance, explicitly calls for "the positing of an ideal world composed of vegetarianism, pacifism, and feminism as opposed to a fallen world of women's oppression, war, and meat eating" (133), and contrasts veganism as a "culture of life" that can (and should) replace the current phallocentric, corpse-consuming "culture of death." Although not essential to the strategy of destabilizing unjust patriarchal systems, the equation of veganism with such positive qualities is prevalent in many discussions of the topic.

This contrast is rhetorically effective in making veganism appealing. At the same time, it echoes the dualistic division of reality that opposes attributes of the transcendent, 'pure' mind, soul, or spirit to those of the immanent, corrupt body—the same dualism that has led to the consistent devaluation of the body, which has been associated with ignorance, death, and war since the time of Plato.[15] This dualism and its negative portrayal of the body has had particularly harmful consequences for women, however, who have been traditionally associated with the body and all its negative characteristics.[16]

The claim that feminists should transcend 'the negative' by refusing to eat bodies—to consume corruption and death—should not, then, be understood in separation from the broader cultural context of the association of women with bodies and all their attendant negative qualities. As Cohn argues,

> this system of dichotomies is encoding many meanings that may be quite unrelated to male and female bodies. Yet once that first step is made—the association of each side of those lists with a gender—gender now becomes tied to many other kinds of cultural representations. (364)[17]

The association of bodies with ignorance, death, violence—and women—runs too deep to be ignored or easily subverted. In fact, taken in this context, the connection of veganism with qualities like knowledge, life, and peace in explicit contrast to their opposites runs the danger of underscoring rather than undermining the somatophobia (body loathing) that is one of the hallmarks of the patriarchy. This consequence should give pause to anyone who rejects the idea that female liberation should involve distancing oneself from or transcending one's physicality.[18]

The dichotomy between male 'oppressor' and female and animal 'oppressed,' male 'subject' and female and animal 'object' that underlies much work in second-wave and eco-feminism is also subject to critique. First, the portrayal of men as agents who exercise domination over women and animals belies the much more complicated lived experience of most men, including those in privileged positions.[19] Second, this dichotomy's emphasis on the parallel positionality of women and nonhuman animals masks important differences between how women and animals fare in the patriarchy. There is a disanalogy between the way that women are exploited as sex objects and animals are exploited for food, moreover, that proves crucial for both understanding and resisting the complex power dynamics of the patriarchy—namely, unlike the animals who are killed or exploited for their products, women are often enthusiastic participants in the systems that disadvantage them. Downplaying this difference ignores the subjectivity of women and the role they play in sustaining and perpetuating patriarchal structures.

Take, for example, the restaurant chain Hooters, whose gimmick is female servers in tight tank tops and short shorts, and whose slogan is an owl with breasts for eyes emblazoned with the phrase "More Than a Mouthful." Adams sees this as an example of 'anthropornography,' where animals are objectified as edible beings in the same context that women are objectified as sexual beings. In her account, Beth Dixon observes, "Adams collapses the differences between animal intentionality and human intentionality" (190) in order to highlight the similarities between them.[20] Yet the objectified animals served up at the restaurant as burgers, wings, and such were given no say in the situation, whereas the objectified women who serve them actively chose that position. Competition among women for jobs as servers at Hooters tends to be fierce: For one thing, you can expect higher tips there than at most 'family-friendly' establishments. In general, women often gain tangible benefits from actively participating in their own objectification, including increased wages, social status, and self-confidence. The fact that the same system that confers these benefits also undercuts their possibilities in other areas makes those advantages no less real or desirable for those women.[21]

Adams, Gruen, Kheel, and others may well be right that sexism and speciesism are oppressions that are linked in significant ways.[22] My focus in this chapter is the more specific claim that rejecting the consumption of animals and animal products is an important (perhaps necessary) step in destabilizing this system. And—as Nancy Bauer, who has written extensively about feminism and the phenomenon of female self-objectification, demonstrates—attempts to change systems that don't take seriously the reasons that people participate in apparently harmful activities tend to fail or even backfire.[23] In this particular case, it is important not to ignore the agency of women who are involved in their objectification or to treat them as victims of the patriarchy in the same way that animals who are used for their products and/or slaughtered for consumption are victims.

In addition, we need to be sensitive to the ways in which advocating veganism as a feminist ideal interacts with existing norms for women's eating and appetites. The refusal of adolescent women to eat—especially to eat meat—has sometimes been read by feminists as an empowered (if unconscious) opposition to patriarchy. Susie Orbach, for instance, has argued that anorexia can be read as a feminist 'hunger strike'; it silently protests the demand to repress female appetite by carrying it to its logical (and visibly harmful) extreme.[24] Observing that oppressed or marginalized groups often turn to nonverbal forms of protest in situations where verbal resistance can lead to recrimination, Carol Adams also discusses 'meat phobia' as a phenomenon that might symbolize young girls' rejection of the phallocracy via their food choices. She suggests that these women can be seen as practicing feminism, "coding their criticism of the prevailing world order in the choice of female-identified foods" (175). On Adams's account, where meat eating is "the" symbol of the patriarchy, the refusal to eat meat is likely to look like a refusal to participate in that system.

This interpretation of teenaged girls' rejection of meat and animals products seems to me, however, worryingly disconnected from an understanding of how this refusal fits into broader cultural attitudes towards female appetite and consumption. The standard myth of female eating—which is exemplified in the lives of anorexics—effectively prohibits regular female consumption of 'male-identified' foods such as meat by linking it to weight gain and a corresponding loss of sexual attractiveness. (Adams herself points out that 'female-identified' foods are typically lower in calories, fat, and protein than 'male-identified' foods.) In this context, the act of 'refusing the male order in food' by rejecting meat, eggs, and dairy products is an act that *reinforces* existing cultural norms surrounding female consumption. For girls who rigidly conform to social norms of female eating and who deny themselves the food rich in protein and fat that their developing bodies require, "the protest collapses into its opposite and proclaims the utter capitulation of the subject to the contracted female world" (Bordo 176).[25] Women who display disordered attitudes towards physical embodiment and/or their own sexuality by avoiding male-identified foods seem to be participating in more than protesting the patriarchal status quo. Indeed, there is some concern in the medical community that at times "vegetarian diets may be selected to camouflage an existing eating disorder."[26]

Women avoiding male-identified foods is the *norm* for sexist myths of gendered eating, not the exception. Women are meant to monitor their food consumption closely, feel guilty about consuming the 'wrong' foods, and satisfy their appetites primarily with fruits, vegetables, and grains. It is unclear how making veganism a moral ideal would destabilize these norms. For one thing, the women who participate in this protest will be indistinguishable from those who are simply participating in disordered patterns of gendered eating. Furthermore, on the global level, women in situations of food scarcity often allow (or encourage) men to consume what little meat is available, cooking and serving it to the adult males while depriving themselves—even if these women perform more physical labor daily than their male counterparts, and even if they are pregnant and/or lactating. These practices lead to a disproportionate number of women dying of starvation in famine situations.[27] Again, it is not clear how advocating veganism as a specifically feminist moral ideal would undercut these realities.

The argument for feminist veganism must, I think, be taken in the larger context of these long-standing, deeply entrenched gendered eating norms. And, in this context, it is difficult to see how the act of feminists refraining from the consumption of animals and their products will destabilize the current system of objectification and oppression in the way that Adams et al. believe it will.

Moral Ideals and Second-Class Citizens

To this point, I have concentrated on how the case for veganism as a feminist moral ideal interacts with existing norms of gendered eating. In this section, I turn to the question of how people fare on this account who cannot meet (or who struggle to meet) this ideal for physiological, economic, or other reasons. There are two common responses to these situations: The first is to grant an exception to the moral rule to those people; the second is to bite the bullet, claim that those people are forced to behave immorally—and accept that this is a regrettable consequence of some people's suboptimal situations. My worry with the first response is that the people who need these exceptions tend to be those already most disadvantaged by the current system, and that giving them moral excuses thus reinforces their status as 'second-class' citizens. My worry with the second is that it has the effect of rendering those already disadvantaged people *immoral* second-class citizens, and that we should object to a moral theory that turns disadvantage into immorality. My response to these concerns is not to reject the idea that dietary choices are moral choices, however, but rather to argue (in the following sections) for an account in which there is no 'one' ideal for ethical eating but rather individual ideals based on particulars of our situations.

The American Dietetic Association has judged that

> appropriately planned vegetarian diets, including total vegetarian or vegan diets . . . are appropriate for individuals during all stages of the life cycle, including pregnancy, lactation, infancy, childhood, and adolescence, and for athletes.[28]

That is, there are no blanket health considerations that rule out veganism as a potentially healthy diet for human beings. At the same time, it is vital for vegetarian or vegan diets to be "appropriately planned." As the same primary author of the ADA report (W. J. Craig) writes in another report specifically on the health consequences of vegan diets,

> eliminating all animal products from the diet increases the risk of certain nutritional deficiencies. Micronutrients of special concern for the vegan

include vitamins B-12 and D, calcium, and long-chain n-3 (omega-3) fatty acids. Unless vegans regularly consume foods that are fortified with these nutrients, appropriate supplements should be consumed. In some cases, iron and zinc status of vegans may also be of concern because of the limited bioavailability of these minerals.[29]

For our purposes, there are two things to note about these reports. First, the specific micronutrients at issue in a vegan diet—especially calcium, iron, and zinc—are ones that women are more 'nutritionally vulnerable' with respect to than men. And the extent to which women are nutritionally vulnerable with respect to these nutrients varies over their life cycle (puberty, menstruation, pregnancy, lactation, perimenopause, menopause, post-menopause). This in no way implies that vegan diets are inappropriate for women. What it does mean is that women need to be more careful about their intake and absorption of these micronutrients on a vegan diet than men do. Second, whether women (and men) are in a position to put the time, money, energy, education, and other resources into adopting a healthy vegan diet depends on their individual situations. The ones who are most likely to be able to dedicate themselves to this lifestyle are people in situations of abundance and who are able to adopt this diet with relative physiological, psychological, economic, and social ease. The people most likely to be able to do this tend to be wealthy men in industrialized countries. Making veganism a moral ideal would require groups that are already economically, socially, and politically disadvantaged to exert a greater amount of time, energy, and resources to living a moral life than those who are already advantaged.

One response to this state of affairs is to grant those disadvantaged people moral 'passes' for being unable to live up to the moral ideal. Yet, in addition to being viewed as morally subpar by others, people who require excuses from the vegan moral ideal would also be likely to internalize their moral 'failings' in the form of feelings of guilt and inferiority, and to view those who can live up to that ideal as morally superior.

Imagine an analogous case in which a person, Devin, believes he has a moral obligation to give money to charity on a regular basis. Devin has, however, recently lost his job and is struggling to make ends meet—selling plasma just to pay rent and buy groceries. Most people are inclined to grant Devin an excuse from that moral obligation and to claim that his inability to meet that requirement does not compromise his moral character.

Now, imagine the effects of this exception from the perspective of both Devin and his community: First, even if Devin fully recognizes that he is not obligated in these circumstances to continue donating money to charity, if he has internalized this moral rule (and we're supposing that he's a sensitive moral agent who takes his obligation to donate money seriously) he is highly likely to struggle with feelings of inferiority and guilt for not being able to act in accordance with it. In addition, even if Devin's community (which we'll narrow just to family, friends, and neighbors for simplicity's sake) recognizes that Devin is excused from the moral rule in these circumstances, they're still likely to judge him negatively (if, perhaps, unconsciously) for being unable to act in accordance with it—and, if they're able to meet that moral requirement, they're likely to view themselves as, in some sense, superior to Devin *even recognizing that he is not obligated to act in accordance with that rule.* The situation becomes exacerbated over time; if Devin continues to struggle financially over the space of years, or even decades, he is increasingly likely to judge himself negatively for failing to be able to give money to charity, and his community is increasingly likely to view Devin as a subpar moral agent in that respect—again, *even if* they believe that he is genuinely excused from charitable giving. Devin would, in practice, be reduced to a second-class moral citizen in this respect.[30]

The parallel to the issue of moral veganism should be clear. Regardless of how we believe the people granted those exceptions are entitled to feel, or what we believe the people who aren't granted such exceptions should believe about those who are excused from the moral rule, it seems almost certain that the actual fact of routinely excusing those groups of people from the vegan moral ideal would have the consequence of morally disadvantaging groups which are already disadvantaged in a number of other ways. This disadvantage is magnified by the fact that many of these people will require exceptions or excuses from the moral rule for the majority of their lives; their biological and/or socio-geopolitical circumstances will entail that they will *never* be able to function in society as ideal moral agents. Claiming that this fact shouldn't impact the way they view themselves or the way that others view them belies the realities of their situation.

Another response to the inequality of these moral demands is to argue that this disadvantage is a tragic result of unjust social structures, and to bite the bullet and claim that the people who are not able to meet the moral vegan ideal are morally subpar. The fact that certain unjust social structures force people to participate in immoral acts is presented as further motivation to change those harmful systems. This response seems even more problematic than the first, however. For one thing, it has an air of adding insult to injury. On this view, people who are for one reason or another unable to flourish (physiologically, psychologically, economically, etc.) on a vegan diet are not just second-class citizens: They are *immoral* second-class citizens that deserve our pity. This puts them in a category of moral disadvantage that would seem to build up rather than break down the various barriers between them and those who are morally privileged on this system.

I believe that we should, instead, think of dietary choices in terms of a mean *relative to us* that falls on a continuum between doing injustice to ourselves, on the one hand, and doing injustice to others, on the other. According to this view, whether it is morally correct for us to engage in or to abstain from eating animals and/or animal products will depend on particulars of our individual physiological, cultural, economic, and relational situations.

Guiding Considerations

Several considerations guide the construction of my account. First, as I've already discussed, existing norms surrounding the consumption of meat are deeply gendered. Rather than overturning patterns of male domination, a more likely result of self-identified feminists—who are predominantly women—rejecting meat and animal products in favor of 'female-identified foods' is the further reinforcement of the current myths of male and female eating. As I've argued in detail elsewhere, more is at stake here than just what types of foods men and women eat: Patterns of meat consumption are only one part of larger gendered patterns of appetite indulgence and repression that permeate Western culture.[31] Men are encouraged to indulge and take pride in their appetites for meat, for sex, and for power, and women are taught to tightly repress their appetites, focusing instead of satisfying the appetites of others. We should be extremely cautious in advising a group that is already predisposed towards harmful repression of appetite to further monitor and restrict its consumption.

Second, eating is a moral activity on my theory insofar as it necessarily involves acting in ways that exemplify a certain relationship both to oneself and to others. One of the most central (and frequent) activities in which we participate, eating is integrally involved in the shape of our lives, and in the shaping of our characters. Dietary choices—whether involving the consumption of animals and animal products or fair-trade practices and fossil fuel use in food production and distribution—are choices that directly impact human and nonhuman animal flourishing on both an individual and community level. My account treats as moral a wide range of attitudes and behaviors not usually thought of as such, but I consider that an advantage rather than a detriment to my theory. To put a complex point very simply, we tend to focus all of our moral attention, energy, and outrage on a very narrow range of activities; in order to counteract systemic injustice, we need to adopt a broader ethical outlook.

Third, the widespread factory farming practices in the current meat, dairy, and egg industries strike me as morally indefensible. Any reasonable theory of ethical eating should advocate the elimination of such practices. Not only does it necessitate the suffering of the 'farmed' animals, but it also harms local environments and contributes to imbalanced and unsustainable agricultural practices (monocropping for feed, the heavy use of pesticide in order to grow nonlocal plants, etc.). The same general difficulties face the factory farm dairy and egg industries. The main reason factory farming has become so prevalent in the last fifty years or so, however, is the increasing demand of the growing global population for meat. In large parts of the industrialized world, factory farmed meat and animal products are the only sort available and/or affordable to the non-wealthy who live in urban areas. 'Free-range' meat, milk, and eggs are, by and large, luxuries available only to the middle and upper classes, who thus gain the upper hand with respect to both moral and health considerations. Any concrete steps towards eliminating factory farming, then, should also take into account negative effects such a move might have on the world's economically disadvantaged and seek to alleviate those effects.

In summary, an adequate feminist account of ethical eating should seek to change the disordered reality of current gendered eating patterns, treat dietary choices[32] as moral choices insofar as they constitute an integral part of our relationships to ourselves and to others, and advocate the end of factory farming practices in ways that don't further disadvantage the urban poor.

Finding the Mean for Ethical Eating

The basic structure of my account is Aristotelian: I think of morality in terms of the actions, attitudes, desires, and beliefs involved in developing and maintaining a good moral character, understood in a robust and meaningful sense.[33] In practical terms, this means that the vast majority of one's everyday choices, actions, and desires—particularly those made on a regular or habitual basis—impact one's character in such a way as to make one either a better or worse moral agent.

I also advocate Aristotle's doctrine of the 'mean relative to us' with respect to moral virtues.[34] That is, I believe that Aristotle was correct in identifying virtue as a mean between two extremes—and that he was right in claiming that human beings do not share a common mean, but rather that where the moral mean falls for each person will be relative to us. In other words, what's virtuous for an individual person will depend (and vary) on their particular external circumstances, physical abilities and limitations, and so on. What's more, this mean can (and will) change as the person's circumstances change. To give a practical example, what bravery for me would look like in the face of an attempted mugging might be cowardly for my friend who's a fourth-degree black belt, and what bravery for her would look like in the same situation might be recklessness for me. It is vital to stress in this connection that it is not a matter of my being *less brave* than my friend, however, or of her being *more brave* than me. Rather, this moral theory maintains that we can both exemplify bravery through different actions—and that it would be morally wrong for either of us to act according to the other's mean.

With respect to the issue of ethical eating practices, then, I believe we should think of the moral mean as falling between the vice of doing injustice to oneself and the vice of doing injustice to others. In thinking about our dietary choices, we should take into consideration both what would facilitate our personal flourishing (physiologically, psychologically, economically, socially, etc.) and what would facilitate the flourishing of those (both human and nonhuman) in our broader communities.

The effects of disordered gendered norms of eating are highly relevant in this context of evaluation. Doing justice to oneself in this case will include, for example, proper respect for our own well-being, which includes viewing ourselves as having equal moral worth with others. Women have, traditionally, been discouraged from viewing themselves in this way. Instead, they have been encouraged to and rewarded for placing the well-being of others ahead of their own, denying their appetites in favor of indulging the appetites of those around them. They have also been taught to fear and repress hunger and to feel constant shame for eating. It would not be surprising, then, if many women needed to move more towards 'doing justice to oneself.' At the same time, doing justice to others will involve respect for their well-being, which includes viewing others as having equal moral worth as ourselves. Men have, traditionally, been encouraged to indulge their appetites without full regard for the impact their actions have on others. It would not be surprising, then, if many men needed to move closer to 'doing justice to others.'

On this account, we should treat all animals (ourselves and others, human and nonhuman) with equal respect and with concern for their flourishing as members of their natural kinds. Treating everyone with consideration for their flourishing will, however, entail a dramatic change in current relationships between human and nonhuman species. We would need to shift from a focus on maximizing the quantity and/or quality of the products we get from the animals we have domesticated for their milk, eggs, and such, to genuine concern for promoting their flourishing. Were we to make this shift, though, I do not believe that living in continued relationships with animals that also involve our consuming their products necessarily harms them. I find nothing inherently objectionable about the consumption of eggs, milk, and other dairy products, for instance, so long as the producing animals live in conditions that allow them to flourish as members of their natural kinds. This will, however, entail a *drastic* reduction in the amount of meat, dairy products, and eggs available for human consumption.

Indeed, one thing that seems certain—especially given the injustices of factory farming and the need to eliminate such practices—is that the mean for almost everyone who lives in wealthy, industrialized cultures will involve the reduction or complete elimination of meat and other animal products. In fact, it seems highly likely that the mean for those who are physiologically, psychologically, and economically able to flourish on diets that do not involve animal products will involve their doing so.

How this will play out in actual practice is complicated, however—and rightly so, for both our own lives and the way they intersect with the lives around us are highly complex. Take the case of Leah, who lives in a position of relative economic and social comfort, with a full-time career as a professional sociologist and primary responsibility for a young child. Leah is capable of flourishing on a vegan diet without compromising her physical, psychological, or economic health, and she possesses sufficient resources to educate herself on how best to live a vegan lifestyle without its consuming undue amounts of time and energy. At the same time, as primary caregiver for her child, Skye, Leah possesses the responsibility to guarantee that her daughter's nutritional needs are met. As a fast-growing girl with a serious allergy to soy and an aversion to beans, kale, and other leafy green vegetables, Skye is not likely to flourish on a vegan diet. Should Leah become a vegan but assume the burden of preparing meals for her daughter that include some animal products? Perhaps, in these circumstances, she should be vegetarian, meeting Skye's nutritional needs with eggs and dairy products while minimizing her own consumption of those products. What is important to note, in any event, is that only she will have access to the full amount of information that determines her mean.

Geographic considerations will also play a role in determining one's mean. If one lives in Southern California, for instance, where the growing season is extended, and one has a backyard suitable for growing vegetables and fruits, one's mean will likely be quite different from one who lives in downtown Cleveland. One's mean can also change with one's geographic and social circumstances. An individual from Maui whose mean in Hawaii is vegan might justly eat meat during an extended stay in rural Mongolia, for instance, while someone from Sierra Leone whose mean is omnivorous there might justly abstain from eating meat and significantly reduce or eliminate her consumption of dairy products when she moves to Tokyo.

My view can be seen as a version of moral contextualism. It differs in at least one important way from versions of contextualism such as Deane Curtin's, however.[35] Although Curtin advocates Contextual Moral Vegetarianism as one aspect of a broader program of nonviolence and does not present that program as a universal rule, Contextual Moral Vegetarianism still presents veganism as the ultimate moral ideal, even if not an appropriate lifestyle for everyone. But, as I argued earlier, this has the net effect of reducing those unable to meet the idea to second-class moral citizens. Thinking of moral ideals (in the plural) as variable according to individuals avoids this effect. What counts as properly ethical eating for an individual person depends on what the mean relative to that person is, whether that involves abstaining entirely from meat and animal products, eating dairy products and eggs but not meat, eating fish but not other animals or animal products, and so on.

Veganism is not uniquely privileged on my account. Although this will be seen by some as a serious flaw, in the context of current disordered gendered eating norms it has at least two distinct advantages. First, the immediate impact of a significant number of men becoming vegetarian or vegan would likely be to weaken that association of meat eating with men and masculinity. This weakening might well lead to a welcome shift in current myths of male and female eating, where the deeply entrenched identification of certain foods (such as meat) as masculine and other foods (such as salads and fruit) as feminine would gradually be deconstructed by actual practice.

Second, the fact that moral dietary choices can vary from individual to individual and from situation to situation should work to prevent any one particular diet from becoming privileged over another. We usually have no direct access to the mean relative to another person, and we would not be entitled to draw definite conclusions about someone's moral character in that area without access to that person's mean. Ideally, one of the long-term consequences of putting this account of ethical eating into practice would be that it would reduce the morally loaded attitudes that we currently hold towards eating—and that significantly contribute to disordered eating. A woman's choice of an ice cream sundae would not, for instance, automatically generate negative judgments about her willpower and/or health status; a man's choice of an Activia yogurt would not automatically generate negative judgments about his masculinity, since those around them would lack access to their means. In general, adopting a virtue-ethics approach to ethical eating would seriously undermine the rigid—and highly gendered— moral judgments that currently guide our thinking about what other people around us should or should not be eating.

This outcome seems deeply desirable to me. Our primary job as moral agents is not, after all, to police the behavior of those around us (except in the case of the very small number of people to whom we have special relations of account- ability); it is to work as best we can to optimize the health of the relations we have both to ourselves and to our communities, to flourish as human beings individually and in relation to others.[36]

Notes

1. These myths are not meant to track actual lived experience. They convey norms against which we measure and judge our eating patterns and appetites, in the way that cultural myths about the American Dream and its 'self-made man' convey norms against which we measure and judge our work ethic and success levels.
2. For a more detailed discussion of this topic, see my "Eating as a Gendered Act: Chris- tianity, Feminism, and Reclaiming the Body," in *Readings in the Philosophy of Religion*, 2nd ed., ed. K. Clark (Peterborough, ON: Broadview Press, 2008).
3. See Carol Cohn's "Wars, Wimps, and Women: Talking Gender and Thinking War," in *The Gendered Society Reader*, ed. M. Kimmel (New York: Oxford University Press, 2000) for a succinct discussion of how 'gendered discourse' impacts our experience of things like food.
4. A quick search on the Internet turns up gems like Epic Mealtime's Christmas "Slaughterhouse" episode, where they construct a gingerbread-style house of meat, filled with Cheez Whiz, topped with bacon, and consumed with eggnog spiked with Jack Daniel's whiskey and bacon grease. The equation of women with low- calorie and fat foods is demonstrated, in contrast, by the 'Women Laughing Alone with Salad' tumblr, or the 'Target Women' episode on yogurt ("the official food of women").
5. Carol Adams, *The Sexual Politics of Meat: A Feminist-Vegetarian Critical Theory* (New York: Continuum International, 1990; 10th anniv. ed., 2000).
6. See, e.g., Greta Gaard's "Ecofeminism and Native American Cultures," in *Ecofemi- nism: Women, Animals, and Nature*, ed. G. Gaard (Philadelphia: Temple University Press, 1993), which also contains Lori Gruen's "Dismantling Oppression: An Analy- sis of the Connection between Women and Animals"; see also Marti Kheel's "The Liberation of Nature: A Circular Affair," *Environmental Ethics* 7 (1985): 135–149, and "Vegetarianism and Ecofeminism: Toppling Patriarchy with a Fork," in *Food for Thought: The Debate over Eating Meat*, ed. S. F. Sapontzis (New York: Prometheus

Books, 2004), 327–343; see also Catharine MacKinnon's "Of Mice and Men: A Feminist Fragment on Animal Rights," in *Animal Rights: Current Debates and New Directions*, ed. C. Sunstein and M. Nussbaum (New York: Oxford University Press, 2004).

7. The idea that one has any real choice over what one eats is, of course, a presumption that comes from a position of wealth and resources. Nevertheless, even in cases where there is little to no range of foods from which to choose, there are likely to remain choices concerning how much to eat in relation to others, etc., that will be moral choices.

8. The question of the means and consequences of this objectification is, on the other hand, more controversial. See Martha Nussbaum's "Objectification," *Philosophy and Public Affairs* 24 (1995): 249–291, for a nuanced discussion of different forms that this can take, and for an argument that not all forms of objectification are morally objectionable.

9. Cohn, "Wars, Wimps, and Women."

10. See, e.g., Simone de Beauvoir's classic treatment of this topic in *The Second Sex,* translated and edited by H. M. Parshley (New York: Vintage Books, 1989); Andrea Dworkin's discussion of objectification in "Occupation/Collaboration," in *Intercourse: Twentieth Anniversary Edition* (New York: Basic Books, 2007), 153–184; Catharine McKinnon's *Feminism Unmodified* (Cambridge, MA: Harvard University Press, 1987); and the introduction to Susan Bordo's *Unbearable Weight: Feminism, Western Culture, and the Body* (Berkeley: University of California Press, 1993), as well as her earlier *The Flight to Objectivity: Essays on Cartesianism and Culture* (Albany: State University of New York Press, 1987).

11. I will be paying special attention to Adams's *Sexual Politics of Meat* in this chapter, as it is both accessible and tremendously influential on current work in this field.

12. MacKinnon, "Of Mice and Men."

13. That men have been systemically advantaged across cultures and time does not, of course, mean that all men have been engaged in a conscious effort to oppress or repress women and nonhuman animals. See part three of the first volume of Foucault's *History of Sexuality* for a discussion of power functions as an interaction of noncentralized forces that both produces and sustains positions of advantage and disadvantage. Michel Foucault, *History of Sexuality*, trans. R. Hurley (New York: Vintage Books, 1990).

14. See Jason Wyckoff's "Linking Sexism and Speciesism," *Hypatia* 29, no. 4 (Fall 2014): 721–737, for a comprehensive and clear discussion of the ways in which oppressions can be linked, as well as a defense of the link between sexism and speciesism.

15. See, e.g., Plato's *Phaedo*, in which Socrates memorably states that

    The body keeps us busy in a thousand ways because of its need for nurture . . . It fills us with wants, desires, fears, all sorts of illusions, and much nonsense, so that, as it is said, in truth and in fact no thought of any kind ever comes to us from the body. Only the body and its desires cause war, civil discord, and battles. (66b–d)

    For a classic argument against essentialism in eco-feminism, see Jent Biehl's *Finding Our Way. Rethinking Ecofeminist Politics* (Montreal: Black Rose Books, 1991).

16. For a particularly trenchant analysis of this phenomenon, see the introduction to Bordo, *Unbearable Weight.*

17. Cohn, "Wars, Wimps, and Women."

18. For an excellent discussion of how somatophobia has functioned in feminist theories, see Elizabeth Spelman's "Race & Gender: The Ampersand Problem in Feminist Thought," chapter five in *Inessential Woman: Problems of Exclusion in Feminist Thought*, ed. E. Spelman (Boston: Beacon Press, 1988), 114–132.

19. See, e.g., Patrick Hopkins's "Gender Treachery: Homophobia, Masculinity, and Threatened Identities," in *Rethinking Masculinity: Philosophical Explorations in the Light*

of Feminism, ed. R. Strikwerda, P. D. Hopkins, and H. Brod (Lanham, MD: Rowman and Littlefield, 2002), in which he explores the fragility of constructions of masculinity as essentially involving strength, confidence, and power. See also Michael Kimmel and Michael Messner's *Men's Lives*, 7th ed. (Boston: Allyn & Bacon, 2006), and Susan Faludi's *Stiffed: The Betrayal of the American Man* (New York: Putnam, 1999).

20. Beth Dixon, "The Feminist Connection between Women and Animals," *Environmental Ethics* 18, no. 2 (1996): 181–194.

21. This is one of Simone de Beauvoir's main explanations in *The Second Sex* for why woman remains Other in a society where she has economic and reproductive liberty: Man still sees woman as Other, and woman has internalized this position and often actively presents herself as Other. For a detailed discussion of this phenomenon, see Susan Bordo's *Unbearable Weight*.

22. Jason Wyckoff, for instance, concludes that the link between sexism and speciesism is best thought of in terms of "what is common to the status of women and nonhuman animals under the law" (734)—namely, less-than-full consideration of their interests and institutionalized subordination. Wyckoff, "Linking Sexism and Speciesism." *Hypatia* 29, no. 4 (Fall 2014): 721–737.

23. See, e.g., Nancy Bauer's "Lady Power," *Opinionator* (blog), *New York Times*, June 20, 2010, http://opinionator.blogs.nytimes.com/2010/06/20/lady-power/?_php=true&_type=blogs&_r=0 , and "Beauvoir on the Allure of Self-Objectification," in *Feminist Metaphysics*, ed. C. Witt (Heidelberg: Springer Verlag, 2011), 117–129. The results of Western feminists' attempts to end female genital cutting in African countries is a prime example of this sort of failure: Rather than the practice ending, it became more common in many areas where it had been declining, began to be carried out on younger girls, and took place more often in nonsterile settings (like hospitals) to avoid official sanction.

24. See Susie Orbach, *Fat Is a Feminist Issue* (New York: Random House, 1978 [vol. 1]; 1982 [vol. 2]). See also Kim Chernin's *The Obsession: Reflections on the Tyranny of Slenderness* (New York: Harper and Row, 1981).

25. Susan Bordo, "The Body and the Reproduction of Femininity," in *Unbearable Weight*.

26. W. J. Craig, A. R. Mangels, and the American Dietetic Association [ADA], "Position of the American Dietetic Association: Vegetarian Diets," *Journal of the American Dietetic Association* 109, no. 7 (2009): 1266–1282. See also A. M. Bardone-Cone et al., "The Inter-Relationships between Vegetarianism and Eating Disorders among Females," *Journal of the Academy of Nutrition and Dietetics* 112, no. 8 (2012): 1247–1252.

27. See Lisa Leghorn and Mary Roodkowsky's *Who Really Starves? Women and World Hunger* (New York: Friendship Press, 1977).

28. Craig, Mangels, and the ADA, "Position of the American Dietetic Association: Vegetarian Diets." Abstract. *Journal of the American Dietetic Association* 109, no. 7 (2009): 1266–1282. http://www.ncbi.nlm.nih.gov/pubmed/19562864.

29. W. J. Craig, "Health Effects of Vegan Diets." Abstract. *American Journal of Clinical Nutrition* 89, no. 5 (2009): 1627S–1633S. http://www.ncbi.nlm.nih.gov/pubmed/19279075.

30. The self-reports of soldiers returning from war (and their reception by their communities) support this claim. Passing over the Vietnam War as problematic for various reasons, interviews with soldiers from WWI and WWII demonstrate that, quite frequently, they struggled with serious feelings of guilt and moral failing for killing other human beings in battle—even when they recognized that they were excused from the general moral prohibition against killing.

31. Van Dyke, "Eating as a Gendered Act."

32. See note 7.

33. I develop this account in more detail in my "Moral Babies, Metaphysical Bathwater" (forthcoming in a special edition of *Res Philosophica* on Virtue and the Emotions).

34. For Aristotle's introduction and discussion of the concept of virtue as a mean relative to us, see Bk. II of the *Nicomachean Ethics*, particularly 1107a, where he presents his full definition of virtue of character.
35. See Deane Curtin's "Toward an Ecological Ethic of Care," *Hypatia* 6, no. 1 (1991): 60–74.
36. This chapter was originally inspired by conversations with Sara Ferguson and Jeanette Bradley, to whom I owe thanks for their individual and collective wisdom on this and many other topics. The chapter has gone through a variety of transformations and been presented in a number of different places, including the University of Wyoming, the Ethics Club at the University of Colorado–Boulder, the Rocky Mountain Ethics Congress, Calvin College Wake-Up Weekend, the underground program at the Bellingham Summer Philosophy Conference, and the Philosophy of Religion reading group at Notre Dame. Each time, it has generated lively discussion and helpful feedback, and I thank those audiences—as well as those I may well be forgetting!—for their generous engagement. Further special thanks go to the editors of this volume for their comments.

3

"EAT RESPONSIBLY"

Agrarianism and Meat

Benjamin J. Bruxvoort Lipscomb

I am going to write about two contemporary "food movements" that have remained largely separate: the movement to reconsider the consumption of meat and other animal products, on the one hand, and the movement to create alternatives to contemporary industrialized agriculture, on the other.[1] I am interested in both, but have been asked to contribute to this collection as a sympathizer with the latter—with the agrarian vision of Gene Logsdon, Wes Jackson, and (especially) Wendell Berry[2]—and to explore what contemporary agrarianism might have to say about meat eating. Though recent agrarians have had little to say about meat eating, things they've said about other topics can be helpful to us in thinking about this one. As anyone who has engaged seriously with agrarianism knows, its implications seldom fit tidily into familiar ideological drawers. That is part of its importance.

This chapter is divided into two parts, corresponding to the two discussions it attempts to bring together. The first part of the chapter is about agrarianism; the second is about meat eating.

Agrarianism

Not all readers will be familiar with the agrarian revival of the past generation, though some now-familiar phenomena—community-supported agriculture, urban agriculture, and locavorism—can be regarded as among its outgrowths. A few words first, then, about (my understanding of) present-day agrarianism—with which I can perhaps make clear to unfamiliar or skeptical readers the attractions of the view. As I already hinted in passing, I will draw especially on the thought of Wendell Berry, agrarianism's most influential living exponent.

Like any serious, wide-ranging practical philosophy, agrarianism does not lend itself to a tidy definition, but the following list of "natural laws" that opens Berry's essay, "Conservation and Local Economy," can serve as a partial list of first principles. I became an agrarian in part because I found this Septalogue so compelling:

I.   Land that is used will be ruined unless it is properly cared for.
II. Land cannot be properly cared for by people who do not know it intimately, who do not know how to care for it, who are not strongly motivated to care for it, and who cannot afford to care for it.
III. People cannot be adequately motivated to care for land by general principles or by incentives that are merely economic—that is, they won't care for it merely because they think they should or merely because somebody pays them.
IV. People are motivated to care for land to the extent that their interest in it is direct, dependable, and permanent.
V.   They will be motivated to care for the land if they can reasonably expect to live on it as long as they live. They will be more strongly motivated if they can reasonably expect that their children and grandchildren will live on it as long as they live. In other words, there must be a mutuality of belonging: they must feel that the land belongs to them, that they belong to it, and that this belonging is a settled and unthreatened fact.
VI. But such belonging must be appropriately limited. This is the indispensable qualification of the idea of land ownership. It is well understood that ownership is an incentive to care. But there is a limit to how much land can be owned before an owner is unable to take proper care of it. The need for attention increases with the intensity of use. But the *quality* of attention decreases as acreage increases.
VII. A nation will destroy its land and therefore itself if it does not foster in every possible way the sort of thrifty, prosperous, permanent rural households and communities that have the desire, the skills, and the means to care properly for the land they are using.[3]

These are only first principles—starting points. Others are needed (extending the concerns of agrarians beyond land to the creatures that live from it).[4] Still, we have here the beginnings of a wide-ranging ethical and political standpoint, whose contrasts to more familiar standpoints are hard to overlook.

Berry's view has precedents. He and other recent agrarians have self-consciously revived a tradition of thought going back to ancient sources, but enjoying special prominence in the United States, first in the thought of Thomas Jefferson, later in various late-nineteenth-century populist movements, and again in the writings of the Southern agrarians of the 1930s. The agrarian political vision—of political liberty secured through a wide distribution of usable properly and the settled attachment of people to place—is an old one.

But there *is* something new about contemporary agrarianism. As Kimberly Smith observes in her study of Berry's political thought, Berry has joined the political vision of Jefferson and Allen Tate (a wide distribution of usable property) to a broad moral and ecological vision. For Berry, the conservation of land and the creatures who live from it depends in part on the very arrangement Jefferson and Tate advocated: a "mutuality of belonging" between people and places that they own and on which they depend.[5]

At the risk of dismembering the view I am describing, which is insistently integrative and holistic, I am going to restrict my focus to the moral and ecological vision of contemporary agrarianism, because it is from this aspect of the agrarian vision that we may anticipate instruction about our treatment of non-human animals.

Present-day agrarianism has some resemblances to a cluster of views in contemporary moral philosophy: the "ethics of care."[6] As the language of Berry's "natural laws" highlights, he starts from an imperative to deal "care-fully" with whatever falls under our potentially damaging influence, and grounds this imperative in individual and communal necessities. His first premise is: We live by using people, places, animals, and other creatures.

Berry's term "use" should be understood in a neutral sense. We need various things, starting with air, food, and water, and get them through interaction with the world and its inhabitants. In some cases, to use is to consume. What is necessary, if we are to survive and thrive, is not to use the world and its inhabitants in ways that degrade or exhaust the sources of our sustenance. This brings us to a second premise: Whatever is used carelessly is put at risk, left open to degradation and exhaustion. It is imperative, then, to investigate and heed the preconditions of careful use. These preconditions, the agrarian maintains, are intimate acquaintance and a sense of mutual belonging between the person and what he or she uses. These preconditions do not guarantee careful use, but neither are they dispensable. And to understand them is already to understand much about the agrarian view.[7]

This discussion is in danger of becoming unhelpfully abstract. Consider, by way of illustration, not an agricultural example, but one as likely to resonate with urban readers as with rural ones: a common fate of residential rental properties. In most cases, these are owned and maintained by people who do not live nearby (within a short walk, so that the owner or steward has occasion to see the rental on a regular basis without going out of his or her way). Sometimes this is because the landlords own many such properties, and can't possibly live near all of them. Sometimes this is because the landlords are corporations and do not *live* anywhere.

What incentives operate in a situation such as this, where there is no intimate acquaintance or sense of mutual belonging? Unless there is an acute housing shortage, the principal users of the house or apartment have little stake in keeping the place up, and the owner can let it degrade badly without thereby degrading his or her own neighborhood (again, if the landlord *has* a "neighborhood"). Typically, some work will be done, now and then, to keep the place marketable, but not the kind of work people do when more than income is at stake. Anyone who has lived in a neighborhood where more than a few houses were used in this manner can testify to the results. Over time, the neighborhood comes to look worse. It sometimes comes to look terrible.[8] Then, following the "broken windows" pattern documented by sociologists James Wilson and George Kelling, the degraded look of the place fosters corresponding forms of communal degradation.[9]

What this example illustrates is that careful use—use that doesn't degrade or exhaust what it depends upon—imposes limits on the scale at which and the distance from which it relates to what it uses. If familiarity can breed contempt, it is nevertheless also a precondition of care-taking. Call this "the first precondition" or "the precondition of scale." Careful use is further supported Berry adds, where there is a sense of mutual belonging: where what is used has a claim on the user and is not merely disposable to him or her. Call this "the second precondition" or "the precondition of belonging." We see right away that the stringency of the first precondition is greater than that of the second. The first precondition is about knowing enough to be able to act carefully. The second gives one a more reliable motive to care.

Before leaving this point, let me pause to enrich the vocabulary with which we can talk about these preconditions and the kind of behavior they enable. A *near* synonym for what we have been talking about is "responsibility," defined not merely as liability to blame or punishment, but as a virtue. I define it as an attentiveness and deliberateness in action that refuses to leave the realization of one's aims to chance or the bad effects of one's actions to be repaired or endured by others—and that thereby leaves one ready to answer for what one does. This introduces notions of obligation, or at least of being held to account, that the language of "care" does not. And it sharpens our sense of what is wrong with negligence—namely, its buck-passing, its unreadiness to give an account. I will frequently use the terms "responsible" or "irresponsible" where I might also have used "careful" or "careless," to accent this morally significant attentiveness, deliberateness, and readiness to answer.

To reiterate the two preconditions of care-taking in terms of responsibility: First, I can only act responsibly toward what I know reasonably well. I cannot be ready to answer for what I cannot anticipate because I know too little. So the gardener who does not know the secondary effects of an herbicide he is applying cannot act responsibly as he applies it. He may get lucky; perhaps nothing will be disrupted besides the weeds he is targeting. But it will only be luck. The gardener does not stand ready to deal with any bad effects of the application of the herbicide. This lesson has the noteworthy consequence that the sphere of potentially irresponsible action is wider than the sphere of potentially responsible action. I can act irresponsibly where I do not know enough to act responsibly.[10]

Second, I am at increased risk of irresponsibility whenever I am using what I regard as merely disposable. The irresponsibility may be large or small. But where the effects of my actions are ones that I do not regard as *attached to me*—where there is no sense of mutual belonging—the danger of irresponsibility increases.

This last point invites us to consider, more closely than we have, this sense of belonging. Earlier writers in the agrarian tradition, interested mainly in politics and economics, stressed not a *sense*, but more official and objective ties: legal ownership, and a direct link (the more direct, the better) between one's own prosperity (in the straightforward economic sense) and the condition of what one owns. They had a point, at least as regards land and other inanimate property. What one controls, and especially what affects one's prosperity, one has an incentive to treat responsibly.

But this is not an adequate motivation to act responsibly even toward land— let alone toward other creatures. Because even if one recognizes a link between one's prosperity and the condition of what one owns, if one does not *inhabit* this knowledge in the right way, one might still choose to degrade or exhaust one's property, judging that this best serves one's interests. One might think of one's property like a mine, the condition of which is, to be sure, linked to the prosperity one can derive from it, but which must someday be exhausted. In any case, the nonreciprocal character of legal ownership makes it an inadequate frame for any *relationship* between creatures. Berry's talk of "mutuality of belonging" hints at what more is needed. Recall how Berry introduces his fifth "natural law": people, he argues,

> will be motivated to care for [land they are using] if they can reasonably expect to live on it as long as they live. They will be more strongly motivated if they can reasonably expect that their children and grandchildren will live on it as long as they live.[11]

In introducing the vocabulary of "responsibility," I already suggested that the agrarian moral vision has an affinity, not just with an ethics of care, but with an ethics of virtue generally.[12] It considers not just actions and outcomes, but the qualities of character that people should cultivate—recognizing that we behave worse when we are not guided by deep habits of action and outlook.[13] And it insists that the habits we form, of care-taking or abuse, will manifest themselves across a wide range of situations, toward a wide range of objects. We must *be* care-takers, and must not *be* abusers. Among the virtues stressed by recent agrarians, besides responsibility, is one that might seem identical with caring, but needs to be distinguished from it: affection.

By "caring," recall, we meant, not a feeling or attitude, but a type of behavior: *taking* care. One can take care (act carefully) without having any particular feeling or attitude toward the object of care. Again, we noted that a sense of mutual belonging provides a reliable motivation to careful behavior, which is nevertheless *possible* without it (though it cannot be relied on very far).

It is noteworthy that, in his recent Jefferson lecture, summarizing the moral vision that has guided him in his work, Berry casts his argument in terms of affection, drawing inspiration (and his title: "It All Turns on Affection") from E. M. Forster's *Howards End*.[14] In Forster's novel, three families of characters from divergent cultural and social backgrounds enter into a web of relations with one another, such that they have great power over one another, for good or ill. Forster, and Berry after him, regards the moral quality of their dealings with one another as traceable to the quality of their imagined (meaning not *made up* but *envisioned*) connections to one another, in particular the affection for one another that these imagined connections do (or do not) ground. Berry's view is that, if we are to be careful and not careless with the land and the creatures that live from it, we must imagine connections between us that ground such affection.

Is this what Berry means by "mutuality of belonging" in the Septalogue I quoted earlier? I am not certain. The expression suggests a reciprocal tie. But one can understand this reciprocal tie in either of two senses—circumstantial or attitudinal—each apparently important to Berry. On the one hand, he is keenly interested in *structural* incentives to responsible behavior, the kind of incentives that operate by subtly (or not-so-subtly) shaping the circumstances within which we deliberate.[15] As he writes, people (by and large) will not be reliably motivated to careful land use "merely because they think they should or merely because somebody pays them." Rather, "people are motivated to care for land to the extent that their interest in it is direct, dependable, and permanent." This sounds circumstantial. The reciprocal tie lies in how one's own well-being and the land's are bound together.

On the other hand, here is how he explains what he means by a "mutuality of belonging" between people and land: "they must feel that the land belongs to them, that they belong to it, and that this belonging is a settled and unthreatened fact." The appeal is to a feeling, a sense—an attitudinal tie. Indeed, when he writes that "people are motivated to care for land to the extent that their interest in it is direct, dependable, and permanent"—that is, to the extent that mutual belonging, in the circumstantial sense, obtains—he makes such belonging a means to an outlook, one he later calls "affection," which is what finally makes us reliable care-takers. And this outlook too is a tie, cultivated through the now-familiar preconditions of care-taking: intimate acquaintance and mutual belonging in the circumstantial sense. This outlook is not properly reciprocal; the land can't share our affection. But it is a way that we can inhabit our truly reciprocal, circumstantial belonging—our dependence on the land, and its dependence on us.

Recasting the agrarian outlook once again, this time in terms of affection, one sees again the importance of scale. It is a mistake to suppose that one can have affection for many, many creatures or places. One can be generously respectful, recognizing all creatures or places as the actual or potential objects of someone's affection, and as important in themselves (not only if someone is affectionate toward them). But one cannot be indiscriminately affectionate, because one cannot indiscriminately imagine the relevant connections between oneself and the world. Berry stands in a classical tradition, then, not only in his sense of the political importance of a wide distribution of usable property but in his insistence that among our most important moral tasks is to combat hubris in ourselves: the failure to appropriately respect our physical, intellectual, and emotional limits.[16]

The topic of affection points toward an essential aspect of contemporary agrarian thought that has not yet emerged in my exposition—or that has emerged only briefly and in passing. I wrote, early on, that we live by using the world and that what we use is thereby open to degradation and exhaustion. And I drew the conclusion that we ought to use the world carefully, to avoid degrading or exhausting what we use. But supposing there were no pressing danger to ourselves: Why not degrade or exhaust?

A virtuous person—a responsible one—might recoil from this question, wanting no explanation of why it is bad to degrade or exhaust. Or someone might rest content with the explanation that the badness of degrading or exhausting what we use lies in its effects on us, which we cannot confidently predict not to be bad. But this would misrepresent the thought of most contemporary agrarians. And it would give only instrumental significance to affection.

The bedrock value for Berry and other contemporary agrarians is not our own well-being but the well-being of the land and the creatures that live from it. There is a basic commitment among contemporary agrarians to the moral significance of the life-sustaining habitat in which we find ourselves, and of the creatures that inhabit it—and thus to the aptness of this habitat (or appropriately scaled portions of it) and these creatures as objects of affection. It is a commitment that *can* be given further explanation—though it might not be possible to argue a determined skeptic into it.

It is, finally, a sense of the sacred in the world, of the world as given to us in *trust* and not as fully or finally ours. This can be given expression in the conceptual vocabularies of various religious traditions. Berry, though his relationship to Christianity is conflicted, has drawn on the conceptual vocabulary of Christianity (actually on the vocabulary, shared between Jews and Christians, of the Hebrew Bible) to articulate this sense of the sacred. Using this vocabulary, he threads between the well-recognized pitfalls of the several major theoretical "camps" in contemporary environmental ethics: an anthropocentrism that sees humans as the only bearers of significance and everything else as existing for us, and various anti-anthropocentrisms that try, quixotically, to conceive the world in abstraction from the human standpoint.[17] Berry articulates, to my mind, a much more stable and satisfactory view, albeit one that is religiously controversial:[18] the world and its inhabitants exist at and for God's pleasure. We are invited to use the world and its inhabitants, but not to degrade or exhaust them. They are not ours to degrade or exhaust.

I will not presuppose in what follows any detailed account of the world's sacredness. Indeed, as I said, a virtuous person might want no explanation of why it is bad to degrade or exhaust what we use. But if one undertakes to explain, and does not rest content with the explanation that it is contrary to our interests to degrade or exhaust what we use, one quickly finds oneself appealing to a moral ontology richer than that of most academic moral theories: theories of self-interest, or of contractual reciprocity, or of the widest possible satisfaction of preferences.

Two final points about contemporary agrarianism, before I turn to the topic of meat eating. One of Berry's distinctive contributions, as I mentioned early on, has been to bring together the political vision of earlier agrarians with the moral and specifically ecological vision that we have been exploring. His insight, in fusing these two visions, had to do with how "thinking small"—limiting the scale of land ownership and land use—enables us to attend more sensitively to the fine-grained interconnectedness of species and their habitats. One of the final points I want to make about Berry and contemporary agrarianism concerns this commitment to ecological holism. Our flourishing, and the flourishing of the world and its inhabitants, depends finally on our thinking about the systems or cycles in which we intervene when we use the world. Since some of our use will be consumptive, we must find ways to consume that allow for the steady replenishment of what we consume. Whatever it means to make sure we do not degrade or exhaust what we use, it cannot mean that we never take the life of another creature. There are better and worse ways to do this, as we will discuss. But just as important as taking life in better ways is the preservation of the patterns by which lives carry on. This is best accomplished, on the agrarian view, by the efforts of many people, each applying the kind of detailed local knowledge that would be impossible on a very large scale.[19]

It remains to say something—less than I would like—about the evident conservatism of Berry's thought: its emphasis on preserving established agricultural communities and practices.[20] This is related to the point of the previous paragraph. A deep knowledge of the land and creatures one uses is necessary for caretaking, but this is hard if one has little history with the objects of one's use. If people are to understand and preserve what they use, the best thing is to proceed by careful, cautious adaptations of means to context, adaptations that might take generations to develop.

This allows us to tie together our overview of contemporary agrarian thought. If intimate acquaintance requires extended association, so too does a sense of mutual belonging and affection. Affection, proceeding from a sense of belonging, is a safeguard against the temptations always supplied by need or greed to degrade the sources by which we live. And a sense of belonging is not something we can will into being, or sustain in isolation from others who share it with us. We evoke and strengthen affection by shared care-taking, by celebration of what we enjoy together, and when necessary, by challenging one another. The best care-taking, then, will be the work of "permanent . . . households and communities that have the desire, the skills, and the means to care properly for the land they are using."[21]

Meat Eating

Like Berry in "Conservation and Local Economy," I begin with a statement of principles. My aim is to draw out some implications of the agrarian outlook I have been discussing. Most of the rest of the chapter will consist of elaboration of these principles:

1. The animals that people hunt or raise for slaughter are fit objects of care, sites of sacred significance. They are not to be treated in ways that degrade them.
2. But since the same is true of the plants we eat, this does not immediately rule out consuming animals or their products.
3. What degrades an animal is to make its life a poor one for the kind of creature it is. It is to deny it a life involving the characteristic activities and satisfactions of its kind, or to cancel these by one's use of it. Thus ethology—the contextual study of the characteristic activities and satisfactions of a kind of animal—is necessary background to any conclusions about what is careful or degrading use of that kind of animal.
4. There are some traditional meat animals, at least, for which killing *per se* does not degrade the animal. This is no guarantee that the same can be said of all traditional meat animals, or of all forms of killing.
5. Along with ethology, the appropriateness of various uses of a kind of animal depends on that animal's role(s) in a responsible agricultural ecology. This is, at least at present, an important role.
6. Killing and eating animals could be cavalier and wasteful, and thus contrary to appropriate respect, even if it isn't *per se* degrading.
7. The vast majority of meat and dairy animals live degraded lives, and the ways in which they are raised degrade the land on which they are raised. But this needn't be so, and it is not unreasonable to suppose that meat could be a modest part of a Western diet without the degradation of land or animals—as it is a modest part of the diet in many parts of the world without such degradation. The necessary departures from conventional agriculture in an agrarian direction, however, are more radical than is often appreciated.

> *The animals that people hunt or raise for slaughter are fit objects of care, sites of sacred significance. They are not to be treated in ways that degrade them.*

The agrarian cannot accept, for *many* reasons, the degradation of these or other animals. But the agrarian's bedrock commitment to these animals as fit objects of care is indispensable—and gives further support to the characteristic agrarian insistence on limitations of scale. One might think I would turn, in defending this principle, to the argument that abuses to the land and creatures from which people live eventually rebound upon those who live from them. It is a horrifically demonstrated fact, though, that a lot of money can be made by the abuse of meat animals when it is done on a grand scale.[22] And in the short term at least, big money enables people to buy their way out of—or at least to leave to others—the ill effects of their abusive behavior. Small-scale animal agriculture is not proof against cruelty, either. But a limitation in scale allows one to feel more fully the effects of one's actions and thus to act responsibly. It allows one to feel the sacredness of the animals one uses.[23]

> But since the same is true of the plants we eat, this does not immediately rule out consuming animals or their products.

Everything subject to our use requires our care. But to use is sometimes to consume. Indeed, we live by consumption, by the deaths of others. To care does not mean *never to consume*, then. There might be other reasons, specific to one or another kind of creature, not to consume it. But there is no path straight from the imperative of care-taking to a ban on consumption. And the ecological holism of contemporary agrarianism focuses as much on the cycle of consumption by which the lives of all creatures are maintained as it does on the lives of individual creatures.

> What degrades an animal is to make its life a poor one for the kind of creature it is. It is to deny it a life involving the characteristic activities and satisfactions of its kind, or to cancel these by one's use of it. Thus ethology—the contextual study of the characteristic activities and satisfactions of a kind of animal—is necessary background to any conclusions about what is careful or degrading use of that kind of animal.

This is the point on which I must do the most to supplement the literature of contemporary agrarianism. For that literature has been content, mostly, to call the gross misuse of animals by name, and—inasmuch as this gross misuse is institutionalized among us—to note its connections to other failures in our common life: the dangerous concentrations of waste that the large-scale confinement of meat animals implies, the concentration of farming in fewer and fewer hands to the detriment of rural communities, and so on. It has not asked by what criteria—however inexact—our use of animals should be judged *degrading* or *not degrading*.

To degrade an animal, I maintain, is to systematically deny it the characteristic activities and satisfactions of its kind, making its life overall a poor one.[24] In working to understand what it is to treat an animal with care or to degrade it, then, abstractions appropriate to just any animal will take us only a very limited way. For any animal, malnourishment, dehydration, physical torment, or other such afflictions can make it impossible for the animal to engage in the characteristic activities of its kind. But having said this, one has said very little about what careful treatment of that animal requires. One must get into the details—its social behavior, its grooming, etc.—particularly if one's interactions with the animal are going to be close. Careful treatment of a raptor is not the same as careful treatment of a chicken. Indeed, careful treatment of an Orpington is not the same as careful treatment of a Sumatra. And even *that*—though it is better than saying "bird"—may be insufficient. To treat *this* chicken carefully I may have to bring together general knowledge of the breed with experience of the bird in question. Again, we are returned to the fundamental agrarian principle that intimacy of acquaintance, possible only on a limited scale, is necessary for care-taking.

Ethology, then, is prerequisite for the careful treatment of animals, as is intimacy of acquaintance with any animals more intensively under one's care.

And careful treatment, especially if the animal is entrusted to our care, will involve at least as much attention to the development and exercise of the animal's powers as to what we might call the "hygienic minimum": seeing to it that the animal isn't—or isn't on our account—starved or frozen or the like. In the case of trainable animals, it may involve training them, so that their energies are developed and focused, not thwarted.[25]

All of the foregoing applies as much to humans as to nonhuman animals. To treat them well, one must of course not deny them the hygienic minimum, but the end of good treatment is to help people develop their powers and to give them scope for exercising them. And one had better know more about people than that they can suffer if one is to provide such care.[26]

Two final notes, on "cancelling" the goodness of an animal's life by one's use of it. First, it is possible to spoil a life that had been going well. Aristotle makes this point in his discussion of Priam, King of Troy. In living to see his family killed and his city overthrown, Priam's life as a whole takes on a different character than it would have had if it had ended a few years earlier. Similarly, one could degrade an animal that *has* lived well by stripping away, near the end, the activities and satisfactions characteristic of its kind.[27] Second, cutting a life short does not cancel its goodness in this way. (Nor does it count as systematically denying it the characteristic activities and satisfactions of its kind.) To degrade an animal is to make its life a mockery of the characteristic life of its kind, through deprivation or other hard treatment. Ending a life is not making a mockery of it—or it does not have to be.

> *There are some traditional meat animals, at least, for which killing per se does not degrade the animal. This is no guarantee that the same can be said of all traditional meat animals, or of all forms of killing.*

Having seen that we cannot live but by consuming other lives, the objection to killing cannot be—or cannot be *only*—that the lives we consume are not ours; it cannot be, "Who are we to live at the expense of other creatures?"

If we are not to degrade, and degradation is giving it a poor life, then the question we must ask is, "Does killing this or that animal give it a poor life?" If it does, we must not do it; it is a misuse of the animal. If it doesn't, then killing the animal remains a moral *possibility*.

Take chickens, an increasingly popular backyard animal. What are the characteristic activities and satisfactions of chickens? Well, scratching for food, establishing and maintaining a social hierarchy that is nevertheless compatible with communal nesting behaviors, mating and brooding as opportunity presents. They nest together, and find it distressing to be separated from the rest of the flock, but do not seem to mourn one another deeply. Is it the case that any of the central goods of a chicken's life are denied or cancelled if members of the flock are, at several months of age (as is typical with broiler hens) killed quickly and relatively painlessly? It would be otherwise if the characteristic activities of chickens included (as they do for humans) narrating their lives to themselves, ritually marking life transitions, reminiscing about youth, and anticipating maturity or senescence or the community of generations. This is the paradigmatic shape of a human life, the shape we must take care not to willfully spoil in the lives of others. It is not the paradigmatic shape of a chicken's life. As Mary Midgley (herself a vegetarian) points out, to notice and respond practically to these details is not speciesism in any vicious sense.[28]

But the foregoing is no blanket defense of meat eating, or of just any methods of killing. It is very possible that ethological investigation of some commonly domesticated animals reveals them to be, if not self-narrators, at least social in ways that leave them degraded (through the cancellation or deprivation of their life goods) when their children or parents are taken from them. If this is so, then it is so. It may well turn out that there are some animals we cannot hunt or raise for slaughter without degrading them. If so, then we must stop.

Likewise, if an animal that could otherwise be killed for meat (without degrading it) cannot be killed in a *way* that does not cancel the goodness of its life, then that too should stay our hands.[29]

> *Along with ethology, the appropriateness of various uses of a kind of animal depends on that animal's role(s) in a responsible agricultural ecology. This is, at least at present, an important role.*

In 2012, the *New York Times* sponsored a competition, soliciting moral defenses of meat eating. Many of the entries were widely at variance with the principles articulated here, defending meat eating on the basis of evolutionary history, or getting in touch with nature, or the fact that humans have canine teeth. But one of the finalists, herself a small farmer,[30] made the distinctly agrarian point that grain and vegetable farming have traditionally existed in a mutually supportive relationship with animal agriculture.[31] If our reflections on care-taking had led to the across-the-board conclusion that killing animals (except for mercy's sake[32]) is degradation, then that would be that. But our reflections did not lead there. And it is relevant to our topic that a highly effective means of maintaining soil fertility is the application of animal waste.[33] One could keep animals purely for their manure (this would already violate the principles of some animal liberationists), but if the killing of these animals is morally acceptable, then this suggests itself as an aspect of a responsible human-plant-and-animal arrangement.

Some critics of animal agriculture have improperly estimated the importance of animals in a responsible agricultural ecology, exaggerating the ecological costs of keeping agricultural animals and neglecting the importance of the cycles of fertilization made possible by the keeping of agricultural animals (and poorly replaced by synthetic alternatives). Two widely quoted statistics concern the inefficiencies of meat production. One suggests that the energy invested is ten times greater than the energy made available for consumption, while the other suggests that water is massively squandered on meat animals (a figure common given: 100,000 liters to produce one kilogram of beef). As Simon Fairlie has shown, both depend on assumptions that are dubious or worse. The energy-in–energy-out statistic presumes that meat animals are eating grains and other foods that humans could eat directly. This is the disgraceful truth as regards most large-scale animal agriculture. But there is nothing inevitable about it, as agrarians would be the first to note. One ecological value animal agriculture can have, when carried on sensitively and with respect for the precondition of scale, is in capturing the energy of grasses and other vegetation not fit for human consumption, on soils and slopes not fit for row crops. The efficiency of meat calories can be equivalent to grain or vegetable calories, if they come from cattle grazing on steep slopes or other marginal lands, from pigs eating slops, and from chickens eating insects.[34] As to freshwater usage, as Fairlie points out, the commonly reported statistic assumes, absurdly, that all the rain falling on pastureland grazed by a cow disappears into the cow, never to be seen again. This is not sober accounting.

Again, though, the most important point to be made about the ecology of animal agriculture concerns the value of manure as the traditional alternative to synthetic fertilizers, with their various drawbacks (ecological and—especially in two-thirds-world contexts—economic and political). This is no direct license to kill and eat agricultural animals. The acceptability of killing animals rests upon the case already presented. Moreover, the place of manure in ecologically attentive agricultures (its being generally cheaper, more effective, and more ecologically benign than synthetic alternatives) is contingent on the state of agricultural science—though it seems likely to remain the case for some time to come.

> *Killing and eating animals could be cavalier and wasteful, and thus contrary to appropriate respect, even if it isn't per se degrading.*

The character-centered ethic of contemporary agrarianism is alert not only to consequential degradation of the material bases of our lives, but also to the outlooks we manifest and cultivate through our actions. Even assuming the in-principle acceptability of killing and eating certain animals, circumstances may render these actions vicious. In particular, given the wicked things that are done to most meat animals in the United States, American consumers who eat meat incuriously are guilty of irresponsibility—even if it luckily happens that the meat they eat was not irresponsibly produced. This is an unhappy feature of life in contemporary America: a behavior that might have been presumptively inno-cent a couple of generations ago is no longer so, because we have allowed a great wickedness to develop in our midst.

> The vast majority of meat and dairy animals live degraded lives, and the ways in which they are raised degrade the land on which they are raised. But this needn't be so, and it is not unreasonable to suppose that meat could be a modest part of a Western diet without the degradation of land or animals—as it is a modest part of the diet in many parts of the world without such degradation. The necessary departures from conventional agriculture in an agrarian direction, however, are more radical than is often appreciated.

The first sentence above is demonstrated so devastatingly and in so many places (including elsewhere in this volume) that I will not bother to argue it. My interest is in the final sentence. Moral arguments for a vegetarian or vegan diet sometimes presume that they represent the only alternative to guilty participa-tion in mainstream animal agriculture, dismissing small-scale animal agriculture in ways strikingly reminiscent of how defenders of industrial agriculture dismiss small-scale agriculture generally. *It is impractical; it can never be practiced on a large scale; so the real alternatives are complicity with the abominations of confinement opera-tions or the refusal of meat.*

This is less and less convincing as an argument for vegetarianism or veganism. Perhaps vegetarianism or veganism is morally compelling on other grounds. But in an era in which more and more urban consumers are demanding conscien-tiously produced meat, and some are even raising their own, it is no idle fantasy that meat could be, as I say, a *modest* part of a Western diet without involving the degradation of land or animals.

Nevertheless, the agrarian would have us reckon honestly with the implica-tions of a careful animal agriculture. It will be small in scale. It will be attentive to ecological context; it will not practice animal agriculture where water is scarce. The meat it produces will be comparatively expensive. Meat will be, as it is in most of the world, a festive luxury or an accent, not the centerpiece of every meal.

Conclusion

A stupid and wearily familiar argument for meat eating goes like this: if we really think meat eating is morally questionable, then coyotes and other predator animals are very wicked beasts; it is sentimental to preach restraint to our fellow humans when we are just doing what nature does anyway. It is, as I say, a terrible argument. Humans are, biologically, omnivorous. But what that means is that, unlike coyotes, we have options. We are also self-conscious, deliberative creatures, who can consider what ways of living we can endorse upon reflection. Vegetarianism and veganism should be (no pun) on the table.

But there is a cousin of the bad argument that merits our attention. It emphasizes that we can only live by taking life, and suggests that we try to reorient our thinking about this. No one (I hope) seriously believes coyotes are wicked. But some believe, or seem to believe, that the order in which coyotes prey upon prairie dogs and rabbits and such is a horrific one, one we should abstain from and perhaps even interrupt. It is a temptation, particularly in Christian and post-Christian contexts, to regard the death by which the world lives with mere horror—as not the way things are supposed to be. But to think thus is to be alienated in one's thinking from the order Darwin uncovered—the order in and by which we live. Christians and non-Christians alike might try to learn to see our condition—not as a merely fallen condition, but as one we can inhabit with gratitude.[35] The point is not that nature has no standards and that therefore we shouldn't either. The point is that we can accept the world as a place where we might try to make ourselves—carefully, graciously—at home.[36]

Notes

1. This is not to deny the presence of many vegetarians and vegans among critics of industrialized agriculture. Neither movement has made much use of the *arguments* of the other, though. Vegetarians and vegans have decried the abuse (and even the use) of animals in contemporary agriculture, but have not generally tied this to a general critique of industrialized agriculture.
2. I might have mentioned also a number of writers indebted to these older ones: Norman Wirzba, Michael Pollan, and Barbara Kingsolver, and many others, less widely known.
3. Wendell Berry, "Conservation and Local Economy," in *Sex, Economy, Freedom, and Community* (New York: Pantheon, 1993), 3–4.
4. Also, for readers at home in the literature of analytic philosophy, Berry's lawyerly rhetoric will sometimes pull them up short. Must a nation really foster the indicated sorts of households and communities *in every possible way?*
5. Kimberly Smith, *Wendell Berry and the Agrarian Tradition: A Common Grace* (Lawrence: University Press of Kansas, 2003).
6. The *locus classicus* for contemporary care ethics is Nel Noddings's *Caring: A Feminine Approach to Ethics and Moral Education* (Berkeley: University of California Press, 1984).
7. For Berry's statement of this argument, see his essay "The Conservation of Nature and the Preservation of Humanity," in *Another Turn of the Crank* (Washington, DC: Counterpoint, 1995), 18–29. It is an argument he has revisited often, including most recently in his 2012 Jefferson lecture. See note 14.
8. There are happy exceptions of course—owners who, though distant, diligently repair and improve their properties. Such exceptions do not disconfirm the point: that the structure of the situation does not encourage careful behavior.

9. James Q. Wilson, *On Character* (Washington, DC: AEI Press, 1995), 123–138.
10. This is an apt moment at which to stress that present-day agrarians, like Jefferson before them, are focused on *usable* property—things with use-value, not merely exchange-value. The preconditions I am discussing do not apply to bank notes. They do apply to the things one buys with them.
11. Berry, *Sex, Economy, Freedom, and Community*, p. 4.
12. Kimberly Smith in *Wendell Berry and the Agrarian Tradition* makes the same point, focusing particularly on the classical virtue opposed to hubris: *sophrosyne*.
13. By this I am acknowledging, to moral philosophers reading this, that I am not proposing an ethics of virtue as a fundamental account of value. The point is that we need virtues, not that there could be nothing more fundamentally important.
14. Available at http://www.neh.gov/about/awards/jefferson-lecture/wendell-e-berry-lecture.
15. A fine introduction to such incentives and how they operate is Cass Sunstein and Richard Thaler's *Nudge* (New Haven, CT: Yale University Press, 2008).
16. As I mentioned in note 12, this is a point of emphasis in Smith, *Wendell Berry and the Agrarian Tradition*.
17. Anthologies in environmental ethics standardly contain examples of the kind of theorizing I have in mind, under headings like "biocentrism" and "ecocentrism."
18. Though what view on these matters could be uncontroversial?
19. There are important questions, which I lack space to address, about the extent to which recent and ongoing developments in "big data" challenge this claim. There is an analogy to this challenge in debates surrounding contemporary medical practice. There too an ideal of experienced judgment has been challenged by advocates of an algorithmic approach. On the latter debate, see James Lindemann Nelson, "Unlike Calculating Rules?," in *Slow Cures and Bad Philosophers*, ed. Carl Elliott (Durham, NC: Duke University Press, 2001).
20. Note how Berry joins this conservatism to a suspicion of moneyed interests (interests that have often been at odds with the interests of small farmers). This opposes him to a certain, familiar sort of free-market or pro-business conservatism. As I observed early on, contemporary agrarian thought fits badly into familiar ideological drawers.
21. Berry, "Conservation and Local Economy," 3–4.
22. If not by the farmer, then by the vertically integrated corporation that holds the farmer in its power.
23. Some of these reflections, plainly, do not apply to the wild animals that people hunt, though the principle about sacred significance does.
24. I am focusing on the "higher" animals—the sort most commonly raised for meat. What I say here, even if it works for these animals, might not work for mollusks and the like, or for plants. There too, I want to say, one should not take charge of a creature (or a community of creatures) and ruin its life. But where the individuality of the creature is harder to fathom, so too are the conditions of its flourishing or ruination.
25. Anyone who has read the work of the animal trainer, poet, and philosopher Vicki Hearne will recognize that I follow her thinking here. See especially *Adam's Task: Calling Animals by Name* (New York: Knopf, 1986).
26. The human case highlights an important point, made in passing above: Not every animal is entrusted to our care—though that does not relieve us of the burden of treating them all carefully. The human case also highlights the point that good lives, even within a species, come in varied forms. So it will be illegitimate to conclude, for instance, that to keep an animal from mating is to spoil its life.
27. Many lives, human and nonhuman alike, end in great deprivation and suffering. This need not cancel their goodness. The length of the deprivation and suffering matters, though it is not possible to say anything too precise.

28. Mary Midgley, *Animals and Why They Matter* (Athens: University of Georgia Press, 1983), 98–111.

29. I assume without argument that, across a wide range of cases, no serious issues arise about *eating* the meat of animals that it is acceptable to *kill*.

30. Stacey Roussel, "We Require Balance. Balance Requires Meat," *New York Times*, April 20, 2012. http://www.nytimes.com/interactive/2012/04/20/magazine/ethics-eating-meat.html?ref=magazine.

31. This is a common model throughout the two-thirds world, where draft and meat animals supply labor and fertilizer as well as fat and protein. They are, for excellent reason, elements of a model widely supported by relief and development organizations.

32. A circumstance that may actually obtain in contexts other than the euthanizing of pets. In my part of New York State, where most large predators besides humans have been eliminated, the deer population has exploded. Browsing down to nothing the understory of regional forests, they are not only starving; they are destroying the habitat of ground-nesting birds. Even for the deer's own sake, it may be best to cull the herd.

33. On this, I highly recommend—and not only for the title—Gene Logsdon's book, *Holy Shit* (White River Junction, VT: Chelsea Green, 2010).

34. Simon Fairlie's *Meat: A Benign Extravagance* (White River Junction, VT: Chelsea Green, 2010) contains copious citations to the popular statistics as well as refutations. See especially chapters 3 and 7.

35. For a Christian articulation of a position like this, see Thomas Aquinas, *Summa Theologiae* I 48.2 ad 3. For a secular (or, rather, Buddhist) articulation, see Gary Snyder's wonderful poem, "Old Woman Nature" at http://uutpoetry.tumblr.com/post/9918941712/old-woman-nature.

36. I am very grateful to the editors for their thoughtful and constructive engagement with an earlier version of this paper.

4

WHY I AM A VEGAN (AND YOU SHOULD BE ONE TOO)

Tristram McPherson

If you are like the vast majority of people, you eat, wear, and otherwise use products made from or by nonhuman animals (hereinafter *animals*). Like most aspects of human life, these actions have an ethical dimension: We can ask what principles ought to guide our interactions with animals, and what implications those principles have for our use of animal products. *Ethical vegans* accept a radical view of our relations to animals: They claim that it is (at least ordinarily) wrong to eat or otherwise use animal products.

Because this view demands a radical change in our lifestyles, it may initially seem implausible, or even absurd. In this chapter, I show that this dismissive attitude is unwarranted. I do this by sketching a clear and compelling case for a version of the vegan view. To be precise, I defend:

Modest Ethical Veganism: It is typically wrong to use animal products.

This thesis is modest in two respects. First, some vegans might claim that it is wrong to use products made from or by any member of the animal kingdom. However, by *animal products*, I mean only those products made from or by mammals, and the birds that are familiar sources of meat (chickens, turkeys, ducks, etc.). (I very briefly discuss how far my argument can be extended to other species of animals in the final section of the chapter.)

Second, unlike the boldest forms of ethical veganism, my thesis claims only that it is *typically* wrong to use animal products, not that it is always wrong. (Unless explicitly noted, I use "veganism" in what follows to refer to this modest form of the view.)

One might argue for veganism in many ways.[1] For example, one might argue that one should become a vegan because it is good for your health, or because of the bad environmental effects of animal agriculture. I will discuss these ideas very briefly in §§ 3 and 4, but they are not central to my argument. Instead, I focus on spelling out some of the ethical consequences of the fact that the industry that provides us with animal products systematically inflicts mind-boggling quantities of suffering and death on billions of animals each year. I develop my argument in three stages. I first argue that the wrongness of inflicting suffering can be partially explained by what it is like to suffer. I argue on this basis that it is typically wrong to make animals suffer (§ 1). I then argue that the wrongness of killing can be partially explained by the fact that killing typically deprives the victim of a valuable future. I argue on this basis that it is typically wrong to kill animals (§ 2). Together with facts about the lives of animals raised for our use, these principles entail that the institutions responsible for providing most of our animal products act wrongfully on a massive scale. I argue that it is typically wrong to use such animal products because doing so constitutes a wrongful form of complicity with these institutions (§ 3). I conclude by discussing some of the implications and limitations of the view that follows from my argument (§ 4).

Before proceeding to my argument, let me clarify the nature of ethical principles, as I will be discussing them in this chapter. Consider a familiar principle: *It is wrong to break your promises.* First, this principle states a typically *sufficient* (but not necessary) condition for wrongness. In this case: If an act breaks a promise, then it is typically wrong. This is compatible with there being many wrong acts that do not involve promise-breaking. Second, ethical principles are typically *defeasible*. There are two ways ordinary principles can be defeated. First, the principle can be outweighed in a given context, by important competing ethical considerations. For example, if I need to break my promise to meet you for lunch in order to save a life, it would not be wrong to do that. Second, some ethical principles can be *undercut*: Ordinary conditions for their holding can be absent. For example, if I only promised you that I would paint a certain bicycle because you led me to falsely believe it was yours, I might have no reason to keep my promise once I find out that you stole the bicycle. I will explicitly signal that the principles I defend may be defeasible in these ways by including the word "typically" in their statement.

1. The Wrongness of Making Animals Suffer

I begin my central argument for veganism in this section, by considering the ethical significance of animal suffering. After briefly explaining how I understand animal suffering, I argue that reflection on why it is bad to suffer and wrong to inflict suffering supports the conclusion that it is typically wrong to make animals suffer.

There are many phenomena that might be grouped together under the heading "suffering," and humans are surely capable of suffering in ways that animals cannot. However, I take it to be clear that animals can suffer in ethically important ways.[2] Consider two examples of what I have in mind by "suffering." The first is intense physical pain, such as a piglet experiences when he is castrated without anesthetic. The second is intense distress, such as a cow or a sow experiences when she is separated from her young far earlier than is natural. I take it to be clear that animal suffering is ethically significant. But it may be useful to consider a vivid case to illustrate that significance. Suppose that I caught a stray dog, took him home, and then repeatedly applied electric shocks to his genitals—shocks so intense that they were just short of life-threatening. My shocking the dog in this way would be very wrong. (Notice that, this claim too is only true holding ordinary assumptions fixed. If shocking the dog were for some reason necessary to prevent hundreds of human deaths, I should shock the dog.)

I seek a plausible and general explanation for why it would be wrong to shock the dog. To begin the search, consider the possibility of accidentally smashing one of your fingers with a hammer. There are many sorts of reasons to avoid such an outcome: Both the pain and the injury would be distracting and would disrupt your ability to pursue your goals, you might be ridiculed for your clumsiness, and so on. These reasons do not compete with each other. Rather, *each* of them is typically a sufficient explanation of why you should avoid smashing your finger. Another plausible typically sufficient explanation of why you should avoid smashing your finger is simply that experiencing the intense throbbing pain of one's injured finger is—just by itself—bad.[3]

Think next about why it is wrong to *inflict* suffering on another person. Again, there are many sorts of reasons why this may be so. For example, inflicting suffering can interfere with your victim's autonomy: her power to live the life that she values, to the best of her abilities. It may also express disrespect for your victim, or some other vicious attitude or trait. However, compare two ways of disrespectfully interfering with someone's agency. On the one hand, you could repeatedly and obnoxiously distract her. On the other, you could inflict intense and prolonged pain on her. The second possible action seems worse, even holding fixed the degree of disrespect and interference. Indeed, if forced to choose between these two actions, it would be wrong to perform the second. The most natural explanation of this fact is that *the way that suffering feels* is a typically sufficient explanation of the wrongness of inflicting it.

Our imagined stray dog can also suffer. In light of this, the explanation just suggested is also a very plausible explanation of why it would be wrong to shock the stray dog: Doing so would make it suffer terribly. But there is nothing special about this case. Rather, the explanation just proposed supports a general principle: *It is typically wrong to make animals suffer.* Notice that this principle and the explanation that I used to defend it are distinct: It is possible for someone to reject my explanation but accept the principle for some other reason.

Both the principle and the explanation I use to defend it are compatible with the plausible view that it is typically worse to inflict similarly severe suffering on an adult human rather than an animal. This could be explained, for example, by the significance of disrespecting or interfering with autonomous agency, which few (if any) animals possess to a significant degree.

One might object that my explanation for the wrongness of inflicting suffering on a human fails, because it ignores the explanatory role of *moral status*. For example, it might be claimed that it is wrong to make a human suffer because of what their suffering is like, together with humans' distinctive moral status. Animals, it might be insisted, lack moral status (or have some sort of second-class moral status), and so the badness of their suffering cannot render wrongful an action that makes them suffer (see Cohen [1986] for something like this idea).

This objection should be rejected for two reasons.[4] The first reason is intuitive. It is very plausible that it would be wrong to shock the dog, and this objection threatens to deprive us of the most natural explanation of that wrongness. The second reason is theoretical: The notion of moral status is associated with at least two different ideas. Once these ideas are distinguished, the objection fails.

The first idea associated with moral status is that moral status is the bundle of ethical powers and protections characteristically possessed by adult humans. The second idea is that moral status grounds the directionality of duties. For example, if I have a duty to care for your treasured vase, it is a duty to you, not to the vase. By contrast, I have a duty *to my son* to care for him. So my son, but not the vase, has moral status in the directionality sense.[5]

While I owe special duties *to* my two-year-old son, he lacks many of the ethical powers and protections that are characteristic of human adults. For example, it is often wrong to paternalistically make decisions for adult humans: We should rather respect their decision-making about their own lives. By contrast, I have a moral duty to my son to be paternalistic towards him.

If this is correct, the objection from moral status fails. The two ideas associated with moral status come apart: My son possesses the second but not the first. Further, the fact that we have duties to children to refrain from making them suffer shows that the explanation of the wrongness of inflicting suffering does not require that the victim have the sort of moral status characteristic of adult humans. Does the wrongness of inflicting suffering require the second (directedness) notion of moral status? I'm not sure. Recall the dog-torturing case. Do we have a duty *to the dog* not to make it suffer horribly? I am much less sure about this question that I am that it would be wrong to torture the dog, because of how it would feel for the dog to suffer. In light of this, I conclude: Either we have duties to animals not to make them suffer, or the badness of their suffering can explain the wrongness of inflicting it, even absent such directed duties.

This section has argued that it is wrong to make animals suffer. This followed from my underlying explanatory thesis: that what it is like to experience suffering constitutes a sufficient explanation of the wrongness of inflicting suffering. This explanation (perhaps amended to include reference to directedness moral status) appears plausible, and reflects the ethically significant similarities between humans and animals, without ignoring the ethically significant differences.

2. The Wrongness of Killing Animals

In this section, I focus on the ethical significance of killing. As in the previous section, I begin by identifying a typically sufficient condition, this time for the wrongness of killing. This principle entails that it is typically wrong to kill animals. The wrongness of painlessly killing an animal is less obvious to many people than the wrongness of making it suffer. In light of this, I complement my primary argument by showing that it is difficult to coherently deny that it is wrong to kill animals while accepting the wrongness of inflicting animal suffering.

My foil in this section is the *ethical omnivore* who suggests that it is okay to use animal products that are produced without inflicting suffering.[6] Because ethical omnivorism accepts the wrongness of inflicting suffering, it is itself a radical view, condemning most forms of contemporary animal agriculture. For example, it denounces the factory farms that provide animals with lives of nearly unmitigated suffering, and the especially egregious cruelties meted out to veal calves and the geese used to produce pâté.

The fundamental disagreement between the ethical omnivore and the modest ethical vegan concerns the ethics of painlessly killing an animal. A clear case shows that the omnivore's position is at least uncomfortable. Suppose that I caught a healthy stray kitten, took it home, and then killed it by adding a fast-acting and painless poison to its meal. I take it that this would be wrong. Suppose that the omnivore disagrees. The right way to adjudicate this dispute is to seek a general explanation of the wrongness of killing.

The ethics of killing is a complex and controversial matter (see McMahan [2002] for a detailed discussion of many of the complexities). However, as with the wrongness of inflicting suffering, we can identify several typically sufficient explanations for the wrongness of killing an adult human. First, killing typically interferes dramatically with the victim's autonomy. Second, nonconsensual killing is also inconsistent with appropriate *respect* for the victim's autonomy: It alters his life—by ending it—without his consent. I will assume here that animals do not have autonomous plans, and thus that killing them is not objectionable in these ways.

There is another important reason why killing a human being is wrong: Killing typically deprives the victim of a valuable future.[7] That is, killing someone deprives them of valuable experiences, activities, relationships, and so on that they would otherwise have had. The significance of this explanation is made especially vivid by considering cases of *life-extending killings* (Lippert-Rasmussen 2001). For example, imagine a drug that, when injected, damages one's heart such that one dies quickly and painlessly a year later. Ordinarily, my intentionally giving you such a drug would be wrongful killing. However, suppose that this drug is also the only antidote to a poison that you have just accidentally ingested, which will kill you within the hour unless treated. Suppose finally that I give you the drug while you are unconscious from the poison, and sure enough, it kills you a year later. This is not a case of wrongful killing. Indeed, I am presumably ethically required to give you the drug in these circumstances, if I can. The crucial difference between this case and the ordinary case is that in the ordinary case, injecting the drug deprives you of your future, while in this case, it extends that future. The contrasting value of these possible futures provide a plausible explanation for why it is wrong to give the drug in the former case, and right to do so in the latter. This explanation entails that the fact that a killing deprives the victim of a valuable future is typically sufficient to explain why the killing is wrong.

It is plausible that the futures of animals can be objectively good (or bad) for them to have. Valuable features of animal lives are not hard to sketch. Animals seem capable of pleasures as well as pains, and it is good to have a pleasant life; pack animals have better lives if they have companions, and so on. Consider a range of things that one might intentionally do to an animal: raising it in isolation, painlessly amputating a healthy limb, or rearing it on a diet lacking essential nutrients. These sorts of acts seem wrong. A natural explanation is that they are wrong because they deprive the animal of aspects of a valuable future such as companionship, the ability to function physically, and the ability to have a pleasant life.

I have just suggested that animals can have valuable futures. And I argued above that one typically sufficient explanation for the wrongness of killing is that it deprives the victim of a valuable future. Because this is a typically sufficient condition, it applies (absent defeating conditions) to killing anything that has a valuable future. For example, it smoothly explains why it would be wrong to kill the stray kitten in the example introduced above: Given that the kitten is healthy, killing it almost certainly deprives it of a valuable future. But there is nothing special about the kitten in this example. So the explanation also entails a general ethical principle: that it is typically wrong to kill animals.

The explanation that supports this principle also provides plausible guidance concerning when it would be okay to kill an animal. For it suggests that (other things being equal) it is permissible to kill an animal if its future will on balance be bad for it to have. For example, it suggests that it would be a mercy, and not wrong, to painlessly kill a cat that is suffering from an agonizing and incurable disease. This is the sort of case where we would rightly say that the animal's continued life was a fate worse than death.

As with the argument against inflicting suffering on animals, it is possible to resist my argument for the wrongness of killing animals by objecting that the explanation that I offer is incomplete. One initially plausible objection here claims that in order for an entity's death to be bad for it, that entity must value its future. With this idea in hand, it could be suggested that many animals cannot value their futures (or at least, not in as rich of a way as humans), and hence that their deaths are not bad.[8]

This objection fails because it can be wrong to deprive a person of a valuable future, even if they do not value it (compare Marquis [1989], 195–196). Suppose that Penelope has temporarily fallen into deep depression: She cannot see the point of anything, except perhaps of dying to end the pointlessness. However, in a few weeks this condition will lift, and she will go on to have a long, rich, and fulfilling life. In this circumstance, Penelope has a valuable future, although her depression prevents her from valuing it. Evidently, killing Penelope now would be very wrong, even if she wanted you to do so.

Nor does the value of an activity for a person depend on their eventually valuing it, or being able to value it. We are all familiar with cases of people who (sadly) never realize how good a relationship or activity is for them. And some such people may be psychologically incapable of recognizing such value due to some prejudice or trauma. This sort of blindness typically makes a person's life worse, but it need not erase the goodness for him of the underlying relationship or activity. If animals are incapable of valuing, this entails at most that they are in a situation analogous to that of such people. We can act wrongly by depriving people of such unappreciated goods: You cannot vindicate theft or discrimination by convincing the victims that they do not value what they lack. This suggests that it can be wrong to deprive a creature of goods even if they do not or cannot value them. And with this the objection collapses.

This argument for the wrongness of killing animals was independent of my case for the wrongness of making them suffer. However, it is also difficult to coherently accept that it is wrong to make animals suffer, while denying that it is wrong to kill them. The difficulty can be dramatized by an example.

Suppose that one could make a commercially or artistically successful video that in part would require performing a painful and unnecessary medical operation on a cow. If we grant that it is typically wrong to make the cow suffer, it is implausible that the commercial or artistic merits of the video outweigh the suffering, and thereby justify performing the operation. So performing the operation here would be wrong. But suppose that performing the same painful operation on a second cow would save that cow's life. Here, performing the operation is clearly permissible—indeed, very nice—if the cow would go on to have a long and worthwhile life after the operation. This pair of cases makes it very difficult to accept that it is wrong to inflict suffering on animals, while denying that it is wrong to kill them. For preserving the life of the cow—and hence its valuable future—is enough in the second case to ethically justify inflicting otherwise wrongful suffering.

This directly refutes the strong view that animal suffering matters but animal death does not: The strong view implausibly entails that it would be wrong to perform the life-extending operation. On the remaining possible view, the valuable future of an animal does not make it wrong to kill the animal, but it can somehow justify inflicting otherwise wrongful suffering on the animal. This view is deeply puzzling: It threatens to entail, for example, that it is okay for me to perform the painful operation, and then decide to slaughter the cow.

The account I have offered in this section provides a better explanation of why the second (medically required) cow operation is permissible: In this case one inflicts *life-extending* suffering. Inflicting life-extending suffering can be permissible for the same reason as life-extending killing: because the value of an animal's future plays a uniform role in determining which ways of treating that animal are right and wrong.

In this section, I noted that killing a person or an animal typically deprives them of a valuable future. I argued that this is a typically sufficient explanation of why a killing is wrong. The upshot is that it is typically wrong to kill animals. Finally, I argued that this thesis garners additional support from cases where we inflict suffering on animals as a necessary means to provide them with better lives.

3. Complicity with Animal Suffering and Death

The arguments of the previous two sections entail that it is typically wrong to kill or inflict suffering on animals. While crucial to my case for veganism, these arguments do not settle the issue. This is because of a central fact about contemporary life: The typical omnivore need not ever see a live cow or pig or chicken, let alone kill or inflict suffering on one. This fact forms the basis for an important objection to Modest Ethical Veganism. In this section, I develop the strongest form of this objection, and then answer it in two stages. First, I argue that the institutions responsible for producing our animal products act wrongly. Second, I argue that veganism is typically required as a response to the wrongful behavior of those institutions.

Consider a preliminary objection: By the time you order a chicken dinner, the chicken it is made from is already dead. Ordering the meal doesn't kill the chicken, and ordering a vegan burger instead won't bring the chicken back. This objection invites a very tempting reply: What matters ethically is not (just) whether you yourself actively *inflict* animal suffering or death, but whether your behavior tends to *makes a difference* to the amount of animal suffering or death. Ordering the chicken dinner—while not harming the chicken you eat—might tend to lead to another chicken being bred, made to suffer terribly, and then killed.

Your ordering the chicken dinner would tend to make a difference to the amount of animal suffering if the market for chicken were a perfectly efficient classical market in the following sense: Every chicken dinner purchased increased the aggregate demand for chicken slightly; this increase in demand would slightly increase the market price for chicken, and this in turn would tend to produce a slight increase in the supply of chicken. Given how chickens are raised, increasing the supply of chicken involves increasing the amount of chicken suffering and death.

This puts me in a position to introduce a stronger version of the objection to Modest Ethical Veganism:

> **Inefficacy**: Even if it is wrong to inflict animal suffering and death, it is not typically wrong to use animal products, because doing so does not tend to make any difference to the amount of animal suffering and death.

Inefficacy combines an empirical claim with an ethical thesis. The empirical claim is that using animal products does not tend to make any difference to the amount of animal suffering and death. The ethical thesis is that veganism could only be ethically required if it made such a difference.

The empirical claim could be defended by rejecting the hypothesis that the actual market for chicken is relevantly similar to a perfectly efficient market. According to the objector, food industry supply chains are so complex, and waste and inefficiency so rampant, that my decision to buy a chicken dinner (or other animal products) tends to have no effect at all on the rate of animal suffering and death. This empirical hypothesis has been challenged,[9] but I will not pursue that challenge here.

The idea that becoming vegan will tend to make no difference to animal welfare is discouraging, but I will argue that it does not undercut Modest Ethical Veganism. This is because the ethical thesis underlying Inefficacy should be rejected, as I now argue.

One initial reason for skepticism about this ethical thesis is that there are plausible ethical principles that require action even in cases where one does not make such a difference. For example, consider the duty of *fair play* (e.g., Klosko 2004): This duty requires that one not benefit from successful cooperative institutions without making a fair contribution to them (i.e., that I not *freeride*). For example, suppose that there is a public bus in my town, which survives by charging its riders a fair price to ride. Because the bus uses the honor system, I can easily ride without paying, if I choose. Suppose finally that the cooperative benefits provided by the bus are not threatened by my failing to pay: There are enough paying riders that the bus system will persist whether or not I pay. In this case, my freeriding does not harm anyone, and yet it still seems wrong. This example only gives us reason to be suspicious of Inefficacy.[10] I now argue that the suspicion is warranted: We can be required to be vegan even if doing so will make no difference to the amount of animal suffering and death.

I begin by evaluating the institutions most directly involved in raising and slaughtering animals for use in making animal products: the farms, animal factories, feedlots and slaughterhouses. To be concise, I will call these the *animal product industry*. This industry inflicts extraordinary amounts of suffering, and then very early death, to the billions of animals it raises (see Mason and Singer [1990] for a sketch of some of the literally gory details).[11] My argument for the wrongness of killing animals and making them suffer constitutes a strong case that the animal product industry thereby acts wrongly.

As I have noted, however, the principles I defend can be defeated by sufficiently weighty competing ethical considerations. Can we find such considerations to ethically vindicate the industry that raises and slaughters animals for our use? We cannot. The most obvious good effects of this industry are the economic benefits to the industry itself, and the enjoyments and meanings that consumers take from using the resulting products. The appeal to these good effects fails for three reasons.

First, economic benefits are rarely the sort of thing that can justify otherwise wrongful acts. For example, suppose that I could make a good living torturing kittens and selling videos of the torture on the Internet. The fact that it would make me money would not justify my actions.

Second, there is a vast array of enjoyable vegan food that most current omnivores could learn to enjoy: While veganism surely requires sacrificing some gustatory enjoyment, it is certainly compatible with a richer gustatory life than most omnivores currently experience. This leaves the value of the cultural meanings that many people attach to food as a significant positive effect. But these meanings surely cannot justify inflicting suffering and death on billions of animals every year.

The third reason that the appeal to the good effects of contemporary animals agriculture fails is that such agriculture has significant negative effects on humans that must also be weighted in the balance.

Consider four points. First, it typically requires far more arable land and water to produce a calorie of meat than to produce a calorie of plant-based food.[12] Animal agriculture thus puts pressure on vulnerable cropland and water resources. Second, the economic incentives facing animal agriculture have led to increasingly industrialized farming practices. This has increased the amount of environmentally toxic by-products generated by farming. This in turn both further damages land and water systems and directly threatens human health (Walker et al. 2005). Third, animal agriculture is a significant contributor to the catastrophic threat of global warming.[13] Finally, the overconsumption of animal products is a central contributor to the unhealthiness of the majority of North American diets, which include too many calories, too much saturated fat, and too few vegetables and whole grains (Walker et al. 2005). Vegan diets tend not to have these features. It is thus arguable that the overall impact of the animal product industry on human health is very negative.[14]

For these reasons, it is very far from clear that the net effect of contemporary animal agriculture on humans is positive.[15] It is thus implausible that these effects suffice to defeat the application of the principles I defended in the previous two sections. Because the institutions that produce our animal products are responsible for the suffering and death of many billions of animals every year, the principles I have defended thus entail that the institutions most directly responsible for animal suffering and death are thereby guilty of massive and systematic wrongdoing.

I now argue that veganism is required because consumption of animal products puts us into ethically objectionable relations to these institutions. The key idea is that one should not aim to benefit from wrongdoing.[16] Let me illustrate this idea with a case. Suppose that Alice has decided to buy a house, and (having small children) desires to live in a quiet neighborhood near an elementary school. It turns out that a certain real estate agent in her town consistently has the best stock of such houses on offer. There is only one catch: This agent is a racist, who uses his business to promote the racial homogeneity of "nice" neighborhoods. He does this by showing houses in these neighborhoods only to members of Alice's race. If there are other agents with reasonable houses on offer, it would be wrong for Alice to work with the racist agent. This seems true even if Alice's doing so will make no difference to the racial makeup of the relevant neighborhoods or to the agent's profits (for example, because Alice can foresee that someone else of her race will happily make use of the agent's services in her place).

The wrongness of working with the real estate agent, even in such circumstances, appears best explained as follows. The agent has a wrongful plan: to promote racial homogeneity by selling desirable homes in a discriminatory way. By using the agent's services to buy a home, Alice would be seeking to benefit by cooperating with that plan. And it is wrong to do that. This suggests that it is typically wrong to seek to benefit by cooperating with wrongful plans.

We can identify a more specific and more stringent principle, however. Suppose that the only local grocer sells two sorts of products: ethically produced food, and nutritional supplements that she makes by painfully extracting bone marrow and tissue from the slaves that she keeps in the basement. If refusing to buy the grocer's food would lead you to starve, it might be too demanding to insist that one not cooperate with the grocer at all. However, this does not give you carte blanche to buy and enjoy the supplements. The right way to explain this is that there is a distinctively wrongful *part* of the grocer's plan: making and selling the supplements. And even if we have no acceptable way to avoid cooperating with her plan overall, we can and ought to avoid cooperating with its distinctively wrongful part.

These cases illustrate the principle that I endorse:

> **Anti-Complicity**: It is typically wrong to aim to benefit by cooperating with the wrongful elements of others' plans.

My talk of "plans" here should not be taken to apply only to official corporate plans, or to patterns of explicit reasoning; rather it should include the pattern of goals that explain an individual's or institution's behavior. For example, suppose that nongovernmental organization (NGO) X's official organizational mission is to dig wells in sub-Saharan Africa, but X's executives in fact systematically use X to funnel donor funds to its Swiss bank accounts. As I am thinking about plans, NGO X's actual plan in this case centrally involves defrauding donors.

Anti-Complicity explains why it is wrong to buy supplements from the grocer, but okay to buy vegetables from her (at least if you lack other adequate sources of food). Buying the vegetables does not cooperate with the wrongful *part* of her plan. Similarly, Anti-Complicity can explain why it is okay to buy vegetables at your local grocery store, despite the fact that this store almost certainly sells animal products, and thereby has a wrongful plan. However, as in the slave-torturing grocer example, you do not typically cooperate with the wrongful *part* of your grocery store's wrongful plan by purchasing their vegetables.

Anti-Complicity similarly explains why it is wrong to work with the racist real estate agent: buying a house from the agent just is cooperating with the wrongful part of his plan. Finally, Anti-Complicity also explains why Inefficacy is false, because it does not require that your use of animal products makes a difference to the amount of animal suffering in the world. This aspect of Anti-Complicity is plausible: In the example just given, it is wrong to buy the supplements from the grocer even if doing so did not lead to more suffering for the grocer's slaves.

I take these points to show that Anti-Complicity has formidable explanatory power. One might worry that this principle is nonetheless objectionable, because it is *too demanding*. Consider for example the hypothesis that virtually every product that we need in order to live our lives is produced as part of a plan that aims to benefit from exploitative labor practices, or wrongful environmental degradation, or some other wrongful act. Given this hypothesis, it might seem that Anti-Complicity tells us that whatever we do is wrong.

There are three important points to make about this worry. First, the suggested hypothesis is boldly pessimistic, and we should not assume that it would survive careful scrutiny. Second, the hypothesis is naturally read as one in which our lives are maintained only at ethically objectionable cost to others. Our ethical obligations *should* be very demanding when applied to such cases. Compare: A slaveholder should typically free his slaves, and compensate them for the exploitation he has inflicted on them, even if doing so requires sacrificing the things he most cares about. Third, the demandingness of Anti-Complicity should not be overstated. Like all of the principles I have defended in this chapter, this principle is explicitly defeasible. This means that it is compatible with there being cases in which competing ethical considerations make cooperation with wrongful plans permissible, or even required. Consider the grocer example again: If my child had a rare medical condition that was devastating if untreated, and the condition could only be treated by using the grocer's noxiously produced supplements, it might be permissible to buy the supplements in order to treat her.

My defense of Anti-Complicity puts me in a position to complete my case for Modest Ethical Veganism. My preceding arguments entail that the institutions that make our animal products have a wrongful plan: They aim to profit financially by selling products made in a way that involves wrongful animal suffering and death. By purchasing the resulting products, you would be seeking to benefit by cooperating with this plan. Anti-Complicity entails that such cooperation is typically wrongful. And—unlike in the medical condition case just discussed—the choice to be vegan does not typically impose large morally significant costs.

4. What the Argument Implies

This chapter has argued for

> **Modest Ethical Veganism**: It is typically wrong to use animal products.

Where *animal products* means products made from or by mammals, and the birds that are familiar sources of meat (chickens, turkeys, ducks, etc.). It may be helpful to review the overall structure of my argument for this thesis:

1. It is wrong to inflict animal suffering and death, unless there are strong competing ethical considerations (§§ 1–2).
2. The animal product industry systematically inflicts massive suffering and death on animals.
3. There are no competing ethical considerations that justify the animal death and suffering inflicted by the animal product industry (§ 3).
4. The animal product industry systematically engages in massive wrongdoing: It has a wrongful plan (from premises 1–3).
5. In the typical case, using animal products involves seeking to benefit from cooperating with the animal product industry's plan (§ 3).
6. It is wrong to seek to benefit by cooperating with others' wrongful plans, absent competing ethical considerations (§ 3).
7. In the typical case, there are no competing ethical considerations that justify cooperating with these institutions.
8. In the typical case, it is wrong to use animal products (from premises 4–7).

This summary of the argument may seem overly pedantic. However, it is intended to be useful. The argument makes explicit each of the claims that together support my conclusion. And the argument is *valid*: If the premises of the argument are true, then the conclusion must be true. This means that anyone wishing to reasonably reject my conclusion must explain which premise they wish to reject, and how my argument for that premise is flawed.[17]

I conclude the chapter by exploring the implications of this argument. In order to clarify its significance, I focus on spelling out its limitations. I first explain that I leave open how far across the animal kingdom my argument extends. I then explain the way that Modest Ethical Veganism is compatible with the possibility of ethically acceptable animal farming practices. Finally, I explore some consequences of the fact that this thesis allows for exceptions, and discuss its application to certain hard cases.

Before explaining these limitations, it is important to emphasize that they limit the implications of *this* argument. My argument does not claim to illuminate the *only* reason to be vegan. Consider just one example: As I noted in § 3, the animal product industry also contributes significantly to global warming and environmental degradation more broadly. Some such contributions may constitute wrongful indifference to human and animal well-being. This in turn could underwrite a second argument that it is wrong to be complicit with this industry. Such an argument, if sound, might have interestingly different scope and limitations. So a vegan could accept my argument, but take veganism to be required for other reasons, in cases where my argument does not apply.

Note first that my argument rests crucially on the fact that animals like cats, dogs, cows, pigs, sheep, deer, goats, rabbits, geese, ducks, turkeys, and chickens can suffer.[18] It is a hard question how far across the animal kingdom this capacity is distributed. The central question is: What sort of brain architecture is needed to underwrite the possibility of suffering, and how widely distributed is that architecture? If we ordered all known animals by the complexity of their nervous systems, humans would be at one end; at the other end are animals like the oyster (which lack a brain) and the sponge (which entirely lacks a nervous system). I am certain that these latter animals cannot suffer.[19]

As I emphasized in the introduction, my argument thus falls short of vindicating veganism, if that is strictly understood to ban use of any animal products.[20] This chapter does not seriously address where on that spectrum the capacity to suffer arises. For example, fish are a salient hard case. However, I will suggest that in the absence of a convincing account of the biological basis for the capacity to suffer, we should be cautious in what we are willing to eat. Merely *doubting* whether an animal can suffer is not an appropriate ground for privileging one's appetite over its possible suffering.

Note next that nothing in my argument rules out animal farming *per se*. It is possible to imagine farming animals in a way that does not involve shortening their lives or making them suffer. My view does not suggest any objection to using milk, wool, and so on that were produced on such farms. Again, some vegans take it to be wrong to *use* animals in any way. This is another respect in which my veganism is modest.

This limitation has little practical import, however. This is because almost all actual animal farming involves killing animals or making them suffer. The reasons lie in the interaction between biology and economics. Consider a single example among many: Even the most humane dairy farm will typically produce as many male calves as female, and almost no such farm will support all of the (largely economically useless) males through their natural lives. Rather, in almost every case, they will be raised for meat. That means that almost any economically viable dairy farming operation participates in the raising of cows to be killed and eaten, a practice that I have argued in § 3 is typically wrong.

This sort of point explains why I take my argument to support a vegan lifestyle, as opposed to a vegetarian lifestyle that permits use of dairy products (for example), but not animal flesh. Even in the best realistic case, using dairy products involves supporting institutions whose practices include the systematic wrongful treatment of male cattle. Using such products is thus typically wrong.

The final limitation to my argument that I want to explore is that my argument for the wrongness of eating animal products allows for exceptions. At least three sorts of exceptions are possible. First, there are possible cases (like those just mentioned) of animal products that are made without inflicting suffering or death. Second, there are cases where the burdens of refraining from using animal products would be exceptionally high.[21]

What is the significance of this second possibility? On the one hand, my arguments do not imply that animal death or suffering is typically *as ethically significant* as human death, or similarly intense human suffering. In fact, in §§ 2 and 3 I emphasized that there is a range of factors that typically contribute to the wrongness of killing humans or making them suffer that are not present in most animals.

I take these considerations to suggest that the most central and pressing human interests typically take ethical priority over nonhuman animal welfare. For example, my conclusion is compatible with it being permissible or even required to harm or kill an animal if doing so is needed to prevent suffering or death to a human being. This may suggest that some lethal medical research using animals can be ethically justified, if we have good reason to believe that it will greatly benefit humans. (However, this weighty criterion suggests that much current medical research using animals is not justified.) Similarly, in various times and places, animal products have been an essential element of the only available adequate human diets. For example, for rural families in many parts of the world, having a cow—or even a handful of chickens—can offer crucial protection against certain forms of malnutrition. I suspect that these considerations are sufficient to justify exceptions to my argument.

My argument for Modest Ethical Veganism thus allows for exceptions. But it bears emphasis that the burdens that I take to justify exceptions to veganism must be very weighty, as those just mentioned were. Here is an imperfect but reasonable heuristic: Some circumstances would warrant torturing the stray dog imagined in § 2, or killing the stray kitten imagined in § 3. I contend that only equally dire circumstances would warrant ordering the sirloin steak for dinner. In light of this heuristic, consider what most of us would give up by becoming vegan. First, one gives up the aesthetic pleasure and rich meaning involved in consuming animal foods. Second, one gives up the ability to participate fully in some culinary traditions and food-centered social occasions. This also has the potential to decrease one's social opportunities. Finally, given the marginal status of vegans in our society, one faces extra burdens of planning and inconvenience in feeding oneself. For those who are severely disadvantaged in other ways—by poverty and discrimination, for example—the additional sacrifices that veganism would require might constitute an intolerable additional burden. But for most of us, the costs of becoming vegan are far from weighty enough to justify omnivorism. After all, you wouldn't torture a dog or kill a cat for these sorts of reasons, would you?[22]

Notes

1. Many philosophers defend views related to veganism within various systematic ethical frameworks. For utilitarianism see Singer (1980); for broadly Rawlsian and Scanlonian contractualist approaches, see, respectively, Rowlands (2002, chap. 3) and Talbert (2006); for a 'rights' view see Regan (2004); for a Kantian approach see Korsgaard (2004); and for virtue theory see Hursthouse (2006). If you find one of these ethical frameworks especially compelling, you should consider reading the relevant paper from this group. My argument does not presuppose such a systematic framework; two important arguments for vegetarianism that share this feature are Rachels (1997) and DeGrazia (2009); this chapter is especially indebted to these last papers.
2. Here I set aside important debates. Should pain be distinguished from suffering? Does the latter require capacities that the former lacks? Is only the latter ethically significant? I take the best work on animal pain and suffering to strongly support the assumption made in the text. See Allen (2004) and Akhtar (2011, 495–501) for helpful discussion.
3. It may be that not every pain is intrinsically bad. Some pains may be essential components of valued or valuable accomplishments or experiences. Possible examples include certain athletic achievements or even masochistic sex. It is arguable that such pains may not be bad at all. Other pains may not be bad because they are imperceptibly mild. Because my claim is about the typical significance of pain and suffering, it is compatible with these possibilities.
4. For related skepticism about the usefulness of 'moral status' talk, see Zamir (2007, chap. 2).
5. A helpful introduction to debates about moral status (Jaworska and Tannenbaum 2013) dubs these two ideas 'full moral status' and 'moral status,' respectively.
6. Compare Pollan (2006, Chap. 17) and especially Chapter 1 of this volume. This view has received significant critical attention. See McMahan (2008), DeGrazia (2009, 160–164), Harman (2011), and Norcross (2012) for alternatives to my reply.
7. Compare Marquis (1989). Marquis suggests that this is the 'primary' thing that makes killing a person wrong. Because the autonomy-based considerations also strike me as important, I reject this stronger claim. For the underlying idea that the badness of one's death is constituted by that death's depriving one of a valuable future, see Nagel (1979).
8. See Tooley (1972) for the closely related idea that the capacity to care about one's continued existence is required for the right to life.
9. This challenge has been pressed by Singer (1980, 335–336). Singer argues for the hypothesis that our consumption has a very small chance of making a difference to animal welfare, but if we do make a difference, that difference will be correspondingly enormous. Singer concludes that we ought to be vegetarian for that reason. Norcross (2004, 232–233) and especially Kagan (2011) develop Singer's idea further. See Budolfson (forthcoming) for an important challenge to the Singer-style argument.
10. One important way to defend the ethical thesis underlying Inefficacy would be to appeal to an influential general ethical theory: *act-consequentialism*. This is the thesis

that the rightness of an act is determined purely by the aggregate consequences of that act (in its most familiar form, how much net happiness will follow from it, compared to other options). If true, act-consequentialism would vindicate the ethical thesis underlying Inefficacy. I take act-consequentialism to be false, but I cannot argue adequately for that claim here.

11. We often hold institutions responsible for acts. For example, US law held BP responsible for the Deepwater Horizon oil spill. However, some philosophers believe that only individuals can act or be morally responsible. If you believe this, feel free to read my talk of institutions with wrongful plans as shorthand for very complex facts about large collections of individuals with wrongful plans.

12. This is only true in the general case; for example, some land is too poor to viably grow plant crops, but can support grazing animals, so environmental consideration may support eating meat grown on such land. For a helpful discussion of this issue, see Fairlie (2010, chap. 3).

13. Estimates of the climate impact of animal agriculture range wildly, from between a twentieth and a half of all anthropogenic greenhouse gas emissions. For competing estimates of the climate effects of animal agriculture, see Goodland and Anhang (2009), Fairlie (2010, chap. 13), and United Nations Food and Agriculture Organization (2014).

14. To be clear, current nutritional science does not find significant health differences between people with 'plant-based' omnivorous diets and those with vegetarian or vegan diets (Dwyer 2013, 318–320). The impact of animal products on health that I identify is a function of actual, rather than ideal, patterns of omnivorous eating.

15. For arguments for vegetarianism that appeal to some of the considerations just mentioned, see Singer (2002, 165–169) and Rachels (2011, § 3).

16. DeGrazia (2009, 157–159) argues for a related idea. Other philosophers (e.g., Rachels 1997) content themselves with the thought that ideas in this neighborhood are deeply plausible.

17. For discussion of the attempt to reject the conclusion of this sort of argument without rejecting its premises see McPherson (2015). For related methodological discussion, see McPherson (2014).

18. Vegans are sometimes challenged to explain how they justify taking the life of plants. While plants can have better or worse lives, they cannot suffer. And it is implausible that their lives are ethically significant in anything like the way the life of a being that can feel is.

19. Armstrong and Botzler (2008, pt. 2) provides a helpful introduction to questions about animal capacities.

20. The animal kingdom is an elegant and salient place to mark the boundary of the ethically edible, but I take ethical veganism to require a more serious vindication than this. Compare Cox (2010), which suggests that vegans ought to be able to eat oysters.

21. Another possibility is that certain forms of animal agriculture might inflict suffering and death on animals, but also have good effects that outweigh the ethical significance of that suffering and death. These effects include overall animal well-being, as well as a range of other values, including agricultural sustainability, environmental sustainability, and fostering meaningful local economies. Consider a possible example. Traditional or organic farming tends to involve much less animal suffering than factory farming. Suppose (1) that such farms could only be economically viable if they involve some killing and inflicting suffering on animals, and (2) supporting such farms had a good chance of bringing about a future in which animals were overall much better off than they currently are, and the deleterious environmental effects of agriculture were mitigated. It might be argued that it is okay or even required to support such farms. I take there to be little reason to believe that supporting such farms has a significantly better chance of promoting the relevant values

than being vegan does. In light of this, I consider such a possibility largely irrelevant to our ethical choices.

22. I am indebted for helpful comments and discussion to David Plunkett, Mark Bryant Budolfson, Andrew Chignell, Tyler Doggett, Sean Walsh, Derek Baker, Tom Dougherty, Gideon Rosen, and Katie Batterman; to audiences who gave me feedback on related work at Rhodes College, Bowling Green State University, Charles Sturt University, and Virginia Commonwealth University; and to many students who have wrestled with previous versions of this chapter. I am also indebted to Liz Harman, whose talk on this topic first started me thinking systematically about it. Parts of this chapter draw significantly on my "A Case for Ethical Veganism."

References

Akhtar, Sahar. "Animal Pain and Welfare: Can Pain Sometimes Be Worse for Them Than for Us?" In *Oxford Handbook of Animal Ethics*, edited by Tom Beauchamp and R. G. Frey, 495–518. Oxford: Oxford University Press, 2011.

Allen, Colin. "Animal Pain." *Noûs* 38, no. 4 (2004): 617–643.

Armstrong, Susan J., and Richard G. Botzler, eds. *The Animal Ethics Reader.* 2nd ed. London: Routledge, 2008.

Budolfson, Mark. "The Inefficacy Objection and the Problem with the Singer/Norcross/Kagan Response." Manuscript (forthcoming).

———. "The Inefficacy Objection to Deontology: From Complicity to Degree of Essentiality in the Ethics of the Marketplace." Manuscript (cited as *ms-b*).

Cohen, Carl. "The Case for the Use of Animals in Biomedical Research." *New England Journal of Medicine* 315 (1986): 865–869.

Cox, Christopher. "Consider the Oyster." *Slate.* April 7, 2010. http://www.slate.com/id/2248998/.

DeGrazia, David. "Moral Vegetarianism from a Very Broad Basis." *Journal of Moral Philosophy* 6 (2009): 143–165.

Dwyer, J. "Vegeterian Diets" [*sic*]. In *Encyclopedia of Human Nutrition*, 3rd ed., Vol. 4., edited by Lindsay Allen, Andrew Prentice, and Benjamin Caballero, 316–322. Amsterdam: Academic Press, 2013.

Fairlie, Simon. *Meat: A Benign Extravagance.* White River Junction, VT: Chelsea Green, 2010.

Goodland, Robert, and Jeff Anhang. "Livestock and Climate Change." *Worldwatch*, November/December 2009, 10–19.

Harman, Elizabeth. "The Moral Significance of Animal Pain and Animal Death." In *Oxford Handbook of Animal Ethics*, edited by Tom Beauchamp and R. G. Frey, 726–737. Oxford: Oxford University Press, 2011.

Hursthouse, Rosalind. "Appling Virtue Ethics to Our Treatment of Other Animals." In *The Practice of Virtue*, edited by Jennifer Welchman, 135–154. Indianapolis: Hackett, 2006.

Jaworska, Agnieszka, and Julie Tannenbaum. "The Grounds of Moral Status." In *Stanford Encyclopedia of Philosophy*. Summer 2013 ed., edited by Edward N. Zalta. http://plato.stanford.edu/archives/sum2013/entries/grounds-moral-status/

Kagan, Shelly. "Do I Make a Difference?" *Philosophy and Public Affairs* 39, no. 2 (2011): 105–141.

Klosko, George. *The Principle of Fairness and Political Obligation.* New ed. Lanham, MD: Rowman and Littlefield, 2004.

Korsgaard, Christine. "Fellow Creatures." In *Tanner Lectures on Human Values* 25/26, edited by G. B. Peterson. Salt Lake City: University of Utah Press, 2004.

Lippert-Rasmussen, Kaspar. "Two Puzzles for Deontologists." *Journal of Ethics* 5, no. 4 (2001): 385–410.

Marquis, Don. "Why Abortion Is Immoral." *Journal of Philosophy* 86, no. 4 (April 1989): 183–202.

Mason, Jim, and Peter Singer. *Animal Factories*. Rev. ed. New York: Harmony, 1990.

McMahan, Jeff. *Ethics of Killing*. Oxford University Press, 2002.

———. "Eating Animals the Nice Way." *Daedalus* 137, no. 1 (Winter 2008): 66–76.

McPherson, Tristram. "A Case for Ethical Veganism." *Journal of Moral Philosophy* 11 (2014): 677–703.

———. "A Moorean Defense of the Omnivore?" In *The Moral Complexities of Eating Meat*, edited by Robert Fischer and Ben Bramble. Oxford: Oxford University Press, 2015.

Nagel, Thomas. "Death." In *Mortal Questions*, 1–10. Cambridge, Cambridge University Press, 1979.

Norcross, Alasdair. "Puppies, Pigs, and People: Eating Meat and Marginal Cases." *Philosophical Perspectives* 18, Ethics (2004): 229–245.

———. "The Significance of Death for Animals." In *Oxford Handbook of Philosophy of Death*, edited by Ben Bradley, Fred Feldman, and Jens Johansson, 465–474. Oxford: Oxford University Press, 2012.

Pollan, Michael. *The Omnivore's Dilemma*. New York: Penguin, 2006.

Rachels, James. "The Moral Argument for Vegetarianism." In *Can Ethics Provide Answers? And Other Essays in Moral Philosophy*, 99–107. Lanham, MD: Rowman and Littlefield, 1997.

Rachels, Stuart. "Vegetarianism." In *Oxford Handbook of Animal Ethics*, edited by Tom Beauchamp and R. G. Frey, 877–905. Oxford: Oxford University Press, 2011.

Regan, Tom. *The Case for Animal Rights*. 2nd ed. Berkeley: University of California Press, 2004.

Rowlands, Mark. *Animals Like Us*. London: Verso, 2002.

Singer, Peter. *Animal Liberation*. Paperback ed. New York: Ecco, 2002.

———. "Vegetarianism and Utilitarianism." *Philosophy and Public Affairs* 9, no. 4 (Summer 1980): 325–337.

Talbert, Matthew. "Contractualism and Our Duties to Nonhuman Animals." *Environmental Ethics* 28 (Summer 2006): 202–215.

Tooley, Michael. "Abortion and Infanticide." *Philosophy and Public Affairs* 2, no. 1 (August 1972): 37–65.

United Nations Food and Agriculture Organization. "The Role of Livestock in Climate Change." 2014. http://www.fao.org/agriculture/lead/themes0/climate/en/

Walker, Polly, Pamela Rhubart-Berg, Shawn McKenzie, Kristin Kelling, and Robert S. Lawrence. "Public Health Implications of Meat Production and Consumption." *Public Health Nutrition* 8, no. 4 (2005): 348–356.

Williams, Bernard. "A Critique of Utilitarianism." In *Utilitarianism: For and Against*, edited by J. J. C. Smart and Bernard Williams, 77–150. Cambridge: Cambridge University Press, 1973.

Zamir, Tzachi. *Ethics and the Beast*. Princeton, NJ: Princeton University Press, 2007.

5

A MORAL ARGUMENT FOR VEGANISM

Dan Hooley and Nathan Nobis

In this chapter, we argue for dietary veganism. Our case has two steps. First, we argue that, in most circumstances, it is morally wrong to raise animals to produce meat, dairy products, most eggs (a possible exception we discuss is eggs from pet chickens), and most other animal food products. Turning animals into food, and using them for their by-products, causes serious harms to animals that are morally unjustified: That is, the reasons given to justify causing these kinds of harms—goods or alleged goods that result from animal farming and slaughter—are inadequate to justify the bad done to animals. This is true for both conventional 'factory farming' methods of raising and killing animals and small-scale, boutique animal farming and slaughter: so-called humane farming is actually inhumane and is wrong.

Some will conclude from this argument that each individual has a moral obligation to be vegan because they are morally obligated not to support wrongdoing. Our second step bolsters that reasoning. It *is* often morally wrong to support those who act wrongly. So, when it is wrong to produce a particular product, it can be wrong to purchase or use that product or otherwise encourage the product's production. We develop a plausible general moral principle concerning when consumers are obligated not to purchase a product. This principle justifies a moral obligation not to support the wrongful treatment of animals by purchasing or consuming animal food products. Thus, it's wrong *not* to be a vegan.

We discuss a variety of attempts to explain why these harms to animals are morally justified, that is, alleged good reasons to justify treating animals badly. Focusing on some of the most philosophically challenging justifications, we argue that none succeed: No defense points to goods that justify the serious harms done to animals, and so these harms are unjustified.

Arguments for veganism often appeal to many other considerations, such as personal and public health, environmental protection, and world hunger, but our arguments do not appeal to them. Some of these concerns support steps *toward* veganism but, unlike harm-based concerns, they do not justify a moral obligation to eat a vegan diet. Concerning personal health, we accept the common view that people are not morally obligated to act, and so eat, in ways that are likely to be best, or at least very good, for their own health. And there is no scientific reason to believe that vegan diets must be nutritionally superior to diets that include some animal products, especially if they are consumed rarely and in limited quantities. And to adequately address environmental, public health, and human social justice problems resulting from animal agriculture, no one must eat a vegan diet: A radically fewer number of animals could be raised in far less environmentally degrading ways that don't compromise public health and the lives of the world's poor. Veganism addresses these concerns, but so do some nonvegan responses. These concerns thereby augment harm-based arguments for veganism, but do not replace them.

Step 1: Raising and Killing Animals for Food

Step 1 in our case for veganism is this argument:

(1)   If a practice causes serious harms that are morally unjustified, then that practice is morally wrong.
(2)   The practice of raising and killing animals for food causes serious harms to animals and some human beings.
(3)   These harms are morally unjustified.
(4)   Therefore, the practice of raising and killing animals for food is wrong.

Unlike arguments for veganism that appeal to 'equality' for animals, animal 'rights' or the 'moral status' or 'standing' of animals, this argument depends on an uncontroversial moral principle that most people already accept: It is wrong to cause serious harms, to make someone worse off in some way, unless those harms are morally justified.

Premise 1: A Moral Principle

Our first premise, then, is a commonsense moral principle that nearly everyone affirms for both humans *and* some animals: Common sense and law affirm that intentional cruelty to animals is wrong because it harms them, which indicates a presumption against unjustified harms.

Nevertheless, the principle requires some clarification. The idea of a 'serious' harm is vague: How bad does a harm have to be in order to be a *serious* harm? We offer no systematic answer here, nor do we establish a clear distinction between

more and less serious harms. We don't do this because it's not practically important since most of the harms done to animals are, unfortunately, among the worst
harms an individual can experience: They are not in any 'grey area' of harms.
We also do not offer a complete theory on what does and would justify harms.
Harms can be justified in cases of self-defense and other defense, and allowing
harms to yourself to avoid future harms or achieve future benefits for yourself can
be permissible also. But we offer no general theory here. Instead we approach the
issue on a case-by-case basis, arguing that actual given justifications (e.g., "Yes,
this seriously harms animals, but it's not wrong because ___") do not succeed.

Premise 2: Harms to Animals

Our second premise is that animals, and some human beings, are seriously
harmed when animals are raised and killed for food. Animals are made worse
off in various and significant ways when raised and killed to be eaten, and some
humans are made worse off for doing this. Is this true? We offer a brief summary of the harms farmed animals are made to experience. All these harms
concern standard practices in farms and slaughterhouses: None is extraordinary
or deemed cruel by the industries.

Harms to Animals in Treatment

Let's begin with how animals are treated during their short lives. The vast majority of meat, dairy, and eggs produced in the US come from animals raised on
factory farms or confined animal feeding operations (CAFOs).[1] Here is a sample
of some standard practices:[2]

- Egg laying hens' beaks are sliced or burnt off; they are crammed in tiny,
  wire cages with other birds, without the space to turn around or spread
  their wings. Many die as a result of their confinement, while others suffer
  broken bones, open cuts and sores, as well as other injuries. Once a hen has
  stopped laying eggs, after a year or two, she is removed from her cage and
  killed, usually by suffocation with carbon dioxide. Her body is often used
  in processed chicken products.
- Male chicks are useless to the egg industry since they don't lay eggs or grow
  big enough to be useful for their flesh. As a result, male chicks are killed,
  either by suffocation or being ground alive. Every year about 200 million
  male chicks are killed in the US.
- 'Broiler' chickens and turkeys (raised for meat) live indoors in crowded sheds.
  These animals have been bred to grow very large, very quickly. In the 1920s,
  a chicken took about sixteen weeks to grow to be over two pounds; now
  they can reach five pounds in just seven weeks.[3] As a result, they suffer leg
  disorders, chronic joint pain, and heart attacks. Injured birds often have their
  necks broken or are clubbed to death.

- Pigs live in crowded pens, and at a young age are castrated and have their tails cut off, all without anesthetic. Young pigs who are injured, or not growing fast enough, are killed, sometimes by being gassed, other times by being slammed to the ground. Sows are confined for the majority of their lives in metal 'gestation crates' barely larger than their own body, where they cannot turn around. Their confinement causes severe physical and emotional distress.
- Female dairy cows are separated from their young after birth, an experience that is often emotionally distressing. Most live confined in cramped sheds on concrete floors. Young dairy cows are branded, dehorned, and have their tails cut off, all without anesthetic. When the cows are 'spent' and no longer produce as much milk, usually at a small fraction of their natural life span, they are sent to slaughter. Here, 'downed' dairy cows, who can no longer move on their own, are often kicked or shocked to be made to move to slaughter.
- Veal calves are a direct product of the dairy industry: Nearly all veal calves are the male offspring of dairy cows. These animals are often confined in individual crates, too narrow for them to even to turn around, where they are tethered by their neck to further restrict their movement. Living like this causes these calves significant stress, fear, and physical pain.
- Cows raised for their flesh are branded, castrated, and dehorned, all without anesthetic. Most spend the last months of their lives in crowded feedlots.

The vast majority of farmed animals raised in the US live in close confinement. This results in injuries, disease, immobilization, boredom, psychological distress, and often death. These animals are also sometimes abused and injured by workers in other ways than the standard industrial practices detailed above. In addition to these *inflicted* harms, these animals are harmed by being *deprived* of many goods crucial to their well-being. By failing to provide the space and resources needed for good lives, we seriously harm them: They are denied what they need for basic, natural, and social behaviors, and to live lives that are good *for them*.

While the vast majority of US farmed animals are on factory farms, some live on smaller farms that provide the animals with more space and better living conditions. But these animals are also harmed in how they are treated. Many smaller farms inflict painful body mutilations (e.g., castration, dehorning, branding) on the animals, and they still face the harms that come from transport to slaughter (such as abuse in handling, severe dehydration and hunger, and suffering from crowding as well as overheating or extreme cold). And all of these animals are harmed by an untimely death.

The Harm of Death for Animals

The final way *all* animals used for food are harmed is when they are killed. Farmed animals are often killed in ways that are quite painful. US law mandates that cows and pigs be rendered unconscious before being slaughtered, most often by using a pistol that puts a bolt through the animal's brain. However, because of the rapid pace at which animals are slaughtered, animals often have their throats slit while they are still conscious. And this law excludes birds, fish, and rabbits. Chickens and turkeys make up the vast majority of animals slaughtered in the US, nearly nine billion are killed every year, and they suffer particularly horrifying deaths. They are shackled upside down, paralyzed by electrified water, and then dragged across a mechanical throat-cutting blade, all while being fully conscious.[4] Every year millions of unlucky birds miss the blades and drown in scalding water.

A painful death is also the fate of animals like fish and other sea creatures that are often not raised for food, but captured and killed.[5] Commercial fishing operations cause fish and other creatures captured substantial pain prior to their death. Trapped in massive trolling nets, many fish suffer as they are dragged along the ocean floor. As they are pulled up to the surface, fish experience excruciating decompression that can rupture their swim bladders and pop out their eyes. Once on board, these fish slowly suffocate or are crushed to death. Other unfortunate fish are still conscious when their throats or bellies are cut open.

The harm of death extends beyond pain animals experience in the process of being killed. Cutting their lives short seriously harms animals because the good lives they could have experienced are taken from them. Nearly all of the animals we eat are killed at a very young age, well before they have come anywhere close to living out a natural life span. Chickens are killed at five to seven weeks, and pigs are killed after just six months, when both types of animals can typically live between eight and twelve years (and sometimes much longer). Cows raised for their meat live a little longer: Usually they are killed after about eighteen months, but they can normally live between fifteen and twenty years.[6]

In cutting their lives short, we seriously harm these animals by depriving them of the possibility of enjoyable and valuable future experiences. This is a deprivation of the most fundamental kind. Nearly all of us would recognize this when it comes to companion animals (and ourselves!). If your neighbor painlessly killed your young, healthy, and friendly dog, you would be upset because your neighbor had harmed the dog, taking away *her* life and depriving *her* of enjoyable future experiences. This is why even killing farmed animals 'humanely' is actually inhumane: the animals lose *everything*, all the good of their future, and are made far worse off because of it. For farmed animals, a 'pain-free' death isn't a harm-free death.

Harms to Human Beings

While our argument's central concern is the serious harms farmed animals are made to experience, some human beings also are harmed when animals are raised and killed for food. Although most of these harms are pervasive across the industry, they are not essential to the practice of raising and killing animals for food. Since, in theory, many of these harms to human beings could be eliminated, our argument does not depend on them.

Some harms to human beings concern public health: For example, air pollution from intensive animal agriculture may cause higher asthma and depression rates for those who live close by.[7] Animal agriculture also increases the number of harmful bacteria that are resistant to antibiotics. To help prevent the spread of disease in such cramped quarters, and increase the rate at which farmed animals grow, most are fed antibiotics. This use has reduced the efficacy of many drugs for humans and may lead to the emergence of novel 'superbugs' that could harm and kill many humans, potentially at pandemic levels. Factory farming is also dangerous work: Workers are sometimes injured or killed by flailing animals and machinery in slaughterhouses and meat processing plants. And there is also evidence that the presence of industrial slaughterhouses in rural communities harms these communities, as they lead to an increase in violent crimes that cannot be explained by other factors, such as population demographics, unemployment, and so forth.[8]

Another way that workers are often harmed is that the work they do contributes to their own attitudes of indifference and hostility towards animals, rather than the respect and care animals are owed. However, the possibility that some ways of raising and killing other animals might not engender disrespect or a lack of concern for other animals suggests that harms to humans may not be *essential* to this practice. We have argued that harms to animals are essential and unavoidable: That is why harms to animals are the basis of our argument for veganism.

Premise 3: These Harms Are Not Justified

To complete Step 1 of our argument we must support premise (3), that that these harms to animals are unjustified. Why believe this? Most simply, because farmed animals are treated very, very badly; some humans are harmed as well; and *either* no good comes from this *or* no good great enough to justify the pain, suffering, frustration, deprivation, death, and other harms done. To defend this claim we must respond to attempts to justify these harms. To begin, however, we argue that common *motivations* that lead individuals to eat animal products cannot justify the harms we inflict on farmed animals.

One common motivation for eating animal products is health: Many people believe that eating animal products is necessary to be healthy. If we need animal products for good health, this might justify harming animals. While common, this claim is not supported by scientific evidence. The Academy of Nutrition and Dietetics, the world's largest organization of food and nutrition professionals, has an evidence-based sixteen-page review of this issue, with hundreds of references to the medical and nutrition literature. They state:

> It is [our] position . . . that appropriately planned vegetarian diets, including total vegetarian or vegan diets, are healthful, nutritionally adequate,

and may provide health benefits in the prevention and treatment of certain diseases. Well-planned vegetarian diets are appropriate for individuals during all stages of the life cycle, including pregnancy, lactation, infancy, childhood, and adolescence, and for athletes. . . . The results of an evidence-based review showed that a vegetarian diet is associated with a lower risk of death from ischemic heart disease. Vegetarians also appear to have lower low-density lipoprotein cholesterol levels, lower blood pressure, and lower rates of hypertension and type 2 diabetes than nonvegetarians. Furthermore, vegetarians tend to have a lower body mass index and lower overall cancer rates. Features of a vegetarian diet that may reduce risk of chronic disease include lower intakes of saturated fat and cholesterol and higher intakes of fruits, vegetables, whole grains, nuts, soy products, fiber, and phytochemicals.[9]

This review states not merely that vegan diets are healthy, but that people may be healthier on a well-planned vegan diet. Our argument does not rest on any expectations for better health, only the well-supported claim that with some effort nearly everyone will be at least as healthy on a vegan diet as they would be an omnivorous diet, and so they are no worse off. If they're better off for being vegan, then all the better.

Another common motivation for consuming animal products is that many people find that they taste good and are pleasurable to eat, and they feel that foods without animal products generally do not taste as good or are not satisfying. So, some argue that not eating delicious meals with animal products would be a very significant loss of human pleasure and this fact justifies the harms we inflict upon animals. Indeed, a common initial reaction to arguments for veganism is, "But meat tastes good!" But there are all sorts of actions that do, or would, produce pleasure, but they are wicked and wrong actions. That an action produces pleasure never, in itself, justifies it morally. All sorts of historical and contemporary examples with human beings confirm this. That we are deprived of some pleasure never, in itself, morally justifies a harmful behavior.

Consider how we would react to similar attempts to justify harming animals when the source of pleasure is not food. Suppose someone raises and kills animals (in similar ways to what we find on factory farms) so he can paint with their blood, which he enjoys immensely. He is no sadist: He does not raise and kill animals *because* he likes seeing them suffer, nor is he pleased that many animals must be killed to get enough blood. But, alas, without any of this he would not be able to gain the pleasure he does in using their blood for art (and other methods of obtaining animal blood are just too costly or inconvenient or don't provide enough blood at once for his artistic proclivities). So, he believes that harming animals is morally justified.

Most would think that such a person is a moral monster. After all, he can enjoy painting without harming other animals. And even if he got significantly less pleasure from using oil or acrylic paint, so what? Clearly, humans, morally, cannot do *whatever* brings them pleasure. The painter's pleasures from using the blood of animals are trivial and insignificant compared to the harms to the animals. Arguably, the painter's pleasures should not count for anything positive in evaluating his actions since they depend on harming animals. The same is true about raising and killing animals for someone's pleasures in eating them. Just as the painter can paint beautiful, interesting paintings with oils or acrylics, all of us can eat foods that are *tasty, pleasurable to eat*, and vegan. Vegans, most of whom were once omnivores, typically agree: They report that eating vegan is pleasurable and satisfying.

Step 2: Buying and Eating Meat, Dairy, Eggs, and Other Animal Products

If we can adequately support our premise (3) that the harms to animals are not morally justified, readers might think that enough has been done to reach the conclusion that each of us shouldn't purchase and consume animal products. After all, if it is wrong to raise and kill animals for food, it might be obvious that we shouldn't support these practices, and that we should all transition to a vegan diet. What else needs to be said?

We offer the following general principle to connect individuals' consumer behavior to the practices of the animal agriculture industry:

If a product is such that

(a) its production causes serious and unjustified harms and so is morally wrong,

(b) the product can be avoided,

(c) avoiding the product would not seriously harm the boycotting individual,

(d) there are readily available alternatives to that product,

(e) the boycotting individual might benefit from boycotting,

(f) the probability that *not* purchasing or consuming the product will lessen or eliminate the wrongdoing is *equal to or greater* than the probability that purchasing or consuming the product will lessen or eliminate the wrongdoing, and

(g) boycotting will make that individual a member of a morally progressive group that opposes a wrongdoing,

then individuals are obligated to not purchase or use that product.

Meat and other animal food products satisfy all these conditions.

Given this principle, each of us is morally obligated not to support the wrongdoing of the meat industry; we are obligated to eat vegan. This is true at least for people who live in societies where their survival and basic health is consistent with a vegan diet. We believe this is true for most people living in developed countries. However, this might not be true for some individuals living in developing countries.

This principle does not make unreasonable demands. If an individual would be seriously harmed by avoiding a product, and if the product cannot be avoided (because it is necessary for human survival, perhaps), then that individual is not obligated to do so. This principle captures many of the obligations we have as consumers. When all of these conditions are satisfied for a product, an individual has an obligation not to purchase or consume that product. We do not claim that there are no contexts where an individual has an obligation but all of these conditions aren't met. Satisfying these conditions is *sufficient* to have a moral obligation, but meeting all of these conditions might not be *necessary* either.

Objections and Responses: "These Harms Are Justified Because . . ."

Step 1 of our argument held that the practice of raising and killing animals for food is wrong. Step 2 concluded that if the principle we specified is fulfilled, an individual has an obligation to not support unjustified harms—either by paying someone to cause these harms or by benefitting from these harms—and thus, to be vegan. To complete our argument, however, we must respond to objections that attempt to justify these harms. There are *many* objections, and our limited space prevents us from discussing many commonly given justifications for eating animal products, such as:

> "Eating meat is natural," "Animals eat other animals," "Animals would eat us if they could," "We *are* animals," "Animals are not equal to humans," "Animals have no rights," "Our bodies were designed to eat meat," "Animals aren't human," "Animals aren't people," "There is a circle of life," "Many traditions involve eating animals," "Cheese is too hard to give up," "Vegan foods just don't taste good," "Eating vegan is too expensive," "Eating vegan would require learning new ways to cook," "People would lose their jobs if people didn't eat meat," "Too many restaurants would go out of business if people didn't eat meat," "It's too difficult to eat vegan," "It's not illegal to eat animal products," "Animals wouldn't exist if we didn't eat them, and they would go extinct," "Animals would overpopulate if we didn't eat them," "We just can't give up eating meat," "They eat cats and dogs in Asia," "What about people in areas where they can't eat vegan?" "Religions approve of eating meat," "We have a right to eat whatever we want," "Vegans are offensive," "It's good enough to eat less meat," "Plants might be harmed too," and more.

We believe that these common justifications, and many others, have been adequately responded to elsewhere.[10] Here we respond to just a few of the more philosophically challenging objections to our argument.

"Harms to Animals Are Justified Because Humans Are Superior"

Some might think the harms we inflict on other animals are justified because animals matter less, morally, than human beings. "They are just animals," one often hears. We can draw on this idea and attempt to justify harming animals to eat them by claiming that human beings are intellectually 'superior' to animals: We are more intelligent than animals, are capable of using complex language, are self-conscious in a way many animals are not, are moral agents who are responsible for what we do, and so on. These characteristics, the argument goes, separate us from other animals, make us morally superior, and so justify our harming animals for our benefit.

Notice first, however, that all of us reject this argument when it comes to other human beings. The fact that one individual might be more intelligent, more rational, or more morally virtuous does not justify that individual in harming less intelligent or rational or virtuous individuals. So while this argument 'justifies' eating animals, the first premise also 'justifies' harming and eating human babies, seriously cognitively disabled human beings, and dementia patients. Any argument to justify eating animals that would also justify eating vulnerable human beings is unsound and should be rejected.

But even if *all* human beings were morally 'superior' to *all* animals (or no animals were 'equal to' humans), that does not, in itself, justify harming animals. Suppose super-advanced aliens arrived on earth to raise and kill humans for food. Even if they were superior to us in a variety of ways—they have powers of rationality and reasoning that far exceed our smartest computers, language abilities that put ours to shame, and moral self-control that far surpasses that of human beings—they would not be justified in killing us for food. So even if humans are intellectually superior to other animals and on this basis matter more, morally, than other animals, this does not justify our harming other animals, especially for trivial ends. Human moral superiority might justify us doing more to *benefit* human beings, and to promote our welfare, but it does not justify actively undertaking efforts to harm other animals, especially when these harms can be easily avoided.

"These Harms Are Justified Because Painless Killing Is Harmless Killing"

Some believe that a painless death does not harm other animals. They claim that death only harms beings who have an interest in continuing to live, and to have that interest that being must have an understanding of his or her self existing in the future, or goals or projects that extend into the future and that are cut off by death.[11] If these claims are true, it might open the door to some morally acceptable forms of animal agriculture (assuming we could find ways to consistently kill animals without causing them pain, terror, or significant distress, and that they were raised in ways that did not seriously harm them).

However, even if we accept this view about who can be harmed by death, there is evidence that farmed animals have an interest in continuing to live. Peter Singer accepts this account of the harm of death, and argues that some animals (such as the great apes) have the cognitive capacities that make it prima facie wrong to kill them. But he also believes that there is strong evidence that many of the animals humans eat, like pigs, chickens, and maybe even fish, may have the sense of their self, existing in the future, that makes it prima facie wrong to kill them, even painlessly.[12] Even if we accept the view that a painless death only harms beings with a sense of themselves existing in the future, some animals deserve the benefit of the doubt. There might be sufficient reasons to think death *may* harm them—and it would still be wrong to painlessly kill them to consume their flesh.

A lot will depend on what we think is the right criteria for having an interest in continued existence. If we require that an animal have an understanding of his or her own death, this would rule out most animals as beings who can be harmed by a painless death. There is some evidence, although it is far from conclusive, which suggest that some animals, like elephants and the great apes, may have some awareness of death and their own mortality.[13] And it is possible that other animals that humans use for food, like pigs and cows, might have some understanding as well. If, however, we only require that an animal has some sense of his or her self existing in the future, this seems to open the door to many more animals, including most of the animals (certainly mammals and birds, and arguably fish) that humans consume or use for food. If these animals have desires that extend hours or days in to the future, then it seems they have some sense of their self existing in the future, and as a result would be harmed by death.

More fundamentally, however, the view that only beings with a strong sense of themselves existing in the future are harmed by death is false. On this account, a painless death would not harm human babies, individuals with very severe cognitive disabilities, and older adults with severe dementia: They often don't have, or have lost, the strong sense of self-awareness that proponents of this view often suggest is needed to be harmed by a painless death. But it would be wrong to kill these individuals, even apart from the effects on others. Part of the reason is that these humans, like other animals, have interests and desires that can be satisfied only if they are alive: They have at least an indirect interest in being alive even if they lack the concepts to understand this. An individual doesn't need a strong sense of themselves existing in the future to be harmed by death or to have an interest in continued existence. Thus, we have good reasons to reject the claim that animals aren't harmed by a painless death, in favor of our deprivation account articulated earlier. 'Happy meat' precludes future happiness for animals, harms them greatly for no good reason, and so is wrong.

"These Harms Are Justified Because Animals Are Not Seriously Harmed"

While some don't deny that animals are harmed by being painlessly killed, they claim that this harm is not serious, and is much less serious than when a human being is killed. So, if we raise animals in ways that don't harm them, or if we hunt or capture animals that have had good lives, then perhaps we are justified in doing this, since we get pleasure from eating their flesh and the harm of death is not as serious for animals. There are different reasons why an individual might think that killing an animal is not a serious harm. But the most compelling draws on two claims: First, animals are not capable of achieving the same quality or level of well-being as humans; second, the strength of animals' psychological unity over time is much weaker than that of most human beings (e.g., animals' capacities for memory and anticipation of the future is weaker than most human beings).[14]

These claims may help to explain common intuitions people have about the comparative harm of killing different beings. Most people think it would be far worse to kill an adult human being than a fish. Why is this? One explanation is that fish seem incapable of achieving or having many of the 'higher goods' that are components in human well-being (creativity, close friendship, long-term projects, intimate relationships, etc.). We also have reason to doubt the strength of the psychological unity between any particular fish now, and that same fish months or years later, is anywhere near the psychological unity of most human beings. The memories of a fish, it seems, do not extend as far into the past as ours, nor do they have a strong, reflective understanding that it was themselves that existed months and years before and will exist months and years in the future.

Taken together, these two claims may suggest that other animals are not seriously harmed by a painless death. If the well-being they are cut off from is of a lesser quality than human beings, and if there is a much weaker psychological continuity between an animal now and that same animal in the future, then it appears they are harmed less than human beings in being killed. So, perhaps this harm is not serious, and we can be justified in killing them by appealing to the pleasure and satisfaction we get from eating the flesh of animals.

We suspect that one reason some find the view that animals are not seriously harmed by death compelling is that they underestimate the cognitive capacities of other animals. If an animal's experience of the world consisted solely in one experience after another—a constant stream of unconnected experiences, like the mythical goldfish with a three-second memory[15]—we might have significant doubts that a painless death would seriously harm such an animal. Without any memory connecting different experiences, and without any continuity between these experiences, we might think this sort of creature is replaceable: Indeed, we might doubt that a real individual or self is snuffed out of the world when this being is killed.

This view of the inner lives of animals, however, is not supported by recent developments in the field of ethology and animal behavioral science. For the vast majority of animals humans eat, particularly mammals, birds, and fish, we have good reason to believe that this is not how these animals experience the world. These animals have shown the ability to recall events well into the past: Rainbowfish, to give just one example, can remember the location of a hole in a net that they have not seen in eleven months.[16] Other animals recognize many other individuals with whom they live, often exhibit preferences for which animals they spend their time with, and even develop friendships over time with other animals. There are good reasons, then, to believe that the psychological continuity of these animals is likely much stronger than the mythical goldfish.

With this, we don't believe the pleasure human beings get from eating the flesh of other animals justifies killing them, *even if* death is less of a harm to them than it is to most human beings. Animals, after all, also get pleasure from eating. So it is unclear why the momentary pleasures humans would get from eating the flesh of an animal should outweigh a lifetime of pleasure an individual animal experiences (both from eating and in other activities).

The claim that other animals are incapable of achieving the same quality or level of well-being as human beings may only illustrate our human prejudice for our form and ways of life. Why are things like human creativity, art, novels, and intimate friendships more valuable or 'higher goods' than the goods and activities that characterize the lives of pigs, cows, or chickens? Is writing a novel or enjoying poetry really more valuable or a higher good than rooting in the mud or enjoying a nice dust bath? Offering a rationally compelling response to this question has proven more difficult than many philosophers might suspect.[17] There is no neutral ground from which we can consider whether or not we would prefer the life of a contented pig or the life of a human being: We can only consider this question from our own human perspective. And even if we think that many of the goods that characterize paradigmatic human lives are more valuable goods than the goods that characterize the lives of other animals, it does not follow that killing these animals does not seriously harm them. After all, the goods that characterize their lives matter to them.[18]

Finally, given the significant objections to the claim that animals are not seriously harmed by death, we think a more cautious approach is required. We have good reasons to reject the claim that death is not a serious harm to other animals. But even if one wasn't convinced of this, given the uncertainty surrounding this account of how serious a harm death is for animals, we ought to err on the side of caution. That death is a harm to animals is part of common sense (since nearly all of us would affirm it with respect to our companion animals), and we recognize it for human beings who lack certain intellectual capacities. And, we do not need to raise and kill animals to survive or lead flourishing lives. Thus, given that those who think animals are not seriously harmed by death very well might be wrong, we should err on the side of caution and not raise and kill animals for food, nor should we purchase meat or animal products.

Pet Chickens

While we do not think we are justified in killing animals for food, we do think there are some circumstances where it is permissible to use chickens for their eggs. This is only the case for companion hens and, in rather limited circumstances, hens used for eggs on 'hobby farms.' If someone had hens whose needs were met, lived good lives, were protected and cared for (including access to veterinary care), and kept free from harm (in particular, they are not killed when their egg production slows or ceases), there doesn't seem to be anything wrong with consuming their eggs. These chickens are not harmed, especially since they do not seem to be at all bothered by their eggs being taken. In these situations, we believe that purchasing and consuming these eggs is morally permissible.

If it can sometimes be permissible to use hens for their eggs, what about using cows for their milk? We believe dairy production is nearly always impermissible. Actions required to produce cow's milk—like forced impregnation, the separation of mother and calf, depriving the calf of his or her mother's milk (so that milk can be sold for humans), and overmilking—harm the cow and her offspring. And dairy cows, as female mammals, must have a calf in order to produce milk. Current practices use male calves (who don't produce milk) for beef or veal, and female calves eventually become part of the cycle of dairy production. These biological realities make morally permissible dairy production highly unlikely: To maintain a 1,000- to 2,000-pound cow for dairy production, without causing serious harms to her and her offspring, would be very difficult and incredibly expensive.

"All Diets Cause Harm, So Veganism Isn't Required"

For almost everyone, no matter what foods we purchase and eat, we still contribute to practices that cause *some* animals to be harmed, including being killed. Modern crop production inevitably kills some animals living in the fields: Rabbits, birds, mice, and other small rodents are killed by tractors and harvesting machines, and other animals are killed by pesticides. There is likely no diet that is free from harm.

Some could appeal to these facts to argue that our arguments imply, absurdly, that each of us has an obligation to grow all our own food, or to eat a diet of only fruits, nuts, and other plants that are produced in a way that avoids harming *any* animals. Since this is too demanding, perhaps each of us is only obligated to take reasonable steps to reduce our consumption of animal products. Maybe our obligations when it comes to what we ought to purchase and eat are much less uniform than we have argued. Our own obligations might depend on our individual circumstances (where we live, how much money we have, our access to plant-based foods, etc.). Given that it can be easier to be vegan in some places, and for some individuals, perhaps not all of us have an obligation to eat a vegan diet.

We agree that our argument would be too demanding if it led to the conclusion that we must grow our own food and not purchase vegetables and other plant food where some field animals are killed. But our argument doesn't lead to this conclusion. What anyone is obligated to do depends on what he or she *can* do, and most people just *cannot* grow all their own food or eat such a diet: That's not realistic. We are only obligated to take *reasonable steps* to minimize harms that we contribute to with our food choices, but this is consistent with an obligation to be vegan. Unlike meat and other animal products, there are no readily available alternatives to vegetables and other plant foods grown in ways that kill some field animals. And foregoing these foods would seriously harm an individual: We all need something to eat. Thus, the claim that each of us has an obligation to grow our food and boycott plants produced in a way that leads to the death of some field animals fails to meet the conditions we outlined in Step 2, for when an individual has an obligation not to buy a product. We recognize that veganism is easier for some than others. It is more difficult to be vegan in rural Montana than in a major American city. Nevertheless, our argument does not make unreasonable demands.

A related objection here involves the claim that a vegan diet will not always result in the least harms to animals and human beings. Since modern crop production kills some field animals, perhaps eating large animals, like cows, that feed on grass would result in the least number of animal deaths. If one lives in a place where the cows are grass fed, perhaps eating beef would contribute the least to the death of animals, than were one to eat a vegan diet that included plant foods where field animals were killed.

There are challenging empirical and mathematical issues here, but it's worth noting, first, that this objection in no way justifies any standard diet involving factory farmed animals, since that clearly results in unjustified harms and fails to minimize the number of animals killed. Factory farmed animals are fed corn and soy: Producing these crops kills some field animals, and then on top of that, the animals on factory farms are killed. If this objection were sound, we would only be justified in eating large animals in situations where our doing this would contribute the least to the death of all animals. Second, and more importantly, the data that has been marshaled in favor of these objections is just not convincing. As far as we know, there is no strong empirical evidence against the claim that the vegan ideal would result in the death of the fewest animals.[19]

Conclusions

In sum, we have argued that each of us is obligated to eat vegan. Step 1 argued that it is wrong to raise and kill animals for food since these practices cause serious harms to animals that are not justified. Step 2 connected this conclusion to our own behavior: It's wrong to support those who act wrongly, when the conditions we outlined are met. We then addressed several attempts to justify these harms and argued that they don't succeed.

But we cannot address every concern or objection, and there are many more than what we have considered here. To evaluate other justifications for eating animal products, or objections to arguments like ours, we recommend identifying the complete pattern of reasoning and carefully trying to determine whether all the essential claims of the justification are true: If any are false, the justification fails.

Finally, we recommend being on guard for, as James McWilliams puts it, the 'tyranny of taste.' As we saw with our earlier 'blood painter' example, human beings have a tendency to privilege the pleasure we get from food over other sources. This is not surprising: Food often occupies a central place in our lives and forms part of our identities and cultural traditions. But this privileged status sometimes leads people to endorse rationalizations for harming animals, and human beings, that they would reject if the source of pleasure were different. A useful corrective, then, is to consider whether or not the justification would be plausible if the source of pleasure were not food, but something else. Seeing that harms inflicted on animals for pleasure or enjoyment from other activities are not justified can help us see that the harms humans inflict on so many animals for food are not justified either.[20]

Notes

1. Approximately 99 percent of all farmed animals in the US live on factory farms. Most of the farmed animals killed in the US for food are chickens, and only 0.44 percent of these animals are raised on 'free range' farms. See the US Department of Agriculture, "The Economic Organization of U.S. Broiler Production," 2008. http://www.ers.usda.gov/media/205671/eib38_1_.pdf.
2. Mercy for Animals' short video, *Farm to Fridge*, gives an excellent overview of many of the harms farmed animals experience, as standard practice, during their lives and in the process of being killed: http://www.mercyforanimals.org/farm-to-fridge.aspx.
3. Humane Society of the United States, "An HSUS Report: The Welfare of Animals in the Chicken Industry," December 2013. http://www.humanesociety.org/assets/pdfs/farm/welfare_broiler.pdf.
4. Humane Society of the United States, "The Welfare of Birds at Slaughter," 2009. http://www.humanesociety.org/issues/slaughter/research/welfare_birds_slaughter.html.
5. The evidence is increasingly strong that fish are conscious creatures who experience pain. See Victoria Braithwaite, *Do Fish Feel Pain?* (Oxford: Oxford University Press, 2010), and Jonathan Balcombe, *Pleasurable Kingdom: Animals and the Nature of Feeling Good* (New York: Macmillan, 2006), chap. 10.

6. Mercy for Animals, *Farm to Fridge.*

7. Pew Commission on Industrial Farm Animal Production, "Putting Meat on the Table: Industrial Farm Animal Production in America," 2009, p. 29. http://www.ncifap.org/_images/PCIFAPFin.pdf.

8. See Amy Fitzgerald, Linda Kalof, and Thomas Dietz, "Slaughterhouses and Increased Crime Rates: An Empirical Analysis of the Spillover From 'The Jungle' into the Surrounding Community," *Organization & Environment* 22, no. 2 (2009): 158–184.

9. "Position of the American Dietetic Association: Vegetarian Diets," *Journal of the American Dietetic Association* 109 (2009): 1266–1282.

10. For a discussion of the many other common objections to veganism, see Nathan Nobis's "Reasonable Humans and Animals: An Argument for Vegetarianism," *Between the Species* 13, no. 8 (2008), http://digitalcommons.calpoly.edu/bts/vol13/iss8/4; Gary Francione and Anna Charlton, *Eat Like You Care: An Examination of the Morality of Eating Animals* (Exempla Press (online), 2013), http://www.abolitionistapproach.com/books/eat-like-you-care-an-examination-of-the-morality-of-eating-animals; and Sherry F. Colb, *Mind If I Order the Cheeseburger? And Other Questions People Ask Vegans* (New York: Lantern Books, 2013). Which objections are most common, which are most influential? This article is the only empirical research on these questions we could find: Hank Rothgerber, "Real Men Don't Eat (Vegetable) Quiche: Masculinity and the Justification of Meat Consumption." *Psychology of Men & Masculinity* (November 12, 2012).

11. See Peter Singer, *Practical Ethics* (New York: Cambridge University Press, 2011), chap. 5.

12. See ibid., pp. 101–103.

13. Elephants have been shown to grieve the death of other elephants that have died, and even engage in death rituals, such as covering the dead body of family members with dirt. See Cynthia Moss, *Elephant Memories: Thirteen Years in the Life of an Elephant Family* (Chicago: University of Chicago Press, 2000). And Koko, a gorilla that was taught American Sign Language, expressed sadness and grieved when she learned of the death of her pet cat, All Ball.

14. See Jeff McMahan, *The Ethics of Killing: Problems at the Margins of Life* (New York: Oxford University Press, 2002), chap. 3.

15. See Colin Allen, "Ethics, Law, and the Science of Fish Welfare," *Between the Species* 16, no. 1 (2013): 68–85, p. 77.

16. See Culum Brown, "Familiarity with the Test Environment Improves Escape Responses in the Crimson Spotted Rainbowfish, *Melanotaenia duboulayi*," *Animal Cognition* 4 (2001): 109–113.

17. See Paulo Cavalieri, *The Animal Question* (New York: Oxford University Press, 2001), chap. 5.

18. For an interesting discussion of these issues, see Christine Korsgaard, "Getting Animals In View," *The Point*, 2012. http://www.thepointmag.com/2012/metaphysics/getting-animals-view.

19. For discussion, see Andy Lamey, "Food Fight! Davis versus Regan on the Ethics of Eating Beef," *Journal of Social Philosophy* 38, no. 2 (Summer 2007): 331–348.

20. We would like to thank the many people, friends and not-yet-friends, who read and commented on the many previous drafts of this paper and offered both critical and supportive comments and suggestions. We especially thank the editors of this volume for the opportunity to be part of this project and for their feedback on previous drafts.

6

NON-IDEAL FOOD CHOICES

Tyler Doggett and Andy Egan

Our lives are full of failures. Some are significant. Some are trivial. Some are reprehensible. Some are laughable. Some are worth responding to. Some aren't. But, as we said, life is full of these things, so let's be gentle about them. Failing is a way of acting non-ideally. Instead of "failure," let's just talk about behaving in a "non-ideal" way. When the New England Patriots won the Super Bowl in 2015, this was, for the Patriots and their fans, ideal. When the New England Patriots won the Super Bowl in 2015, this was, for the fans of the Cleveland Browns, non-ideal: There can be only one Super Bowl winner and the Browns failed in pursuit of the ideal of winning it. Again.

When Aurora resolves to do ten push-ups a day and only does seven, this is non-ideal.

When Beth breaks her promise to attend her best friend's wedding simply to finish a book she's reading, this is non-ideal.

Many choices about food—what to eat, what to buy—are clearly not ideal. In Cormac McCarthy's *The Road*, some of the few human survivors of the apocalypse form cannibalistic gangs, roving the highways, capturing and eating other survivors. This is non-ideal because it is obviously morally wrong.[1]

At least one of us invariably eats too much Halloween candy and ends up nauseated. This is non-ideal because it is imprudent.

One day after starting an attempt at vegetarianism, one of us had an Egg McMuffin, not realizing they contain ham. This is non-ideal because the policy of being vegetarian and eating ham is obviously incoherent.

Some food choices are non-ideal in, we think, more interesting ways. This chapter is about some such departures from the ideal. Not all of these departures are *failures*. One might fall short of an ideal without failing. Some ideals are so difficult to achieve that simply approximating them counts as success: The ideal in baseball is getting on base *every* time, *never* making an out. So someone who only gets on base half the time is falling well short of the ideal; yet such a hitter is *extraordinarily* successful. When a doctor performs a less risky surgery at the cost of producing a less satisfactory result, this is non-ideal because it isn't the best possible outcome. But, still, the doctor might not have failed at all. She might have done just as she should have.

Also, not all failings to act ideally are fallings short. One might miss the ideal mark by exceeding the ideal. Eating a seventh burrito isn't ideal but also doesn't exactly fall short of some nutritional mark. Donating so much of your income to famine relief that you don't have enough left to feed yourself isn't ideal, but also doesn't fall short of the moral mark. (Though perhaps both of these are properly characterized as cases in which exceeding one standard—for example, charity—results in falling short on another—for example, a duty of self-care.)

Our main goal in what follows is to map out (part of) the landscape—to identify, and provide examples of, several of the interestingly different ways in which we miss the ideal mark, food-wise. Some of these call for correction; some don't. Some are easy to fix; some aren't. Some are easy to see; some aren't. This chapter isn't about fixing.[2] It is about how we get things not quite right: *believing* more or less than our evidence warrants, under- and over*committing*, and under- and over*performing*. It is clearly, sadly, possible to fail in more than one of these ways at the same time—one can believe less than one's evidence supports, undercommit relative to one's moral beliefs, and underperform relative to one's moral commitments. By getting clearer on various ways we get things not quite right food-wise, we can figure out ways to improve, just as by getting clearer on whether it's the carburetor or the gas pedal or the windshield wipers that have gone wrong, we can figure out how to fix the car. But there's another lesson: Some ways of not acting ideally are actually helpful and defensible. There's sometimes quite a bit to be said for getting things not quite right.

Carl knows he needs to get out of bed by 7 a.m. The ideal thing to do is sleep until then and bolt up. But, he knows, that almost never works for him, he finds getting out of bed too hard. He reluctantly sets his alarm for 6:45 a.m. to make sure he's out of bed by 7 a.m.

Delia knows the best thing for her to do is eat only a few pieces of Halloween candy. She also knows that once she starts, she usually can't stop and ends up with a bad stomachache. So she forgoes the best thing just to avoid the stomachache.

Eva thinks she should exercise more to be healthier. She treats herself to unhealthy candy every time she exercises. It would be better just to exercise, but Eva knows that that'd never work, that the unhealthy enticement is crucial to getting to the gym.

These behaviors are all non-ideal and all defensible, even laudable. Understanding the ways in which, and the reasons why, people can fall short of various ideals, can help to take a bit of the heat out of at least some of the debates about the ethics of eating. There's a sort of fury and superiority that attaches to some of the vegan/vegetarian rhetoric, which doesn't typically seem to help advance anybody's understanding of the issues, or improve anybody's behavior. (Often it hinders progress by making those in the crosshairs defensive and unreceptive to the substance of the criticism behind the outrage.) Sometimes this sort of harsh judgment of those in other camps might be justified, but other times not. Some people who aren't, for example, vegan might have excellent reasons for not being so. Relatedly, there's a sort of complacency and smugness about some omnivore rhetoric, often accompanied by a not especially helpful sort of outrage and/or contemptuous dismissal. Sometimes this sort of strong reaction might be justified, but other times not. The chapter helps to pinpoint when and why.

Doing Things (More or Less Ideally)

Some people are dietary vegans, people who eat neither animals nor animal products. Some of these people never consider the issue and just eat that way because they were raised that way. Others carefully consider the issue and come to believe they *should not* eat any animals or animal products because it would be *morally wrong* to do so. So they commit not to do any such eating; they adopt a policy of doing so. And then they hold to that commitment, stick to that policy.

Other people are omnivores, people who eat animals and animal products as well as plants. Some of these people never consider the issue and just eat any old thing. Others carefully consider the issue and come to believe they *may* eat any old thing—more or less—because it is morally permissible to do so. So they adopt a policy of eating any old yummy thing, flesh or not. And then they hold to that policy.

What is going on here comes in three parts: There's what the agent believes he should or may do. There's a commitment to action, or adoption of a policy, based on that belief. Finally, there's the action he then carries out based on that policy.

Not everything we do is so thoughtful or systematic. Some action is not produced by beliefs about what you should do or may do. When we idly drum our fingers on the table, this isn't produced by such beliefs.

Some action issues from a belief you should do it without issuing from a commitment. It's a one-off.

Other actions are repeated without being commitment based. Where do you put your right ring finger when you are plugging in a microwave? For some people—for the two of us, at least—this action, though repeated, does not issue from commitments we make, or general policies we adopt, about how to act. Neither does our habitual behavior of checking the mailbox on the way into the office: It's something we do. We know we're doing it. We think it's the thing to do. But it doesn't issue from a belief about what we should do or a commitment to do such a thing—it's an act but also just a habit we have.[3]

Some things our bodies do aren't acts at all: hiccups, muscle twitches, fainting spells. These are things that happen rather than things we do.

Yet, we think, some of what we do with regard to food has the tripartite structure we introduced at the beginning of this section. We need to eat to survive. Sometimes, satisfying this need, we just eat. Other times, it's more complicated. We need to eat and then think about what to eat: Should it be this or that? That or this? We consider the evidence. We form a belief about what we ought to eat. We set a policy: Veganism or omnivorism or the paleo diet. For some of us, these policies are an important part of who we are. For some of us, the policies match up with our beliefs about what we ought to do. For some of us, the beliefs about what we ought to do match up with our evidence. The rest of the chapter is about the rest of us.

Belief

Some deviations from the ideal come at the first stage when we form bad beliefs. A belief can be bad in all sorts of ways. We'll focus on beliefs that are bad because they are beliefs that are supported by evidence that warrants a *stronger* belief. For example, we learn that pandas are a type of mammal and that some people love all mammals. The evidence warrants the conclusion that some people love pandas. If, instead, we conclude only that some people love *female* pandas, we, to use an unlovely word, underbelieve.

For another example, we learn that the power is out. On this evidence, we are justified in concluding that we can turn on neither the TV nor the radio nor . . . If, instead, we conclude only that we can't turn on the TV, that's underbelieving.[4]

There's underbelief and then there's underbelief. When you look out your window and see a car, you might well have evidence about what its hubcaps are like, but, typically, you form no such belief. You thereby underbelieve. And that's okay. What the hubcaps are like is neither salient nor important in this case and so underbelief here isn't, we think, objectionable. It's non-ideal because it falls short of what an ideal cognizer would believe based on the same evidence, but falling short of this ideal is not, in this case, objectionable. Yet it is in some cases. Consider Fred. He believes it is morally wrong to buy factory farmed meat. His argument for that conclusion is that factory farming produces a huge amount of suffering and what people get out of that sort of farming—food—is not sufficient justification for the suffering. Because of this, he thinks, *buying* the meat produced by factory farms is wrong.[5] Basically, Fred reasons like this:

> Factory farming causes a great deal of suffering for animals for very little gain for humans and animals. Hence,
> It is morally wrong to factory farm. Hence,
> It is morally wrong to buy factory farmed meat.

Yet Fred's evidence for the claim that it is wrong to buy factory farmed meat is evidence for the stronger conclusion that it is wrong to buy all factory farmed food, not only meat but factory farmed dairy and eggs, too. He believes morality requires him to X but does so on the basis of arguments that support a more-demanding requirement to X+. His evidence *obviously* supports the requirement to X+, and the requirement to X+ is a conclusion that's importantly relevant to what he's trying to figure out. In particular, Fred holds it is wrong to hurt animals just to produce cheap, yummy, nutritious food. Because of this, he holds it is wrong to buy animal *flesh* produced in that way. But if this argument that it is wrong to buy factory farmed flesh is a good one, then it shows that it is wrong to buy any products of factory farmed animals—it's not just meat that's problematic.

After all, meat animals aren't the only animals that suffer in factory farms in order to produce food for humans. Most obviously, there are hundreds of millions of factory farmed egg-laying hens, hens who live in no better (and often worse) conditions than chickens raised for meat (and who live in such conditions for longer than meat birds do).[6] There are millions of factory farmed dairy cows, cows who live in no better (and often worse) conditions than cattle raised for beef (and who live in such conditions longer than beef cattle do). These animals are hurt just in order to produce food. Unlike, say, the cattle that made your burger, they produce food without being killed, but Fred's argument for his food policy has nothing in particular to do with killing animals. Fred thinks it is wrong to cause animals much suffering in order to produce food. Because of this, he concludes it is wrong to buy factory farmed meat. But he does not draw the more general conclusion that his premises warrant: that it's wrong to buy *any* factory farmed food products. It is as if he is convinced by an argument the key premise of which is that causing pain to innocent people is wrong; and then, because he is thereby convinced, draws the conclusion that poking innocent people in the eyes is wrong, but then does not accept that kicking innocent people in the shins is wrong, too. Fred's is a common sort of failure, one of moral underbelief. Again, schematically, Fred believes that morality requires X, but on the basis of arguments that saliently support a more demanding requirement to do X+.

A related failure is the failure of moral *overbelieving*. Consider Gabby. Gabby believes that eating meat is wrong on the basis of a belief that factory farming is wrong. If her argument is this simple:

> Factory farming is wrong. Hence,
> All meat eating is wrong,

she clearly draws a conclusion that goes well beyond what is warranted. Conclusions about *eating* don't follow straight from premises about *production*. You need a premise linking the wrongness of producing food a certain way to the wrongness of consuming such food. But even the more subtle

> Factory farming is wrong.
> Eating products that are wrongly produced is wrong. Hence,
> All meat eating is wrong

is not a good argument, and, if Gabby goes in for it, she believes more than her premises warrant. If factory farming were the only way of producing meat, then the argument would be better, but that isn't the only way. There are free range–farmed animals. There are hunted animals. There are road-killed animals. Consider Jonathan McGowan, an English taxidermist. McGowan eats meat but only animals that have been accidentally killed. Is he doing wrong? Gabby's premises don't show this. McGowan gets no meat from animal farming or hunting. (He, in fact, thinks both activities are morally wrong.) All he does is clean carcasses off roads and, rather than trashing them, consumes them.[7]

Because she overlooks the possibility of eating meat without eating meat that is wrongly produced, Gabby overbelieves and thereby fails to draw the food-based conclusion that her argument warrants. At most, from this argument, Gabby should believe that it is wrong to eat meat from places that wrongly produce it and that, in particular, it is wrong to eat factory farmed meat. But that is consistent with it being permissible to eat meat produced in some other way.

Commitment, Part One

Besides under- and overbelief, there's also the phenomenon of *under- and overcommitment*.

Consider Hope. She believes morality requires not eating any factory farmed animals and because of this believes the ideal food policy for her is the policy of never eating a factory farmed animal. Yet Hope *under*commits by committing to a less demanding policy of not eating any factory farmed animals except those prepared at great restaurants and at family gatherings. If the steak tartare at Very Wonderful Restaurant comes from a factory farmed cow, so be it, she'll eat it. If Grandma's turkey comes from a factory farm, so be it, she'll eat it.[8]

In one way, what's going on with Hope looks like what is going on with Fred. Hope seems to endorse an argument that looks like this:

> Factory farming causes a great deal of suffering for animals for very little gain for humans and animals. Hence,
> It is morally wrong to factory farm. Hence,
> It is morally wrong to eat factory farmed products.[9]

So it might look like Hope makes a mistake like Fred's. It might look like she simply overlooks the fact that this argument implies that it is wrong to eat factory farmed products at great restaurants and family gatherings. But this is an illusion. Hope makes no oversight. She knows full well that animals factory farmed for great restaurants and for her grandmother's turkey casserole are no different from other animals. She knows full well that the conclusion of her argument is that eating factory farmed food is wrong and knows full well that certain things she does are, by her own lights, morally wrong. Still she does them. And she doesn't do them absent-mindedly or out of weakness. Her failure is not one of performance or belief. She deliberately and consciously adopts a policy that she thinks is not the one that's best supported by the moral arguments. She thinks there's a sound moral argument against eating factory farmed food, but she commits to a policy that permits eating factory farmed food.

Because of this, the policy Hope follows is clearly, by Hope's own lights, morally inferior to a policy it is *possible* for Hope to follow. That is, there is an eating policy Hope could be pursuing—strict abstention from factory farmed food—that is more coherent and, by her own lights, morally superior to the policy she in fact pursues. Hope *could* do this. She needn't eat any old meat at great restaurants or family gatherings. Abstaining would, however, be hard for Hope. It would require abstaining from her grandma's factory farmed turkey casserole and foregoing the delicious factory farmed steak tartare at Very Wonderful Restaurant.[10] And so she commits to the less difficult policy.

Doing so is a deviation from the ideal, for Hope commits to a policy that is, by her own lights, morally wrong and less coherent than a policy she could commit to. It could be her commitment is contemptible. It could be that what is going on with Hope is that she is "self-indulgent, essentially wishy-washy, . . . morally lazy . . . [and] suffers from the vices of ethical lethargy, hedonistic selfishness, and intemperance."[11] In some cases like Hope's, the grounds for the undercommitment are simply that committing to the more coherent, more morally defensible policy is difficult, and there is little to be said for such policies. For example, at least one of us promised himself to eat only twenty-five Christmas cookies last year. Could he have committed to doing better? Of course! But doing so would have been hard. So one of us undercommitted. That's not an impressive justification. When a young child tries to get out of tying his shoes on the grounds that doing so is hard, one might empathize without being impressed. Yet Hope's justification might well be quite a bit better than that, even quite good. It could be that her undercommitment, while non-ideal, is really quite defensible.

Why would anybody adopt a policy that, by their own lights, fell short of the requirements of morality? One reason: They just don't care about morality. Or—more likely—they just don't care *that much* about morality. More generously, they don't *just* care about morality, and they adopt a policy whose dictates are sensitive both to their moral views and to the other things they care about.[12] For example, a kid might adopt a policy of stealing cookies every once in a while even though she knows she shouldn't and might adopt it just because despite caring about not stealing and caring about doing right, she cares more about satisfying her own interest in having a cookie.

If Hope's motivation is like that, her actions are understandable but somewhat hard to defend. Her policy might, however, be better defended. Her case might be like this: She thinks that following a morally suboptimal policy is, morally speaking, the best that she probably *would* do. As we said, while the policy Hope follows is morally inferior to policies it is *possible* for her to follow, it is morally superior to the policies she would *actually* follow if she didn't follow hers. Hope, reflective, self-knowing, knows that if she failed to give herself the great restaurant escape clause and the family gathering escape clause, she would as a matter of fact follow policies she thinks are morally *much* worse: She'd too often give in to temptation, become discouraged, give up any effort at imposing moral constraints on her eating habits, and eat a totally unrestricted diet, including a lot of factory farmed animal products. She is not, we stipulate, just eagerly seizing on any justification for not doing the more demanding thing. She is thoughtful, earnest, and undeceived. She has been down these roads before. She has powerful evidence about her track record with these sorts of commitments, and no evidence that this time will be different. Her confidence in what she would do is high and is warranted.[13]

So the policy she does follow—the one with the escape clauses—might be the best she *would* do—or the best she would be likely to do—out of the options that are realistic for her. That is, it might be the policy that is closest to the ideal, the one with the fewest and least serious deviations. Yet following that policy isn't the best she *could* do. Again, it is *possible* for her to strictly abstain from factory farmed food, just like it'd be possible for the two of us to do one hundred push-ups a day or run marathons every year. It's possible. It's just not going to happen. And it's not crazy to think that it's reasonable for us to make our plans and decisions, and choose our policies, based on the assumption that it's not going to happen. Perhaps something stronger is true: It would be unreasonable for us *not* to make our plans and decisions, and choose our policies, based on the assumption that it's not going to happen.

Here's a way of making the point: Suppose we have the option of signing up to serve on an alpine rescue team next summer. It's a high-stakes job and one that requires a very, very high level of fitness. We could make it the case that we're at that level of fitness by the time next summer rolls around, by adopting and sticking to a very, very demanding training regimen. We could do it! Yet we both know that neither of us will in fact stick to such a regimen, and so we won't have the level of fitness that we'd need to have in order not to be dangerous liabilities on the alpine rescue team. The *ideal* thing for us to do is to sign up for the job, do the fitness program, and then go do a great job as alpine rescuers. And it's *possible* for us to do that. But we are quite reasonably very confident that that is not what will actually happen if we sign up for the job. If we sign up for the job, we will fail to stick to the fitness program, and we'll be dangerous liabilities as alpine "rescuers."

The alpine rescue case is similar to (because based on) Jackson and Pargetter's (1986) Professor Procrastinate case, in which a professor is asked to review a book. He knows that the best thing for him to do is to say "yes" and then write the review, and that the worst thing is to say "yes" and not write the review. He also confidently predicts that if he says "yes," he won't write the review. The Procrastinate case, the mountain rescue case, and the class of cases of choosing a food policy that we're presently concerned with all have the same troublemaking structure: There's a commitment one can choose to undertake now, or not, and there's follow-up on the commitment that one can perform later, or not. The best thing to do is to undertake the commitment and then follow up. The worst thing to do is to undertake the commitment and then fail to follow up. That precipitates the review not being written and the editor and author being left in the lurch. It precipitates incompetent and dangerous mountain rescue workers endangering people's lives. It precipitates the agent with Hope's sort of motivational structure becoming discouraged and giving up on the project of improving moral dietary improvement altogether. The case for choosing the second best, and undercommitting relative to what you take to be the morally best course, is that you expect yourself to do better, morally speaking, by adopting the second-best commitment than by trying, and failing, to abide by the best commitment. The best *you* will do is second best.[14]

Our knowledge that we won't, in fact, follow through on the optimal course can quite appropriately inform our decisions about what to do, and so the thing for us to do is to choose the second-best option of not signing up for the alpine rescue team in the first place. Something like this idea is at work when G.E.M. Anscombe claims that some people think that they should be pacifists, try to be pacifists, find that they are not living up to their ideals and, disheartened, give up on even approximating the ideals. Even if one acknowledges that pacifism is the ideal, committing to a less pacific life might make sense.[15]

Peter Singer, in his work on famine relief, makes a similar point. His view is that the affluent should give up quite a bit to help the poor. How much? He doesn't make too many demands of the affluent, for he fears that they will see what his view requires, come to believe it's right, and, since they aren't going to comply with it, just say "forget it" and ignore the poor entirely.[16]

Peter Abelard suggests that a policy of assiduously avoiding minor sins leads to a commitment of major sins. One plausible way of explaining why: Since, realistically, you're going to commit a minor sin every now and again, straining to avoid them might just weaken your self-control so much that you end up committing a major one.[17]

One of the ideas behind the claim that the perfect is the enemy of the good is that striving for an ideal can be counterproductive in that it can stop you from doing even pretty well and lead to your, instead, doing worse. Hope's food policy is pretty good, though imperfect.[18]

Commitment, Part Two

Choosing the not quite best is a way of undercommitting oneself. It's also possible—and it's plausibly sometimes *reasonable*—to *over*commit yourself. You might believe morality requires merely X and nevertheless adopt a more demanding policy of doing X+.

Parents commonly adopt more restrictive policies than they think they need to. They are opposed just to letting their youngest kids watch certain R-rated movies but impose a policy of no watching R-rated movies. They are opposed just to bags of Cheetos consumption but impose a policy of no Cheetos consumption.

The monks of Mount Athos generally eat a significantly more restrictive diet than they think their faith requires of them.[19]

And consider Isaiah. He believes it is typically wrong to kill sentient animals. Because of this, he believes it is typically wrong to *eat* sentient animals.[20] However, the policy he follows is not of abstaining merely from eating *sentient* animals killed for food. Rather, the policy he follows is not eating any animals: He doesn't eat nonsentient animals that have been raised and killed for food, like farmed clams. Isaiah also doesn't eat sentient animals that weren't killed for food, such as road-killed deer or wild boar struck by lightning.

Like Hope's, Isaiah's case involves a mismatch between moral argument and behavioral policy. Unlike Hope's, Isaiah's policy is *more* restrictive than the policy that his argument supports. All the same, there is something non-ideal about it: By not eating various foods that, by his own lights, it is morally permissible to eat, Isaiah deprives himself of lots of pleasurable experiences that are not, by his own lights, wrongful. He also imposes costs on others: He is unable to coordinate with his fellow diners on a shared order of mussels to accompany dinner, for example, and it's not enough, for a restaurant to qualify as a place to meet Isaiah for lunch, that it does a great oyster po'boy. That restaurant has to offer, for example, a really good seitan burrito. Isaiah's argument permits him to eat more (kinds of) food than he in fact does. Isaiah is, like Hope, adopting a policy that he doesn't regard as lining up with the moral facts.

Yet, like Hope's position, Isaiah's, while not by his own lights ideal, is defensible. In fact, like Hope's policy, Isaiah's makes a great deal of sense.[21] How so?

Generally, adopting an overdemanding policy makes sense if you predict that you will underperform if you adopt the less demanding, morally ideal policy and predict you'll be able to do better if you adopt the more demanding one. Maybe you think you'll do this because you think you're just the kind of person who systematically underperforms relative to commitment, and so you need to overcommit in order to perform on target. Maybe you think this because you think underperformance (or particular kinds of underperformance) is especially likely in this case. For example, you think it's okay to eat humanely raised meat a couple of times a week. But if you adopt a policy of doing that, you'll eat humanely raised meat five or six times, and a factory farmed burger once or twice. If you adopt a vegetarian policy, you'll still fall short, but the way you'll do that is by eating free-range meat once or twice a week. For a non-food-related example, you might commit to going to the gym ten times a month because you're happy with going eight times but know that you also won't *quite* meet whatever goal you set for yourself.[22]

It's fairly common to find vegans or vegetarians who don't think that absolutely all meat/animal product-eating is impermissible. They think there is nothing wrong with eating roadkill or eating discarded food the eating of which definitely won't contribute to demand.[23] Some even think there is nothing wrong with eating the products of certain presently uncommon methods of animal agriculture. But applying the policy that tracks this tortuous moral boundary is cognitively demanding, requires more research, introduces space for self-deception and rationalization, and introduces opportunities for bad action based on bad information or misapplication of the more complex rule. By adopting a strict, say, vegetarian policy, one avoids a lot of complication in one's food decisions, for the overdemanding policy might be easier to *stick to*: The clear, never-to-be-crossed bright line makes the policy easy to follow and, importantly, easi*er* to follow than the ideal policy, a policy that casts a line of less brightness.

The more demanding policy might be psychologically easier to *keep in mind*: It's not just a bright line. The bright line is also cast by a simple, easy-to-keep-in-mind rule.

The more demanding policy introduces fewer potential sources of error: If it's an animal, you can't eat it. If it isn't, you can. By contrast, the less demanding policy leaves you open for making mistakes on the basis of all sorts of errors about the provenance of this particular bit of flesh: Was the animal sentient? Was it killed for food? and so on. And avoiding those errors requires research. By contrast, the more demanding policy necessitates no check on the provenance of what you're eating—whether the animal was killed for food, for example. Also, there's no need to check on the mental status and cognitive capacities of the animal—whether, for example, it's sentient, like a cow, or not, like a mussel. And there's no need to put trust in research that is not settled.[24]

Adopting the more demanding policy might help in avoiding temptation. Attempting to adhere to the ideal policy might tempt Isaiah to act badly. (Isaiah's more restrictive policy puts up a buffer between him and the animals he thinks it's actually wrong to eat.[25]) If Isaiah allows himself to eat any sentient animal as long as it isn't killed for food, he might get into the habit of eating, say, road-killed chicken. This might tempt him to eat non-road-killed chicken: If you're eating chicken already, why would this one farm-raised chicken hurt? So the ideal policy might be harder to adhere to because it makes certain deviations so tempting.

There is also likely to be an *epistemic* advantage to the more-demanding policy: The more demanding policy might well be one Isaiah is *certain* is okay. Even if he is pretty sure eating Niman Ranch[26] bacon is permissible, he might still want to play it safe because he is not *completely* sure, and it's a big deal if he's wrong.[27] Compare: You are somewhat sure it's safe to eat food weeks after the sell-by date but are much more sure it's safe to eat food by the sell-by date. It makes sense to adopt the more demanding policy of eating food by the sell-by date. (It's more demanding because you have less time to get your eating in.)

Also, in some cases following the more demanding, more cautious, bright-line policy will be likely to have better effects on others than the ideal policy. Peter Singer thinks some meat eating is permissible but instead follows a vegan diet in part because that has better effects on others than a free-range one.[28] If you're visibly a vegan, this might lead to conversations with one's dining companions in which they might be exposed to ideas, arguments, and examples that change their behavior, conversations they wouldn't go in for if you were following the ideal eating policy.

Also, eating meat very rarely and under very strict conditions might signal to others that all meat eating is okay, and that might be a bad effect. When Isaiah and Singer instead adopt a policy of never eating meat, they signal that they are against eating animals. In the US, at least, not eating meat signals that one is against killing animals. These are the signals that are in fact picked up whether or not they are the signal Isaiah and Singer mean to send and whether it is a signal they endorse. Sending out this signal might make sense even if a policy of eating animals sometimes has more to be said for it than a policy of never doing so. When you signal that, you signal you are on a certain side of an issue. There might be value in that that cannot be reduced to the value of its effects on Isaiah or Singer or the effects on those who pick up the signal.[29]

Performance

Besides missing the mark with our belief and commitment, we can miss the mark with our performance.

We focus on *underperformance*.[30] Juan believes that morality requires that he do X, he commits to a policy of doing X, but he doesn't do X. There are more and less interesting ways this might happen. For example, Juan believes he shouldn't eat Cheetos, he commits to a policy of not eating Cheetos, and then, when he's out and about, he eats some trail mix with well-hidden Cheetos in it. This is underperformance due to (understandable) confusion. Not so puzzling.

In another not-so-puzzling example, Juan believes he shouldn't eat Cheetos, he commits to a policy of not eating Cheetos, and then, when he's out and about, someone puts a gun to his head and tells him that he had better eat Cheetos. So he does. This is underperformance due to coercion. Again, not so puzzling.

In a third example, Juan believes he shouldn't eat Cheetos, he commits to a policy of not eating Cheetos, and then, when he's out and about, he's given a drug that makes him irresistibly crave Cheetos. So he eats some. This is underperformance due to addling. Again, not so puzzling.

A more puzzling example of underperformance is this: Juan believes it's morally wrong to eat Cheetos, that he shouldn't—morally shouldn't—eat Cheetos, he commits to a policy of not eating Cheetos, and then, when he's out and about, under no coercion or illusion, not addled, harboring no relevant false beliefs about them, he eats a bunch of Cheetos.

What is going on here? What exactly is happening in situations where we do something other than the thing that we sincerely judge we should do? To answer this is to solve the traditional philosophical puzzle of *akrasia* or weakness of will.[31] Juan's Cheetos-eating and other, less frivolous food cases raise a puzzle right next door to the traditional puzzle, one about cases in which we fail to follow through on our sincere commitments or intentions.

There are a number of different things that could be happening. Here is a (very incomplete!) sample: Juan might think that he *morally* should not eat the Cheetos, but think that other, nonmoral considerations outweigh the moral ones, so all things considered he should eat them. Reasoning like this goes on with regard to veganism sometimes. People are sometimes convinced that *morally* they should be vegan and also think that nutritionally veganism is inadequate for them and so think that veganism is *imprudent*. They then think the prudential considerations are weightier than the moral ones and decide that, all things considered, they should not be vegan. Such cases do not, it turns out, raise a puzzle about failing to carry out one's sincere commitments. In such a case, it turns out, one's sincere commitment is to eat the Cheetos or not to be vegan and that's what one does. But such cases *do* raise questions about how forceful moral considerations are. Sometimes those considerations seem to be decisive? "Should I lie to him?" "No. That would be wrong." But other times, maybe they aren't. When aren't they? Why?

Alternatively, Juan might be fragmented—part of him thinks he should X, part of him thinks he should Y, and it's the first part that adopts the policy and the second that pulls the behavioral trigger at the crucial moment. We aren't thinking of Juan as having a split personality. Rather, we think of him as being a normal, complex person who's torn about something. He's like you when you get home from some terrifying movie. You know there is no goblin in your basement. Yet you find yourself unable to go down to it to scoop the kitty litter. There's a rational part of your soul that's forming a belief. And an arational part of it that's driving your behavior, keeping you from going downstairs. Juan might show a different but related split. So, too, might people who keep botching their diets or, to return to an earlier example, keep eating too many cookies.[32]

Alternatively, Juan's behavior might be the product of a behavior-guidance system that's not sensitive, or not just sensitive, to Juan's reflectively endorsed ends, and his reflectively endorsed beliefs about what's likely to best satisfy those ends. J. M. Coetzee suggests that "the level of behavior [Juan wants] to change is too elementary, too elemental, to be reached by talk."[33] There is a fair bit of research suggesting that a lot of our eating behavior is driven by systems of behavior guidance that largely short-circuit our rational, reflective systems of deliberation and decision.[34] You might have a commitment to not eating any more hors d'oeuvres at the party, but your eating of them is insensitive to that, automatic.

Finally, Juan might be discovering that his commitment, after all, wasn't really a commitment not to eat Cheetos. It was, instead, some more subtle commitment to mostly avoid eating Cheetos or to avoid eating Cheetos when at home or . . . Relatedly, imagine you find yourself both avowing that you eat no animals and yet also occasionally eating oysters or mussels. This could be a case of not following through on your commitment or, instead, it could be a case of discovering that you have been misunderstanding or misdescribing your own commitments: What you're against is eating *sentient* animals rather than eating animals.

Plausibly, there's no one-size-fits-all account to be given of all cases in which we fail to do what we've committed to doing. Plausibly, different theories explain what is happening to different people on different occasions of moral underperformance. Plausibly, too, more than one theory might correctly characterize the same person on the same occasion. Because of this, the steps to take to deal with underperformance—your own or someone else's—will vary from case to case.

Conclusion

Unlike breathing or sleeping, eating is both an activity we need to do to survive and one that routinely raises pointed ethical questions. It might well be that the eating policies that dominate the globe are morally wrong and *ipso facto* non-ideal. It might be that the food production policies that dominate the globe are wrong and *ipso facto* non-ideal. If so, multiple times a day, huge numbers of people act non-ideally and objectionably so.

Also, it might be that the right policy will be hard to follow, whereas the wrong one will always tempt. Compare this with, say, stealing or killing innocent people. Doing so is non-ideal, but comparatively few people, comparatively infrequently, are tempted to steal or to kill people.[35] By contrast, eating meat might be non-ideal and powerfully tempting. Generally, acting non-ideally food-wise might be tempting in a way that acting non-ideally theft-wise or murder-wise is not.

In this chapter, we have identified, and provided examples of, several of the interestingly different ways in which we can fall short of an ideal, be that ideal moral, prudential, or rational. We also provided ways in which we can fail to hit the mark by *over*shooting it. We can *underperform* relative to our commitments: We can identify some policy as best, set out to follow it, and then fail to do so. So, too, we can *overperform*: We can identify some policy as best and some more stringent policy as above and beyond the call of duty, we can set out to follow the less stringent policy and yet find ourselves following the more stringent policy. We can *undercommit* relative to our beliefs: We can identify some policy as best but then set out to follow some policy that is by our own lights less stringent. And so, too, we can *overcommit*: We can identify some policy as best but then set out to follow a policy that is by our own lights even more stringent. Finally, we can *underbelieve* relative to what the considerations we bring to bear on our thinking support: We can come to believe less than our evidence supports. And so, too, we can *overbelieve*: We can come to believe more than our evidence supports.

By identifying some different ways we can act in non-ideal ways, we are trying to identify different ways we go wrong and are tempted to go wrong. This taxonomical project helps to make sense of why people act in ways that we mightn't immediately understand and yet, on reflection, might make good sense.[36] The taxonomical project helps, too, with fixing these deviations from the ideal when they crop up. It helps formulate more realistic policies, too, policies that are easier to follow and easier to stick to. These policies accommodate the fact that we are weak and limited in various ways. Because of this, there will be some deviations from the ideal. There are better and worse ways of deviating. *Worstward Ho*'s advice to "fail better" is sound.[37]

Notes

1. A short account of human cannibalism is in chapter 2 of Fernández-Armesto (2002). A short philosophical discussion is in Diamond (1978).
2. For help with that, see Halteman and Halteman Zwart in this volume.
3. Here's a failure to act ideally that we will not be talking about: Sometimes you *should* form some commitment to act but do not do so. In such a case, you might act and this action isn't issuing from any sort of commitment, but, really, it should issue from a commitment. For example, you know you should limit your candy intake and know you should form a commitment to do this, a commitment to some sort of candy diet. But you don't. That's non-ideal. Similarly, you might fail to form a belief when, really, you should. You might, for example, be studiously uncommitted about whether the Earth's climate is changing despite having all the evidence that any reader of this book has. That's non-ideal. Such failures to attend to evidence and failures to form thoughtful commitments are important in food ethics. For discussion, see Nolfi (2015). What we focus on are mostly cases where you *do* believe, *do* commit, *do* act and these goings-on are non-ideal.
4. The philosophical terminology here might be confusing: The belief that some people love all pandas is stronger than the belief that some people love female pandas in exactly this way: That some people love all pandas implies that some people love female pandas. That some people love female pandas does *not* imply that some people love all pandas.

   The belief that we can turn on neither the TV nor the radio is stronger than the belief that we can't turn on the radio in exactly this way: That we can turn on neither the TV nor the radio implies that we can't turn on the radio. That we can't turn on the radio does *not* imply that we can turn on neither the radio nor the TV. (Maybe the radio is broken and so can't be turned on but the TV works fine and can be turned on.)
5. There are some suppressed premises in Fred's reasoning. One is the moral principle that licenses the move from the fact that factory farming causes a lot of suffering for very little gain to the conclusion that it's morally wrong to factory farm. The other

is the principle that licenses moving from the wrongness of factory farming to the wrongness of buying factory farmed meat. Both principles are potentially contestable, but the second more so than the first. Fred's view is that *buying* factory farmed products is typically wrong and his argument for this view flows from a premise about *factory farming* itself being wrong. Why is that a valid argumentative move? Why is it wrong to buy factory farmed products just because the farming itself is wrong? This question is worth considering—and is considered in this volume in the chapters by Terence Cuneo, Elizabeth Harman, Adrienne M. Martin, and Ted Warfield.

6. The awfulness of certain forms of egg production is well detailed in Singer and Mason (2006) and the documentary *Fowl Play: The Untold Story Behind Your Breakfast* (Adam Durand, Mercy for Animals, New York, 2009).

7. For more on McGowan, see his "Experience: I Eat Roadkill," *Guardian*, March 25, 2011, http://www.theguardian.com/lifeandstyle/2011/mar/26/i-eat-roadkill, and Joe Satran, "Jonathan McGowan, 44-Year-Old UK Man, Lives Off Roadkill for 30 Years," *Huffington Post*, October 17, 2011, http://www.huffingtonpost.com/2011/10/17/jonathan-mcgowan-roadkill_n_1016108.html.

8. Almost all the turkeys do: 97.43 percent, according to Foer (2009): 271. That's a good book for Hope since it is insightful on food and family.

9. Maybe we need to make these arguments subtler in various ways in order to make it reasonable for Hope to be convinced by them. At any rate, keeping the arguments simple makes it easier to make our main points here, and we could make those points using more subtle arguments.

10. We assume that what we are *going* to do doesn't affect what we are *morally permitted* to do in the way that what we *can* do, arguably, does. So the fact that one of us is not *in fact* going to refrain from stealing this bar of soap does not show that it is morally permitted for us to steal the soap or even that it is *not wrong* to steal the soap. It is wrong. One of us is going to do wrong.

    By contrast, the fact that one of us *cannot*—truly cannot—refrain from stealing the soap might show that it isn't wrong for that person to steal it. It wouldn't show that it is *permissible* to steal the soap; rather, it'd show that stealing isn't a morally evaluable action at all. It's like a reflex, a baby's instinctive action, or a meteor shower: something that happens that is neither right nor wrong.

    See note 15 for a bit more discussion and some references. For an introduction to issues about the relation between what you morally ought to do and what you can do, an argument about that relation, and a wealth of references to work on the topic, see Vranas (2007).

11. This was an anonymous referee's description of her.

12. Generally, different values can pull you in different directions. You value community and self-interest. Should you join your friends in eating a tub of ice cream? There's a community-based reason to do so. There's a prudential reason not to do so. Should you keep serving your guest drinks? There's an etiquette-based reason to do so. There's a moral reason not to do so. (The example is from Foot [2002].) Sometimes it is easy to weigh up these competing values: Should you steal the apple just to see what it feels like? There's a prudential reason to do so. There's a moral reason not to do so. But the moral reason is obviously stronger—you shouldn't steal the apple. In other cases, the weighing up is tougher. In some cases, you might worry the values cannot be weighed against each other. On this, see Anderson (1993) and Chang (1997) and the references therein. Also, see Ruth Chang's TED talk, "How to Make Hard Choices," June 2014, https://www.ted.com/speakers/ruth_chang.

13. Hope is in some ways like the sociopathic serial killer, Dexter Morgan, from the TV series *Dexter*. Dexter follows a policy of killing only serial killers and other especially dangerous individuals. Part of his justification for this is that if he failed to kill

serial killers regularly, he would do something by his own lights much worse: He would kill innocent people. (Hope, less so than Dexter, would benefit from reading the Halteman and Halteman Zwart chapter in this volume.)

This example shows that a policy though morally *superior* to some alternative need not be morally *good*. This should be uncontroversial. Some actions are morally superior to others without being good. Stealing is morally superior to stealing and then lying about it, but stealing isn't morally good.

On the relations between what you *probably would do* and what you *should* do, see, among others, Goldman (1976), Goldman (1978), Jackson and Pargetter (1986), and Louise (2009).

14. Some moral theories imply that each of us is morally required to do what is best. Others are skeptical that *the best* makes sense. See Thomson (1997) and (2008).

Still others accept that some actions are best but imply that some actions are morally permissible—or even required—even though they are not best. These theories sometimes carve out space for a category of action that is *supererogatory*, permissible, praiseworthy, but above and beyond the call of duty. For an overview with lots of references, see Heyd (2012).

15. Anscombe writes, "The truth about Christianity is that it is a severe and practicable religion, not a beautifully ideal but impracticable one." The false view of Christianity moves pacifists and "pacifism has corrupted enormous numbers of people who will not act according to its tenets. They become convinced that a number of things are wicked which are not; hence seeing no way of avoiding wickedness, they set no limits to it" (1991: 56–57).

16. See Singer (1972) and (2009). In the latter, Singer writes,

> Asking people to give more than almost anyone else gives risks turning them off, and at some level might cause them to question the point of striving to live an ethical life at all. Daunted by what it takes to do the right thing, they may ask themselves why they are bothering to try. To avoid that danger, we should advocate a level of giving that will lead to a positive response. (151)

17. Abelard (1995: 29–33). Thanks to William Mann for the reference. Note that a policy of *routinely* going in for minor sins might also weaken one's self-control and one's resolve to resist major sins. On this, see the *Catechism of the Catholic Church* 1876: "The repetition of sins—even venial ones—engenders vices, among which are the capital sins." This sort of issue is discussed in the next section.

18. As we said, there are ways of describing the Hope case so that her policy is not so good. It's an important part of the case that she knows that following this policy is the best she's likely to do. What if we change that detail? Imagine if Hope simply deceives herself into thinking that the policy she does follow—and is very content to follow!—is the best she *would* do when, in fact, she could and would (if she set out to) follow a more severe, less pleasurable policy. She might, for example, tell herself that in all the nearby possible worlds where she tries to be an exceptionless freerangetarian, she fails and ends up stuffing her face with McNuggets. But she might be fooling herself about that or simply wrong: There might be some nearby worlds in which she's a strict freerangetarian. But these worlds are less appealing to her since they involve no turkey at Thanksgiving, no steak at Very Wonderful Restaurant. That saddens her. And that affects her view of what would happen. If that's what's going on, then Hope's policy becomes no less understandable but quite a bit less impressive.

19. When they fast, the monks

> generally follow a strict pattern and abstain from any consumption of meat (which monks never eat anyway), dairy products, fish, wine, and oil. The notion is that through fasting the body shares in the work of prayer; and fasting gives the faithful a sense of freedom and lightness . . .

> The monastic diet is much the same as the traditional Greek peasant diet and consists largely of vegetables, bread, olives, salads, cheese, soya and fruit. On non-fast days there is usually plenty of food on the monks' table and an ample supply of wine; and on feast days there is often fish. (Speake 2002: 222)

20. For that matter, he doesn't eat sentient animals that were killed for certain other reasons—for fun, say—and then offered up as food.
21. The policy might be more defensible than Hope's. It might be an Anscombean rejoinder to Hope, a "severe and practicable" policy that reveals that she lets herself off the moral hook too easily. Whether this is so depends on whether Hope is right about what she would do if she weren't a freerangetarian with exceptions. Would she actually eat any old factory farmed thing? Or could she stick to strict freerangetarianism?
22. By adopting a more demanding policy, you guard against a more insidious sort of underperformance. This comes from the phenomenon Richard Holton calls "judgment shift," in which what temptation does is not just get you to want something but also to adjust your valuation of whether you *should* do it. So, for example, when you're tempted by cigarettes, sometimes what happens is you know you shouldn't smoke but just can't help yourself, then smoke. (We discuss cases like this in the section "Performance.") Yet temptation sometimes works differently: Sometimes what happens is that the temptation gets you to revise your view about what you should do, so you end up thinking, "It's fine for me to smoke this one." So you do. This is underperformance by the lights of your past self rather than underperformance by lights of your current self. See Holton (2009) on judgment shift and Korsgaard (1989) and Parfit (1984) on present underperformance by lights of your past self.
23. See Rachels (2011) and some papers discussed in Warfield's chapter in this volume.
24. Allen and Trestman (2014) cover recent research on animal cognition. They give a good feel for how interesting and tricky it is and suggest that when we make mistakes about which things are sentient, these mistakes are typically cases of false negatives: We falsely believe certain things aren't sentient and they turn out to be sentient.
25. Compare the Talmud's advice to "make a fence around the Torah" (Avot 1:1). Thanks to Arthur Kuflik for the reference.
26. On Niman Ranch, see Foer (2009) and Niman (2010). For more on similar farms, see Kingsolver (2007).
27. Cf. Guerrero (2007).
28. Cf. Singer (1999).
29. On signaling and symbolism, see, among many others, Adams (2002) and chapters in this volume by Andrew Chignell, Terence Cuneo, and Adrienne M. Martin.
30. Compare with overperformance. Overperforming is believing you should X but need not X+, committing to X rather than X+, and then doing X+. You overperform when you believe you should clean your office once or twice a month, commit to doing so, and then clean it daily. ("I can't stop.") We focus on underperformance because, as far as we can tell, dietary overperformance is usually pretty *philosophically* uninteresting and unproblematic. Counterexamples are, of course, always welcome.
31. Whether *akrasia* and weakness of will are the same thing is disputed. For discussion, see Holton (2009) and Stroud (2014).
32. For this sort of story about *akratic* action, see Davidson (1970, 1982). For other discussions of the general phenomenon of fragmentation, see, for example, Lewis (1982), Stalnaker (1984), Schwitzgebel (2001), Egan (2008), Greco (forthcoming), and Elga and Rayo (manuscript).
33. Coetzee (2004: 103). The point recurs several times in the book.
34. See Farley and Cohen (2008) and Wansink (2010) and the references therein.
35. That said, the ideal of not killing humans may well have become easier and easier for people to follow, and maybe centuries from now people will look back at our food

practices with the sort of horror and incredulity with which we now regard cultures in which routinely killing people is normal.
36. Compare this with Elizabeth Harman's project of making sense of a certain sort of vegetarian accommodation. See her chapter in this volume and also her "Morally Permissible Moral Mistakes" (forthcoming).
37. "All of old. Nothing else ever. Ever tried. Ever failed. No matter. Try again. Fail again. Fail better" (Beckett 1983: 7). This paper fails in fewer ways than it would have due to the efforts of friends who commented on drafts, suggested readings, and improved our ideas. Thanks, Andrew Chignell, Terence Cuneo, Matthew Halteman, Elizabeth Harman, Arthur Kuflik, and Kate Nolfi.

References

Abelard, Peter. *Ethical Writings*. Indianapolis: Hackett, 1995.

Adams, Robert. *Finite and Infinite Goods*. New York: Oxford University Press, 2002.

Allen, Colin, and Michael Trestman. "Animal Consciousness." In *The Stanford Encyclopedia of Philosophy*. Summer 2015 ed. Edited by Edward N. Zalta. http://plato.stanford.edu/archives/sum2015/entries/consciousness-animal/.

Anderson, Elizabeth. *Value in Ethics and Economics*. Cambridge, MA: Harvard University Press, 1993.

Anscombe, G.E.M. "War and Murder." In *Ethics, Religion, and Politics*, 51–61. Oxford: Blackwell, 1991 (originally published in 1961).

Beauchamp, Tom, and R. G. Frey, eds. *The Oxford Handbook of Animal Ethics*. New York: Oxford University Press, 2011.

Beckett, Samuel. *Worstward Ho*. London: John Calder, 1983.

Chang, Ruth, ed. "Introduction." In *Incommensurability, Incomparability, and Practical Reason*, 1–34. Cambridge, MA: Harvard University Press, 1997.

Coetzee, J. M. *Elizabeth Costello*. New York: Vintage, 2004.

Davidson, Donald. "How Is Weakness of the Will Possible?" In *Essays on Action and Events*, 21–42. New York: Oxford University Press, 1970.

———. "Paradoxes of Irrationality." In *Philosophical Essays on Freud*, edited by Richard Wollheim and James Hopkins, 289–305. Cambridge: Cambridge University Press, 1982.

Diamond, Cora. "Eating Meat and Eating People." *Philosophy* 53 (1978): 465–479.

Egan, Andy. "Seeing and Believing: Perception, Belief Formation and the Divided Mind." *Philosophical Studies* 140 (2008): 47–63.

Elga, Adam, and Agustín Rayo. "Fragmentation and Information Access" (manuscript).

Farley, Deborah, and Thomas Cohen. "Eating as an Automatic Behavior." *Preventing Chronic Disease* 5, no. 1 (2008): A23.

Feinberg, Joel, ed. *Moral Concepts*. New York: Oxford University Press, 1970.

Fernández-Armesto, Felipe. *Near One Thousand Tables*. New York: Free Press, 2002.

Foer, Jonathan Safran. *Eating Animals*. New York: Little, Brown, 2009.

Foot, Philippa. "Are Moral Considerations Overriding?" In *Virtues and Vices*, 181–188. New York: Oxford University Press, 2002.

Goldman, Holly Smith. "Dated Rightness and Moral Imperfection." *Philosophical Review* 85 (1976): 449–487.

Goldman, Holly Smith. "Doing the Best One Can" in A. Goldman & J. Kim (Ed.), *Values and morals*. Dordrecht: Reidel, 2978.

Greco, Daniel. "Iteration and Fragmentation." *Philosophy and Phenomenological Research*, forthcoming.

Guerrero, Alexander. "Don't Know, Don't Kill." *Philosophical Studies* 136 (2007): 59–97.

128 Tyler Doggett and Andy Egan

Harman, Elizabeth. "Morally Permissible Moral Mistakes." *Ethics*, forthcoming.
Heyd, David. "Supererogation." In *The Stanford Encyclopedia of Philosophy*. Winter 2012 ed. Edited by Edward N. Zalta. http://plato.stanford.edu/archives/win2012/entries/supererogation/.
Holton, Richard. *Willing, Wanting, Waiting*. New York: Oxford University Press, 2009.
Jackson, Frank, and Robert Pargetter. "Oughts, Options, and Actualism." *Philosophical Review* 95 (1986): 233–255.
Jamieson, Dale, ed. *Singer and His Critics*. Boston: Wiley-Blackwell, 1999.
Kingsolver, Barbara. *Animal, Vegetable, Miracle*. New York: Harper, 2007.
Korsgaard, Christine. "Personal Identity and the Unity of Agency: A Kantian Response to Parfit." *Philosophy and Public Affairs* 18 (1989): 101–132.
Lewis, David. "Logic for Equivocators." *Noûs* 16 (1982): 431–441.
Louise, Jennie. "I Won't Do It! Self-Prediction, Moral Obligation, and Moral Deliberation." *Philosophical Studies* 146 (2009): 327–348.
Niman, Nicolette Hahn. *Righteous Porkchop*. New York: William Morrow, 2010.
Nolfi, Kate. "Food Choices and Ethical Character" (manuscript, 2015).
Parfit, Derek. *Reasons and Persons*. New York: Oxford University Press, 1984.
Rachels, Stuart. "Vegetarianism." In *The Oxford Handbook of Animal Ethics*, edited by Tom Beauchamp and R. G. Frey, 877–905. New York: Oxford University Press, 2011.
Schwitzgebel, Eric. "In-Between Believing." *Philosophical Quarterly* 51 (2001): 76–82.
Singer, Peter. "Famine, Affluence, and Morality." *Philosophy and Public Affairs* 1 (1972): 229–243.
———. "Reply to Hare." In *Singer and His Critics*, edited by Dale Jamieson. Boston: Wiley-Blackwell, 1999.
———. *The Life You Can Save*. New York: Random House, 2009.
Singer, Peter, and Jim Mason. *The Ethics of What We Eat*. Emmaus, PA: Rodale, 2006.
Smith, Holly. "Doing the Best One Can." In *Values and Morals*, edited by A. Goldman and J. Kim, 185–214. Dordrecht: Reidel, 1978.
Speake, Graham. *Mount Athos: Renewal in Paradise*. New Haven, CT: Yale University Press, 2002.
Stalnaker, Robert. *Inquiry*. Cambridge: MIT Press, 1984.
Stroud, Sarah. "Weakness of Will." In *The Stanford Encyclopedia of Philosophy*. Spring 2014 ed. Edited by Edward N. Zalta. http://plato.stanford.edu/archives/spr2014/entries/weakness-will/.
Thomson, Judith Jarvis. "The Right and the Good." *Journal of Philosophy* 94 (1997): 273–298.
———. *Normativity*. Chicago: Open Court, 2008.
Vranas, P.M.B. "I Ought, Therefore I Can." *Philosophical Studies* 136 (2007): 167–216.
Wansink, Brian. *Mindless Eating*. New York: Bantam, 2010.
Wollheim, Richard, and James Hopkins, eds. *Philosophical Essays on Freud*. Cambridge: Cambridge University Press, 1982.

7

PHILOSOPHY AS THERAPY FOR RECOVERING (UNRESTRAINED) OMNIVORES

Matthew C. Halteman and Megan Halteman Zwart

Philosophy "comes to dinner" most often in this volume as a valuable tool for constructing and criticizing arguments that can help us to discern our dietary obligations and evaluate various action plans we might adopt in striving to fulfill them. Recourse to a variety of well-constructed arguments is undoubtedly a significant strategic asset for cultivating more ethical eating habits and convincing others to follow suit.

Nevertheless, common obstacles often prevent even the best arguments from getting traction in our lives. For one thing, many of us enter the discussion hampered by firmly entrenched but largely uninvestigated assumptions about food that make it difficult to imagine how even well-supported arguments that challenge our familiar frames of culinary reference could actually apply to us. When an argument contests our cherished food ways, we are inclined almost reflexively to dodge, downplay, or dismiss it, and all the more anxiously if we suspect it's a good one. Moreover, even when we find such arguments convincing and resolve to change, we often discover to our chagrin that, when the buffet is open, we lack the will to act on our convictions. Whether the obstacle is a lack of imagination or a failure of will, the way to concrete moral progress is blocked.

Our aim here is to consider how other modes of philosophical inquiry can help us to overcome these two obstacles that arise at the margins of philosophy's argumentative contributions to food ethics. First, we diagnose these obstacles as common moral malaises—we call them the *malaise of imagination* and the *malaise of will*—that create existential unease for moral agents that can curtail their ability to eat in accordance with what they learn from philosophical arguments. We then propose that other modes of philosophical inquiry can serve as therapy for these malaises. Next we argue that philosophical hermeneutics (exemplified by Hans-Georg Gadamer) can treat the malaise of imagination by helping us to excavate and revise hidden prejudices that interfere with our ability authentically to engage arguments that challenge entrenched assumptions about food. Finally, we argue that philosophy as care of the self (exemplified by Pierre Hadot) can treat the malaise of will by helping us to identify habits of thought and action that hamper concrete progress toward new dietary ideals and to replace them, through repetitive exercises, with transformed habits. In a brief conclusion, we identify some benefits of this approach.

Two Common Moral Malaises and the Prospect of Philosophical Therapy

The Cases of Karla and Augusto

Imagine that Karla learns in her ethics seminar that pigs are as intelligent as dogs. She has a bulldog herself—the irreplaceable Mr. Chauncey "Chum" Thickleston III—and is horrified by the thought of eating him, not just because she loves him but also because he clearly seems to have an interest in avoiding a one-way trip to the deli case. This situation worries Karla because she wants to be consistent and her newly minted awareness of porcine intelligence raises the possibility that she shouldn't eat pigs anymore. She mulls things over at lunch while enjoying the dining hall's much-lauded pulled pork sandwich.

As Karla considers the class discussion, various thoughts occur to her that allay her concern somewhat. Pulled pork is delicious, and she and her father have a fifteen-year history of relishing the legendary barbequed version at her church's annual pig roast. Were Karla to go vegetarian, her father would be crushed; he always boasted that *his* daughter could keep pace with the footballers when it came to devouring barbeque. And if her church deems it suitable to celebrate the season with a pig on a spit, the practice can't be that bad. Didn't God give human beings dominion over animals along with direct permission to eat them? Besides, from a practical perspective, going vegetarian is expensive, judgmental of others, and probably unhealthy, so it would be bad stewardship of her finances, her relationships, and maybe even her body. Notwithstanding these consolations, Karla still feels remarkably unsettled when her classmate Augusto offers an articulate case for veganism in a follow-up class discussion. As compelling as his argument seems, though, she just can't imagine how it could be right.

Now consider the case of Augusto, Karla's classmate. He has always had a heart for animals and chokes up every time he sees a commercial on mistreated dogs or a truck full of cows en route to slaughter. The article discussed in class has hit Augusto hard, convincing him that eating meat is often morally wrong, and that all things considered, he shouldn't do it. He swears off eating animals and resolves to choose a veggie burger over meatloaf at lunch. Approaching the cafeteria, he smells the pulled pork. He notices his friends at a nearby table, gleefully gorging on the vaunted sandwiches. His conviction is weakened by the pork's irresistible aroma, combined with the knowledge that he'll take a pummeling from the guys if he turns up with an anemic veggie burger.

He guiltily swipes a pork sandwich and consoles himself that *this* sandwich is already prepared and would probably just go in a landfill if he doesn't eat it. Besides, it's Shotz-n-Wingz night at Baloneez and he'll surely have better luck breaking old habits at the start of a new day. Or maybe a new month, given that his grandparents will want to take him to Admirals Wharf for his birthday. Actually, it might just be best to wait until semester's end, given that learning to cook will take time, and he's locked into a meal plan at this green-forsaken cafeteria anyway. At the next class discussion, he compensates by speaking up for veganism, silently lamenting that the argument that so readily changed his mind has been decidedly less transformative of his will.

In certain respects, the cases of Karla and Augusto are similar. Both are moved by philosophical arguments to question the moral adequacy of some of their current beliefs and behaviors. Both feel significant discomfort, even anxiety, when confronting these argumentative challenges. And both find the consolations of continued argumentative engagement alone to be insufficient means for quelling their anxiety and moving toward concrete moral progress. Maybe Karla and Augusto just haven't happened upon the game-changing argument yet, and a more rigorous engagement with the right counterexample could provide the cure for what ails them. But suppose that even after significant grappling with the arguments and counterarguments, they still find themselves stymied in the ways just described. Beyond helping them to discern the strengths and weaknesses of the arguments they encounter, does philosophy have any additional resources at its disposal to aid them?

We think the answer is yes. To prepare the way for explaining how philosophy can help, it is instructive to distill the differences between Karla's and Augusto's predicaments into two common moral malaises that offer a clearer picture of the specific obstacles to moral progress they confront.

The Malaises of Imagination and Will

Karla suffers from a malaise of imagination. Her anxiety is a function of the bewilderment caused by feeling the pull of a provocative argument for eating otherwise while simultaneously being unable to imagine a world in which eating otherwise is possible for her without compromising important aspects of her identity. Her imagination is limited thus in part because her identity has been shaped by a number of largely uninvestigated but nonetheless pervasively influential assumptions about the world (and its human and animal denizens) that are inhospitable to the prospect of changing her diet. For instance, she has religious assumptions about divine designs for human/animal relationships that render her wary of views that seem to accord inordinate moral importance to subordinate creatures; in the back of her mind, she worries that policing her meat consumption would mean impiously holding animals in higher esteem than God does. She also has gendered assumptions about eating and personal and familial attachments to particular foods that regulate her self-understanding and self-esteem; how could she dash her father's pride and jettison tradition for bunny-hugging? Karla has been shaped, too, by an economic system in which cheap, convenient foods are often products of industrial farm animal production (IFAP), and by a popular-scientific outlook that deems animal protein essential for health, so she is inclined to assume that replacing animal products would be unaffordable and unhealthy.

Unlike many of her classmates who succumb to this malaise without becoming aware of the assumptions generating their unease, Karla identifies them and even pits them against the proposed argument to mitigate her anxiety. But her eagerness to defeat an argument that has genuinely piqued her moral concern nonetheless betrays a kinship with her less reflective colleagues: Her identity-framing background assumptions are interfering with her ability to be as open to the argument as she would be if there weren't so much at stake. Karla would have a hard enough time imagining herself as 'Karla the vegetarian' or 'Karla the agrarian' even if it were just a matter of choosing veggies over animal products most of the time. But in her malaise of imagination, she worries that adopting such ideals could compromise cherished religious, personal, familial, economic, and physical aspects of her identity. She suspects, even if she can't bring herself to believe, that she has good moral reasons to change her diet. But her malaise obscures potentially liberating interpretations of the world—of her religion as enjoining her to more compassionate eating, of her family as able to benefit from her example, and of her economic and physical circumstances as enhanced by eating less meat—and thus it dampens her fledgling inclination to follow her moral curiosity into new and potentially transformative experiences.

Augusto, by contrast, suffers from a malaise of will. His anxiety is a function of his unwillingness to initiate and/or consistently maintain daily adherence to a dietary ideal he feels morally inspired and/or obligated to live out. His failure to follow through is hardly mysterious; it results from a potent cocktail of all the usual challenges that thwart best intentions: peer pressure, bad faith, aesthetic preferences, wish fulfillment, laziness, dubious traditions, placation of loved ones, entrenched habits, lack of experience, and the demotivating inertia of society's pervasively compromised institutions.[1]

But if Augusto's malaise is initially easier to identify than Karla's, it is potentially more debilitating to endure. Like Karla, he experiences existential unease: he is discomfited by cognitive dissonance and anxious about what to do next. But unlike Karla, whose identity-framing assumptions render her initially unreceptive to argumentative indictments of her diet and offer a semblance of plausible deniability against them to boot, Augusto *is* receptive to the indictment and feels convicted by it. He now believes that a specific behavior modification is required and he desires to respond accordingly. Whether his conviction that this modification is obligatory is in fact supported by the proposed argument is not our concern here. The point is that Augusto's strong belief that he should change his behavior and his earnest desire to do so combine to make his unease over failing to do so all the more acute.

Philosophical Therapy for Moral Malaises

Most moral agents will recognize these predicaments from experience. Indeed, both malaises are ubiquitous obstacles to moral progress. For many, moreover, philosophical argumentation alone won't budge these obstacles because of entrenched and often unconscious attitudes and behaviors that interfere with their ability to engage and apply arguments. To help dispel these malaises, we recommend engagement with other modes of philosophical inquiry—hermeneutics and care of the self—that can, respectively, increase receptivity to moral arguments for dietary modification by reframing assumptions that hamper one's ability to imagine new dietary possibilities, and facilitate concrete striving toward dietary goals by habituating practices of thought and action that supplant bad habits with new and better ones. In these ways, the modes of philosophical inquiry we consider may serve as therapy for the malaises in question and as welcome supplements to philosophical arguments.

A few clarifications are in order before we proceed. First, we understand 'therapy' here as a strategy or set of strategies that aims to help one recover from some ill or set of ills that compromises well-being and that represents a falling away from a health ideal.[2] The health ideal we have in mind is a moral life in which an agent reflects on and feels appropriately satisfied with the degree of harmony between her beliefs and actions, and in which she has the tools to identify and assume beliefs and actions that authentically reflect her values. The malaises in question threaten this ideal. Though they can arise in the context of any moral issue, we're concerned here with how they pertain to the challenges of ethical eating.

Within this context, our proposed therapy is explicitly *philosophical.* This clarification is important in order to distinguish our project from *psychological* approaches, which we do not engage here. Our therapeutic is philosophical because it prescribes philosophy as an antidote to a common problem in ethics that is especially widespread where arguments for dietary changes are concerned. People see that such arguments have great force—and genuinely have no objection, though they might still strain to think of one—and yet are curiously unmoved by such arguments. This stagnancy is curious because in cases concerning, say, voting ethics or the ethics of deception, people are typically moved by forceful arguments. Vis-à-vis such arguments, we distinguish two ways one might be moved: moved to accept the conclusion (Karla is unmoved in this way); and moved to modify one's behavior in response to accepting the conclusion (Augusto is unmoved in this way). Then, we distinguish two corresponding strategies for using philosophy (namely, hermeneutics and care of the self) to move one in these respective ways. Because philosophical confusion of various kinds is the source of the problems that Karla and Augusto face, philosophical therapy is an appropriate response.[3]

We hope this exercise in diagnosing a moral ailment and observing how philosophy can help cure it is interesting in its own right to a variety of audiences. One audience that might benefit especially, however, is a group we call "recovering unrestrained omnivores." By 'unrestrained omnivore' we mean someone whose dietary habits are such that even when she has many options available to her, she mainly chooses, by default or design, products of IFAP. By 'recovering' unrestrained omnivores, we mean those within this demographic who believe (or at least suspect) that dietary changes are morally requisite and want to change on some level, but whose progress is hampered by one or both of the malaises.[4]

In proposing philosophical therapy for these malaises, we take for granted that many people see unrestrained omnivorism as an obstacle to moral well-being. We do not argue here for the moral inadequacy of unrestrained omnivorism, nor do we defend any particular set of 'restraints' as an alternative to it.[5] Our aim is rather to show how philosophy can help those who, challenged by one or more of the numerous arguments against IFAP or in favor of some alternative dietary ideal, sensibly take themselves to have good moral reasons to restrain their consumption in particular ways (whether by avoiding eating and/or purchasing IFAP products, eating and/or purchasing them more selectively, or becoming agrarian, vegetarian, or vegan) but lack the imagination or will to do so.

We set the scope of our project thus because, as other chapters in this volume illustrate, there is widespread agreement that IFAP is morally problematic but considerable debate about what this consensus means for our dietary obligations. By targeting unrestrained omnivorism generally, we take aim at a common moral foe and preserve the prospect for alliances with many arguments advanced in this volume. If one finds Hooley and Nobis or McPherson compelling, one might undertake the proposed therapy in pursuit of veganism. If Budolfson or Van Dyke strikes a chord, altruistic omnivorism might be the goal, whereas agreement with Lipscomb may find one striving for the agrarian ideal. In each case, the proposed therapy aims to aid those struggling with the challenges of improving on unrestrained omnivorism, either by broadening their imaginations in ways that increase receptivity to these arguments or by strengthening their wills to live out the commitments to which the arguments give rise, or both.[6]

Readers will have noticed, finally, that ethical concerns regarding animals take center stage in our diagnoses of the malaises and in our framing of related worries about IFAP and unrestrained omnivorism. This trend continues throughout the chapter and is largely a function of the limits of our personal interest and professional expertise. In emphasizing the animal-related dimensions of the struggle to eat more ethically, however, we do not wish to minimize important objections to IFAP and unrestrained omnivorism issuing from serious concerns about the environment, human health, or worker justice. We hope the proposed therapy is useful, pending relevant modifications, to those whose malaises are prompted by reflection on these other important pieces of the food ethics puzzle.

Treating the Malaise of Imagination: Philosophical Hermeneutics

Gadamerian Insights for Hermeneutic Therapy

Let's return to Karla, who suffers from a malaise of imagination. Recall that she is moved to serious reflection by a class discussion on ethical veganism. The argument intrigues her and she suspects it has merit, but it provokes anxiety because she's unable to imagine a world in which it could apply to her without challenging a variety of seemingly nonnegotiable identity-framing assumptions. Our task now is to draw on Gadamer's philosophical hermeneutics to identify a treatment plan to help Karla reframe the uninterrogated assumptions she brings to bear on new experience, thereby opening the way to less defensive, more authentic engagement with arguments and experiences that challenge even her most deeply held beliefs and attitudes. Gathering the relevant Gadamerian insights requires a short hike into higher altitudes than we have had to ascend thus far, but the goal is to be back on the ground with Karla in a few paragraphs, bearing some down-to-earth therapeutic advice.

When asked to characterize his approach to philosophy in a nutshell, Gadamer once said: "Philosophy is the way not to forget that man is never God."[7] The guiding insight here is that philosophy's perennial task is to illuminate human finitude in order to curb our self-forgetful and often self-defeating inclination to overestimate the objectivity and extent of our knowledge. This reminder issues from Gadamer's writings as a descriptive account of the essentially hermeneutic (i.e., interpretive) character of finite human understanding. Such understanding is neither impartial nor complete because it is always already shaped in advance by the interpretive legacies of its evolving historical and linguistic inheritances. Simply put, human beings understand on the basis of what we have already understood, and shaping forces like history, language, and tradition drive this 'hermeneutic circle' of understanding forward, handing down interpretations of the world that both *facilitate* and *limit* our ability to understand it.[8]

These shaping forces put the world before us and orient us within it by inculcating us with 'prejudices' through which we 'have the world in advance' even as we remain beholden to the incomplete understanding of it inherited from the past. Prejudice-dependent understanding is thus always both underway and as yet unfinished; it is simultaneously indebted to a formative past and open to an amorphous future. Gadamer is careful to add that these prejudices need not be false or unfounded judgments (as the term's pejorative sense in English conveys); they are best understood, rather, as guiding prejudgments of experience that can have positive or negative value but that provide, in either case, a necessary starting point for interpretation.[9] If prejudices are a necessary condition of understanding, however, *uninterrogated* prejudices can distort our understanding of things and limit our receptivity to new experiences that could redress such distortions.

Gadamer calls this blinkered condition "the tyranny of hidden prejudices" and argues that it "makes us deaf to what speaks to us in tradition."[10] When this tyranny prevails in our understanding of the world, we remain beholden to uninterrogated assumptions even when new experiences challenge them in potentially edifying ways. In the event of such provocative new experiences, an individual in thrall to hidden prejudices—call her hermeneutically 'inexperienced'—feels anxiety resulting from the tension between her assumptions and her new experience. Because she is naïve of the influence of her hidden prejudices, however, she has difficulty bringing them reflectively to the fore and reevaluating them in light of new information. Instead, her anxiety prompts her to seek the comforts of the familiar, thereby foreclosing the opportunity to learn from ongoing experience. The more acute her anxiety becomes, the more tightly she clings to her untutored prejudices.

In contrast to the inexperienced person who shrinks from the new, the strange, and the challenging, Gadamer holds out the 'experienced' person who has learned through hermeneutic training how to be tutored by these provocations. Such a person responds very differently to the anxiety that arises from having her prejudices brought up short by challenges to their interpretative adequacy. Rather than fleeing from anxiety into the safety of past understanding, the experienced person moves toward the source of her unease, expecting to learn something and recognizing that such provocations are necessary for making her governing prejudices conscious to her.[11] The experienced person thus sees her anxiety as the harbinger of an opportunity to learn what her prejudices are and to observe how they both enable and curtail her current understanding. As a result of her careful attention to the dependence of her understanding on revisable prejudices that must be tested against and reframed in accordance with experience on an ongoing basis, the experienced person is "radically undogmatic": "because of the many experiences [s]he has had and the knowledge [s]he has drawn from them, [she] is particularly well equipped to have new experiences and to learn from them."[12]

Overcoming the Tyranny of Hidden Prejudices

If her pulled-pork coma has subsided and Karla has been listening in, she's already gleaned the lesson: She is Gadamer's inexperienced person! She resists the provocation of an argument that intrigues her because she is unprepared to recognize her anxiety as a symptom of her dependence on contestable (and now contested!) assumptions. She finds it easier simply to cling to these assumptions uncritically than to commit to the daunting work of riding out the experience and risking them to evaluation and revision. In short, Karla's malaise is a function of the tyranny of hidden prejudices: The very prejudgments whose experiential revision could prompt her to imagine new possibilities for moral flourishing are functioning, in this case, as obstacles to her piqued moral interest in following experience where it leads.

The therapy is already working. Even this dawning of a clearer sense of why she feels so anxious is liberating. But in realizing that her malaise is in part a symptom of inexperience, Karla has also attained a new health ideal: Where arguments about ethical eating are concerned, she wants to become the experienced person. And she sees how to do it: She will employ this argumentative provocation to illuminate her uninterrogated assumptions and test their interpretive adequacy by seeking out new experiences that eventuate their ongoing evaluation and revision.

Karla quickly discovers that certain of the assumptions contributing to her malaise are little more than defense mechanisms. For instance, the worries that eating differently would be unaffordable and unhealthful are—for her, if not for everyone—easily revised beliefs. However expedient these were for keeping her guard up, her new openness allows repressed or overlooked experiences to take retroactive effect and now counterexamples abound, from her (modestly compensated) math teaching assistant who eats meat only from trusted sources to the (ultra-fit) vegan marathoner she saw on *Oprah*.

Her anxiety around the church barbeque, however, leads to murkier depths. She realizes that her religious upbringing has primed her to believe that humans have divine permission to use animals, including for aesthetic enjoyment. With this assumption foregrounded, she sees just how much hangs on it. For argument's sake, she brackets recourse to divine permission and finds it difficult to see how she would otherwise justify ranking her superfluous pleasure in eating pork above the pig's most basic interest in living. That a benevolent creator would prefer this arrangement now seems worth reconsidering. In nosing around online, Karla discovers that many religious people—in her tradition and most others—are thinking about these issues too: There is an ever-expanding scholarly literature,[13] growing concern in religious magazines and blogs, and even major activist organizations enjoining faith groups to eschew IFAP on religious grounds.[14]

But her barbeque-induced anxiety isn't just about religion. It's also rooted in her identity as a lifelong community member at her particular church, and as a friend, a daughter, and a woman. She has always assumed that anything widely supported by her trusted community is morally permissible. Wouldn't her concern over the provenance of the meat be judgmental of her fellow congregants? Interrogating her anxiety over potential fallout with loved ones is even more daunting, but as the process unfolds, Karla comes to see how beholden she is to the assumption that she has an obligation to engage in communal meat-eating traditions that outweighs many good reasons to abstain. As for her father, she has always just accepted that he is justifiably proud of her ability to "eat like a man."

Under scrutiny, though, this belief seems to rely on the assumption that eating in accordance with 'masculine' norms makes a person more praiseworthy, and she now realizes that her delight in transcending Dad's gendered expectations is both a bigger source of self-esteem than she'd prefer and a questionable motive for overeating barbeque.[15]

As her awareness of these governing assumptions grows and her openness to questioning them increases, Karla notices something they all have in common. They are unreflectively anthropocentric: if they countenance the possibility that 'food animals' have interests at all, they inevitably assume that these interests are less important than the human interests putatively served by using animals. More concretely, whether Karla's dietary interests lie in avoiding expense, maintaining health, demonstrating piety, experiencing gustatory pleasure, preserving community, following tradition, or boosting self-esteem, she has always just assumed that these interests take precedent over any interests 'food animals' may have. Moreover, perhaps *because* of this anthropocentric prejudice, she's assumed thus without ever really contemplating whether these dietary interests can be met in other ways that take better account of animals' interests.

But do animals have morally significant interests? If so, what are they? And how are we to weigh them against competing human interests? In arriving at these critical questions, Karla makes a major breakthrough: It's not just her individual prejudices that are under discussion now, but the broader anthropocentric frame of reference they share. At the same time, however, these questions bring her up against perhaps the biggest obstacle to moral progress erected by the tyranny of hidden prejudices: the tendency to render invisible the possibilities and interests of the very beings who are most harmed by the attitudes and actions these prejudices suborn.

To wit, a culture dominated by androcentric prejudices diminishes the possibilities and interests of girls and women; in such a culture, a woman herself, or men around her, may dismiss a passion and aptitude she feels for a leadership role, because it is widely accepted that women are ill-suited to such roles. Similarly, a culture dominated by anthropocentric prejudices diminishes the possibilities and interests of nonhuman animals; in such a culture, a cow who expresses intense distress over separation from her calf may not be recognized as grieving because it is widely accepted that cows are incapable of forming such bonds.[16] For some, it might even be difficult to conceive of cows as unique individuals at all (much less as individuals capable of grief) rather than as merely interchangeable members of the bovine species.

Reframing Anthropocentric Imagination through Experiencing Animals

Reframing inadequate prejudices about animals is thus a challenging prospect. Given the pervasiveness of unreflectively anthropocentric attitudes toward them, the present culture provides few opportunities for animals—especially 'food animals'—to appear in lights that would provoke the requisite imagination-expanding conflict between our prejudgments of them and our experiences with them as more than sentient underlings at best and mere resources on the average.

Interestingly, one of the very few opportunities the present culture *does* provide for provoking this conflict is precisely the one that initially prompted Karla's anxiety, namely the horror associated with projecting the deep moral concern—even love—she feels for her canine companion onto the animals she eats. But just as her moral indignation was dawning in the thought that pigs, like dogs, might be irreplaceable individuals, the tyranny of hidden prejudices deflected her horror into defensive consolations that prevented deeper engagement with the argument.

That was then. But now she's in a different position vis-à-vis these prejudices; she's aware of what some of the more influential ones are, she's seen through and revised some of them, glimpsed the revisability of others, and gained insight into both the human-centered frame of reference they share and the moral risks of operating unreflectively within that frame. These experiences, moreover, have increased her confidence; she's no longer intimidated by further investigation. Now, wishing to be tutored by the anxiety provoked in attempting to imagine her cherished Mr. Chauncey and a nameless pig as moral equals, Karla undertakes an intentional examination of why other animals shouldn't be accorded the same levels of care and compassion that her companion enjoys.

Toward that end, she does some reading about other animals—both domesticated and free-living—and discovers that their inner and social lives are rich and complex.[17] She's not entirely surprised, given what she already knew of Mr. Chauncey, but she is delighted and comforted, too, that science corroborates her experience of animals as sentient creatures capable of caring about their own and others' lives; she isn't just bunny-hugging here. But what if she were? Frankly, her anxiety over being labeled a 'bunny-hugger' has all but dissipated, thanks to her realization via feminist literature that minimizing the compassion we feel for vulnerable fellow creatures (and mocking those who display it) is one of the oldest tools in the oppressor's kit for concealing injustice to suffering others.[18] This emerging sense that animal advocacy is something she could actually support surprises Karla, but she must admit that few things presently agitate her more than images of animals—both suffering and flourishing—presented in the work of activist artists like Jo-Anne McArthur and Sue Coe.[19]

She follows this growing compassion and courts the company of other animals about whom she's been reading. She visits some local places that keep pigs and carefully considers the differences between those she encounters at petting zoos, county fairs, local farms, and a farm sanctuary (where she ends up volunteering on weekends). She visits the city zoo, famed for its conservation work, and is surprised by how much more sensitive an observer of animal behavior she has become since her previous visit. Last year, she would have assumed that pacing lions and arm-biting chimpanzees were just 'doing what animals do.' Now she sees the telltale signs of boredom, frustration, and stress. Having observed what these creatures' lives are actually like, Karla is incredulous that she recently believed they were dim-witted, antisocial, or uninterested in their own lives. Her experience now confirms the contrary.

Karla can't deny that this experience has furnished a powerful corrective to her untutored assumptions both about animals (and their prospects) and about human beings (and the relative importance of our uses for animals). By experiencing animals as they are, she has cultivated compassion, appreciation, respect, and wonder that have helped her to overcome her inclination to see them— at least those outside her self-interested sphere of concern—as mere resources. Animals in their fullest flourishing, she has discovered, are not always or only vulnerable like industrially farmed or other exploited animals are; they can be and are mysterious, beautiful, forceful, ingenious, and autonomous (in species-appropriate ways).

When Karla revisits her notes from that fateful class discussion, the arguments that seemed bewildering just six months ago now seem crystal clear, even persuasive. Though she hasn't figured out exactly where her reframed perspective will lead her, she *can* now imagine herself as 'Karla the agrarian' or 'Karla the vegan' or even 'Karla the animal rights activist.' Her malaise of imagination has lifted, but her state of unease is now even more pronounced. Previously, her fleeting anxiety upon eating pork was readily assuaged by wistful memories of church picnics; she could even laugh it off with a bacon joke at the expense of vegetarian friends. Now, such jokes seem perverse. Doing nothing feels deeply wrong. But adopting new habits seems like harder work than she can manage. Karla, like Augusto, now suffers from a malaise of will.

Treating the Malaise of Will: Care of the Self

Hadot's Itinerary from Philosophical Exercises to Transformed Living

Let's return, then, to Augusto's case. Recall that he's convinced that he should (at least) avoid eating meat. He lacks the will, however, to make this major change in the face of many obstacles, including entrenched preferences and habits, lack of experience, bad faith, laziness, and peer pressure. What he needs are role models and practical strategies that will fix his attention on the self-defeating consequences of being beholden to these bad excuses and empower him to think and act authentically in accordance with his conviction.

He can find these resources in abundance in Hellenistic philosophy's emphasis on care of the self. In engaging this tradition via its contemporary appropriation by Pierre Hadot, moreover, Augusto can get a compelling introduction to a rich and complex historical literature from a single trusted source. Following Hadot and the ancients, he can approach philosophy as a type of training for living, and as a potentially transformative way to engage the world.[20] As Hadot explains,

> philosophy then [in antiquity] appears in its original aspect: not as a theoretical construct, but as a method for training people to live and to look at the world in a new way. It is an attempt to transform mankind.[21]

Philosophy is thus a way of life—a process aimed at transforming one through a regime of practices—and it opens a compelling way forward for those, like Augusto, who are intellectually committed to changing but lack the will to do so.

What sorts of therapeutic practices might Augusto employ, then, to cure his unrest and modify his behavior? Care of the self aims to help one cultivate an authentic, consistent, satisfying life, in part by requiring close attention to and reflection upon one's actions. This attention demands the application of repetitive daily exercises—some intellectual and some practical—that serve to heighten his consciousness of the world beyond himself, and through habituation, transform his seeing and being within it.[22]

The intellectual exercises will look familiar even to contemporary philosophers; these include reading, listening, and investigation.[23] These exercises occur for Augusto in the context of further class discussions, conversations with professors and peers, and efforts to seek out articles that bolster or challenge his existing views. Such exercises can help to dislodge the obstacles of lack of experience and bad faith that threaten to stymie his progress. To broaden his experience, for instance, Augusto seeks out arguments from various perspectives, reflecting on what new challenges they pose for his evolving understanding of ethical eating. To keep bad faith at bay, he discusses these issues with a community of others who take his concerns seriously, help him sharpen his thoughts, and keep him intellectually honest and consistent.[24]

To convert the discoveries of these intellectual disciplines into authentic behavior modification, however, Augusto must undertake other complementary exercises in tandem. In the Stoico-Platonic tradition of philosophical therapy,[25] attention and meditation are valuable practices that help one assimilate arguments in a way that is truly transformative, converting intellectual information that merely enables us 'to know' into wisdom that helps us to 'be in a different way.'[26] For the Stoics, attention meant a vigilant focus on the present moment—a constant self-awareness of one's thoughts and actions and of how they reflect one's principled commitments. Such attention guards one against acting mindlessly in ways that undermine one's commitments and lead to distress or cognitive dissonance.

As Augusto enters the cafeteria, for example, he might strive to keep present to mind the connection between the meat there and the individual animals that meat used to be. He can remind himself that his self-conception as 'Augusto the vegetarian' is important to him, and that actions inconsistent with it will ultimately cause him discomfort and degrade his authenticity. Careful attention to these realities of the present moment can aid Augusto in his pursuit of behavior modification[27] by reminding him of the urgent nature of his concerns, thereby staving off the convenient excuse that his desired behavior modifications are best left for some future occasion. His vigilance can thus offer an antidote to the laziness that threatens to undermine his resolve and hasten his return to entrenched habits.

But if he is to face the cafeteria with such attention and conviction, it behooves him to prepare in advance. Here, the exercise of meditation is useful. Ancient philosophers meditated by imagining themselves experiencing poverty or illness in order to be ready to respond appropriately should these afflictions befall them.[28] While this practice might seem morbid to contemporary sensibilities, the idea of mentally preparing oneself for a difficult situation need not be. Augusto might begin his day with a reflection on why he wishes to avoid eating meat, mentally reviewing the arguments for adopting this behavior, and imagining what situations may arise on a particular day to test his resolve.[29]

To take it further, he might follow the Stoic model of adopting a particular practice he initially finds difficult for a prescribed period of time. Seneca counseled others to adopt temporary poverty as a way of "toughening the soul," cautioning that it should be undertaken as "a test of yourself instead of a mere hobby."[30] In that spirit, Augusto could adopt veganism (the most stringent dietary regime) for an appointed time as an exercise in cultivating the most vigilant attention to what he is eating, even if he is unwilling or unable to maintain that level of vigilance indefinitely.

Habituating Self-Mastery and Accomplishment of Duties

Augusto can also benefit from adopting repetitive practical exercises that promote "self-mastery," in Hadot's language. It is instructive to note that ancient philosophers often compared living philosophically with honing athletic skills. Living philosophically, much like developing athletic ability, involves repetitive, daily, practical exercises that may be mundane in themselves, but that train the individual to achieve loftier goals.[31] In Augusto's circumstances, these daily, repetitive practices may prove the most powerful remedies for many of the obstacles he encounters.

A simple practice like grocery shopping at an appointed time each week can preempt the laziness that might otherwise find him cruising the Frank-n-Burger's drive-through on his way home to an empty fridge. Packing a lunch every evening that is ready to grab on his way to campus each morning can dampen the siren song of the pork and diminish the threat of cafeteria peer pressure. Planning regular outings with sympathetic friends to exciting new veg-friendly restaurants can broaden his experience and supplant alienating interactions with encouraging fellowship. By the next birthday dinner, hopefully, he'll have both a variety of new eateries he loves and the confidence to recommend them to his grandparents. In the longer term, learning to cook a variety of delicious plant-based meals for all occasions could liberate him from dependence on convenience foods that might otherwise erode his resolve. Practical exercises like these may seem trivial, but in the context of adopting a new behavior, they can help Augusto to form habits that make the difference between success and failure.

In addition to habituating self-mastery, practical exercises emphasize the "accomplishment of duties"—the assumption of positions of leadership or responsibility and the fulfillment of their associated obligations.[32] Augusto could volunteer for a student organization or convene a meatless cooking demonstration, even and especially if such measures take him outside his comfort zone. He might consider donating monthly to an animal advocacy nonprofit, carefully reading the stories of the animals who benefit from his contributions. By taking on obligations to others in ways that stretch him and require him to live up to his own aspirations, Augusto raises himself above his individual perspective, and begins to see the implications of his actions for the whole.

If all goes well, once he initiates some of these exercises, the combination of good reasons and repetitive actions has a transformative effect over time, supplanting entrenched behaviors that both caused unease and degraded his moral integrity with new and better habits. To the contemporary philosopher, the practical exercises that have brought Augusto to this point may not look much like 'philosophy.' But in the tradition of care of the self, "doing philosophy meant practicing how to live" by training oneself to adopt actions that are "just and in conformity with reason."[33] Philosophy thus serves as a "therapeutic" that can cure the "anguish" of failing to live up to one's aspirations.[34]

The role for philosophy sketched here may sound idealistic or unattainable, but its advocates are not naïve of the fact that it is always a process we undergo as moral progressives, never an end point reached by the elusive sage.[35] This should prove heartening rather than discouraging for those inclined to worry that their strivings to eat ethically are futile, causally impotent, or impossible to uphold consistently.[36] Because care of the self focuses on transforming how an individual sees and acts in the world, it is possible for one to make real moral progress even without achieving sage-like wisdom, a life of purity, or large-scale institutional reform. Though the measurable effects of one person's actions may be insignificant, that person may experience the very significant transformational effects of a life lived with enhanced attention to consistency between thought and deed.[37] For Augusto, pursuing this consistency requires him to stand in symbolic solidarity with oppressed animals by refusing to use them as mere instruments. His focus on holistic moral transformation in the areas of his life that he *can* control mitigates lingering anxiety about not making a quantifiable impact in ways he *can't* control.

For care of the self, acknowledging this distinction between what one can and can't control is key for facilitating personal transformation, but also for extending the individual's circle of concern beyond his or her own interests.[38]

If achieving statistically significant results in terms of 'animal lives saved' or 'people converted to vegetarianism' is beyond Augusto's control, he is nonetheless very much in control of his own attitudes and responses, and finds that his new solidarity with animals alleviates his feelings of unrest and enables him to live up to his own vision of authenticity.

As his anxiety abates and solidarity with animals becomes a way of life, he notices that the disciplines of intellectual and practical attentiveness that have transformed his attitudes and actions concerning animals are affecting other aspects of his vision, too. His consistent attention to the interests of animals, to wit, has heightened his awareness of the interests of other individuals exploited by our food system. He finds himself contemplating the circumstances of people who work in slaughterhouses, tomato fields, and coffee plantations. He starts taking note of the distance traveled by produce purchased at the grocery store, begins paying attention to the vast swaths of corn and soybeans in the fields beyond campus, and initiates research on the impact of these practices on everything from topsoil erosion to climate change. What began with occasional, unpredictable uprisings of compassion for cows nuzzling the vents of transport trucks has expanded into a systematic and holistic vision of the impact of his food choices for the world at large. Hadot might describe this change as Augusto's achievement of a more cosmic view of the whole.[39]

Although striving for this cosmic vision may seem quaint to many contemporary philosophers, Hadot maintains that aspiring to this frame of reference is as relevant for us today as it was for the ancients. Following thinkers in the phenomenological tradition, including Husserl, Heidegger, Merleau-Ponty, and Bergson, Hadot argues that our daily struggle to cope with finite existence inclines and often requires us to envision the world as a collection of disconnected objects and to act as if its denizens were mere resources for accomplishing our myopic ends.[40] Practicing care of the self, however, can serve as an important corrective to this pervasive tendency to instrumentalize and consume the constituents of our world. Says Hadot,

> [This] utilitarian perception we have of the world, in everyday life, in fact hides from us the world qua world. Aesthetic and philosophical perceptions of the world are only possible by means of a complete transformation of our relationship to the world: we have to perceive it for itself, and no longer for ourselves.[41]

Ancient though this wisdom may be, it is difficult to imagine advice more pertinent to the present situation, in which the collective impact of our shortsighted decisions at dinner is now well known to threaten the oceans, the atmosphere, and everything between. Those who, with Karla and Augusto, can imagine the flourishing of the whole and resolve to act in accordance with it have a world to gain—for humans, animals, and the planet.

Conclusion

We hope to have offered a helpful diagnosis of common moral malaises of imagination and will, as well as to have made a good case that therapeutic philosophy can help people overcome these obstacles that might otherwise prevent them from authentically engaging and responding to argumentative challenges to their eating habits. Though we have focused here on food ethics, we believe that readers who resonate with the predicaments of Karla and Augusto in other arenas of moral discernment may find hermeneutics and care of the self illuminating and even liberating complements to argumentative challenges in those other arenas, too. We see an added benefit in the opportunity our approach affords to pay increased attention to philosophical traditions that are underrepresented in contemporary food ethics, but that have significant resources to contribute to the discussion.[42]

Notes

1. A discussion of the complex and often contested ways in which these obstacles figure into philosophical and social scientific accounts of weakness of will is beyond the scope of this chapter. For much more on these topics, see Stroud and Tappolet (2008) and Mele (2014).
2. Diverse thinkers from antiquity to the present have argued that philosophy has therapeutic value. Western philosophers in this tradition include Plato, Aristotle, Hellenistic philosophers, Wittgenstein, Foucault, and Hadot. For discussions of philosophy as therapy and of these figures and others, see Banicki (2014) and Fischer (2011). For discussion of the Hellenistic tradition, see Nussbaum (1994). Nearly all accounts of philosophy as therapy, Banicki maintains, have in common the notions of "the health ideal, disease (or illness), and the process of treatment" (14). We borrow Banicki's language in referring to a "health ideal" above (Nussbaum calls this the "norm of health," 19). Note that both Fischer (2011, 50) and Nussbaum (1994, 5) stress, as do we, that philosophy as therapy is not incompatible with philosophy in its argumentative mode, but rather includes argumentation. We agree with Nussbaum, too, that philosophy as therapy must respect the agent's conception of her own health, rather than simply promote a norm of health that is "'out there' to be discovered and then applied to [her] case" (19). Accordingly, we operate with the very broad understanding of "health ideal" identified above.
3. We are grateful to Terence Cuneo and Tyler Doggett for help framing this clarification.
4. We treat each malaise in turn without addressing the complexities of their relations, which—space permitting—would be interesting to explore. For instance, sometimes anticipation of a malaise of will (say, anxiety over the difficulty of taking action if one becomes convinced one should) might (un)consciously exacerbate a malaise of imagination (by leading one more trenchantly to protect uninvestigated assumptions for fear that investigation would only increase unease and inauthenticity).
5. This territory is well surveyed in the literature, including numerous chapters in this volume. For an overview of the wide array of moral problems associated with IFAP, see Rossi and Garner (2014).
6. See Van Dyke, chapter 2; Lipscomb, chapter 3; McPherson, chapter 4; Hooley and Nobis, chapter 5; and Buldofson, chapter 9. The proposed therapy may prove useful as well for those struggling with some of the "food failures" discussed by Doggett and Egan, see chapter 6.

7. Pyke (1993).
8. Gadamer (1992) develops this account of the hermeneutic character of understanding at great length in his magnum opus. He addresses its therapeutic applications more explicitly in Gadamer (1996).
9. Gadamer (1992, 265–300).
10. Ibid., 270.
11. Ibid., 299.
12. Ibid., 355. Gadamer is not claiming that experienced people are bereft of (even strong) commitments; his point is that their awareness of the influence of hidden prejudices keeps these from acting as immovable obstacles to learning from assumption-challenging experiences.
13. On Christian discussions, see Halteman (2013). On world religions more broadly, see Kemmerer (2012).
14. Humane Society of the United States Faith Outreach, for instance, offers resources on ethical eating for Buddhists, Christians, Hindus, Muslims, Jews, and Unitarians. See http://www.humanesociety.org/about/departments/faith/facts/statements.
15. For a classic treatment of the gendered aspects of meat eating, see Adams (1990). Van Dyke (this volume, chapter 2) draws on and contests aspects of Adams' account.
16. As an example of the anthropocentric bent of the institution of language, "autocorrect" suggests depersonalizing animals from "who" to "that" even as we type these words.
17. Balcombe (2010).
18. Donovan and Adams (2007).
19. McArthur (2014) and Sue Coe, http://graphicwitness.org/coe/enter.htm.
20. Philosophical discourse is certainly an important tool, but it must be understood as propaedeutic to living the philosophical life. Hadot (1995, 107).
21. For an overview of the diverse range of thinkers and traditions that approach philosophy thus, see Chase, Clark, and McGhee (2013).
22. For a full discussion of these exercises, including Hadot's illuminating account of why he calls them 'spiritual' exercises, see Hadot (1995, 79ff).
23. Ibid., 86.
24. Seneca speaks of the value of "fellowship of wise men," noting that a true friend will help one keep "his virtues . . . and point out to him opportunities for honourable action" (1925, CIX, 3).
25. Hadot (1995, 84).
26. In Hadot's language, "real wisdom does not merely cause us to know: it makes us 'be' in a different way." Ibid., 265.
27. See Marcus Aurelius (2011, 20 [3.10.1–4]): "Remember, furthermore, that each of us lives only in the present, this fleeting moment of time, and that the rest of one's life has either already been lived or lies in an unknowable future."
28. Hadot (1995, 84).
29. As Marcus Aurelius (2011, 10 [2.1.1 ff]) advises,

> Say to yourself at the start of the day, I shall meet with meddling, ungrateful, violent, treacherous, envious, and unsociable people. [. . .] But I, who have observed the nature of the good, and seen that it is the right, [. . .] I, then, can neither be harmed by these people, nor become angry with one who is akin to me, nor can I hate him.

30. See Seneca's letter XVIII to Lucilius, "On Festivals and Fasting" (1917), where Seneca describes the importance of this practice and highlights that Epicurus used to do the same.
31. Seneca compares the virtuous sage to a wrestler in top form (1917, CIX); Epictetus invokes an archer hitting his mark (1928, *Enchiridion* 27); Marcus Aurelius says, "in the application of one's principles, one should resemble [a boxer]" (2011, 116 [12.9.1]).

32. Hadot (1995, 86).
33. Ibid., 86. Hadot and the ancients he follows go to great pains to make clear that the exercises themselves are not distinct from 'philosophy' but are a key part of it, since "the philosophical act is not situated merely on the cognitive level, but on that of the self and of being." Ibid., 83.
34. Ibid., 266. "Wisdom, then, was a way of life which brought peace of mind (*ataraxia*), inner freedom (*autarkeia*), and a cosmic consciousness. First and foremost, philosophy presented itself as a therapeutic, intended to cure mankind's anguish."
35. Hadot quotes Quintillian on this point: "We must . . . strive after that which is highest, as many of the ancients did. Even though they believed that no sage had ever yet been found, they nevertheless continued to teach the precepts of wisdom." Ibid., 265.
36. See Warfield, (chapter 8) and Chignell, (chapter 10) in this volume.
37. According to Hadot, for the ancients, "each school had its own therapeutic method, but all of them linked their therapeutics to a profound transformation of the individual's mode of seeing and being. The object of spiritual exercises is precisely to bring about this transformation" (1995, 83).
38. For Stoic philosophers in particular, becoming aware of this distinction is the first and most important step one can take. Epictetus begins *Enchiridion* with this insight: "Some things are under our control, while others are not under our control . . . If you believe the things which are slavish by nature are also free . . . then you will be hindered" (1928, *Enchiridion* 1.1).
39. Hadot (1995, 252).
40. Ibid., 258.
41. Ibid., 254.
42. Thanks to Andrew Chignell, Terence Cuneo, Tyler Doggett, Dan Hooley, Ben Lipscomb, and Nathan Nobis for their helpful advice. We are grateful, also, to the Schlegel brothers—Karl Wilhelm Friedrich and August Wilhelm—for their inspiration as pioneering philosopher siblings.

References

Adams, Carol J. *The Sexual Politics of Meat.* New York: Continuum, 1990.
Balcombe, Jonathan. *Second Nature: The Inner Lives of Animals.* New York: Palgrave Macmillan, 2010.
Banicki, Konrad. "Philosophy as Therapy: Towards a Conceptual Model." *Philosophical Papers* 43, no. 1 (2014): 7–31.
Chase, Michael, Stephen R. L. Clark, and Michael McGhee, eds. *Philosophy as a Way of Life: Ancient and Modern: Essays in Honor of Pierre Hadot.* Oxford: Wiley Blackwell, 2013.
Donovan, Josephine, and Carol J. Adams, eds. *The Feminist Care Tradition in Animal Ethics.* New York: Columbia University Press, 2007.
Epictetus. *Epictetus Vol. 2.* Translated by W. A. Oldfather. Cambridge, MA: Harvard University Press, 1928.
Fischer, Eugen. "How to Practice Philosophy as Therapy: Philosophical Therapy and Therapeutic Philosophy." *Metaphilosophy* 42, nos. 1–2 (2011): 49–68.
Gadamer, Hans-Georg. *Truth and Method.* New York: Crossroad, 1992.
———. *The Enigma of Health.* Stanford, CA: Stanford University Press, 1996.
Hadot, Pierre. *Philosophy as a Way of Life.* Oxford: Blackwell, 1995.
Halteman, Matthew C. "Knowing the Standard American Diet by Its Fruits: Is Unrestrained Omnivorism Spiritually Beneficial?" *Interpretation* 67, no. 4 (2013): 383–395.
Kemmerer, Lisa. *Animals and World Religions.* Oxford: Oxford University Press, 2012.

Marcus Aurelius. *The Meditations with Selected Correspondence.* Translated by Robin Hard. Oxford: Oxford University Press, 2011.

McArthur, Jo-Anne. *We Animals.* Brooklyn, NY: Lantern, 2014.

Mele, Alfred R. *Backsliding: Understanding Weakness of Will.* Oxford: Oxford University Press, 2014.

Nussbaum, Martha C. *The Therapy of Desire.* Princeton, NJ: Princeton University Press, 1994.

Pyke, Steve. *Philosophers.* London: Zelda Cheadle Press, 1993.

Rossi, John, and Samual A. Garner. "Industrial Farm Animal Production: A Comprehensive Moral Critique." *Journal of Agricultural and Environmental Ethics* 27, no. 3 (2014): 479–522.

Seneca. *Seneca Epistles 1–65.* Translated by Richard M. Gummere. Cambridge, MA: Harvard University Press, 1917.

———. *Seneca VI, Ad Lucilium Epistulae Morales.* Translated by Richard M. Gummere. Cambridge, MA: Harvard University Press, 1925.

Stroud, Sarah, and Christine Tappolet, eds. *Weakness of Will and Practical Irrationality.* Oxford: Oxford University Press, 2008.

PART II
Puzzling Questions

8

EATING DEAD ANIMALS

Meat Eating, Meat Purchasing, and Proving Too Much

Ted A. Warfield

Factory farming is morally awful. I doubt that there is room for serious debate about this claim. I refer those wanting to explore some of the background that helps support this position to the work of others.[1] My focus in this chapter is not factory farming.[2] My main attention is on meat eating and the related but distinct issue of meat purchasing.

My focus is on the following issue which will be refined further as I move along. What argumentative connection can be made between the horrors of factory farming and the moral status of the consumption and use (often abbreviated with the phrase "meat eating") of the products of factory farming? For this occasion I set aside issues about the products of so-called friendly farms; there are several interesting issues in that general area that would require separate discussion.[3] I also set aside for the present occasion arguments not relevantly grounded in appeals to the moral status of factory farming practices. There are certainly arguments of this sort that deserve careful attention. I hope to address these issues in later work.

In asking what argumentative connection, if any, can be made between the wrongness of industrial farming practices and the moral status of meat eating, I reject the claim that the wrongness of the latter follows immediately from the wrongness of the former. Fortunately, few philosophers make the mistake of thinking that this implication does hold. The mistake, or something very much like it, however, does appear in some deservedly classic texts on animal issues. Here I'll take note of two examples, one from the work of Tom Regan and one from the work of David DeGrazia.

In Regan's case, we find in his classic book *The Case for Animal Rights* (Regan 2004) a section called "Why Vegetarianism Is Obligatory," which exclusively focuses on the rights violations he argues are involved in meat processing. Regan argues at length that various rights violations are occurring in industrial farm practices. Regan leaves unaddressed, however, how one is supposed to conclude further that "vegetarianism is obligatory." It is easy to see why Regan might have thought that it followed that the rights-violating acts should not be performed, but Regan did not argue in that chapter that meat eating was such a rights-violating act. He seems to have thought that the wrongness of meat eating follows immediately from his conclusion that various rights-violating acts take place in meat processing.

DeGrazia makes a similar error in his deservedly celebrated book *Animal Rights: A Very Short Introduction* (DeGrazia 2002). DeGrazia's chapter, called "Meat Eating," has almost no discussion of the ethics of eating meat. Instead, the chapter is a sustained discussion leading up to DeGrazia's conclusion that financial support for institutions like and including factory farms is morally unacceptable. DeGrazia seems here to presuppose that if financial support for industrial farming is morally problematic, then an anti-meat-eating conclusion follows. But this implication does not hold (as we'll shortly see, DeGrazia himself agrees in other work that the implication does not hold).

As both Regan and DeGrazia are surely aware, eating meat does not imply providing financial support of any kind for the meat industry and purchasing meat does not imply eating meat. One can eat without purchasing and purchase without eating. Argumentatively, an invalid argument for the conclusion that one should not eat meat cannot be improved solely by strengthening the conclusion of the argument. The invalid argument I have in mind is the argument from the premise of the wrongness of factory farming to the conclusion that one ought not eat meat. It would not improve this argument to strengthen its conclusion by adding "and one ought not financially support factory farming" to it.

I have said a couple of times that an argument moving directly from the wrongness of factory farming to the wrongness of eating the products of factory farming is invalid. I also say that the same is true of an argument from that premise moving immediately to the conclusion that purchasing the products of factory farming is wrong. Am I right to say these things? Yes, I am, and I take it that all parties to the contemporary debate about these topics agree.

I pause to quote just one involved party because he puts the point so clearly. Here is David DeGrazia from a recent paper: "Factory farming is morally indefensible. What follows for individuals' responsibilities? Nothing follows straightforwardly, so we will need arguments to cross the bridge from institutional wrong to individual obligation" (2009, p. 157).[4] I agree completely, and I think that this is one place where the important action is in these debates. Let me quickly remind everyone why the simplistic argument is invalid. I'll then move on to critically evaluate attempts at strengthening the arguments by supplying the "bridge" material that DeGrazia notes is needed.

Here are two points about the invalidity of the simple argument. First, though in some ways inferences from collective (or group) obligations to individual obligations are notoriously complex, in other ways they are simple to evaluate. Inferences from institutional wrongs (of factory farming or other kinds) to conclusions about individual behavior are invalid on their face. Even inferences from collective wrongs involved in allowing the existence of large evils (such as factory farms) to the wrongness of particular individual actions are invalid.

If one requires more to see this obvious first point, the following second point usually convinces. Various kinds of "causal impotence" observations illustrate why the immediate move from collective wrong to individual wrong is invalid. Assume that factory farming practices are morally wrong. One might think that it follows that one who consumes the products of factory farming practices is therefore obligated to cease doing so on grounds that one's consuming the products immorally supports the morally wrong factory farming practices. Causal impotence objections call this point into question.

One causal impotence point here is the point that it is *purchases* of products that support the factory farming industry and not *consumption* of such products. This suggests at a minimum that the above argument should perhaps be reframed with a conclusion about "not purchasing" instead of a conclusion about "not consuming" factory farm products.[5]

A related though distinct causal impotence issue focuses on the likelihood (in some discussions this is put forward as "the fact") that an individual consumer who changes from consuming (or purchasing) factory farm products to refraining from doing so will make no change to the factory farming practices themselves. The overall market, it is commonly claimed, is wholly insensitive to such small individual changes. One pushing this line would likely be denying the premise that consumption supports factory farming practices. One might also use this observation to deny the claim that individual purchases relevantly support factory farming practices. I will return to this issue.

A final causal impotence issue that helps illustrate the invalidity of simple inferences from the wrongness of factory farming to the wrongness of individual meat eating is perhaps best called "causal isolation" rather than "causal impotence." Consider, for example, those who consume factory farm products only after retrieving them from the garbage. And consider those who consume such products only after obtaining them just before they are placed in the garbage. Most writings on this topic remember to include a footnote indicating that they do not oppose the practice of eating factory farm products found in dumpsters and do not object to eating meat just about to be thrown into the garbage. For example, in the context of arguing against the purchasing of factory farmed meat, Stuart Rachels (2011, p. 883) writes, "if someone is about to throw food away you might as well eat it"—I confidently assume that Rachels also wouldn't object, at least on moral grounds, to eating the food after it has been thrown away. Most seem to concede that this sort of isolation of the consumer from the factory farming practices is morally important and breaks in favor of the permissibility of factory farmed meat consumption in these sorts of contexts.[6]

Here is what these three quite different "causal impotence" claims have in common. They illustrate ways of rejecting the inference from the wrongness of factory farming to the wrongness of consuming the products of such farming.[7]

It is at this point that discussions in the contemporary literature diverge. Most everyone acknowledges that there is work to do explaining how to argue from the wrongness of factory farming to any conclusion about individual moral obligations. Most of what I judge to be the best discussions note the separability of the meat-eating and meat-purchasing issues and focus mainly on working toward the conclusion that it is wrong to purchase the products of factory farms. Since most consumption of such products is associated with purchasing (the products are purchased by the consumers), the idea seems to be that this is in the right neighborhood of a "pro-vegan" conclusion. The sensible thought seems to be "yes, we'll leave freegans and some other types of free riders outside the scope of our main line of criticism and focus upon those who purchase the products (including those who purchase and consume the products)."

Two quibbles about this. I raise these points only to set them aside for another day. First, not all free riders are created equal. Compare the freegan dumpster diver with the freeloader who simply never pays for a meal but instead convinces others to do so. This free rider never purchases a steak. He instead causes others to do so in a way that most would want to argue importantly and negatively distinguishes him from the freegan who also never purchases steak. Second, though most defenders of "pro-animal" positions would be quite happy with a strongly defended "no purchasing" conclusion there is something quite odd about the insistence in some quarters that this would be a pro-vegan position. If this is veganism, do not conclude that one eating steak at your meal is not vegan until you see who pays.[8]

The shift in focus to defending a "no purchasing" conclusion is, as I say, the most common choice made by those attempting to argue from the wrongness of factory farming to the immorality of individual conduct involving the products of such farming. Some, however, aware of the independence of these issues construct their arguments so as to keep the "no eating" conclusion firmly in view. After one final remark about the common shift from a conclusion target of "no eating" to "no purchasing," I'll have a look at one main argument of each type.

Most of what I take to be the best discussions of this issue come from philosophers who I think correctly discuss these issues in an at least broadly consequentialist framework. I have in mind Alastair Norcross, Stuart Rachels, Peter Singer, and a few others. If one favors a different approach, then for today I set such approach aside for another occasion. David DeGrazia does not clearly belong in this group, though his "broad basis" (see DeGrazia 2009) approach is one that he takes to involve commitment to the view that he can provide an argument consequentialists will be comfortable with. So I include him as part of the present conversation. This focus on broadly consequentialist argumentation makes it natural to shift the focus of discussion from meat eating to meat purchasing. In setting aside "stain of the past" and/or "symbolism" arguments from the wrongness of factory farming to the wrongness of eating the products of factory farming, one puts the focus on future directed support for a wicked industry and/or on future directed issues about making a difference concerning the welfare of animals. *Purchasing* drives these kinds of issues. *Eating* does not. There are serious issues worth discussing about the other kinds of argument (past directed and symbolic), but I set these aside so as to now engage with the kinds of arguments I judge to be the best in this area.[9]

The remainder of my discussion will focus on two important attempts to argue from the wrongness of factory farming to some important conclusion about individual obligation. In doing so I will look at one argument that keeps the focus on the "no eating" conclusion (the conclusion that consuming the products of factory farms is morally unacceptable) and then examine an argument that focuses instead on the "no purchasing" conclusion (the conclusion that purchasing the products of factory farms is morally unacceptable).

The first argument I will discuss is from Alastair Norcross.[10] This argument keeps the focus on meat eating in a relevant and important way. Norcross tells the story of Fred who tortures puppies to produce a hormone necessary for Fred's experiencing the taste of chocolate. Norcross argues by analogy from the wrongness of Fred's actions in the story to the wrongness of consuming the products of factory farming. Though one consuming these products does not thereby horribly mistreat animals (as Fred does), Norcross claims that one consuming these products is closely enough connected to the mistreatment of animals to be considered morally on a par with Fred.

The first objection Norcross considers is this: "Fred tortures the puppies himself, whereas most Americans consume meat that comes from animals that have been tortured by others." He continues: "But is this really relevant?" and quickly concludes that it is not relevant. As Norcross rhetorically asks: "What if Fred had been squeamish and had employed someone else to torture the puppies?" The thought is that a typical consumer is relevantly like someone who pays someone else to torture animals so that the consumer can eat them. And this makes the consumer relevantly like the torturer because, according to Norcross, paying someone to torture so that one can benefit is no better than torturing for one's own benefit. Because that is unacceptable, so is what the ordinary consumer does in consuming factory farm products.[11]

After that response to the objection, Norcross moves on to discuss other objections to his argument from analogy. The initial issue, however, requires more discussion. Begin with this point: The typical consumer can surely deny "paying for someone else to torture," as Norcross's analogy seems to require. The typical consumer is, for one thing, causally downstream from the torture of the animals she consumes and not causally prior to it as Fred is. But even setting this nontrivial issue aside, the argument that Norcross is endorsing seems to generalize too far. Let's see why this is so.

Even setting aside the issue of causal order, the typical consumer does not pay someone to torture chickens. She pays someone who pays someone who pays someone who pays someone who pays someone . . . to do so. (Further precision would require replacing some of the instances of "pays someone" with "is paid by someone"—the chain is complex and it is long.) This far longer and more complex chain more accurately describes the relation between the typical consumer and the animal mistreatment. One might ask in reply, "So what? The longer, more complex chain between the consumer and the animal mistreatment isn't relevant to the argument, is it? The torture is still wrong, and so is paying someone to torture, and so is standing in the more complex relation to the mistreatment." Answer: This last point is not so clear.

Consider what happens when a vegan (or anyone else) pays his phone bill (call this the "phone bill" problem). In paying one's phone bill, one pays someone who pays someone who pays someone who pays someone who is paid by someone . . . who pays someone to torture chickens. The same sort of chain between individual behavior and animal mistreatment exists linking many other normal transactions (compare: buying rice at the grocery store instead of buying chicken).

Much more is needed to sort out what sorts of connections and ties and causal chains and dependence relations do and do not transmit moral properties such as wrongness. Those pushing the view that factory farmed meat consumption is "just like" and so "morally like" paying someone to torture for one's benefit need to say much more about this, and they have not done so.[12] Their explicit argument generalizes badly—it overgeneralizes in ways that they will not find acceptable.

I pause to note that those offering a similar kind of argument from analogy to defend the conclusion that one should not purchase the products of industrial farming face related issues about overgeneralization. For example, David DeGrazia (2009, p. 157ff) argues toward the conclusion that one should "make every reasonable effort not to provide financial support to institutions that cause [the harms of factory farming]" in part by analogy to the case of causing those harms directly. DeGrazia (2009, p. 159) further points out that doing this isn't even inconvenient for most people: They can "buy non-meat substitutes at the very grocery stores they currently shop." Doing things this "convenient" way would provide financial support to those who pay people who are paid by people who pay people . . . to torture animals. The same goes for the convenient option of ordering a vegan option at a restaurant one already frequents.[13]

Unless defenders of these arguments from analogy want to conclude that a near total isolation from the mainstream economy is morally required, I conclude that they have more work to do to defend the arguments from the objection that they prove too much. They must address the phone bill objection.

I turn now to the second argument I will examine from the wrongness of factory farming to a conclusion about individual obligation. This argument pushes for the conclusion that one should not purchase the products of factory farming. The main consideration in play is that financial support drives the industry and that one can in some way(s) make a difference toward decreasing the morally awful conduct of the industry by refraining from such support. I'll focus on Stuart Rachels's excellent discussion of this issue (Rachels 2011).[14]

Rachels argues convincingly for the (sub)conclusion that "industrial farming is wrong." His main idea for moving from that point to the conclusion that individuals should not purchase the products of factory farming is summed up this way: "Boycott cruelty," where the boycott he calls for involves withdrawing financial support from the factory farming industry.

Somewhat oddly, Rachels immediately claims that if we have soundly reached this boycott/no purchasing conclusion, we will have to face up the argument's "taxing implications: you may eat almost no meat, dairy, or seafood sold in restaurants and grocery stores" (2011, p. 883). He says this after explicitly saying just one paragraph earlier that the conclusion of his argument is about purchasing and not about eating. But this is only somewhat odd. As noted earlier Rachels is explicitly aware of causal isolation points against this broad conclusion—recall from earlier: "If someone is about to throw food away you might as well eat it." Rachels presumably means this even if the food in question comes from a factory farm. In stating these "taxing implications," Rachels is leaning on the fact that almost all individual meat/dairy/seafood consumption is contingently tied to personal purchasing of products from factory farms. After all, typically those who eat meat purchase it.[15] Though there are some further issues worth exploring in an attempt to clarify exactly what conclusion Rachels is pursuing, let's set this aside and instead focus the evaluation on the main line of thought he provides.

Rachels recognizes that the argument from the wrongness of factory farming to the conclusion that individuals should not purchase products from factory farms is not concluded simply by introducing the guiding idea of boycotting cruelty. Because Rachels works within a consequentialist framework he recognizes the importance of responding to the following kind of causal impotence objection: "My [boycotting] actions won't make a difference, so I might as well enjoy my [factory farmed] meat and hope that someday" industrial farms are shut down.[16]

Rachels's response in a nutshell is this. Sufficient for mandating a personal boycott is that one's behavior "*might* make a difference: the meat industry might produce less meat next year if I don't buy meat this year.[17] After all, my behavior might determine whether a threshold or tipping point of sales is reached prompting a reduction in production" (Rachels, 2011, 886). The basic point is familiar enough (the issue has been widely discussed in the literature). Even if the industry is insensitive to Rachels's refraining from purchasing twenty chickens this year, there will be some threshold—10,000? 1,000? 1,000,000? He'll argue it won't matter—such that industry is sensitive to that threshold and will decrease future production if that many fewer chickens are purchased this year. And there is a chance that Rachels's refraining will take the industry past the tipping point. If industry sensitivity is high (unlikely), his refraining will be more likely to trigger a threshold that prevents a relatively small number of chickens from being produced next year. And if, as is more likely, industry sensitivity is low, it will be less likely that Rachels's boycott triggers the threshold but, when it does do so, the "payoff" in reduction of chicken suffering will be correspondingly higher. The expected payoff, in either case, we are told, is the same or at least similar (Rachels, 2011, 886).

Some details about this "might" or "threshold" response vary from author to author. Some (e.g., Norcross 2004) take it to be a rejection of the premise of the causal impotence objection. Norcross's thought is that whether your action triggers a threshold of production or not, your action is difference making: It either takes us to a threshold or takes us closer to one, and in either case the action makes a difference. Rachels does not seem to think he is denying the premise that an individual boycott will not always make a difference (consistent with that it might is, after all, that it will not). Rachels instead seems to deny that actual difference making is needed for the inference he is defending. He seems to think that the fact that one's boycott might make a difference suffices to defend the inference.

I will make two points objecting to the Rachels version of this "might make a difference" response to the causal impotence objection to Rachels's call for boycott. The first point is that I worry that the response might generalize beyond what Rachels wants to defend. Concede that Rachels's refraining from purchasing chickens might make a difference to future chicken production. Increasing (or decreasing for that matter) rice purchasing or corn purchasing or gasoline purchasing *might* do this too—these proposed changes might also make a difference to chicken production. They might decrease chicken production. Speculative "might" claims are surely too weak on their own to play the argumentative role that Rachels wants them to play.

Here is a sensible reply to that first point that almost certainly more accurately captures Rachels's thinking. Though Rachels's point is initially stated using a "might" claim, the argument really does not rely on a bare speculative "might" claim about the relation between Rachel's refraining from purchasing chickens and future chicken production. The argument is explained more fully, after all, in terms of "expected payoff" rather than simply what "might" be the outcome.

This sensible reply leads to my second objection to the argument. The appeal to *expected outcome* ratchets up the pressure considerably on the required defense of the "might" claim needed for the argument. If we focus only on the contribution that Rachels's boycott makes to demand, we might quickly conclude that this one factor tends to promote an overall drop in demand. The same point holds for any others who join Rachels in boycotting factory farmed chicken. So focusing only on these effects of the boycott suggests that overall demand for factory farmed products will go down as a result of the boycott. This observation seems to return us to Rachels's claim that this lowered demand might result in a production decrease, where the "might" is now clearly understood in terms of expected outcome. This seems to put Rachels's position in a more favorable and persuasive light. But the issue is not thereby settled in Rachels's favor.

The reply does seem to helpfully clarify Rachels's position. In doing so, however, it reveals some further work that is needed before one should find the argument persuasive. One does not reason adequately about an expected (as opposed to a merely possible) outcome by focusing on a limited range of factors relevant to the overall evaluation. This, however, is what Rachels has provided, and this is not an adequate defense of his "might make a difference" claim interpreted as a claim about expected value.[18] In general, it does not follow from the fact that demand will go down if we focus just on the contributions of those who choose to boycott production that overall demand will go down (or that overall expected demand will decrease). This depends on a much wider range of issues than just the expected contributions of those new to a boycott.

Here is a somewhat flippant illustration of this fact. Several of my students who went vegan in high school have reported to me that mainly this led to their siblings and parents eating more meat.[19] The general point is one familiar to consequentialists thinking about a variety of issues. Consequentialists almost always stress the importance of thinking about "wide" outcomes in considering what to do rather than looking narrowly at how one's individual available courses of action would likely effect the outcome. Five people are in danger of drowning in the pool. If I attempt a rescue, I can rescue one of them. If I do not attempt a rescue, I will rescue no one. Attending solely to my possible contribution to a rescue effort, my attempting a rescue will do more good than my refraining from doing so. Does it follow that I should attempt a rescue? Those working broadly within consequentialism are quick to note that this conclusion does not follow. If my attempting rescue would result in my saving one but also result in fewer total being saved, then I should refrain from attempting rescue. How could this happen? Perhaps my efforts would hinder the efforts of other would-be rescuers who, without my interference, would rescue more total than are rescued by all of us if I attempt rescue. To properly evaluate "expected outcomes" we must attend broadly to all sorts of considerations. It is not adequate to consider only a few factors that seem to tend in one's preferred direction of argumentation. This appears to be what Rachels has done in defending his claim about the expected outcome of an individual beginning a boycott of the products of factory farming.

I have not here defended the view that Rachels's key "might" claim is false. Interpreted as the "bare possibility" claim, my position is that the claim is true but does not relevantly support the inference that Rachels is defending. Interpreted in this way it would prove far too much. Interpreted more naturally and I think faithfully as a claim about "rationally expected outcome," Rachels's "might" claim requires a far more sophisticated defense than has been provided for it. It certainly requires this before Rachels can conclude that his "no purchasing" conclusion is "fully rational" given the argument he has provided.

Conclusion

I think that if there is a strong argument to be had for the conclusion that it is wrong to consume the products of factory farming or for the conclusion that it is wrong to purchase the products of such farming, the argument should take a certain form. The argument should begin with a premise about the wrongness of factory farming practices and attempt to move from there to the desired conclusion about individual behavior. Using arguments from Alastair Norcross, Stuart Rachels, and David DeGrazia as examples of such attempts, I hope to have displayed some of the complexities involved in figuring out how best to state and defend such an argument. I conclude that these arguments as I have so far encountered them are unpersuasive. I do not speculate about whether or not the needed improvements are forthcoming in the near future.[20]

Notes

1. For some of the background information relevant to supporting this claim, see Singer and Mason (2007) and also Rachels (2011), which significantly leans upon Singer and Mason while providing some updated information. These resources are more up-to-date than older material from classic sources such as chapter two ("Down on the Factory Farm") of *Animal Liberation* (Singer 2009).
2. If factory farming were my focus, I would take up two issues. First, I would criticize arguments for the conclusion that what happens to animals during industrial animal processing is not properly called "torture," because "torture" is an essentially political concept and politics is not involved in industrial animal processing. I would deny both premises. Second, and more importantly, I would explore the question of what kinds of violence and destruction are morally permissible against industrial farming facilities. I would with some confidence defend the position that many such kinds of acts are morally permissible. So, if I'm the enemy of many mainstream "pro-animal" philosophers because of the conclusions I reach later in this chapter about a large class of arguments for mandatory personal veganism, then I am also the enemy of the enemy of these philosophers on many moral issues about factory farming.
3. For one brief but helpful discussion see DeGrazia (2009, p. 160ff).
4. See also Rachels (2011, pp. 884–885) with similarly clear and correct remarks about the need to say more about the connection between the institutional wrong of factory farming and any conclusion about individual obligations.
5. As will be discussed later, one might try to keep these issues connected via the observation that though purchasing and consuming can come apart, they typically go together.
6. Similarly, when the focus of a discussion is on meat eating generally rather than more narrowly on the issue of factory farmed meat, it is common to see acknowledgements such as this one from David DeGrazia (2009, p. 148): "My position does not oppose the consumption of, say, a dead animal one finds in the woods." Some who might object to freegan dumpster diving and the consumption of factory farmed products about to be thrown away are those who object to typical consumption on symbolic grounds rather than on the broadly consequentialist grounds I am focused

on in this chapter. Such symbolic arguments and related "stain of the past" arguments deserve attention they will not receive on this occasion. I do note, though, that the symbolism involved in freegan consumption does not seem to me to be the sort of symbolism that even fans of symbolic arguments for broadly pro-vegan positions should find objectionable.

7. Causal impotence objections have received some attention in the literature. The literature, however, focuses mostly on debates about the second item on my list of three "causal impotence" points. I would like to see more attention to various aspects of the causal isolationism issue (e.g., discussions of the difference between freegans and freeloaders raised shortly) and I would also like to see more explicit attention to differences in evaluating meat consumption and meat purchasing.

8. Philosophers who want to defend a mandatory veganism position via arguments that focus on purchasing might of course choose to take the no purchasing conclusion as a subconclusion on the way to a further conclusion (supported with one or more additional premises) to mandatory veganism. They might instead choose to defend a conclusion about "typical" meat eating (of factory farmed meat) rather than a universal no-meat eating conclusion. There are other options as well. My primary advice is therefore this: Be precise about what conclusion you are trying to defend in laying out arguments you call "pro-animal" or "pro-vegan." I also advise being clear about what one means by "vegan" if one claims to be arguing for something like "mandatory veganism." Is veganism consistent with freeganism? Is veganism compatible with purchasing but not consuming animal products?

9. I can't help observing how odd it will be if the best arguments for individual obligations to refrain from eating and/or purchasing the products of factory farms manage to float free from considerations about future directed considerations, such as the mistreatment of animals processed in that setting.

10. Norcross (2004), especially pp. 229–231. There is brief related discussion in DeGrazia (2002, p. 74) and also DeGrazia (2009, pp. 157–159).

11. Norcross (2004, p. 231). Norcross is well aware that freegans do not do anything like this. He therefore should charitably be read as arguing that typical consumers are acting wrongly in consuming factory farm products—freegans are not typical. I do not know what Norcross thinks about nonfreegans who never pay for meat they consume. I suspect he would not approve of their behavior.

12. I'm sure Norcross would be with me in advising those who want to try to solve the phone bill problem to refrain from attempting to do so by appeal to the differing *intentions* of the rice purchaser compared with the meat purchaser.

13. Let's also take note of the fact that nonmeat substitutes at stores and vegan options at restaurants typically have higher *profit margins* for the industry.

14. DeGrazia (2009, p. 158) has a brief but helpful discussion of the same main point as Rachels. Norcross also discusses a closely related point (2004, pp. 232–233).

15. I do not know what Rachels would say about those who consume factory farmed products only when those products are purchased by others. I'm confident that he would not want to give all such people a moral free pass, because I'm confident he would be sensitive to the points made earlier in comparing the freegan and the freeloader.

16. Rachels (2011, p. 885) actually puts this more narrowly, with the objection including an expression of hope that "the government will force agribusiness to change," but presumably the objection needn't express hope in government-driven change specifically.

17. Rachels (2011) defends this response after persuasively objecting to other responses to the argument that one finds in the literature. See especially his discussion at pp. 885–886.

18. I doubt that Rachels would disagree. The Rachels paper in question covers a wide range of issues and is not exclusively intended for specialists on these issues. Indeed,

the paper is probably not intended primarily even for philosophers. It is to his great credit that the paper contains discussions of importance to those with all sorts of differing backgrounds on the issues. This likely led him to sacrifice a bit of relevant detail on issues of most importance to the philosophical debates about central arguments.

19. Rachels (2011, p. 901) shows an awareness that he is oversimplifying when he notes that "if one group of consumers exits the market, prices will drop, and then the remaining consumers will buy more." He might also have added that new consumers may well enter the market. He makes this point in observing that eliminating twenty chicken purchases through boycott does not imply reducing overall demand by twenty. But he doesn't consider that such a move might not reduce overall demand *at all*.

20. This text closely descends from a talk delivered at the Central Division Meeting of the American Philosophical Association in 2012 as part of a lively symposium organized by Anja Jauernig on "meat eating" and related issues. The paper retains some of the conversational style of that presentation and includes minimal references. The other speakers in the session were Alastair Norcross and David DeGrazia, and so my remarks make special reference to the work of these fine philosophers. I have presented related material in various places, including, most memorably, the University of Missouri and Calvin College. I have benefitted from discussions of these issues with far too many people to thank individually. Matt Halteman, Amelia Hicks, and Graham Leach-Krouse are singled out for special mention as I have learned as much about these issues from them as almost anyone else. The co-editors of this volume provided impressively detailed feedback on an initial draft. Anja Jauernig helped me sharpen my thinking about these and related topics over several years of enjoyable discussion. I dedicate my chapter to Anja, who probably cares a bit too much about the issue, and to Leopold Stubenberg, who probably does not care quite enough.

References

DeGrazia, David. *Animal Rights: A Very Short Introduction*. Oxford: Oxford University Press, 2002.

———. "Moral Vegetarianism from a Very Broad Basis." *Journal of Moral Philosophy* 6 (2009): 143–165.

Norcross, Alastair. "Puppies, Pigs, and People: Eating Meat and Marginal Cases." *Philosophical Perspectives* 18 (2004): 229–245.

Rachels, Stuart. "Vegetarianism." In *The Oxford Handbook of Animal Ethics*, edited by T. L. Beauchamp and R. G. Frey, 877–905. Oxford: Oxford University Press, 2011.

Regan, Tom. *The Case for Animal Rights* (updated ed.). Berkeley: University of California Press, 2004.

Singer, Peter. *Animal Liberation* (reissued ed.). New York: Harper Perennial Modern Classics, 2009.

Singer, Peter, and Jim Mason. *The Ethics of What We Eat: Why Our Food Choices Matter*. Emmaus, PA: Rodale Books, 2007.

9

CONSUMER ETHICS, HARM FOOTPRINTS, AND THE EMPIRICAL DIMENSIONS OF FOOD CHOICES

Mark Bryant Budolfson

Food, Consumer Ethics, and Arguments Based on Harm Footprints

Consider the following pro-vegan reasoning, which is often endorsed by philosophers such as Peter Singer:

> Would you ever open your refrigerator, pull out 16 plates of pasta, toss 15 in the trash, and then eat just one plate of food? How about leveling 55 square feet of rain forest for a single meal or dumping 2,400 gallons of water down the drain? Of course you wouldn't. But if you're eating chickens, fish, turkeys, pigs, cows, milk, or eggs, that's what you're doing—wasting resources and destroying our environment.[1]

Like many arguments about consumer ethics, and like almost all pro-vegan arguments, this argument begins with an empirical premise about the harm footprint of actions of a particular type—namely, the action-type of *eating animal products*—and then draws the (implicit) conclusion that it would be wrong to perform actions of that type because of that harm footprint. However, even if we grant that the empirical premise is correct (as we should), there are a number of important objections to such footprint-based arguments.

To see the first objection, note the similarity between the pro-vegan argument just displayed and the following anti-vegan argument:

> Would you ever dump thousands of gallons of water down the drain, dump pollutants into our rivers, kill the creatures that inhabit our ecosystems, and impose the risk of debilitating injuries and serious violence on other human beings? Of course you wouldn't. But if you eat a vegan

meal—such as a familiar vegan meal that combines quinoa, greens, avocados, berries, and nuts—then that's what you're doing—wasting resources, destroying our environment, and harming people. Therefore, it is wrong to eat a vegan meal because of this serious harm footprint that lies behind a vegan meal.

Presumably, no one would think that this anti-vegan argument is a good argument, despite the fact that it relies on the same reasoning as the pro-vegan argument. So then what is wrong with this anti-vegan argument? Is the problem merely that its empirical premise is false about the harm footprint of vegan staples, whereas the empirical premise of the pro-vegan argument is true about the harm footprint of animal products?

Unfortunately for the pro-vegan argument, that cannot be the relevant difference between these two arguments, because the empirical premise of the anti-vegan argument is actually true—in particular, it is true that vegan staples have a surprisingly high harm footprint, just like animal products.[2] This is true, in part, because contemporary agriculture is surprisingly intensive in terms of the land, water, chemical fertilizers, pesticides, fossil fuels, migrant labor, and other inputs that it requires, where that intensity—even in the production of vegan staples— causes serious harms to humans, nonhuman animals, and other aspects of nature. Furthermore, some vegan staples are delivered by supply chains in which rape, torture, and murder of those who produce those goods is a common occurrence due to the predatory acts of the criminal gangs that control those supply chains.[3] And there is also a host of other harms that may also lie behind a vegan meal—for example, as one recurring example, demand from developed nations for a particular vegan staple might harm humans in lesser developed nations by pricing their hungry citizens out of the market for that nutritious staple, as has allegedly happened with staples such as quinoa, and other commodities such as corn that are also used in biofuel production.[4]

This points to a structural problem for the pro-vegan argument we started with, because even after the empirical facts become clear about the surprisingly high harm footprint associated with vegan meals, it does not immediately follow that it is wrong to eat such a meal—but such an inference seems to be exactly the inference that is made by the pro-vegan argument. Upon reflection, the underlying problem for such an inference is that the conclusion that it is wrong to consume X does not follow from the premise that X has a high harm footprint because, for one thing, the alternatives to X might have an equally high harm footprint or worse. This explains why it does not follow from the high harm footprint of vegan staples that it is wrong to eat those staples—but by the same token, it then does not immediately follow from the high harm footprint of animal products that it is wrong to eat them.

In light of this problem, defenders of the pro-vegan argument will presumably insist that the harm footprint of vegan staples is still *much lower than* that of animal products, which provides grounds for a more charitable reconstruction of the argument they endorse based on harm footprints:

Pro-Vegan Argument Based on Harm Footprints

Empirical Premise: The harm footprint of animal products is much worse than the alternatives—in particular, it is much worse than the harm footprint of vegan staples.

Conclusion: So, it is wrong to be a consumer of animal products when vegan alternatives are available.

Note that this argument is an instance of a more general form:

Consumer Ethics Argument Based on Harm Footprints

Empirical Premise: The harm footprint of X is much worse than the alternatives.

Conclusion: So, it is wrong to be a consumer of X when those alternatives are available.

As the empirical premise makes clear, a crucial question we need to ask in evaluating such arguments based on harm footprints is a *comparative* question about the difference in harm footprints between the good in question and its alternatives—for example, we need to ask what exactly is the difference in harm footprints between vegan staples and the alternatives involving animal products. This comparative question about vegan food and animal products will be my main focus in the rest of this chapter, along with analogous questions about the harm footprint of organic versus conventional food, and locally produced food versus food delivered by the conventional global supply chain.

But before delving deeper into these comparative, empirical questions about the harm footprints of food, it is worth noting a few general points that arise from the discussion so far: namely, that the crucial questions to ask when evaluating any consumer ethics argument based on harm footprints are, first, the empirical question of how the footprint of a particular good compares with the footprints of the alternatives; second, how important it is that we consume that general category of goods in the first place; and finally, whether and in what exact way ethical conclusions about how we should behave follow from facts about footprints.

To get a better feel for this last issue, which is the most philosophical issue in the neighborhood, it is worth taking the time to identify an important kind of general objection to arguments based on harm footprints: namely, that even if it were true that, for example, vegan staples always had a much lower harm footprint than the alternatives, it still wouldn't obviously follow that we should prefer to consume those goods, because it isn't obvious that minimizing our harm footprint is ultimately the best way to promote our ethical goals. This kind of objection arises from two independent considerations.

First, the harms captured in the notion of a harm footprint are only a subset of the things that ultimately matter, which means that at best harm footprints provide only *defeasible* reasons for choices—defeasible in the sense that those reasons can be outweighed by other reasons that derive from other things that matter more. For example, if there are occasions where vegan food can only be purchased at great expense to other things that matter more (e.g., where vegan food would require a two-hour detour to the nearest city center, which would take you away from projects that are very important from an ethical point of view), then vegan food may not be what it would be best for you to choose on that occasion, even if there are some genuine considerations based on harm footprints that tell in favor of vegan food, because those considerations, although genuine, can be outweighed. In other words, the idea that we should always act to minimize our harm footprint is mistaken because it overlooks the opportunity cost of doing so—sometimes minimizing the harm footprint of our food would be the wrong thing to do because it would come at the cost either of not doing nearly as much good as we could have done, or not avoiding doing nearly as much harm as we could have avoided doing.

Second, a deeper problem arises from the fact that the *footprint* of a particular act X is essentially a measure of the *average effect* of *all acts of the same type* as X—but there are impressive reasons to think that when making decisions, the average effects of the possible actions open to you are not what matters, and instead what matters are the *actual effects* of your specific acts (as opposed to the average effects of everyone's acts of that type). To illustrate the importance of this in the current context, consider John Robbins's claim in *The Food Revolution* that a pound of beef raised in California has a larger water footprint than taking a shower each day for six months; from this he immediately concludes that you can save more water by not eating a pound of beef than by not showering for six months.[5] The problem is that such a conclusion does not follow, because even if Robbins is correct about the footprint of eating a pound of beef—that is, the average effect of eating a pound of beef—it does not follow that you should expect the actual difference made by your action as a single individual to be equivalent to that average effect. Instead, what you do as a single individual might make no difference at all, or at least might make a difference that should be expected to be much less than the average effect. This example suggests that it is a fallacy to think that your decisions should be based on what the average effects of such actions would be, rather than what the actual effects of your actions would be—a fallacy that might be called the *Average Effects Fallacy*—and to avoid this fallacy, when making decisions what really matters are the actual effects of your actions, not the average effects as measured by footprint analyses.

With this objection in mind, we should be particularly worried about the *Inefficacy Objection* that what you do as a single consumer generally cannot be expected to have any effect on the harms that lie behind the goods you consume. This worry is particularly pressing, because it may seem to show that rather than engaging in futile *direct consumer action* such as boycotting goods with a high harm footprint, you can often do much better by ignoring the harm footprint of your actions and investing your resources more productively elsewhere, such as in *political advocacy* to change 'the system' that perpetuates those harms, or in charitable giving.[6] In short, the worry is that if your choices as an individual consumer cannot make any difference to the harms that lie behind the goods that you consume, and those harms are also not your fault in any ethically interesting sense, then perhaps they should not affect your consumer choices, and instead you should focus on what would actually be an effective way to make the world a better place.[7]

In what follows I set aside the general objections to arguments based on harm footprints that arise from the Average Effects Fallacy, the Inefficacy Objection, and other worries about the basic relevance of footprints to decision-making. I set aside these objections partly because I discuss them at length elsewhere, and partly to focus attention in the remainder of this chapter on the empirical facts relevant to pro-vegan, pro-organics, and pro-locavore arguments. So, in what follows, I will simply assume for the sake of argument that your primary concern should be the harm footprint of your actions, contrary to what the objections just discussed might seem to show.

I also set aside the other objection above based on the fact that the harms captured by harm footprints are only a subset of what ultimately matters, except to note that such an objection does seem to show that your ultimate goal in the domain of food should not generally be to *minimize* the harm footprint of your food choices, but rather to *optimize* your footprint given the other things that matter and thus the trade-offs that you will have to make to best promote our ultimate ethical goals.

As a result, in what follows I assume that your goal in the domain of food should be to keep your harm footprint below some threshold determined by the all-things-considered facts of what ultimately matters—in other words, your goal should be to keep your harm footprint *under budget*. This notion of keeping your footprint under budget is what we should expect not only on consequentialist views, but also on deontological views, where on such views the budget will be determined by the footprint of harm that can be justified to others, which on any plausible view will generally be greater than the minimum possible harm footprint you could obtain. And this notion of keeping your footprint under budget in the food domain is also consistent with the idea that you nonetheless have a duty to bring your overall harm footprint to zero by taking *offsetting* actions outside the domain of food—such as by purchasing carbon offsets. However, those actions and obligations outside the domain of food are beyond the scope of our concern here and would require a longer discussion to address adequately, and so I set them aside. I also set aside important questions about offsetting *within* the domain of food, such as whether it is permissible to continue to consume food that you enjoy very much if that food has a very high harm footprint, as long as you make offsetting sacrifices elsewhere in what you eat that keeps your overall harm footprint under budget within the domain of food—or whether instead there are some kinds of harm that lie behind food and other goods that create something more like a *permanent ethical stain* on anyone who consumes them, where that stain cannot be removed by offsetting. Again, I simply set aside these interesting and important issues in order to focus attention on the crucial empirical issues in the remainder of this chapter.[8]

The Empirical Dimensions of Vegan versus Omnivore

So, turning then to the crucial empirical issues, what should we make of the claim that the harm footprint involved in eating animal products is worse than the harm footprint involved in eating vegan staples?

It turns out that even if we ignore all of the other possible objections to the pro-vegan argument, this empirical claim is itself problematic, and is false in many cases. The source of the problem is the same as noted earlier: that even vegan staples have a surprisingly high harm footprint as a result of the land, water, chemical fertilizers, pesticides, fossil fuels, migrant labor, and other inputs that they require that cause serious harms to humans, nonhuman animals, and other aspects of nature. And when we carefully investigate the empirical facts about the harm footprints of vegan staples and compare them with the footprints associated with animal products, it turns out that many vegan staples do *worse* than animal product alternatives, and so it appears that an ethical consumer will reject the idea that food choices should be based simply on vegan principles. As a result, instead of being a *typical vegan*, it appears better to be an *altruistic omnivore* who pays careful attention to the particularities of the food products consumed, and who periodically judges that eating animal products is best.

To begin to see why, consider Figure 9.1, which compares the main kinds of harms that lie behind many general kinds of food.[9]

This chart expresses the harm footprint of various kinds of food in terms of their footprint *per unit of nutrition* along various dimensions, which paints a much more accurate picture than the presentations favored by pro-vegan sources in terms of footprint *per unit of product weight*, because animal products contain much more nutrition per unit of product weight than vegan alternatives. So, a presentation of footprints by product weight introduces a highly misleading pro-vegan bias.[10]

As the chart shows, there are regularities such that if your goal is to keep your harm footprint *under budget*—or if your goal is to *minimize* your harm footprint—you can do much better than by simply being a vegan, and you can

FOOTPRINT / UNIT OF NUTRITION

Mark Bryant Budolfson

	GHG		Land	Water		Other Pollution	Animal Harm	Human Worker Harm
	kg CO2eq / kg protein	kg CO2eq / 10,000 kcal	sq. meters / kg protein	liters / kg protein	liters / 10,000 kcal	(judgment) / unit of nut.	(judgment) / unit of nut.	(judgment) / unit of nut.
Beef	102	93	656	75969	60645			
Lamb	160	133	120	66985	42348			
Pork	46	51	51	30231	26104			
Chicken	25	29	28	11925	10316			
Farmed Salmon	54	58	7					
Mussels	6	8	2					
Eggs	38	31	36	12468	10951			
Milk	60	31	34	25270	13049			
Cheese	54	33	34	15843	9789			
Butter	42	3		131091	8669			
Lentils	10	8	20	22767	17125			
Beans	22	14	20	23590	14562			
Rice	116	24		28960	6000			
Tomato	125	61		24318	11889			
Potato	155	33		14208	3727			
Broccoli	71	59		10106	8382			
Carrots	33	8		20968	4756			
Oranges	51	8		80000	12174			
Bananas	45	6		72477	8876			
Peaches	45	11		100000	23333			
Strawberries	75	16		51791	10844			
Grapes	63	6		96508	9075			
Apples	135	7		316154	15808			
Almonds	11	4		76099	27798			
Peanuts	5	2		15403	7009			
Cabbage	25	13		21875	11200			
Lettuce	25	23		17426	15800			

FIGURE 9.1 The harm footprint along several dimensions for many common types of food.

Source: Author's calculations, available at HYPERLINK "http://www.budolfson.com/footprints" www.budolfson.com/footprints, based on data from Nijdam 2012, Hamerschlag 2011, CleanMetrics, and Mekonnen et al. 2011 and 2012 (see footnote 9).

do so by internalizing a strategy for eating that is much less costly to you than being a typical vegan. This is because in the food domain, as in every domain, the empirical facts really matter, and it can be surprising what really best promotes our ethical goals. As the numbers here indicate, adopting the simple intuitive strategy of eating vegan is highly suboptimal, and a more nuanced strategy is much better.

For example, suppose you have to decide between four meals that are on offer, where those meals are: (a) the vegan meal described above, combining pasta, quinoa, greens, avocados, berries, fruit, and nuts; (b) macaroni and cheese with vegetables—namely, carrots, beans, and greens; (c) grass-fed beef with the same vegetables; and (d) factory farmed chicken with the same vegetables. Suppose these four meals all cost the same and contain comparable protein, calories, and micronutrients—in other words, assume that they are comparable nutritionally, as could be the case if the portions of meat and cheese are modest. If we know nothing further about the source of these meals, it appears that we should expect (d) to have the best overall footprint, even though it is the farthest from the vegan ideal of the four options. Meal (d) is likely to be best because (a) has a high human harm footprint, due to the harm suffered by farm workers, especially in picking the berries and fruit, and in the supply chain that lies behind quinoa and especially avocados—and at the same time (a) also has a very high environmental footprint, due to the water and greenhouse gas footprint associated with many nuts, fruits, and vegetables, which are comparable or worse than, for example, the footprints of the factory farmed chicken per unit of nutrition. Meal (b) also appears inferior to (d), because the cheese that is at the center of the meal is as bad or worse than factory farmed chicken along every relevant dimension. Similarly, (c) appears worse than (d) because it is worse along every relevant dimension. Of particular note, (c) has a much worse environmental harm footprint than all of the other options, and some negative human-welfare footprint due to the injuries suffered by those who work in slaughterhouses, as well as an animal welfare footprint that is in the neighborhood of (a) and (b).

The upshot that this example illustrates is that, based on regularities in the harms that lie behind the food we eat, you can do much better by being an altruistic omnivore than by simply being a vegan, in the sense that the best meal to choose in our nonideal world is sometimes one that involves factory farmed meat even when nutritionally comparable vegan, ovo-lacto vegetarian, and humanely raised meat options are available at the same cost. Importantly, this is true even if we ignore the Average Effects Fallacy, the Inefficacy Objection, and other objections—which, if sound, only serve to further undermine pro-vegan arguments based on harm footprints.

The Importance of Considerations beyond Animal Welfare

One key issue highlighted by the discussion in the previous section is that trade-offs have to be made between human harms, animal harms, and environmental harms, and in making these trade-offs, everyone should grant the general ethical point—as do even utilitarians like Peter Singer—that suffering by a human, per unit of time, is generally much worse than the same duration of suffering by a chicken, in part because humans have capacities that chickens don't, which makes the suffering of a human worse, other things being equal.[11] In addition, most ethical views imply that humans count for more than chickens, and that humans have more ethical constraints on what can be permissibly done to them. As a result, any plausible view must be open to the idea that the harms to humans that lie behind many vegan staples might be worse than the harms to animals that lie behind a meal that involves, say, factory farmed chicken.

All of this is further supported by the fact that factory farms are becoming gradually more humane, led by both consumer pressure and regulation by progressive states like California that have enacted stricter regulations on factory farm conditions, such as regulations that require cages of approximately twice the size of the national average.[12] Furthermore, all of this is also consistent with thinking that the overall harm footprint associated with, say, pork is still worse on balance than the overall harm footprint of all fruits and vegetables, on the grounds that pigs have sufficiently higher moral status than chickens. The main point here is that *some* animal products such as chicken present a particularly pressing challenge to pro-vegan arguments in light of the trade-offs that have to be made—because although chickens are clearly sentient, they are also clearly not of anything like the same level of moral status as pigs or even cows (even on a utilitarian view like Peter Singer's),[13] and so it is at best unclear why their interests are always be taken to trump the interests of, for example, human workers in pro-vegan arguments.

Here it is important to emphasize—as it is not emphasized nearly enough—that in our actual food system many of the fruits and vegetables that we consume require intensive backbreaking work by humans to harvest, where that work is ultimately debilitating to many of those farm workers before they reach middle age (especially when harvesting involves constant bending over and other 'bad posture' movements, as in many kinds of berry harvesting), and is performed under conditions that also involve constant exposure to very large amounts of pesticides and harassment, very little access to medical or psychological treatment of any kind, and inadequate access even to basic requirements for human dignity, such as bathrooms.[14] In the case of female farm workers, this also includes a pervasive environment of sexual harassment and sexual assault.[15] With these serious harms to humans clearly in mind, it is difficult to see how harms to chickens could be thought to outweigh these human harms in a way that is so obvious that it requires no further argument, as pro-vegan arguments generally presuppose.[16]

In response, it could be argued that migrant farm workers have freely consented to the work that they perform, and so that work must make them better off by their own lights—and thus no harm is done to them, at least not in the sense that a utilitarian should worry about. However, the actual testimony of migrant workers suggests that this argument is mistaken in a number of important ways.

For example, even setting aside the question of whether migrant workers should be interpreted as *freely consenting* to their labor market choices, when people choose to become migrant workers, they are typically mistaken about how this will actually benefit or harm them in the future, because they often have highly misleading evidence about what to expect.[17] When they are subsequently asked, after working as migrant workers for several years, whether they would make the same choice if they could do it all over again, they often emphatically insist that they would not—instead, common complaints are that (1) they are not actually making the kind of money that they expected; (2) they have become trapped in this labor market, far away from home, with no feasible way out; and (3) they are suffering significant and unexpected harms. So, they often do not see their choice to become a migrant worker as having made them better off by their own lights. In addition, the most serious harms that they will suffer will manifest themselves only later, insofar as they are incapacitated either by chronic illness or injury, and so are not yet even taken into account. In light of this, and the magnitude of the harms at issue, it would be a dramatic mistake to assume our current system of migrant farm labor makes those workers better off by their own lights.[18]

Furthermore, even if your only goal was to minimize your animal harm footprint (and so you didn't care at all about human harm or other kinds of harm), nonetheless vegan staples generally have a worse animal harm footprint than some specific animal products, such as mussels (as the chart above indicates). This is because many vegan staples have substantial land and water footprints, which means that they take away land and water from wildlife, which can lead to serious harm to those animals. In contrast, mussels have essentially no animal harm footprint at all—partly because mussels are not conscious and so harvesting them does not involve animal harm that has any important weight, and partly because the land and water footprint of mussels is miniscule, and much lower than many vegan staples.[19]

This illustrates perhaps the most important general point in this chapter, which is that the empirical details really matter and things are far more complicated than they initially appear, even for a conscientious ethical thinker. If one aspires to be an ethical consumer, it is crucial to investigate the nuances and counterintuitive facts that are essential for doing what is genuinely best, rather than unintentionally doing what is worse.

Effective Altruism, Information, and Individual Action

It is important to emphasize that many of these important nuances are obscured by the chart above, which does not offer the kind of 'disaggregated' data that choices should be based on when available—disaggregated data such as, for example, the footprint of Roma tomatoes from a particular producer in Mexico purchased in August 2012 in Williston, North Dakota, when considering buying tomatoes of that type at that time and location—and data on how that footprint compares to the other specific substitutes available at that time and location. As another example, consider that grass-fed beef has a much worse environmental footprint than the numbers indicate in the chart above, because the numbers in the chart are essentially based on the footprint of conventional beef—whereas the environmental footprint of grass-fed beef is many times worse than conventional according to most calculations. In contrast, the environmental footprint of organic chicken is only about 10 percent worse than conventional factory farmed chicken.[20] (Conventional production is essentially the basis for the numbers in the chart, as the numbers in the chart are based on an average for all goods of the general type actually produced, where actual production is dominated by conventional production.) As a result, if you believe it is permissible to sometimes eat meat beyond fish and mollusks, but you also believe (as you should) that animal welfare is a very important consideration, then it is important to know that organic chicken appears to be a better choice than the organic meat alternatives along every dimension relevant to harm footprint, especially with respect to environmental footprint.

At this point, an important objection to consider is that the costs of obtaining this kind of nuanced information is prohibitively high, given that investing scarce resources of time and attention elsewhere might yield greater returns. In response to this objection, it should be granted that insofar as it is true that investing elsewhere should be expected to pay greater dividends even when what ultimately matters is taken properly into account—which might, on some ethical views, include 'agent-relative' prohibitions on performing particular acts *yourself* that have a high harm footprint—then it is true that you should not invest further in gathering information in the domain of food.

But at the same time, becoming a more educated and more responsible consumer is not difficult, and appears ethically required up to some threshold, partly because of its low opportunity cost up to that threshold, and partly because there is a general ethical requirement that we educate ourselves enough to be confident that when we act, we are not doing unjustifiable harm, at least when the cost of educating ourselves is low. As anyone who investigates supply chains can attest, although it is generally difficult or impossible to get *fully* satisfactory information on the harms that lie behind the goods we consume, nonetheless there is a large amount of information that is easily available and sufficient to draw *some* ethical conclusions. For example, even if it is difficult to get fully satisfactory information on all of the food options available to us, nonetheless there is enough information easily available to show that, for example, eating veal is a mistake from an ethical point of view. More importantly, as the discussions in this chapter indicate, there appears to be enough information available to know a number of more surprising and counterintuitive facts about what food choices are best: for example, that vegan staples are often much worse than some animal products, that organics are generally worse for the environment than conventionals, and other facts that emerge from the considerations discussed in this chapter.

In general, there is often no more significant cost to becoming educated about the nuanced facts about the footprints of food than there is to becoming educated on more specific facts about animal harms on factory farms—and it is often possible to access even the kind of highly disaggregated information about the footprint of food that is an ideal basis for decision-making.[21] In other words, even if you are not required to know everything about the harm footprints of food, you should still know—based on easily accessible facts, including facts about migrant workers—that strawberries have a much worse harm footprint than mussels. Similar remarks apply to a wide range of food. The fact that it is impossible to know everything is no excuse for not knowing anything, especially if the harm you impose on others increases with your ignorance.

With the ideal of highly disaggregated information in mind, a public policy initiative should be to require such information to be made readily available regarding most of the food and other goods that we purchase. Despite initial appearances, this initiative would not be as costly as it may initially appear, because most of the relevant infrastructure is already in place and much of the relevant data are already tracked throughout the supply chain by the firms involved, either for purposes of profit-maximization or for other regulatory purposes, and could thus be made readily available in machine-readable format to consumers and others at little additional cost. This could be done simply by requiring, for example, a link to that information via an optical code on goods, which consumers could scan with smartphones. (Japan has already done this for beef, and some other consumer information.) Social entrepreneurs could then build applications to read this data and aid in our food choices, partly by performing comparisons and calculations that import additional data from academic, government, and nonprofit research—perhaps also offering 'ethical algorithms' for making trade-offs between different kinds of harm footprints and arriving at an all-things-considered recommendation about what to buy.[22] As with other increases in transparency and consumer consciousness-raising, the collective result would be a shift in demand sufficient to make a large positive difference that significantly reduces the harms that lie behind the food and other goods that we consume, and this shift can be accelerated by this kind of virtuous social entrepreneurship.

As this sort of example reinforces, as a single individual you might be able to do much more good by carefully investing in promoting these kind of policy changes and entrepreneurship than by taking more direct consumer action to lower your harm footprint—which illustrates that advocacy toward policy change and entrepreneurship are often better from an ethical point of view than direct action—and, again, this is true even if we ignore the Inefficacy Objection.

The Empirical Dimensions of Organic-Local versus Conventional-Global

In response to all of the preceding, some people would insist that the correct lesson to draw is very different than what has been suggested so far, and that instead the correct lesson is that we need to shift away from contemporary intensive agriculture and move back toward more traditional organic farming methods that avoid chemical fertilizers, pesticides, and the inputs that drive many of the surprisingly high harm footprints of vegan staples.

There are two main objections to this pro-organics view. The first objection is that such a pro-organics view is mistaken about the relevant empirical facts. In particular, although it is true that organics may be better for the environment than conventionals *in some locations and with respect to some food products*, and although it may be generally true that organic methods produce less environmental harms *per cultivated acre*, nonetheless, all things considered, organics are generally *worse* for the environment than conventionals, because organics have lower yields, and when the lower yields per cultivated acre are taken into account, it is generally true that organic methods produce more environmental harms of most kinds *per unit of product* than conventional methods—which, according to this objection, should surely be the relevant measure of whether organics are better for the environment than conventionals.[23] This is true because the lower yields of organics imply that shifting toward organics means increasing the amount of the Earth's land that must be devoted to agriculture, which is bad for the environment in myriad ways—from destruction of ecosystems and loss of biodiversity as a result of increased land use, to turning carbon sinks into sources of carbon emissions, and many others.[24] Furthermore, some studies indicate that in addition to being generally no better *for the environment*, organics are also generally no better *for human consumers* than conventionals: Organics are generally no more nutritious than conventionals (with exceptions in some locations with respect to some particular products), and organics do not help avoid pesticide levels that have been found to be a threat to human health (with exceptions in some locations with respect to some particular products).[25]

The second main objection to the view that we should move heavily to organics is that even if such a pro-organics view were not mistaken about the empirical facts, it would still be mistaken as an answer to the question of what we should do, because it mistakenly assumes that we have no important goals beyond simply minimizing our footprint on the environment. But on the contrary, we have a number of additional goals that are much more important—for example, we have the goal of *feeding the entire world*, and not merely feeding wealthy people who can afford to shop at farmers' markets. This leads to a serious problem for the pro-organics response, because if we shifted heavily toward organic methods of farming, it appears that we would not have nearly enough food to feed the world, given the world's growing population and growing affluence, which makes for a growing demand for meat, as well as a growing demand for renewable energy, which is provided in part by biofuels, which subtract from the agricultural output available as food.[26]

In reply to these arguments that we need more intensive agriculture to feed the world, many on the pro-organics side insist that such arguments assume that too many regrettable aspects of our current world are unchangeable, including regrettable facts about increasing consumption of meat, regrettable facts about climate change, and perhaps also other regrettable background facts such as the use of biofuels and the general background of the congressional-agribusiness-industrial complex. Instead of taking these things as fixed, many on the pro-organics side insist that the only sustainable way forward is to turn away dramatically from these aspects of the status quo: In particular, they insist that we must reduce our consumption of meat and we must combat climate change effectively, which would then allow us to feed the world via organic farming methods. More generally, along these lines it could be argued that a world with dramatically reduced meat consumption and global organic agriculture is a key part of the outcome that is ideally best for the world, because it represents the food system that is part of the best possible outcome for humanity given the basic physical constraints of our world.

On the other hand, it could be noted that even if we agreed that the ideally best outcome would involve organics heavily in this way, nothing would immediately follow about what we should actually do. In particular, even if we agree that the ideally best outcome would involve the conjunction of (a) reducing people's preferences for meat, (b) reducing people's preferences for fossil fuels, and (c) moving our agricultural production heavily toward organics, nonetheless it does not follow that we should actually try to bring about (a), (b), and (c). That is because if the predictable effect of a policy portfolio that aims for (a), (b), and (c) is that we will fail to succeed in bringing about both (a) and (b), then insofar as we do succeed in bringing about (c), the main effects will be to malnourish the world's poor while the rich continue to eat meat, and to increase use of land for agriculture, and thus accelerate destruction of ecosystems and increases in atmospheric greenhouse gas concentrations. As a result, trying to adopt such a portfolio of policies does not seem to be what we should actually do even if we agree that it aims most directly at the ideally best outcome.

Furthermore, because it is foreseeable that such a simple-minded approach to policy making would have this downside with no realistic upside, such policy making would be an example of *counterproductive altruism*, in which well-intentioned idealism is paired with a lack of serious concern for the empirical facts in a way that makes our goals much worse achieved than they could have been, and at worst is catastrophically counterproductive.[27]

With counterproductive altruism in mind, it is useful to consider Marion Nestle's answer to the question of what food choices you should make:

> When you choose organics, you are voting with your fork for a planet with fewer pesticides, richer soil, and cleaner water supplies—all better in the long run. When you choose locally grown produce, you are voting for conservation of fuel resources and the economic viability of local communities, along with freshness and better taste. Once you consider such

things, the choices in the produce section are much easier to make. Whenever I have the choice, here are my priorities in that section: (1) organic
and locally grown, (2) organic, (3) conventional and locally grown, (4)
conventional.[28]

Unfortunately, the pro-organic and pro-locavore strategy that Nestle advocates appears to be counterproductive altruism: As we've just seen, voting with
your fork for organics is much less like voting in favor of admirable environmental goals and much more like voting in favor of starvation and greater destruction of the natural world. That is because, first, as we saw above, a move toward
organics should be expected to make things worse for both humanity and the
overall environment, which are ultimately more important than the other narrow goals that Nestle mentions—which in any event are not clearly better promoted by organics given a close examination of the evidence.

Second, it is also generally counterproductive to be a *locavore* and strongly
prefer consuming locally produced foods, because those foods generally have a
higher carbon footprint than their nonlocal substitutes, given lesser efficiencies in
the supply chain for production and transportation of local foods.[29] For example,
because the miles you drive back and forth to buy your food are a disproportionately large part of the transportation-related footprint of what you buy, biking to
the store is a more effective way of reducing the carbon footprint of your food.
And with that in mind, it turns out that biking to the conventional grocery
store and buying food generally has a lower carbon footprint than biking to the
farmers' market and buying the same basket of food, because the local food at
the farmers' market will generally have a higher carbon footprint independent
of your own transportation choices.[30] As a result, it appears that an ethical consumer should not generally follow Nestle's advice—and, to a first approximation,
should generally follow the opposite advice instead.

Conclusion

In sum, we've seen that in the domain of food, as in every domain of practical
ethics, the empirical facts really matter and things are far more complicated than
they initially appear, and it is crucial to investigate these nuances in order to
determine what actions are genuinely best, and to avoid unintentionally doing
what is worse. Beyond that, some more substantive conclusions have been suggested. For example, we've seen that there are fundamental objections to the
ethical relevance of harm footprints. And, even if we set those objections aside,
as individual consumers we've seen why it is better to be an altruistic omnivore
than a typical vegan.

As a final note, it is worth noting that the strategy outlined here of being an
altruistic omnivore may not be the best strategy to preach to the world, even if it
represents the truth about what individuals ought to do. For one thing, here as in

many cases in social philosophy, 'morality may not be enough,' in the sense that what is needed most are diverse initiatives from social entrepreneurs and activists who act in the public good above and beyond the call of ethical duty, where their collective actions change the system and move us in the right direction.[31] Many of these innovators are motivated by a higher calling than mere ethics, while some others are motivated by a mistakenly demanding conception of what ethics requires. Furthermore, with respect to even the educated masses who will not take the lead in these ways, the truth about ethics is probably insufficiently inspiring and catchy to motivate them in the way that is best. So, it is important to consider what 'short attention span' principles are most likely to capture their imagination and motivate them with the best results. In light of all the preceding, and with some inspiration from Michael Pollan, perhaps the best message to preach is something like the following:

> Eat food, mostly plants—but not too much food, and not too much harm in the background: keep both under budget.[32]

Notes

Thanks to Tyler Doggett, Ben Miller, Tristram McPherson, Eliot Michaelson, and David Plunkett for especially generous discussions of these issues. Thanks also to Henrik Ahlenius, Agi Andor, Alexander Berger, Andrew Chignell, Terence Cuneo, Johannes Findl, Blake Francis, Sarah Hannan, RJ Leland, Genoveva Marti, Emily Martin, Conor McHugh, Alison Nihart, Rob Reich, Danny Shahar, Peter Singer, and an audience at the Universitat de Barcelona. For a more in-depth discussion of these and related issues, see my paper "Effective Altruism, Food, and the Environment," forthcoming in the *Oxford Handbook of Food Ethics*, edited by Anne Barnhill, Mark Bryant Budolfson, and Tyler Doggett (Oxford: Oxford University Press).

1. This is a quote from People for the Ethical Treatment of Animals (PETA), "Meat and the Environment," http://www.peta.org/issues/animals-used-for-food/meat-environment. Compare Singer, P., *Practical Ethics* (3rd ed.), Cambridge: Cambridge University Press, 2011, pp. 54–56; Singer's conclusion is that we should endorse something "very close to a vegan way of life" (p. 56). See also Singer, P. and Mason, J., *The Ethics of What We Eat*, Emmaus, PA: Rodale, 2007, especially chapters 17 and 18.
2. For more detail, see Figure 9.1, along with the ensuing discussion and references.
3. De Cordoba, J., "The Violent Gang Wars Behind Your Super Bowl Guacamole," *Wall Street Journal*, January 31, 2014; Holmes, S., *Fresh Fruit, Broken Bodies*, Berkeley: University of California Press, 2013; Waugh, I. M., "Examining the Sexual Harassment Experiences of Mexican Immigrant Farmworking Women," *Violence Against Women* 16, no. 3 (2010): 237–261.
4. Romero, S. and Shahriari, S., "Quinoa's Global Success Creates Quandary at Home," *New York Times*, March 19, 2011; for some critical discussion, Paarlberg, R., *Food Politics* (2nd ed.), Oxford: Oxford University Press, 2013.
5. Robbins, J., *The Food Revolution* (10th anniversary ed.), Berkeley, CA: Conari Press, 2010, pp. 236–237.
6. Note that there is not an interesting "but what if everyone did that?" objection to this advice, because if everyone followed the advice not to take direct action but merely to politically support the best policies and otherwise do what is best, the

world's problems would largely be solved by policy supported by all—which appears to be the best solution to these problems that we could hope for.

7. I discuss these issues at length in a number of papers. For a focused discussion of the Inefficacy Objection and evaluation of an important reply to that objection by Peter Singer (which has also been endorsed by Alastair Norcross and Shelly Kagan), see my paper "The Inefficacy Objection to Consequentialism and the Problem with the Expected Consequences Response," forthcoming in *Philosophical Studies*; see also "The Inefficacy Objection to Deontology," and "Collective Action, Climate Change, and the Ethical Significance of Futility," both unpublished.

8. I discuss some related ethical questions about offsetting in my paper "Global Justice, Political Realism, and the Ethics of Collective Action," unpublished.

9. The spreadsheet that contains the relevant calculations, data sources, and a description of the methodology behind this chart is available at http://www.budolfson. com/footprints. In brief, the numbers are based on the best data easily available, including in peer-reviewed sources, and the cells that do not have numbers are based on my own judgment, which aims for empirical accuracy, which the reader can judge for himself or herself, perhaps in conjunction with my more detailed explanation of the methodology. The shading is done by the default three-color shading algorithm in Microsoft Excel 2010. Main sources of numerical data are Nijdam, D. et al., "The Price of Protein: Review of Land Use and Carbon Footprints from Lifecycle Assessments of Animal Food Products and Their Substitutes," *Food Policy* 37, no. 6 (2012): 760–770; Hamerschlag, K., "What You Eat Matters," Environmental Working Group, 2011, accessed at static.ewg.org/reports/2011/ meateaters/pdf/report_ewg_meat_eaters_guide_to_health_and_climate_2011.pdf; CleanMetrics greenhouse gas footprint data, accessed at http://www.foodemissions. com/foodemissions/Calculator.aspx; Mekonnen, M. et al., "The Green, Blue, and Grey Water Footprint of Crops and Derived Crop Products," *Hydrology and Earth System Sciences* 15 (2011): 1577–1600; Mekonnen, M. et al., "A Global Assessment of the Water Footprint of Farm Animal Products," *Ecosystems* 15 (2012): 401–415; and the USDA National Nutrient Database for Standard Reference, accessed at http:// ndb.nal.usda.gov. Of particular note, the specific numbers for greenhouse gas footprints that I use from Hamerschlag and CleanMetrics are near the median estimates reported in Nijdam, which is a survey of the peer-reviewed literature on land and greenhouse gas footprints, are also in line with the numbers reported in other peer-reviewed publications, and the numbers in Hamerschlag are used for the main goal of advancing a pro-vegan argument; so, for all of these reasons, there is no risk that these numbers have an anti-vegan bias.

10. It is standard in the peer-reviewed scientific literature (such as the articles cited in note 9) to express the footprints of food in per unit of nutrition terms.

11. Singer, *Practical Ethics*, pp. 51–53.

12. See Strom, S. "Wishing They All Could Be California Hens," *New York Times*, March 3, 2014.

13. Singer, *Practical Ethics*, pp. 101–104.

14. Holmes, *Fresh Fruit, Broken Bodies*; Eric Schlosser, *Fast Food Nation*, Boston: Houghton Mifflin, 2001; Barry Estabrook, *Tomatoland*, Kansas City, MO: McMeel, 2012.

15. Waugh, I. M., "Examining the Sexual Harassment Experiences of Mexican Immigrant Farmworking Women," *Violence Against Women*, 2010.

16. For example, Peter Singer's main pro-vegan argument in *Practical Ethics* is: "In considering the ethics of the use of animal products for human food in industrialized societies, we are considering a situation in which a relatively minor human interest must be balanced against the lives and welfare of the animals involved. The principle of equal consideration of interests does not allow major interests to be sacrificed for minor interests. . . . [Therefore, the correct conclusion is to live] very close to a vegan way of life" (pp. 54, 56).

17. For more theoretical discussion of how this sort of situation, and related situations, can lead people to freely choose options that predictably make them worse off, see the literature in economics on asymmetric information and market failure—for example, Stiglitz, J., "Information and the Change in the Paradigm in Economics" (Nobel Prize Lecture), *American Economic Review* 92, no. 3 (2002): 460–501.

18. For further discussion and evidence for these claims, see Holmes, *Fresh Fruit, Broken Bodies*. A question noted by an anonymous reviewer, which I lack the space to discuss here, is the extent to which some farm workers might be seen as partially ethically responsible for harms (e.g., slaughterhouse workers), despite their poverty and diminished labor options.

19. Peter Singer and Jim Mason agree that it is *permissible* to eat mussels and other sustainably sourced mollusks in *The Ethics of What We Eat* (Emmaus, PA: Rodale, 2007), but beyond this judgment of mere permissibility, they do not seem to appreciate the *substantial superiority* of mussels and some other animal products to many vegan staples, even on a purely utilitarian view.

20. For discussion of these numbers regarding grass-fed beef and organic chicken, see Nijdam et al., "The Price of Protein," especially pp. 763–764; see also Herrero, M. et al., "Biomass Use, Feed Efficiencies, and Greenhouse Gas Emissions from Global Livestock Systems," *Proceedings of the National Academy of Sciences* 110, no. 52 (2013): 20888–20893.

21. For example, see the Environmental Working Group application and website "Food Scores," http://www.ewg.org/foodscores; the Monterey Bay Aquarium campaign "Seafood Watch," www.seafoodwatch.org; and the Buycott application available at www.buycott.com. The "Food Scores" app was released after the initial version of this paper was submitted, and may be the closest real-world example in the domain of food to the kind of social entrepreneurship suggested here—but still falls short of the ideal, as it does not take into account some important dimensions of harm footprints, such as animal welfare and human worker harm footprints—and is not based on fully disaggregated information (although it does an admirable job moving us in that direction given limited publicly available information).

22. See the examples of applications using this data in the previous footnote. Compare also Cass Sunstein on the importance of government data being made readily available in machine readable format in *Simpler: The Future of Government*, New York: Simon & Schuster, 2013.

23. Tuomisto, H.L. et al. "Does Organic Farming Reduce Environmental Impacts? A Meta-Analysis of European Research," *Journal of Environmental Management* 112 (2012): 309–320; Mondelaers, K. et al., "A Meta-analysis of the Differences in Environmental Impacts between Organic and Conventional Farming," *British Food Journal* 111, no. 10 (2009): 1098–1119; Fischer, T. et al., *Cropyields and Global Food Security*, Canberra: ACIAR Press, 2014.

24. Seufert, V. et al., "Comparing the Yields of Organic and Conventional Agriculture," *Nature* 485 (2012): 229–232; Fischer, *Cropyields and Global Food Security*; Burney, J. et al., "Greenhouse Gas Mitigation by Agricultural Intensification," *Proceedings of the National Academy of Sciences* 107, no. 26 (2010): 12052–12057.

25. Smith-Spangler. C. et al., "Are Organic Foods Safer or Healthier than Conventional Alternatives? A Systematic Review," *Annals of Internal Medicine* 157, no. 5 (2012): 348–366. Again, there are sometimes wide differences with respect to nutrition between particular items bought at a particular time at a particular location, due partly to the fact that nutrients decay quickly after harvest in some foods; for some of these, see Frith, K., "Is Local Food More Nutritious? It Depends," Harvard Center for Health and the Global Environment, 2007, accessed at http://chge.med.harvard.edu/resource/local-more-nutritious. Similarly there are sometimes wide and systematic differences with respect to pesticide levels; for some of these, see the Environmental

Working Group report on pesticides in food, accessed at http://www.ewg.org/food-news/summary.php.

26. Godfray, H.C.J. et al., "Food Security: The Challenge of Feeding 9 Billion People," *Science* 327 (2010): 812–818; Foley, J., "A Five-Step Plan to Feed the World," *National Geographic*, May 2014.

27. The intended contrast with counterproductive altruism is *effective altruism*. For discussion of these issues and related issues through the lens of effective altruism, see my paper "Effective Altruism, Food, and the Environment," forthcoming in the *Oxford Handbook of Food Ethics*, edited by Anne Barnhill, Mark Bryant Budolfson, and Tyler Doggett (Oxford: Oxford University Press).

28. Nestle, M., *What to Eat*, New York: North Point Press, 2006, p. 66.

29. For a good overview of why this is true, see Venkat, K., "Do Organics Have a Lower Carbon Footprint?," *CleanMetrics* (blog), April 11, 2010, http://cleanmetrics. typepad.com/green_metrics_clean_metri/2010/04/do-organics-have-a-lower-carbon-footprint.html; Sexton, S., "The Inefficiency of Local Food," *Freakonomics* (blog), November 14, 2011, http://freakonomics.com/2011/11/14/the-inefficiency-of-local-food; see also Wakeland, W. et al., "Food Transportation Issues and Reducing Carbon Footprint," in Boye, J. and Arcand, Y., eds., *Green Technologies in Food Production and Processing*, New York: Springer, 2012, and the discussion and references in Fischer, *Cropyields and Global Food Security*.

30. Wakeland, W. et al., "Food Transportation Issues and Reducing Carbon Footprint."

31. I discuss philosophical reasons why everyone doing what is required sometimes does not lead to our goals being satisfied in my paper "Why Morality and Other Forms of Normativity Are Sometimes Dramatically Directly Collectively Self-Defeating," unpublished.

32. Compare Pollan, M., *Food Rules*, New York: Penguin, 2009, where the main advice is "Eat food, mostly plants, not too much," but where "not too much" is meant only to mean 'not too much food.' Keeping your harm footprint under budget can also be aided by minimizing food waste, minimizing consumption of packaging that itself has a high footprint when there are not strong reasons for consuming such packaging, and other actions that I lack the space to discuss at length here, but which are important parts of a more complete discussion of harm footprints and the ethics of food choices.

10

CAN WE REALLY VOTE WITH OUR FORKS?

Opportunism and the Threshold Chicken

Andrew Chignell

> Becoming a vegetarian is not merely a symbolic gesture. . . . Becoming *a vegetarian is a highly practical and effective step one can take toward ending both the killing of non-human animals and the infliction of suffering upon them.*
>
> —*Peter Singer, Animal Liberation*

Opportunism

Consider Oppy, an average, middle-aged guy who skims a few of Mark Bittman's pieces in the *New York Times* and starts to worry that what he buys and eats somehow contributes to the global supremacy of the industrial "meat-guzzler."[1] One day he comes across Michael Pollan's *Omnivore's Dilemma* in an airport bookstore and spends his whole flight devouring it. As he learns more about the industrial food system from Pollan, he becomes increasingly alarmed by its treatment of animals and workers, its reliance on government-subsidized corn and soy, its use of lobbyists to gain preferential treatment from lawmakers, and its effects on family farmers, local economies, and the environment.[2] Oppy gets off the flight feeling genuinely engaged by the issue for the first time: He now regards much of the treatment of animals and workers in the industrial agriculture system as wrong, and as a result he intends to donate to an animal sanctuary and spend his free time advocating on behalf of local undocumented workers.

But despite Pollan's apparent optimism about our ability to vote against the industrial food system with our forks (or pocketbooks),[3] Oppy's subsequent research makes him aware of an important, sobering fact. The industrial food system is not only massive, global, and opaque to most individual consumers, it is also *deeply insensitive to slight changes in demand*. In other words, the purchasing choices of an individual consumer are extremely unlikely even to *register* in such a way as to effect any change at the level of production.[4]

So one day Oppy finds himself in a faraway town where he knows no one, and also finds that he *really* wants one of those spicy deep-fried golden-brown fast-food chicken sandwiches. Although he is morally opposed to the system that produces such food, and deeply invested in bringing about its reform or demise, he also knows, given the empirical facts about how purchase orders are made and how much waste and buffer there is at each step, that his individual purchase will *almost certainly have no effect at all* on the larger system. To him, the purchase of a chicken sandwich in that faraway town is equivalent, morally speaking, to eating a sandwich that just fell out of a speeding delivery truck.[5] So Oppy seizes the opportunity to purchase, take, and eat.

How should we evaluate Oppy's decision? Is it wrong to *benefit by consuming the products* of wrongful activities on the part of others?

Note that this question is different from the question of whether it is wrong to benefit *in any way* from wrongdoing on the part of others. The answer to that question is almost certainly "No": Most of what we use and value, including our very existence, is the result of past wrongdoing (my parents wouldn't have met if the Germans hadn't invaded Poland in 1939, for example). The focus here is rather on this question:

> Is it wrong to benefit by consuming the *products* of an activity that we know to be morally wrong, where *a constitutive aim of that activity is to generate those products*?[6]

By "constitutive aim" I just mean an aim that is an explicit part of the rationale for engaging in the activity. For example: Many of our cheap vegetables come from large farms that employ undocumented workers in abject working conditions, and arguably the main goal in employing those workers in such conditions is to produce those vegetables cheaply and sell them to consumers. If we assume that the people running the farms in that way are doing something wrong, we can then ask: Is it also wrong for the rest of us to benefit by consuming the products of that activity?

I will use "opportunistic" here to characterize acts in which

(a) the agent *benefits* by
(b) *consuming* products of activity on the part of others that
(c) the agent *knows to be morally wrong*, and where
(d) generating those products is a *constitutive aim* of the activity in question.[7]

Reflection on cases in which someone receives a gift, wins a prize, or finds something in a dumpster reveals, I think, that most of us take opportunistic eating to be permitted in some circumstances. "Freegans," for instance, have no problem consuming food that results from what they regard as wrongful activities on the part of others, even though they would never produce, hunt for, or purchase those items on their own.[8] To them, and to most of us who consider cases like these, *receiving* and *finding* kinds of opportunism seem intuitively permissible.[9]

The most natural and obvious way to account for this intuition, I think, is in terms of *economic nonparticipation*. The gift-recipient, roadkill-itarian, or freegan is not *financially supporting* the wrongful activity but rather merely absorbing its excess products. In fact, these ways of being involved in the system might make the whole situation *better*, since they at least prevent the products of the system from going to waste.[10] But, again, what about those of us who benefit from a morally wrongful system or activity by *purchasing* its products? Can *that* ever count as a form of permissible opportunism?

My main goal in this chapter is to discuss this question—the question of whether and why opportunistic *purchasing* is different from opportunistic *accepting* or *finding*. It turns out (or so I will suggest) that in a massive, global system that is insensitive to slight changes in demand, it is hard to find a good argument according to which it is always wrong to *purchase* the products of what one knows to be a morally wrongful activity. A key case to consider here is that of a choice on a "threshold"—that is, a choice that, even in an insensitive supply system, does have a significant causal effect on the human workers or nonhuman animals involved in that system. It turns out (or so I will suggest) that even in that case it is surprisingly hard to find a good argument for the claim that we ought to strictly refrain from purchasing, provided we do not *know* that we are on the threshold. In the final section of this chapter, I briefly consider whether the notions of *symbolic value* or *collective obligation* provide additional resources against the purchasing variety of the opportunistic urge.

A final preliminary note: Oppy is not merely the inhabitant of an arcane philosopher's thought-experiment. My own nonscientific surveys of dozens of college students and friends suggest that "it won't really make a difference" (given the insensitivity of the present system) is *often* cited in the moment as the morally sufficient reason for occasional purchasing, even by those who are otherwise concerned about human and animal welfare in the industrial food system. So Oppy is not unusual: opportunism of this sort is widespread, tempting, and plausible-seeming to many of us (present author included).

Opportunistic Purchasing: The Basic Argument in Favor

As we have seen, here is what Oppy is thinking:

> *Opportunistic Purchasing*—Given the insensitivity of the industrial food system (IFS), the occasional purchase of a factory farmed (FF) product makes no individual animal or person worse off than if no purchasing had taken place. Thus, other things being equal, it is morally permissible to benefit by privately[11] purchasing a FF-product occasionally.

One way to spell out this argument relies on the following account of moral wrongness:

> *Causal Consequences Principle (CCP)*: Action A is morally wrong only if the causal consequences of A are worse than they would have been if some readily available alternative to A had been performed.

This principle articulates the core idea of the "act consequentialist" tradition in ethics: what matters, from a moral point of view, is whether your act causes something worse to happen than what would have happened if you had acted in some other readily available way.[12]

In addition to CCP, this version of the basic argument for *Opportunistic Purchasing* cites the empirical fact, mentioned above, that the IFS is deeply *insensitive* to slight changes in demand. So the argument as a whole looks like this:

Basic Argument

(1) The IFS is insensitive: Given the huge numbers of products involved, and the waste and built-in buffers at many stages along the way, the occasional purchase of a FF-product does not cause any bad consequences that would not have occurred if the purchase hadn't happened. [empirical claim]
(2) CCP is true. [premise]
(3) Therefore the occasional purchase of a FF-product is morally permitted. [from (1), (2)]

Note that this argument may *not* go through with respect to food purchased from small family farms, since those operations are *much* more sensitive to slight changes in demand and so there won't be a counterpart for (1). This means that someone like Oppy might reasonably hold that occasionally consuming factory farmed meat is morally permissible, whereas occasionally buying family farmed meat is not. Interestingly, this is the precise opposite of what a lot of people these days want to defend—that is, that purchasing family farmed meat is sometimes permissible but purchasing factory farmed meat never is.[13]

I will leave as homework the question of whether versions of the Basic Argument could be developed within other leading ethical frameworks as well. It seems clear, at least, that a framework in which the infringement of rights is the morally relevant factor could accommodate a version of the Basic Argument—Oppy could plausibly point out that no additional rights are infringed by his opportunism than would have been infringed if he had purchased nothing. Here, however, I will leave that open and focus on the consequentialist version above, since that is the ethical framework within which much of this discussion tends to occur.

Arguments against Opportunistic Purchasing

Pollan, Marion Nestle, some freegans, and many others who work on food issues find it intuitively plausible—indeed obvious—that we can vote with our forks (or our wallets).[14] What they seem to mean by this is *not* that our food choices have about as much of a chance of influencing the outcome as a single vote in a presidential election. Rather, they mean the opposite: by boycotting a system that we regard as morally wrong, we not only avoid doing something morally wrong, but also do something morally right by contributing to a beneficial change in the system.

Most of us share these intuitively plausible thoughts: we think that by withholding our orders (or dollars), we will have a good effect on the system, or at least avoid having a bad effect. These intuitively plausible thoughts then lead (in a consequentialist framework, anyway) to the conclusion that we ought to financially boycott the products of a system or activity that we know to be morally wrong.

I have already highlighted the challenge that the insensitivity of certain systems poses to these intuitively plausible thoughts and the financial boycott conclusion that they underwrite. Oppy and others who are drawn to some version of CCP can appeal—reasonably enough—to such insensitivity as the key premise in their Basic Argument for *Opportunistic Purchasing*. In this section I examine four objections to the Basic Argument; each of them seeks to vindicate the intuitively plausible thought that we do make a difference, and should thus vote with our forks (or wallets).

But What if Everyone Did It?

> **Objection 1**: Opportunistic purchasing is morally wrong, even when performed privately in an insensitive system, because we couldn't coherently will a world in which "everyone did it."

This objection employs the sort of "universalizing" idea that we learn from our parents and teachers, and find encapsulated, in different ways, in the Golden Rule and Kant's Categorical Imperative. The idea is that the activity described in *Opportunistic Purchasing* is underspecified—there is no indication of which and how many people can be involved in it, how often, and under what circumstances. So when Oppy is in that faraway town one afternoon and pulls up to the drive-through, he might be endorsing a "free-riding" version of the principle that applies just to *him*. In other words, he might be thinking this:

> Given the insensitivity of the IFS, it seems clear that *my* occasional purchase of a FF-product makes no individual animal or person worse off than if no purchasing had taken place. Thus, other things being equal, it is morally permissible *for me* to benefit by privately purchasing a FF-product occasionally.

Objection 1 says that Oppy's principle here is arbitrarily focused on him, and cannot reasonably be invoked by *everyone*. And with respect to opportunistic purchasing, it's true: If all 7.2 billion of us do what Oppy does—even just once a week, say—that would result in a *huge* difference in demand, a difference to which even an insensitive supply system would quickly respond. In the case of animal agriculture, the IFS would respond by arranging for the production and slaughter of millions more animals whose flesh could constitute these 7.2 billion weekly meals. So the objection, in a nutshell, is that the *Opportunistic Purchasing* principle cannot be universalized. That is, it makes no sense to say this:

> *Everyone test*: Given the insensitivity of the IFS, it seems clear that *everyone* could occasionally purchase a FF-product and still make no individual animal or person worse off than if no such purchasing had taken place. Thus, other things being equal, it is morally permissible *for everyone* (including me!) to purchase a FF-product occasionally.

This does seem incoherent. But a well-known problem with these "what if everyone did it?" tests is that they result in some overly demanding conclusions. Consider Denny, a recent college grad who is deciding whether or not to become a dentist. It would be crazy to suggest that in order for his action to pass the universalizability test, he has to consider what a world would be like in which *everyone* (all 7.2 billion of us!) becomes a dentist. Neither Denny nor anyone else can coherently want *that* to occur (as good as it would be for our collective teeth). But surely that doesn't make Denny's choice to become a dentist incoherent or morally questionable. Like Oppy, Denny merely needs to make sure he's not making an unfair or arbitrary exception of himself. And it looks like he's not: He can reasonably say that it's fine for *anyone* in his general situation to choose to become a dentist, even if he wouldn't will a world in which *everyone* does it.

The Denny case indicates that the "everyone" test may not be the best way to respond to the basic sense of fairness or nonarbitrariness that is expressed in the Golden Rule or the Categorical Imperative. For it seems that Oppy could just as well universalize his decision at the drive-through via an "anyone" statement.[15] In other words, he could say:

> *Anyone test*: Given the insensitivity of the IFS, it seems clear that anyone in my general situation could occasionally purchase a FF-product and still make no individual worse off than if no such purchasing had taken place. Thus, other things being equal, it is morally permissible *for anyone in my general situation* (including me!) to purchase a FF-product occasionally.

The shift from "everyone" to "anyone" obviously makes a huge difference. If the shift is acceptable (and I realize this is controversial among Kantians), then it looks like Oppy *can* universalize his principle in at least this way. In other words, he can say that in a massive, globalized, industrial food system like ours, it is a near certainty that if *anyone* in his general situation purchases the relevant FF-product occasionally, that action is not going to cause any more harm (or rights-infringement, etc.) than if no purchase had occurred. Thus *anyone in Oppy's general situation* (including Oppy!) can be an opportunist without falling into self-defeating incoherence.

But You Might Be on the Threshold!

> **Objection 2**: Opportunistic purchasing is morally wrong, even when per-formed privately in an insensitive system, because there is a threshold at which a purchase *does* make a genuine causal difference and, for all Oppy knows, his present choice occurs precisely on such a threshold.

This second objection to the Basic Argument for opportunism plausibly assumes that, even in a deeply insensitive supply system, there must be some sort of "threshold," "trigger," or "tipping point" at which the purchase of a FF-product leads—via a complicated causal process involving clerks and computers and managers and purchase orders—to another lot of avocadoes being produced under backbreaking conditions, or another lot of broiler chickens being hatched, debeaked, grown, slaughtered, defeathered, dismembered, reconstituted into patties, and so forth.[16] Furthermore, because the threshold purchase occurs in an insensitive system, it will have disproportionately huge results: Oppy's buying that one chicken sandwich, when it is a threshold purchase, triggers a process that results in the miserable lives and deaths of a huge number of birds.

The objection to *Opportunistic Purchasing*, then, is that since we never *know* when we are facing a threshold choice, we should err (other things equal) on the side of caution. Even if there is only a 1 in 1,000,000 chance that Oppy is facing a threshold choice, the moral badness of being causally involved in the miser-able lives and deaths of, say, 100,000 chickens is *so* serious that no decent person would want to risk it.[17]

In order to grasp the point here, let's go back to the Basic Argument that we considered above:

(1)   The IFS is insensitive: Given the huge numbers of products involved, and the waste and built-in buffers at many stages along the way, the occasional purchase of a FF-product does not cause any bad conse-quences that would not have occurred if the purchase hadn't hap-pened. [empirical claim]
(2)   CCP is true. [premise]
(3)   Therefore the occasional purchase of a FF-product is morally permit-ted. [from (1), (2)]

Objection 2 simply points out that the first premise is false, and needs to be replaced with:

(1′) The IFS is insensitive: Given the huge numbers of products involved, and the waste and built-in buffers at many stages along the way, it is *extremely unlikely* (but not certain) that the occasional purchase of a FF-product causes any bad consequences that would not have occurred if the purchase hadn't happened. [empirical claim]

This change, in turn, requires an adjustment to the conclusion. For even given the truth of CCP, the opportunist can only get to

(3′) Therefore the occasional purchase of a FF-product is *extremely unlikely* to be morally wrong. [from (1′), (2)]

The strategy embedded in Objection 2, then, is to claim that the truth of (3′), together with a reasonable "err on the safe side" principle, renders *any* act of opportunistic purchasing morally impermissible.

Michael Almeida and Mark Bernstein appear to adopt this strategy: They suggest that any action that raises the likelihood of an extreme harm by even 0.0001% is morally impermissible, and support this suggestion by appeal to the example of a nuclear explosion that kills 1 billion people. Other things being equal, they say, it would be wrong to do something that makes it even 0.0001% more likely that such an event will occur; instead, we should err on the safe side. The same goes, according to Almeida and Bernstein, for purchasing the animal products of the IFS.[18]

I don't propose to dispute the "err on the safe side" impulse when the consequence in question is a nuclear explosion over a major city. But I disagree with Almeida and Bernstein in thinking that this is clearly relevant to Oppy's situation. We have granted that workers and especially the animals in the industrial system do indeed suffer badly. But no one is going to view the suffering (or rights violations) involved in the production and death of 100,000 chickens as being in anything close to the same category as what results from a nuclear explosion over a major city.[19]

Considered more closely, then, (3′) seems toothless unless it's combined with an "err on the safe side" principle that is implausibly demanding. It is true of almost *any* action that it is *possible though very unlikely* that it will cause some bad consequences that would not have occurred if the action had not been performed. As Almeida and Bernstein themselves point out, when I order the vegan entrée at a restaurant, it is possible though very unlikely that the chef makes a mistake and prepares the dish with real chicken instead of mock chicken and that, tragically enough, this real chicken is in fact a threshold chicken whose purchase triggers, via the complicated causal chain mentioned above, the production and destruction of 100,000 new chickens. But unlike Almeida and Bernstein, few of us will be tempted to think, in light of this far-flung possibility, that I should err on the safe side and refrain from ordering even the vegan entrée (and thus never go to restaurants that serve real chicken).[20]

Similarly, if Oppy's choice to order the chicken sandwich raises the likelihood of 100,000 new chickens being produced and slaughtered by a mere 0.0001%, few of us will view his act as morally impermissible. The odds are just too long and the harm is too slight (keep in mind that 50 *billion* land animals in addition to billions of fish and sea creatures are raised and slaughtered each year in the current food system—the blood of another 100,000 birds is merely a drop in that bucket of woe).

A slightly better version of Objection 2, I think, looks at this situation comparatively. Perhaps the objection is not that we should *always* avoid doing anything that makes something very bad 0.0001% more likely. That would be incredibly demanding. Perhaps, instead, the suggestion is that if action A makes something very bad 0.0001% more likely, and an available alternative action B makes it less than 0.0001% more likely—and has at least as many positive consequences—then we should go for B. This seems a bit more plausible, though still very demanding.

A third and even better version of Objection 2 focuses on how the odds improve over time. We are supposing that Oppy has a 1 in 1,000,000 chance of making a threshold choice in any *particular* instance. So the odds of causing harm are the same as the odds of a particular number $N \leq 1,000,000$ coming up when throwing a million-sided die.

But suppose that Oppy is forty years old and typically eats three times a day, and also that he will live for another fifty years. That means that he has $50 \times 365 \times 3 = 54,750$ meals left (round up to 55,000 total food choices in order to account for the occasional snack). If someone throws a million-sided die 55,000 times, the chance of coming up with some number N in any *particular case* is, of course, 1 in 1 million = 0.0001%. But the chance of coming up with N at least once over those 55,000 throws is quite a bit better: $55,000 \times 1/1,000,000 = 5.5\%$. Likewise, although the odds of making a threshold choice in any particular instance are a deeply demoralizing 0.0001%, Oppy's sustained vegetarian purchasing practice over the next fifty years will improve his odds of encountering a threshold to a much more inspiring 5.5%.

Some people will be moved by the reasoning here. And perhaps Oppy in particular *should* be moved by it. After all, he's a healthy middle-aged male of reasonable means who lives near a farmers' market and a sustainable whole foods co-op, plus he has a small yard on which he can grow his own vegetables. Adequate nutrients for people like Oppy are easily secured without recourse to the animal products of the IFS, and the financial cost of abstaining from such products is not significantly higher than that of purchasing them.[21] Thus there are no real nutritional or financial costs *for someone like Oppy* that would come with strict abstinence from factory farmed products for the next fifty years.[22]

If that's right, then the only goods that Oppy would give up are aesthetic and sociocultural: the taste of bacon, the ability to participate fully in various familial and cultural institutions (hot dog–eating contests, neighborhood barbecues, Mom's meatloaf, chips and guacamole at the bar, Thanksgiving dinners, and so forth). But even with respect to these goods, developments in the produce and "mock meat" sectors have made the losses seem increasingly negligible. Oppy can now just grill up some tempeh bacon or an aesthetically-indistinguishable "Beyond Meat" patty[23] on the Fourth and enjoy a tofu-turkey feast at Thanksgiving, while at the same time notching a relatively robust 5.5% chance of saving a lot of animals from miserable lives and deaths.

This all sounds correct. But even for people in Oppy's relatively privileged position, I suspect that a 5.5% chance of making a causal difference over five decades will seem a bit slim. Morality may be so demanding as to require that someone in Oppy's position be moved by such odds; I'm not sure. I am sure, though, that many people will reject the idea that this argument shows that strict abstinence from FF-products over a full fifty years is Oppy's only permissible course of action. In other words, I think this second kind of objection shows us why it might be morally *good* or *admirable* to refrain from opportunism, but not that opportunistic purchasing is morally *impermissible*. Our reflection on this objection, however, naturally leads to the following related one.

But You Are Putting Someone Else on the Threshold!

> *Objection 3*: Opportunistic purchasing is morally wrong, even when performed privately in an insensitive system, because there is a threshold at which a purchase *does* make a genuine difference. For any purchase, either it is a purchase on such a threshold, or it is a purchase that brings the system one step closer to the threshold. So in choosing to purchase, Oppy is morally responsible for the amount of harm caused by a threshold purchase divided by the number of purchases required to go from one threshold to the next.

This is a complicated objection, so let's return to the chicken case for illustration. Suppose, again, that there are around 1,000,000 purchases between each threshold, and that each threshold purchase leads—via a complicated causal mechanism—to the production and processing of 100,000 new chickens. We have seen that this means that Oppy's choice has a 1 in 1,000,000 (0.0001%) chance of being causally involved in the process by which 100,000 broiler chickens are produced and processed.

Objection 3 effectively suggests that we can divide through and conquer by thinking of *each* purchasing choice—at the threshold or not—as having a $(100,000 \times 0.0001\%) = 10\%$ chance of resulting in the miserable life and death of *one* chicken. That's because even if a particular purchase is *not* on the threshold, it is part of the process by which the system is brought to the next threshold, and so it is the moral equivalent of purchasing a 10% chance of mistreating a chicken (or the moral equivalent of mistreating one-tenth of a chicken, whatever that means).

Shelly Kagan develops this idea in his influential paper, "Do I Make a Difference?" In Kagan's scenario, the agent is faced with the choice of ordering (or not ordering) an entire chicken. If we let N be the number of chickens that will be killed if this is a threshold choice, Kagan says, we can simply divide through to get the expected animal cost of this choice. In other words, each choice—on the threshold or not—has a $1/N$ chance of killing N chickens, and so the expected cost of each choice is $(1/N \times N) = 1$ chicken.[24]

Mark Bryant Budolfson has pointed out that Kagan's setup here is flawed because it does not take into account an important empirical fact—namely, that there is a lot of excess and waste at almost every step in systems as complex and enormous as the real-world IFS. This implies, according to Budolfson, that the chance an agent takes of killing an individual chicken, even when we do divide through, is going to be *much*, much lower than $1/N$.[25]

My articulation of the case also aims to take an important empirical fact into account—namely, that we almost never order or purchase an *entire* chicken, as opposed to *parts* of a chicken mixed together with lots of other ingredients. This means that the number of purchasing choices that will bring the real-world system to a threshold is much higher than the number of chickens that are killed once it surpasses a threshold. I have no clear idea what the numbers actually are, but it seems closer to the truth to set the numbers up the way I just did, where Oppy takes on at *most* a 10% chance of killing one chicken when he orders the chicken sandwich.

If this is right, then Objection 3 faces a problem similar to that which plagued Objection 2. A 10% chance is a lot higher than a 0.0001% chance, of course, but now the harm involved is much less serious (i.e., the production and death of one chicken). Some moral saints may be moved by this, but in a world where millions of birds are killed every day (and millions of others are regularly culled in order to prevent avian flu outbreaks), I suspect that most people won't find this sufficiently worrisome to regard the purchase as morally wrong. Indeed, some chicken-meat lovers might even argue that the pleasure and nourishment Oppy gets from eating the chicken sandwich is equal to or greater than one-tenth of the suffering endured by one average broiler chicken.

So far we've looked at responses to *Opportunistic Purchasing* that try to meet the challenge head-on by suggesting that such activity takes on an unacceptable chance of causing significant suffering (or violating significant rights). A fourth sort of response, by contrast, looks at the effect that opportunism has on Oppy *himself.*

But It's So Demoralizing!

Objection 4: Opportunistic purchasing is morally wrong, even when performed privately in an insensitive system, because it is motivated by a thought (i.e., that individual actions under such circumstances are extremely unlikely to make a difference) that is prone to have a profoundly negative effect on the psychology of the average moral agent, and impede or undermine other important moral efforts.

In order to understand this argument against opportunistic purchasing, consider an alternative principle that we might call *Optimistic Purchasing*:

> *Optimistic Purchasing*—Despite the insensitivity of the IFS, strictly refraining from purchasing FF-products will make some individual animals or persons better off than if FF-purchasing had taken place. Thus, other things being equal, it is morally wrong to benefit by privately purchasing FF-products occasionally.

As with the *Opportunistic Purchasing* principle, the reference to purchasing behavior is embedded here. There might be other kinds of optimistic principles that would advise strictly refraining from all *eating* of FF-products, too. But *Optimistic Purchasing* is focused on economic exchange, and is compatible with opportunism of the *accepting* and *finding* kinds (freeganism, etc.).

Notice that the principle says that *strictly* refraining (that is, refraining over the long haul as one is confronted with choice after choice) is what is key, and that only that sort of effort can license the thought that one will make a difference. But given the huge numbers and slim chances we were looking at above, what sort of argument could justify us in accepting *Optimistic Purchasing*?

The one I want to consider is inspired by the "practical arguments" utilized in a very different context by Immanuel Kant. This kind of practical argument, at least on one interpretation, moves from broadly psychological facts about what would be seriously "demoralizing" for the average human agent to a conclusion about what it is practically rational for such a person to accept (or try to accept). Kant, for instance, thought that without adopting some kind of faith that the virtuous will ultimately be rewarded with happiness (by God in the afterlife, say), all but the most stoical among us will become discouraged or demoralized—we will see the wicked continuing to prosper, and ultimately lose hope for the establishment of justice—and thus find it difficult to be steadfast in fulfilling our moral obligations.[26]

So how does a practical argument from the threat of "demoralization" work in the case of the optimistic purchaser? Let's focus again on the threshold chicken, just for simplicity, and consider Oppy's optimistic alter ego (call him Opti). Like Oppy, Opti is morally concerned about the suffering and death of animals in the present IFS, and believes that it should stop. In other words, Opti wills a world in which no such animal suffering (or violation of significant rights) takes place. But it would be deeply demoralizing for Opti to will such a world—that is, to want it to be realized and strive consistently to bring it about—without also holding (as an article of faith, at least) that *his own* strivings will contribute in some measurable way to realizing such a world. Given that such demoralization is morally undesirable, there is a clear moral or practical advantage for Opti in holding such an attitude. Thus, according to this form of argument, it is *practically* if not epistemically rational for Opti to accept that a long-standing policy of refraining from purchasing chicken will significantly reduce the amount of harm (or rights infringement) in which he is causally involved. Given the insensitivity of the system, this suggests that it is practically rational for Opti to accept (as an article of faith, at least) that one of his choices will be a threshold choice.[27]

This sort of objection to the Basic Argument for *Opportunistic Purchasing* is intriguing, but it also raises a host of questions. First, why must Opti hold that one of *his own* purchasing actions will make the difference? Why couldn't he avoid demoralization by holding simply that the purchases of *some consumers or other* will make such a difference, whether or not he is one of them? If that were an option, then perhaps he could go out and encourage everyone else to refrain from purchasing chicken, all the while enjoying the occasional bit of private opportunism on the sly.[28]

More pressing, the argument leaves it open that Opti could remain fully psychologically committed to his ideal—fully moralized—simply by accepting (as an article of faith, at least) that *one* of the instances in which he chooses to refrain will be on the threshold, even if he doesn't *always* choose to refrain. This indicates that as long as he *occasionally* chooses to refrain, he would also be able occasionally to purchase and privately eat a chicken sandwich in a faraway town without the threat of demoralization.

A proponent of practical arguments might reply to these two points by noting that Kant's idea, anyway, was that the agent employing the practical argument not only wills the good result (in this case, the eradication of chicken suffering at the hands of the IFS) but also wills that the realization of that result is connected in an important way to *his own ongoing activity* as it is sustained and habituated over time. Thus Kant focuses on agents who are trying to "promote with all our powers what is best for the world" by being *completely* virtuous, where a completely virtuous person is someone who wills the good end with complete consistency, even in the face of the longest odds and the most treacherous obstacles. Kant sometimes suggests that the conclusion of a practical argument like this can only be rationally accepted ("in good faith," we might say) by someone who is at least striving to approximate complete virtue of this sort.[29]

But, third, it is not yet clear why Opti has to hold that his choices about what foods to *purchase* are the ones that will contribute in some small way to the actualization of the end he is envisioning. After all, Opti is an engaged activist working hard to curb the abuses of the IFS. The result of the practical argument could thus be simply that it is practically rational to accept that one of *those* actions, rather than any of his purchasing choices, will have an effect on the insensitive system such that a large number of individuals will avoid harm or a large number of rights violations won't occur. This too, it seems, might keep Opti "moralized," while also allowing him to indulge in the occasional bit of delicious private opportunism.

Finally, fourth, even if Opti rationally accepts (as an article of faith, at least) that, if he stays the vegetarian course, he will—at least once!—stand upon the threshold, and thus—at least once!—have a real chance to refrain from causal involvement in a significant harm, it is not clear that this is equivalent to accepting that he will make an overall difference. For in a system involving as much demand as the present industrial agricultural one, the fact that Opti is on the threshold but chooses to refrain merely means that the next person in line will make the threshold purchase instead, a mere matter of seconds later. And while it may be important psychologically for Opti to accept (as an article of faith, at least) that *he* had the chance to be causally involved in significant harm and then chose to refrain, it doesn't bring the world that he wills—one in which there is no such suffering—any closer to being realized. Once he becomes aware of that, a different but still very familiar kind of demoralization might set in. One sees this in exhausted former activists quite a bit: "I simply have to accept that I made a difference, given all the work I put in, but on the whole the world seems none the better for it."

Symbolic Disvalue and Collective Obligations

We have now considered four objections to the Basic Argument for *Opportunistic Purchasing.* Although there is more to be said about each, we have also encountered reasons to think that none of them is clearly compelling.

In these final sections I want to look much more briefly at two other kinds of responses that do not fit very well within a consequentialist framework but are still worthy of consideration (though I won't be able to do either of them justice here). The first invokes the notion of "symbolic value" and argues that purchasing the products of a wrongful activity is itself wrong because of the symbolic disvalue of being economically associated with something that has those origins. The second focuses on *collective* obligations: it says that, other things equal, we ought to dissociate ourselves from actions that violate such obligations, and that this rules out opportunistic purchasing.

Symbolic Disvalue: Dirty Hands

> Our passionless age substitutes the symbols of action for real action.
> —*Kierkegaard*

Symbolic value is a concept that is less familiar in philosophy than it is in disciplines like anthropology, religious studies, and those parts of sociology that deal with production, exchange, and consumption. The basic idea, however, is simple enough: An object might have far more "symbolic" value to a certain individual than its exchange or monetary value on some market or other, typically because of its causal origins or history. The copy of *Catcher in the Rye* given to you years ago by a now deceased high school friend (who used to act a lot like Holden Caulfield) might have far more symbolic value for you than the monetary or exchange value that it would fetch if you put it up on eBay. The reason for this, presumably, has to do with where that particular book *came from*—its origin in the generosity of a friend who has since died, its ability to invoke his memory, and so on. Other objects might have symbolic value because of who owned them, which associations and memories they bring up, and so forth.

Symbolic *disvalue* works in an analogous way. Some objects might fetch a certain exchange value on an open market (that 99-cent chicken sandwich, say), but have much more significant *disvalue* to those who know that they are the products of activities that are deeply morally wrong. This disvalue might be significant enough to make purchasing that product morally wrong, even if such purchasing is extremely unlikely to lead, causally, to any harm or rights infringement.[30]

An initial issue to consider here is whether the appeal to symbolic value can handle the gift-recipient and other freegan cases. Recall that in these cases, too, the agents benefit by consuming a product of an activity that they regard as morally wrong. But we don't, I have suggested, see their benefitting as morally wrong. The symbolic value theorist will either have to reject this intuition at the cost of giving all of us very dirty hands most of the time, or emphasize the difference in the nature of the consuming relation: in these cases, the agent merely *accepts* or *finds* the product before consuming it, but in the *purchasing* case he somehow *supports* the morally wrongful activity. The problem with this second response is that it either leaves the nature of that support *entirely mysterious*, or else makes symbolic disvalue depend on the existence of a *causal* connection between the purchasing and the wrongful activity, a connection that's likely to make a genuine difference. But the latter is precisely what the opportunist calls into question.

A variation on this sort of account says that occasionally purchasing the products of a morally wrongful activity amounts to *cooperating with* that activity, whether or not it supports or causally contributes to that activity. The opportunistic purchaser does something wrong, on this view, by cooperating with the wrongful activities of others (or, to use McPherson's phrase, by cooperating with the "wrongful parts of others' plans").[31]

A worry about this variation is that it too makes symbolic disvalue too easy to come by, and threatens to leave all of us with extremely dirty hands. When I use my email account or make a phone call, I cooperate with what I know (thank you Edward Snowden!) to be the morally wrongful activities and plans of my Internet service provider, my phone company, and the government. I know that these entities are monitoring emails, tapping calls, selling personal information, and so forth, and so by signing up I am knowingly providing more emails to monitor, more calls to tap, and more personal information to sell. This isn't just affecting me—by opening an email account or a phone line, I knowingly cooperate with their wrongful plan to monitor and sell the information of *others* who will email or phone me (presumably I wouldn't open the account or the phone line if I didn't expect others to write or call back). In short, by sending and receiving emails, making phone calls, using social media, and so on, I am knowingly cooperating with the wrongful parts of others' plans, even when there are readily available alternatives (I could sign up for the Tor Project, for instance). Thus, my hands are dirty too—they are tainted with symbolic disvalue.[32]

But this result seems implausibly strong: Other things being equal, it does not seem wrong, even in our current state of surveillance, to use email or make phone calls.

Collective Obligations: Many Hands

> Where all are guilty, no one is.
>
> —*Hannah Arendt*

There is more to be said about symbolic value theories, but in conclusion I propose to turn to a more promising route that invokes the notion of a *collective obligation*. Let's suppose that *we*—the group of food purchasers—have an obligation not to financially support activities on the part of others that are morally wrong. Suppose, too, that this means that *we*, collectively, have an obligation not to purchase the products of a morally wrongful activity whose constitutive aim is to generate those products.

What happens if we food purchasers have this collective obligation, and then some members of the group go ahead and purchase anyway? What should the other members of the group do? Unless we become steadfast freegans, it will be impossible to remove ourselves from the group of food purchasers. But one plausible suggestion is that we each now have an individual obligation to *dissociate ourselves* from those actions on the part of others in the group. In other words, I now need to do something that shows that I do not sanction the actions of the other members of the group—the actions that have led to a violation of our collective obligation.

There may be many ways to dissociate from such actions, but one clear, obvious, and (I would argue) minimally necessary way is to strictly refrain from participating in them ourselves, at least when a viable alternative is readily available. If I only *usually* refrain, or only in public refrain, then I don't succeed in fully dissociating myself from the part of the group whose actions led us to violate the collective obligation. Even if I protest against their actions and try to get them to change, I fail (I am suggesting) to fully dissociate from those actions if I still occasionally perform them myself. Dissociation of this sort, then, is not merely a function of what other people witness or think.[33]

By way of illustration, consider the (apparent) collective obligation that one race of humans has to refrain from systematically oppressing another race. This is not an individual obligation for most of us—we can't, all by ourselves, systematically oppress an entire race. Rather, if it is an obligation at all, then it is an obligation that we members of the race have as a collective. But now suppose that some members of that collective perform actions that lead to our obligation being violated. Suppose those actions include, among others, enslaving members of another race, setting up laws that systematically oppress them, routinely threatening them with physical violence or humiliation, and using racially charged epithets to describe them.

Under such circumstances, what is my individual obligation by way of response? I can't remove myself from the group (the race) that has failed to meet its obligation. But I can dissociate myself *from the actions* that led to our downfall. My suggestion here is that such dissociation requires *strictly* refraining from performing those actions myself whenever possible. The strictness seems important. If I hurl the occasional epithet in the privacy of my own home where there are no witnesses, I won't have harmed or influenced anyone else, but (I submit) I will still have failed fully to dissociate myself from the actions on the part of others that led to our collective moral failure.

If this is right, it might also offer a way to make sense of the intuition that was motivating the symbolic value theorists—the intuition that we have an obligation to "stand with the good" or to refuse cooperation with the wrongful parts of others' plans, even when doing so makes no causal difference. But here there is no need to invoke a mysterious notion of symbolic support to explain what it means to "stand with the good," and there is also no need to cash it out in terms of refusing to cooperate with the wrongful plans of others. What it is to stand with the good is to fully dissociate from the actions of those in the group that led to the violation of our collective obligation. And fully dissociating, I want to suggest, requires strictly refraining.

The main problem with Oppy's opportunistic purchase, then, is that it renders him unable to dissociate fully from the actions of others that led us—as the group of food purchasers—to violate our collective obligation not to financially support systems that treat animals and workers with needless cruelty.

Although I've said that this route seems more promising as a response to *Opportunistic Purchasing*—as well to related ethical concerns about futility, impotence, complicity, and so on—what I have just offered is obviously a mere sketch. There are deep controversies about what a collective obligation is and how it could be binding, about whether a group so disparate, unofficial, and unstructured as "the group of food purchasers around here" counts as a collective in such a way as to have an obligation,[34] and about how collective obligations (if they exist) devolve to individuals (if at all).[35] Still, despite what Arendt suggests in the quotation above, my sense is that this general area is where we are most likely to find an objection to *Opportunistic Purchasing* that has some genuine teeth.

Conclusion

Most of us share the conviction that we shouldn't benefit by purchasing the products of activities that we know to be morally wrong, provided that one of the constitutive aims of the activities is to generate those products. It seems clear that some of the activities involved in modern industrial food production (especially meat production) are morally wrong, and that they are aimed at producing those food products. Once we come to know that, it is natural to think that we have an obligation to refrain from purchasing those products.

I have pointed out here, however, that the real-world facts about our massive, opaque, and deeply insensitive supply systems open up moral space for the occasional opportunistic purchasing of those products. I have also argued that some of the initially promising objections to such consumer behavior seem inadequate. Finally, I have suggested that an appeal to collective obligations and the requirement to dissociate fully from the actions that led us to violate them seems (to me anyway) to offer the most traction against this sort of opportunism.[36]

Notes

1. See Mark Bittman, "Rethinking the Meat-Guzzler," *New York Times*, January 27, 2008, Week in Review, http://www.nytimes.com/2008/01/27/weekinreview/27bittman.html, accessed May 1, 2015.
2. For a recent assessment of the ills of the industrial system, see John Rossi and Samuel A. Garner, "Industrial Farm Animal Production: A Comprehensive Moral Critique," *Journal of Agricultural and Environmental Ethics* 27, no. 3 (June 2014): 479–522. See also the chapters by Hooley and Nobis, Cuneo, Halteman and Halteman Zwart, McPherson, and McMahan in this volume.
3. Michael Pollan, "Voting with Your Fork," *New York Times*, May 7, 2006, http://pollan.blogs.nytimes.com/2006/05/07/voting-with-your-fork/, accessed May 1, 2015.
4. This is sometimes referred to as the "causal impotence" or "inefficacy" objection to moral vegetarianism and veganism. See the chapters by Warfield, Martin, Hooley and Nobis, and Harman in this volume as well as Shelly Kagan, "Do I Make a Difference?," *Philosophy and Public Affairs* 39, no. 2 (2011): 105–141; Julia Nefsky, "Consequentialism and the Problem of Collective Harm: A Reply to Kagan," *Philosophy & Public Affairs* 39, no. 4 (2011): 364–395; and Mark Bryant Budolfson, "You Don't Make a Difference: The Inefficacy Objection to Consequentialism, and the Problem with the Expected Consequences Response" (forthcoming).
5. The delivery truck example is from Hud Hudson, "Collective Responsibility and Moral Vegetarianism," *Journal of Social Philosophy* 24, no. 2 (1993): 89–104. Singer, too, endorses roadkill-itarianism and other kinds of freeganism in Singer, "Utilitarianism and Vegetarianism," *Philosophy and Public Affairs* 9, no. 4 (1980): 325–337; see pp. 327–328.
6. Tyler Doggett asks in correspondence whether the "benefitting" part is important. If you hate the taste of foie gras and avocado and are allergic to sausage, then you can't really benefit from their nutrients. So are you still doing something morally wrong

in accepting the "Deluxe Avocado, Foie Gras and Summer Sausage Basket" prize that comes with being selected as employee of the month? I don't propose to address that question here, though my guess is that in real-world cases most people wouldn't accept unless there was at least some benefit to be gained (appearing to be a collegial team player, gaining gratitude from the sausage-loving colleagues with whom you share the prize, etc.).

7. The term "opportunistic carnivore" is used in zoological circles to describe animals that are typically herbivorous, but will at times eat carcasses and other meat that are the by-products of the activity of normal carnivores. Such opportunists include hyenas and vultures. As far as I know, Almeida and Bernstein are the first philosophers to use the term to refer to certain kinds of humans. See Michael J. Almeida and Mark H. Bernstein, "Opportunistic Carnivorism," *Journal of Applied Philosophy* 17, no. 2 (2000): 205–211.

8. From Freegan.info:

> Freeganism is a total boycott of an economic system where the profit motive has eclipsed ethical considerations and where massively complex systems of productions ensure that all the products we buy will have detrimental impacts most of which we may never even consider. Thus, instead of avoiding the purchase of products from one bad company only to support another, we avoid buying anything to the greatest degree we are able (Freegan.info, http://freegan.info/, accessed May 1, 2015).

9. Someone might reasonably worry that the situation is less clear when we add a certain kind of *witness* to the situation. Suppose you have a retired peeping capitalist as a neighbor (Tom, naturally) who has recently adopted the irritating habit of observing your activities from his deck much of the day. For all you know, when Tom notices how much you enjoy Grandma's gift of homemade guacamole on your deck, he might be inspired to use his spare capital to start an industrial avocado farm that relies on cruel labor practices to produce cheap products. Thus, for all you know, your public opportunism will play an important role in leading someone *else* to do something that is clearly morally wrong. But as long as you perform your opportunism *privately*, even the most vehement critic of the evils of the industrial avocado system is likely, I think, to admit that you aren't doing anything wrong.

10. From Freegan.info:

> As freegans we forage instead of buying to avoid being wasteful consumers ourselves, to politically challenge the injustice of allowing vital resources to be wasted while multitudes lack basic necessities like food, clothing, and shelter, and to reduce the waste going to landfills and incinerators which are disproportionately situated within poor, non-white neighborhoods, where they cause elevated levels of cancer and asthma (Freegan.info, http://freegan.info/, accessed May 1, 2015).

11. Make it as extreme as you like: Maybe Oppy decides to wear a ski mask, a scarf, and a large jacket as he uses the drive-through, and always pays in cash—that way, he thinks, no one could possibly recognize or identify him, even using closed-circuit television cameras. Perhaps he also slobbers and rants in an unattractive way while ordering the chicken sandwich so that any witnesses to the act (the employees at the drive-through, for instance) are repulsed and (Oppy hopes) associate that repulsion with the act of ordering industrial meat.

12. I leave it as a merely necessary condition here, though many consequentialists will view some version of CCP as providing both necessary and sufficient conditions for moral wrongness in an action. Compare Almeida and Bernstein, "Opportunistic Carnivorism," 206. The set-up of the Basic Argument here is otherwise very similar to theirs.

13. See, for instance, the chapters by Cuneo and Lipscomb in this volume.
14. See Marion Nestle, "Ethical Dilemmas in Choosing a Healthful Diet: Vote with Your Fork!" *Proceedings of the Nutrition Society* 59, no. 4 (2000): 619–629. See also Nestle's interview in the MOOC on "The Ethics of Eating" (https://www.edx.org/course/ethics-eating-cornellx-phil1440x).
15. Compare Almeida and Bernstein, "Opportunistic Carnivorism," 208–209.
16. Singer, Norcross, and Almeida/Bernstein use "threshold," Stuart Rachels uses "tipping point," and Shelley Kagan uses "trigger." See Alastair Norcross, "Puppies, Pigs, and People: Eating Meat and Marginal Cases," *Philosophical Perspectives* 18, no. 1 (2004): 229–245; Stuart Rachels, "Vegetarianism," in *Oxford Handbook of Animal Ethics*, eds. Tom Beauchamp and R. G. Frey (New York: Oxford University Press, 2014), 877–905, and Kagan, "Do I Make a Difference?"
17. See Singer, "Utilitarianism and Vegetarianism," 336; Norcross, "Puppies, Pigs, and People," 233.
18. Almeida and Bernstein, "Opportunistic Carnivorism," 207. In the case they discuss the difference is actually 1/10,000 = 0.001%. But the point is presumably the same.
19. Perhaps Almeida and Bernstein do—they start their article by calling the situation of animals in the industrial system a "Holocaust" and then defend their use of that term (p. 205). For comparisons to the Holocaust, see also Rachels, "Vegetarianism," 900ff.
20. Almeida and Bernstein, "Opportunistic Carnivorism," 210.
21. For the nutrition and cost and references here, see Hooley and Nobis (this volume).
22. See Van Dyke (this volume) for an argument according to which this is not true for members of other demographic groups.
23. Consider for instance the taste test conducted on the *Today Show* on April 25, 2014, in which all five hosts participated in a blind taste test involving a piece of "Beyond Meat" mock chicken and a piece of real chicken. Each of them was asked to guess, based on flavor, texture, and appearance, which was mock and which was real. Each of them guessed wrong. Today.com, http://www.today.com/food/today-puts-meatless-meat-test-does-it-taste-chicken-1D79579619, accessed Sept 1, 2014. Thanks to Matthew Halteman for this reference.
24. Kagan, "Do I Make a Difference?," 123–124.
25. Budolfson, "You Don't Make a Difference." For more objections to Kagan, see the chapters by Harman and Martin in this volume, as well as Nefsky, "Consequentialism and the Problem of Collective Harm."
26. See Immanuel Kant, *Critique of Judgment* 5:445–446n; 5:450–451n, and the discussion "the righteous man (like Spinoza) who takes himself to be firmly convinced that there is no God" in Immanuel Kant, *Gesammelte Schriften*, 29 vols. (Berlin: Deutsche Akademie der Wissenschaften zu Berlin, 1902–), 5:452. See also the exploration of the psychology of commitment and overcommitment in the chapter by Doggett and Egan in this volume, as well as the discussion by Anscombe that they cite from her 1961 piece "War and Murder," in G. E. M. Anscombe, *Ethics, Religion and Politics: Collected Philosophical Papers* (Oxford: Wiley-Blackwell, 1991).
27. For this way of interpreting at least some of Kant's practical arguments, see Robert Merrihew Adams, "Moral Arguments for Theistic Belief," in *Rationality and Religious Belief*, ed. C. F. Delaney (Notre Dame, IN: University of Notre Dame Press, 1979).
28. In Kant's own discussions of practical arguments, it often seems like an "empirically conditioned" question whether, when, and by what a given agent will be seriously demoralized. See, e.g., Kant, *Critique of Judgment*, 5:453–454.
29. Ibid. For more on this broadly Kantian argument, see Chignell, "Practical Arguments against Opportunistic Carnivorism," in *Kant and Animals*, ed. Lucy Allais and John Callanan (Oxford: Oxford University Press, 2016).
30. See Cuneo's chapter in this volume for an invocation of "symbolic value" along these lines. Norcross may be using an appeal to symbolic value on p. 232 of "Puppies, Pigs,

and People." For more on symbolic value generally, see Robert Merrihew Adams, *Finite and Infinite Goods: A Framework for Ethics* (New York: Oxford University Press, 1999) and Thomas E. Hill, "Moral Purity and the Lesser Evil," *Monist* 66, no. 2 (April 1, 1983): 213–232.

31. See McPherson (this volume).
32. See Warfield (this volume) for a different kind of "phone bill" objection.
33. Compare Thomas E. Hill Jr., "Symbolic Protest and Calculated Silence," *Philosophy & Public Affairs* 9, no. 1 (October 1, 1979): 83–102.
34. See Virginia Held, "Can a Random Collection of Individuals Be Morally Responsible?," *Journal of Philosophy* 67, no. 14 (July 23, 1970): 471–481.
35. An excellent collection of new papers on the topic of "forward-looking collective responsibility" was published just as this volume was going to press. See Peter A. French and Howard K. Wettstein (eds.), *Midwest Studies in Philosophy* 38 (2014), especially the essays by Marion Smiley and Carol Rovane.
36. For helpful comments on earlier drafts, I am grateful to Terence Cuneo, Tyler Doggett, Matthew Halteman, and Vivek Mathew and to members of audiences at Cornell University, Colgate University and the University of Vermont.

11

FACTORY FARMING AND CONSUMER COMPLICITY

Adrienne M. Martin

The Puzzle about the Badness of Buying Factory Farmed Meat

Many people who become vegetarians do so first out of a concern for the welfare of factory farmed animals. "Factory farming" refers to production that employs high stocking density, which deprives animals of the opportunity for even minimal movement and causes many animals to engage in self-mutilating behavior and to attack nearby animals. Controlling such harmful behaviors involves further cruel tactics such as debeaking chickens and clipping pigs' teeth without the use of anesthesia. Breeding for extremely fast growth rates and high meat productivity, along with poor nutrition, results in animals that are extremely unhealthy and often die of heart, liver, or lung failure, well before they are big enough to be slaughtered. "Broiler" chickens are bred to be so top-heavy that, sometimes, they literally cannot walk a step, and will die of dehydration because they cannot reach water a few inches a way. Thus, a daily part of the factory farmer's routine is culling the dead from their stock. I could go on, but I will simply assume this is enough to establish that factory farming involves the wrongful treatment of non-human animals.

Factory farming mistreats humans too. Factory farming mistreats contract-capable creatures, too. Take the poultry industry, now dominated by two massive companies, Tyson and JBS. As these companies have increased their market share, their contract farmers have had to increase production in order to be competitive. This means the farmers have to invest in larger facilities, usually funded by debt. The result for many farmers is that, to avoid financial ruin, they must accept increasingly demanding contracts that often last for only the life of one flock, that is, five to seven weeks, along with decreasing net income (Philpott 2011). Worse, these companies have not hesitated to take exploitative advantage of vulnerable populations: As Monica Potts (2011) documents in the *American Prospect*, many Hmong contract farmers for Tyson exist in a condition tantamount to indentured servitude. At the other end of production, meatpacking and poultry processing plants systematically exploit vulnerable immigrant labor forces, provide predictably and preventably unsafe work environments, and obstruct their employees' rights to freedom of association and organization (Compa 2004).

Thus, there are many reasons to think factory farming is wrong. There are more reasons than I have named here—for example, factory farming is also bad for the environment. For simplicity's sake, I will focus just on the wrongful treatment of animals. As I noted at the beginning, many people who become vegetarians are initially motivated by the sense that there is something bad about purchasing meat produced through such a cruel practice. But here is the puzzle: The individual consumer isn't the person stuffing the animals in the cages or setting corporate policy regarding stocking density. Indeed, given the great demand for inexpensive meat, the individual's choice to refrain from buying a package of chicken breasts appears to make *no difference at all* to whether factory farming continues. So why is there anything bad about buying it?

Maybe there isn't. Maybe, since the individual consumer isn't herself a factory farmer, and since her purchases make no difference to whether other people factory farm, there is nothing bad at all about buying factory farmed meat. Maybe the wrongness of factory farming means that we should work to oppose the system by, for example, developing and pushing legislation to reduce factory farming, but not that there is anything bad about buying factory farmed meat.

Here the puzzle reasserts itself, because many people have the sense that there would be something *hypocritical* about simultaneously working to reduce factory farming through legislation and buying factory farmed meat. My main thesis in this chapter is that this sense is right, because even if buying factory farmed meat makes no difference to whether other people continue factory farming, it nevertheless makes the consumer *complicit* in animal suffering.

A word on my methodology: I am proposing a linked set of concepts. When we say someone is "complicit" in a wrong, we say she *shares responsibility* for someone else's wrong. And that implies she is *liable to be blamed* for the other's wrong. Liability to be blamed for another person's wrong in turn leads back to the concepts of shared responsibility and complicity—this is a conceptual circle rather than a linear definition. I consider it a virtuous circle because it seems informative to me to explicitly connect these concepts, especially given the further conceptual connection between being liable for blame and being the appropriate target of so-called reactive attitudes like resentment, indignation, and guilt. On this methodology, we can test against each other our intuitions about complicity and our intuitions about when such attitudes are appropriate.

Distinguishing the Accomplice and Collectivity Features of the Puzzle

The puzzle regarding what could be bad about buying factory farmed meat has two features we can pull apart: First, the consumer is not herself a factory farmer; *other people* make animals suffer. Second, the consumer *doesn't make a difference* to whether these other people make animals suffer. It is useful to think about other cases where each of these two features is isolated.

Start with what I'll call *pure accomplice* cases. These are cases where one person becomes complicit in another's wrongful deed by aiding or abetting her. Hiring an assassin is one such case. The hirer doesn't kill anyone, but something about the way she is related to the killing means she shares responsibility for it.

Then consider what I'll call *pure collectivity* cases. These are cases where a group of people collectively produces a wrongful harm, and no individual's contribution to the collective action makes a difference to the harm. The firebombing of Dresden is one such case. Each individual bomber of course produced the harms of dropping a single bomb, but it was only the mass, collective bombing that caused the city to burn. Or consider the individual driving a car that produces fluorocarbons. That individual makes no difference to whether the ozone layer is damaged; this damage is caused by mass, collective action.[1]

The case of buying factory farmed meat is a *mixed* case. It is like contributing to a collective fund to hire an assassin. More, since individually buying factory farmed meat doesn't make a difference to whether factory farmers continue, it is like contributing to an *already flush collective fund* to hire an assassin. I think we can make progress in understanding the consumer's responsibility by first treating the accomplice and collectivity features of this mixed case separately, and then putting them together.

What Makes a Moral Accomplice? Culpable Negligence

Because of the collectivity feature, individual consumers of factory farmed meat do not make a difference to whether factory farmers continue to cause animal suffering. In order to simplify our inquiry and allow us to focus on the accomplice feature, let's imagine a superconsumer, whose individual purchase is causally sufficient to fulfill the demand necessary to incentivize others to continue factory farming. This puts us in the familiar territory of, to borrow a phrase from criminal law, "aiding or abetting" a wrongdoer.

The criminal accomplice's act is to aid or abet another agent's crime. However, some acts of assistance or encouragement are clearly not sufficient to establish an agent as an accomplice: If one employee tells another the security code, nonculpably unaware that the burglar is eavesdropping, her act contributes to the burglary, but she is not an accomplice. In criminal law, the usual view is that an accomplice is either someone who *intends* to aid or abet, or who *knows* she

206 Adrienne M. Martin

is aiding or abetting. There is also some movement in common law countries, and in the US with regard to certain crimes such as terrorism, toward allowing that that reckless or even negligent aiding or abetting is sufficient to make one an accomplice. So what we want to consider here is whether the superconsumer of factory farmed meat is a moral (as contrasted with criminal) accomplice to factory farming only if she intends to facilitate and incentivize it, or if some other mental state suffices. Is it enough if she knows her purchases facilitate and incentivize factory farming or knows there is a risk of this or, even, if she ought to know?

I think it is relatively easy to see that, to be moral accomplices, an agent needn't intend to facilitate or incentivize a wrongful act; nor does she need to know she is doing so. She only need be culpably negligent.

If there were an intention condition on moral accomplice complicity, then, insofar as I am concerned to avoid liability to be blamed for another person's wrongdoing, I need not hesitate to (1) lend my baseball bat to the person I know will use it to assault someone (my intention is only that he use it in a game this afternoon); (2) leave the store window unlocked when I know someone plans to burgle the store this evening (my intention is only to get on the road to home as quickly as possible); (3) give Kickstarter funds to a stranger working on a project I know will employ immoral means (my intention is only to enable her to develop a valuable project, not to support the particular means she plans to use); or (4) give a rousing speech on the radio expressing a desire for the brutal murder of the ruling class, knowing it will spark a genocidal revolution (my intention is only to call attention to injustice).

If there were a knowledge requirement on accomplice liability, it would mean that, at least insofar as I am concerned to avoid being liable to be blamed for another person's wrongdoing, I need not hesitate to: (1) lend my gun to a stranger without asking why she wants it; (2) fail to double-check that I locked the window, knowing that I tend to forget; (3) give Kickstarter funds on the basis of a project's title alone (or vote for a ballot initiative on the basis of its title alone); or (4) give a rousing speech on the radio expressing a desire for the brutal murder of the ruling class without considering the possibility that some of my listeners may take me literally.

These results are obviously mistaken. There is such a thing as "epistemic irresponsibility" regarding the consequences of our action—failing, that is, to be attentive enough to the changes we are likely to bring about. This is what I am calling *culpable negligence*. Moreover, it is commonplace to "beat oneself up" over such epistemic irresponsibility, and also to feel guilt to a degree that tracks the degree of negligence. Thus, rejecting negligence as a sufficient condition for accomplice complicity would require a substantial overhaul of our usual approach to both deliberation and backward-looking self-assessment. It makes sense to hold ourselves to relatively high standards of epistemic responsibility, when our concern is to be good deliberating agents who learn from our mistakes. A fully decisive argument for the sufficiency of negligence for accomplice complicity would require, among other things, a compelling account of epistemic negligence and its moral significance. This is more than I can attempt here—but, anyway, all I aim to establish is the strong initial plausibility of this principle.

Return now to the superconsumer, whose purchase is sufficient to fulfill the demand necessary to incentivize others to continue factory farming. If she ought to know that her purchase has this result, then she is a moral accomplice in factory farming. She would share responsibility for the wrongful means of production, even though it is other agents who carry out these means. This leaves open the question of what degree, strength, and quality of blame is appropriate to level at a moral accomplice—for example, how guilty should the accomplice feel? Many factors are relevant here, including what other options are available to the accomplice. As far as resolving our initial puzzle about the badness of factory farming is concerned, however, we have completed the first step in analyzing the accomplice feature. Now we turn to the collectivity feature.

The Failure of Causal Accounts of the Collectivity Feature

Of course, none of us is a superconsumer. Our individual purchases do not facilitate and incentivize factory farming except as parts of a collective. Put another way, we've established in the previous section that negligently facilitating and incentivizing factory farming makes an agent an accomplice to animal suffering, but what should we say when this facilitation and incentivization is a collective act?

There is a fair amount of literature on responsibility for collectively produced harms and injustices, though less so on those produced not though intentional coordination among individuals but simply through the accumulated effects of many actions. Here, I will consider two recent promising causal analyses. Their shortcomings, I want to suggest, are reason to think a good analysis of the collectivity feature doesn't start with claims about the consumer's causal role.

Kagan's Subjective Probability Analysis

Now, from the start of this discussion, I have essentially stipulated that the individual consumer *does not make a difference* to the continuation of factory farming. In his recent article, "Do I Make a Difference?," Shelly Kagan (2011) argues that *some* individual purchases *do* make a difference, and that it is morally unacceptable on utilitarian grounds to risk that your purchase will be one of those that makes a difference. A purchase that makes a difference is what we might call a "trigger" purchase, such as the trigger for the meat department to order another shipment from the supplier. If the department orders a new crate of N chickens every time N chickens are sold, then the trigger purchase is every Nth chicken.

Every purchase has a $1/N$ chance of being a trigger purchase, and whatever pleasure the consumer anticipates deriving from eating the chicken has to be weighed against this risk. On Kagan's analysis, the risk trumps.[2]

Although this analysis is compelling, there are some reasons to doubt that it is a good basis for assigning responsibility to the consumer. In particular, it is doubtful that Kagan's analysis applies to all meat departments; many probably do not use such determinate algorithms for their purchasing strategies.[3] Suppose there are two butchers, one who does order in keeping with Kagan's analysis, and one who maintains a standing order of two hundred chickens per day, adjusting it only in response to major shifts in demand that last longer than two weeks. If moral responsibility traces the expected utility of individual purchases, then one should, insofar as one is concerned to avoid responsibility for factory farming, buy a chicken from the second butcher, rather than the first. But that is a strange result—after all, a purchase from the second store still is a way of participating in the collective practice that supports factory farming. While Kagan's analysis does an admirable job of identifying a way that an individual purchase might make a difference to how much factory farming goes on, the peculiarity of this result is, I think, a clue that it might be a mistake to insist that consumer responsibility for the means of production is to be explained by the risk of making a difference. Let's now look at Elizabeth Harman's proposal.

Harman's Joint Causation Proposal

Harman doubts Kagan's analysis can ground compelling reasons not to purchase factory farmed meat and points out that we do not always have to make a difference to have a reason not to participate in collective wrongs. All else being equal, one should not join in bullying, even if one's contribution makes no difference to how badly the victim is hurt, and one might benefit from one's participation. This is surely correct. Harman proposes that the morally significant factor is participation as a *joint cause*. A *joint* cause is neither necessary nor sufficient for an effect—for example, any one of six pallbearers is a joint cause of carrying a coffin bearable by four. She proposes that it can be wrong to participate as a joint cause in a collective wrong, and also to fail to participate as a joint cause in a collective good action. She further proposes that sometimes it is not *wrong*, but rather a *moral mistake* to participate as a joint cause of a wrong, or to fail to participate as a joint cause of a good. (See Harman's chapter in this volume for discussion of "moral mistakes"—the central idea is that making a moral mistake is permissible, but that there are still moral reasons not to make moral mistakes; thus, the appropriate attitudinal and social responses to moral mistakes differ from the appropriate responses to morally impermissible actions.)

Now, I find Harman's arguments for the existence of this deontic category "moral mistake" persuasive. However, I doubt that moral vegetarians who tolerate meat consumption by others do so because we think of meat consumption as a moral mistake. I think it more likely that tolerance is explained by some combination of a belief in a duty of tolerance and simple weakness of will when faced with the prospect of making others uncomfortable and being disliked. More importantly, though, I also think that it is not a causal relation doing the moral lifting in the bullying case or in many analogous cases, including the individual's participation in the support of factory farming. Harman is right to think that what matters in such cases is *participation*, but describing this participation as causal doesn't get at the heart of what matters, morally speaking.

Joint Causation without Complicity, and Vice Versa

Here is a case where it seems plausible that a person is a joint cause of factory farming but is not complicit: Suppose a company that factory farms finds a way to use the soy by-products of farming to make tasty meatless burgers, and a vegetarian (knowingly) buys these burgers. This purchase is a joint cause of the facilitation and incentivization of factory farming, since it makes the venture more profitable. Yet, unless we are already in the grip of the theory that joint causation is sufficient for complicity, it's not particularly intuitive to say the vegetarian is complicit in the factory farming.

An analogous bullying case would be that of the kid who does not join in on the bullying but does keep a low profile in order to avoid getting bullied herself. The bullies know that one by-product of their bullying is that the other kids let them rule the school—the bullies would bully even if this didn't result, but it is certainly part of the incentive for bullying. The meek kid in this scenario is a joint cause of the bullying but, again, it doesn't seem like she's *complicit* in the suffering of the kids who get bullied—at least she is not *as* complicit, even though we can stipulate that she makes the same causal contribution as the active bully.

Here is a case where it seems plausible that a person is complicit in a wrongful harm but not in virtue of being a joint cause: A volunteer Army enlistee plays a support role that individually contributes little if at all to the unjust war effort. She is surely complicit in the unjust war (assume for now she knows it is unjust), even if she makes little or no causal contribution at all. In particular, she is surely *more* complicit than a civilian who makes a minimal yet equivalent contribution. This suggests that it cannot be causal contribution underwriting complicity.

The case of the volunteer Army enlistee has been the subject of recent discussion by just war theorists. The specific puzzle these theorists are concerned to solve is why the enlistee who makes little or no causal contribution to an unjust war effort is liable to be killed by the enemy (assuming the enemy is prosecuting a just war), while a civilian who makes an equivalent causal contribution is not.[4] Saba Bazargan's proposed solution is a "collectivized account" of combatant liability. On this account, unjust combatants but not civilians are liable to be killed because only the former *willingly adopt a role designed to contribute to the unjust war effort*, even if they do not in fact make an effective contribution.

I think this concept of *adopting a role* is the key to solving the remaining piece of the puzzle about consumer complicity in factory farming, as well. To preview, rather than focusing on the causal contribution made by the individual consumer, we should focus on the role she adopts. Specifically, she willingly participates as member of a consumer group that has the function of signaling demand. If we understand the collectivity feature of the puzzle in these terms, we can see why the consumer is liable to be blamed for the collective facilitating and incentivizing of factory farming. Putting this together with the account of the accomplice element, we have a complete story about individual consumer complicity in factory farming.

Extending the Collectivized Liability Account— the Consumer's Role

A collectivized liability account of responsibility in the bullying case is eminently plausible. Everyone who voluntarily joins thereby participates in a cooperative project aimed at making the victim suffer, and it is surely right that each individual participant is thereby liable to be blamed for the victim's suffering, even if the suffering would be just as bad if the ringleader (say) were the only tormentor. What matters here is not whether there is some chance that an individual will make a difference to the suffering, or even that each individual is a joint cause. What matters is that the individual willingly adopts the role of *participant* in a group, knowing or at least suspecting that the group has the function of making its victim suffer. The individual is thereby liable to be blamed for what other group members do qua participants, including succeeding in the group's purpose; this liability stands even if the individual does not actually contribute to the victim's suffering.

Thus we should ask whether there is an analogous role one willingly adopts in virtue of purchasing factory farmed meats, whether one willingly becomes a participant in a group that one knows (or, I will argue, ought to know) serves a function that can then be linked to the provision of means and incentive to factory farmers. Most clearly, the individual consumer joins the group, *consumers of factory farmed meat.*

One might doubt whether this a "group" in the sense relevant to the combatant and bullying cases, because it might seem to lack an organizing principle or function. It is true that the military is a group with quite explicit organizing principles and purposes, and further that a significant portion of the members of this group explicitly intend to structure and direct it accordingly—this is why it makes sense to describe the role of combatant as "designed" to cooperatively serve the function of furthering the war effort, as Bazargan does.

But notice that the group in the bullying case needn't have an organizing principle or function in any sense that might be missing from the consumer group. The group might form spontaneously, without any of its members being aware of each other in advance. Moreover, it is feasible that the group could form and proceed to bully its victim without any of its individual members having the aim or intention of making the victim suffer—each might have only the intention of staying with the in-crowd or avoiding being bullied herself—and yet it still makes sense to describe the group as *having the function of* or *aiming at* making the victim suffer. Having this function is not equivalent to having the *effect* of making the victim suffer, either, for suppose the victim is thick-skinned and able to brush off the bullying without suffering; it nevertheless continues to be appropriate to call the group a *group of bullies*, and to attribute to it this function or aim. I cannot provide a theory of group function here, but the notion I am relying on is that the relevant roles and group activities are to be conceptualized in terms of their function—we understand the concept 'bully' partly in terms of its function.

The group I have in mind is a *consumer group*. Consumer groups are an important element of a free capitalist market economy. It is true that free (or partially regulated) capitalist markets do not have the same degree of deliberately developed structure and organization as the military. However, they are institutions, with individual designers involved in their inception and ongoing maintenance and development. And such economic systems do have aims. It's a matter for philosophical and political debate what the aims of such systems are and ought to be. Some candidates are middle-class prosperity, wealth consolidation in the upper tiers, and maximal growth regardless distribution. Whatever the market aims at, it is clear that its aims depend in part on constituent organizations pursuing a subset of aims. Many constituent organizations are corporations that in turn rely on being able to roughly predict consumer demand for their product. Individual consumers don't matter much for this purpose, except insofar as their buying patterns combine with those of others—insofar, that is, as they are members of consumer groups. A consumer group is defined in part by its function or aim of *signaling demand* for a product, fulfilling a crucial need of the economy's operations.

Just as the group of bullies has the function of causing the victim's suffering, regardless the intentions of the individuals in the group, the function of the consumer group does not depend on members' intentions—one can be a member of a consumer group without intending to signal demand. Also as before, having the function is independent of whether the group actually causes producers to believe there is such-and-such demand for their product (suppose through some strange chain of events the fact of a group of purchases was invisible to the producers). When one purchases a product in the ordinary way, one takes up the role of consumer; one becomes a member of the group of consumers of those products, a group that signals demand to the producers. However, it is a further question when one counts as *willingly* taking up that role.

Willingly Taking Up a Role

Volunteer combatants voluntarily take up their designated role within the military, and thereby become complicitously liable for the actions of other voluntary members of the military, regardless their causal contribution to those actions or to the war effort more broadly. Bazargan grants, however, that a volunteer combatant might not be aware that the war effort in which she is engaged is an *unjust* one, and so we might wonder whether she thereby becomes liable in the manner of an unjust combatant—that is, liable to be killed by those justly opposing her. In other words, while we must grant that she willingly takes up the role of *combatant*, perhaps her ignorance of the war's immorality means she does not willingly take up the role of *unjust combatant*. Similarly, we might wonder whether a young child who willingly joins in mocking a classmate without really understanding how it hurts her should be considered as willingly taking up the role of bully. And we might wonder whether someone making a purchase while ignorant of the basic operations of the market and motives behind market production, lacking the concept of consumer demand in particular, counts as willingly taking up the role of consumer, as I have characterized it above.

Bazargan's answer regarding the combatant is that any reasonably epistemically responsible person volunteering for military service should be aware of the high risk that the war effort will be at best a blend of just and unjust. Ignorance due to culpable negligence does not exempt the combatant from complicitous liability. In other words, to *willingly* take up a role one needn't intend to take it up or even know one is doing so—if one *ought to know* one is taking it up, then one does so willingly. This is useful for thinking about the bullying case. We can ask whether the child ought to know that what she is doing is taking up a role within a group that has the function of causing suffering. We get the intuitively right answers here, I think: For example, if she is on the cusp of awareness of other people's experience and the possibility of having an effect on that experience, then she is only partially liable to be blamed for the classmate's suffering. The appropriate response might be to be disappointed in her but not angry at her, and to work on supporting her development as a moral agent.

Similarly, we should ask whether the individual purchasing a product *ought to* be aware that she thereby joins the group that has the function of signaling demand to the producers. I think the evidence is that the average American consumer (for example) *is* aware of this fact. Consider the "buycott" defense of Chick-fil-A restaurants in 2012, when equal rights activists and supporters boycotted the chain in response to the owner's anti-equality remarks and activities. Taking in the spectrum of people represented by the buycotters and the boycotters, we see people ranging from the poorly educated and relatively impoverished to the highly educated and highly affluent clearly understanding that, by publicly joining a group that chooses to purchase or refrain from purchasing (factory farmed!) chicken, they signal support or opposition, demand or its absence. Now, a consumer group's signal is amplified by the media and perhaps more causally efficacious in the context of an organized public buycott or boycott—the role the purchaser adopts in this context is not just *consumer* or *nonconsumer*, but *public supporter* or *opposer*. Nevertheless, the fact that most of us would feel it hypocritical to participate in a buycott or boycott one day and then turn around and reverse our purchasing habits the very next day (without any change in the producer's stance or practices) indicates that we see a connection between the public declaration of organized consumption or its rejection and relatively private purchases made on a more ordinary day. The most likely connection is that consumer groups have the function of signaling demand: a signal that receives media amplification in one context, but is no less a signal in less dramatic contexts.

If the average American consumer *does* in fact understand the nature of the consumer role adopted in virtue of making a purchase, then it's fair to say that failing to understand this is a failure of epistemic responsibility. There are no doubt exceptions: people who are extremely socially isolated, for example. Nevertheless, the average consumer ought to understand this aspect of her role, and should be considered as *willingly* adopting the role in virtue of her voluntary purchases.

Conclusion

It might be helpful at this point to work backward from where we've arrived to where we began, putting together the full account of what's bad about purchasing factory farmed meat: First, by purchasing factory farmed meat, the consumer willingly joins the consumer group that has the function of signaling demand for that product. She is thereby complicit in the group's collective acts, regardless her actual causal contribution to them. Among the collective acts of the group is facilitating and incentivizing high-density stocking, and the animal suffering involved. Thus, the consumer shares responsibility for this facilitation and incentivization. This is an account of what I have called the collectivity feature of the puzzle.

Next, as we saw earlier, if an epistemically responsible agent would know that by performing a certain action she was facilitating and incentivizing a wrong, then anyone who performs that action shares responsibility for that wrong. It seems fair to assume that an epistemically responsible consumer knows not only that she is part of a consumer group that has the function of signaling demand, but also that the group, *consumers of factory farmed meat*, facilitates and incentivizes factory farming. Thus, the individual consumer is related through her participation in a collective to an action that in turn means she shares responsibility for animal suffering. This is how the collectivity and accomplice features connect to explain how the individual consumer is complicit in factory farming.

Our sense is correct, that by buying factory farmed meat (or, for that matter, other products of wrongful means) we are doing something bad. Specifically, our purchase makes us complicit in animal suffering and the other wrongs involved in factory farming. I don't think we can infer from this it is *morally impermissible*

214 Adrienne M. Martin

to buy factory farmed meat. Modern life involves adopting a great many roles, many of them participatory roles in groups organized by function—so there are a great many opportunities for sharing responsibility in collective wrongs. Modern life also affords the opportunity to influence others in many ways, some of them ways an epistemically responsible agent can anticipate—so there are numerous opportunities to be an accomplice to others' bad choices and wrongful actions. The moral terrain we traverse on a daily basis is diverse enough that there is no algorithmic guide; moreover, this particular bit of territory, where collectivity features large, has been only sketchily mapped. I hope the account developed here fills in an important piece of this sketch.

Notes

I'm very grateful for comments on earlier drafts from Saba Bazargan, Andrew Chignell, Terence Cuneo, Tyler Doggett, Matthew Halteman, Elizabeth Harman, Eliot Michaelson, David Plunkett, participants in the UVA Food Ethics Workshop 2014, and participants in the Penn Animal Ethics and Cognition Group.

1. See Kagan (2011) for a different analysis of these kinds of cases.
2. Specifically, the negative expected utility of each purchase is equivalent to the suffering of one chicken. I leave out a complexity in Kagan's analysis. He incorporates the fact that the number of purchases on a given day may not be a multiple of N, so that one may avoid being the member of a cohort of N purchases. The final result of accommodating this fact, however, is that the individual purchase still has a $1/N$ chance of being a trigger purchase, so that the expected utility of the purchase is the suffering of an individual chicken. This, by hypothesis, outweighs the expected positive utility of eating the chicken.
3. See Budolfson (forthcoming).
4. See Lazar (2010).

References

Bazargan, Saba. "Complicitous Liability in War." *Philosophical Studies* 165, no. 1 (2012): 177–195.
Budolfson, Mark. "The Inefficacy Objection and the Problem with the Singer/Norcross/Kagan Response" (forthcoming).
Compa, Lance. "Blood, Sweat, and Fear: Workers' Rights in U.S. Meat and Poultry Plants." *Human Rights Watch*, 2004. http://www.hrw.org/node/11869/section/1.
GRAIN. "Contract farming in the world's poultry industry," *Seedling* (January 2008): 12–17.
Kagan, Shelly. "Do I Make a Difference?" *Philosophy and Public Affairs* 39, no. 2 (2011): 105–141.
Lazar, Seth. "The Responsibility Dilemma for Killing in War—A Review Essay." *Philosophy & Public Affairs* 38, no. 2 (2010): 180–213.
Philpott, Tom. "Poultry Industry Smothers Immigrant Farmers and Abuses Antibiotics." March 16, 2011. http://grist.org/factory-farms/2011-03-15-poultry-industry-smothers-immigrant-farmers-abuses-antibiotics/.
Potts, Monica. "The Serfs of Arkansas." *American Prospect* (March 2011), http://prospect.org/article/serfs-arkansas-0.

12

EATING MEAT AS A MORALLY PERMISSIBLE MORAL MISTAKE

Elizabeth Harman

A Puzzle about Accommodation

Many people who are vegetarians for moral reasons nevertheless accommodate the buying and eating of meat in many ways. They go to certain restaurants in deference to their friends' meat-eating preferences; they split restaurant checks, subsidizing the purchase of meat; and they allow money they share with their spouses to be spent on meat. This behavior is puzzling. If someone is a moral vegetarian—that is, a vegetarian for moral reasons—then it seems that the person must believe that buying and eating meat is morally wrong. But if someone believes that a practice is morally wrong, it seems she should also believe that accommodating and supporting that practice is morally wrong; many moral vegetarians seem not to believe this. In this chapter, I will offer a solution to this puzzle: I will offer a possible explanation of why people who are vegetarians for moral reasons nevertheless do accommodate the buying and eating of meat. I will offer an explanation of this accommodation behavior on which it is reasonable and it makes sense. I will argue that moral vegetarians may see the buying and eating of meat as a *morally permissible moral mistake.* They may see the practice as one that one should not engage in, for moral reasons, but that is not morally wrong. Thus, they may see their accommodation of the practice as accommodation of behavior that is not morally wrong, while it is still the case that they are *moral* vegetarians who see themselves as *required* to be vegetarians.[1]

I will begin my discussion with an examination of the ethics of buying and eating meat. In order to know what moral positions might lie behind the accommodation practices of moral vegetarians, we must directly examine the morality of the buying and eating of meat. Later, I will explain the notion of a morally permissible moral mistake in more detail.

The Morality of the Farming of Meat

Is it morally wrong to buy or eat meat? One natural thought is that it is morally wrong to buy meat because one is *contributing to* a process that is morally wrong—namely, the farming of meat. Some people think that factory farming of meat is morally wrong because it causes great animal suffering. I will assume that that is so. Nevertheless, some people think that so-called "humane farming" is not morally wrong, because it does not cause great animal suffering. So-called "humane farming" involves raising animals in good conditions and then painlessly killing them in the prime of their lives. (Let's suppose that there is some actual farming like this.) If "humane farming" is morally permissible, then it would seem that buying and eating meat from "humane farms" would also be morally permissible. So it would not be true that buying or eating meat is morally wrong in all cases.

While "humane farming" is morally better than factory farming, I will argue that "humane farming" is nonetheless morally wrong. In particular, if we believe that factory farming is morally wrong *because we have strong reasons not to cause animal suffering*, then we should believe that "humane farming" is morally wrong as well.

If factory farming is morally wrong because we have strong reasons not to cause animal suffering, then that is so because:

> Animals have moral status.
> Factory farming significantly harms animals.
> Any action that significantly harms something with moral status is thereby pro tanto morally wrong.
> There is no sufficient justification available to justify factory farming in the face of its pro tanto moral wrongness.

In my view, these four claims provide the correct explanation of why factory farming is morally wrong. However, they also imply that "humane farming" is morally wrong, because the following is also true:

> Painlessly killing an animal in the prime of its life significantly harms the animal.

"Humane farming" painlessly kills animals in the prime of their lives, significantly harming them. This makes the practice pro tanto morally wrong. No sufficient justification is available to justify the practice, so the practice is all things considered morally wrong. That is my argument.

If someone wanted to deny that "humane farming" is morally wrong while acknowledging that factory farming is morally wrong, she would probably challenge my claim that painlessly killing an animal in the prime of its life significantly harms the animal. I will mention two ways this claim might be challenged, and briefly state my responses to these objections.

First, someone might claim that killing an animal is not *harming* the animal but is rather *depriving* the animal of a *benefit*; and that it is not pro tanto morally wrong to deprive a being of a benefit. I agree that there is a moral asymmetry between harming and depriving of benefit. However, we can see in the case of persons that killing is harming even though what makes killing bad for someone is that the person is deprived of future life. Furthermore, while some deprivations of benefit are not also harmings, when a person deprives another being of a benefit by actively injuring her, this is always a case of harming.

Second, someone might claim that animals' futures have no value to those animals in their present states, because animals lack the right psychological connections to their futures. Note that we are considering this objection from someone who grants my claim that it is pro tanto morally wrong to cause animals to suffer. The problem for this objection arises from considering cases in which an animal has a medical condition which does not bother it now but will cause it to die prematurely several years from now, depriving it of five years of life. It is clearly morally permissible to cause the animal to suffer now in a surgery that will significantly extend its life. The explanation of the permissibility of the surgery is that although an animal currently has an interest in not suffering now, it also currently has an interest in living a longer rather than a shorter life; some current suffering can be morally justified by the extension of the animal's life. This shows that animals do have an interest in surviving, and so that they are harmed by their deaths.

In this section, I have argued that if factory farming is wrong (as I assume it is), then so-called "humane farming" is wrong too.[2]

The Morality of Buying and Eating Meat—Difference-Making

I have argued that all farming of animals for meat is morally wrong, even so-called "humane farming". What are the implications for the morality of buying and eating meat?

One naïve thought is the following. Supply is sensitive to demand. Suppose I buy a chicken at the supermarket today. That is an increase in demand for chicken (as compared to my refraining from buying the chicken today), so it leads to an increase in supply: one more chicken is slaughtered as a result of my purchase. This thought is naïve for several reasons. First, food production is not sensitive to very small differences in demand; second, that there will be some waste is expected and built into the process. It is very unlikely that whether I buy a chicken today will have any effect at all on how many chickens are killed, because it is very unlikely that whether I buy a chicken today will have any effect on how many chickens my supermarket orders. My supermarket is used to small fluctuations in the demand for chicken, and is used to having some waste. If my not buying a chicken today were to result in an extra chicken that went unsold, my supermarket would probably not order fewer chickens. So it is not very likely to be true that how many chickens are slaughtered counterfactually depends on my purchase today of one chicken. My purchase is unlikely to make a difference.

Nevertheless, Shelly Kagan has argued, difference-making considerations may still provide compelling moral reasons against my purchase.[3] For my supermarket is not wholly insensitive to demand. The supermarket would order more chickens if chicken demand greatly increased, and it would order fewer chickens if chicken demand greatly decreased. This means (Kagan argues) that there must be some threshold such that if that many chickens are purchased, my supermarket will order a certain number of chickens, but if fewer chickens had been purchased, my supermarket would order fewer chickens. Suppose that if such a threshold is just missed, my supermarket would order N fewer chickens. Kagan claims that I should take my chance that my chicken purchase is one purchase among a group of purchases that exactly meet that threshold as not very likely, but as $1/N$. Assuming that chicken production is perfectly sensitive to demand from supermarkets, it turns out that the expected animal cost of my purchase of one chicken is $(1/N) \times (N \text{ chickens}) = \text{one chicken}$. Although it is very unlikely that any animal deaths depend on whether I buy a chicken today, there is a small chance that many animal deaths do depend on whether I buy a chicken today: there is a small chance that my purchase makes a big difference.

Kagan's argument is seductive, but a serious worry has been raised by Mark Bryant Budolfson. Budolfson emphasizes two things: there is a great deal of waste in the production of meat, and there are many stages of the process from production to consumer. Waste occurs at each stage. This makes it incredibly unlikely that one's chicken purchase today has any effect at all on actual meat production. Not only is it incredibly unlikely, but there is also no reason to think that if one's purchase did have an effect, it would be a big effect. So difference-making considerations give us only very weak reasons to refrain from meat purchases. The expected animal cost of my purchase of a chicken today is $1/M \times (P \text{ chickens})$, where M is very high and P is low. (Budolfson's point does not depend on the phenomenon of *waste* in particular, but rather on the more general facts that the supply chain is long and that there is *noise* in the information transfers along the way. The information that there has been one fewer meat purchase will not transmit to the other end of the long supply chain, given that there are many steps along the way and the information transfer from step to step is noisy.)[4]

One might react to Budolfson's objection by making a different argument against the moral permissibility of eating meat. One might employ a deontological moral principle that takes *directly causing* the death of a being with moral status to be pro tanto wrong, such that even *taking a chance* at directly causing such a death is pro tanto wrong; and one might hold that simply getting pleasure from eating meat is not the kind of thing that could justify such an action. According to this new argument, it does not matter that the chance is low, because we are not Utilitarians—this is simply the kind of risk we should not take.

This deontological argument is interesting and I discuss it more elsewhere.[5] But here is a response that could be offered. Ordinary human life often involves taking very small chances of directly causing deaths of people. For example, driving to the corner store involves taking such a chance. But this does not make driving to the corner store pro tanto wrong; I do not need a particularly morally weighty justification to do so.

Largely on the basis of Budolfson's objection, I am unsure whether Kagan's argument works. (Though I am not sure that it fails.) For the purposes of this chapter, I will assume that Kagan's argument does fail. Suppose there is no difference-making basis for a strong moral reason against buying and eating meat. Are there nevertheless compelling moral reasons against buying and eating meat?[6]

The Morality of Buying and Eating Meat—Beyond Difference-Making

For the rest of my discussion, I will assume that acts of buying and eating meat make no difference to the amount of suffering in the world (and that we should not have a small credence that such an act will make a huge difference). Nevertheless, sometimes actions are morally wrong (or have moral reasons against them) because they involve *jointly causing* a bad outcome. More specifically:

  (i)   Sometimes it is morally wrong to participate as a joint cause in an act of harming.

Suppose twelve-year-old Jimmy sees some bullies harassing little Timmy on the playground. Jimmy can see the lay of the land: he can't save Timmy, but he can make it less likely that he himself will ever be bullied by joining in on the bullying; Timmy is so upset that he isn't really watching who's talking and it won't make any difference to Timmy whether Jimmy chimes in too. Here Jimmy's bullying won't make things worse for Timmy, and would make things better for Jimmy. But it would be morally wrong for Jimmy to participate in the bullying of Timmy.

Here is another way that one might face a moral requirement, though one's action will not make a difference:

  (ii) Sometimes it is morally wrong to fail to participate as a joint cause in a morally good act or outcome.

Suppose there is a great injustice in one's town or country, and many brave people are protesting, risking injury and imprisonment to stand against the state. It may be wrong to stand idly by and not participate in the protest, even though there are costs to oneself and one more person at the protest will not make any difference.

It is hard to say when it is morally wrong to participate as a joint cause in an act of harming. It is hard to say when it is morally wrong to fail to participate as a joint cause in a morally good act or outcome. But the following two claims do seem to be true:

> If acting in a particular way would be participating as a joint cause in an act of harming, then there is a moral reason against acting in that way.
> If acting in a particular way would be participating as a joint cause in a morally good act or outcome, then there is a moral reason to act in that way.[7]

These claims have implications for the morality of buying and eating meat. When one buys meat, one's action is one of many actions that together cause the production of meat. While there are hard questions (discussed earlier) about whether individual meat purchases ever make a difference to whether meat production occurs, it is clear that the sum total of meat purchases makes a difference to whether meat production occurs: if meat purchases ceased, meat production would cease as well.

Let me now offer some thoughts about vegetarianism. When a person refuses to eat meat, she is participating in a social movement, whether she intends to be doing so or not. There is now—and there has been for quite some time—a social movement of people who refuse to eat meat out of concern for animal welfare. This movement raises awareness of several things: that much animal production involves animal cruelty, that meat production involves animal killing, that it is possible to eat healthily without consuming meat, that some people refuse to eat meat for these reasons, and that there is consumer demand for vegetarian options. This movement has had a huge effect in the United States. Vegetarian options are now more widely available. So-called "humanely farmed" meat is advertised. Efforts to improve the experiences of farmed animals are being made.

The vegetarian movement is doing a lot of moral good. It is addressing an urgent moral problem—our treatment of the animals we raise for food. There is thereby a moral reason to be a vegetarian and to participate in this movement. Some people participate more actively than others, by arguing and urging people to be vegetarian, or simply by saying "I'm a vegetarian for moral reasons." But even those who do not offer their reasons for being vegetarian are participating in the movement.

So we have isolated two moral reasons to be vegetarian: that by buying and eating meat, one is participating as a joint cause in practices that cause animal suffering and/or animal death, and that by buying and eating meat, one is failing to participate in the vegetarian movement, which is doing a lot of moral good.

There is a third reason against buying and eating meat, which arises from consideration of the following:

> (iii) Sometimes it is morally wrong to *benefit* from another being's suffering, though one's behavior will not affect whether any future suffering occurs.

For example, suppose that Sam discovers that his favorite movie, which is a coming-of-age story about some fourteen-year-olds, was made in circumstances in which the children were kidnapped and forced to work in the movie, though they were scared and miserable. It would be morally wrong for Sam to continue to enjoy the movie, even though the story itself is unchanged by facts about the circumstances of its creation. Allowing oneself to benefit in a case like this has expressive significance; it may seem to express approval or acceptance of the harming of the people in question. Allowing oneself to benefit seems to involve taking up a problematic moral relationship with the people who suffered. While it is not always morally wrong to benefit from another being's suffering, the fact that one's action would involve benefiting from another being's suffering does seem to provide a reason against the action.[8]

Some people may think that these three reasons make it *morally wrong* to buy and eat meat; they think that being vegetarian is one of the instances that makes true either (i), (ii), or (iii)—or more than one of these claims.

But that may not be right. Perhaps the situation is as follows: there are these three morally weighty reasons not to buy or eat meat. These reasons are compelling. Indeed, all things considered, one should not buy or eat meat, for these moral reasons. But buying or eating meat is not morally wrong. On this view, buying or eating meat is a *morally permissible moral mistake.*

Morally Permissible Moral Mistakes

It might seem that it is incoherent to suppose that there are morally permissible moral mistakes (behaviors that one should not engage in, for moral reasons, that are not morally wrong). There could not be any if the following principle were a necessary universal truth:

> * If S should not φ, all things considered, and the reasons against φing that make it the case that S should not φ are moral reasons, then S's φing is *morally wrong.*

This principle may seem plausible, but it is false. To see that it is false, I will offer two kinds of counterexamples, one involving the supererogatory, and one involving the suberogatory.

Some actions are supererogatory: they are above and beyond the moral call of duty. These actions are morally good to do, but not morally required. Each of us has many supererogatory actions available to us every day. Many of these actions are not such that we should perform them, all things considered. Some of them are such that we *should not* perform them, all things considered. For example, when I am rushing to Fenway Park for a rare chance to see my beloved Red Sox in person, that is not the time to stop and write a kind note to an old teacher I remember fondly from years before. That would be a nice thing to do, and it would mean a lot to her, but it would be a mistake to do that *now*. (I will use "mistake" to refer to any way of behaving that is such that the agent in question *should not* behave that way, all things considered (in light of all her reasons).[9])

Some supererogatory actions that we could perform are *not* such that we *should* perform them, all things considered (in light of all of our reasons); surely most fall into this category. Some supererogatory actions are such that we *should not* perform them, all things considered (in light of all of our reasons); they are mistakes. But some supererogatory actions are such that we *should* perform them, all things considered (in light of all of our reasons). Here is an example:

> I'm about twenty years out of high school. My friend Moggie and I are chatting about our old English teacher Sally Gilbert, and how much she meant to us. She moved away long ago but we know that another teacher, still in town, would know how to reach her. "We should write her a letter, telling her what she meant to us. We should write it right now, before we get distracted by other things and forget. She would appreciate hearing from us," Moggie says. And she is right.

Sending a note of appreciation to our long-ago teacher would be a nice thing to do, but it isn't morally required. Nevertheless, Moggie speaks truly when she says that we *should* do it. In light of all of our reasons, that is the thing we should do right now. What is there to be said in favor of doing it? That it would make Sally happy, and that it would express our gratitude. These are *moral* considerations.

This example isn't special. Often, when one performs a supererogatory action, one doesn't just think "this would be a nice thing to do, so it's available as something I might reasonably do now," but one thinks "I should do this, even though I don't *have to* do it, even though it wouldn't be morally wrong not to"—and often, one is right about that.

Plugging in *failing to perform the supererogatory action in question* (such as writing the note to Sally) for φ, these cases yield counterexamples to principle (*). This failure is a way of behaving that one should not engage in, for moral reasons, but it is not morally wrong to behave that way.

Now let's turn to the suberogatory.[10] It is more controversial whether this category of action exists, but I think it does. Suberogatory actions are actions that are morally bad to do, but not morally wrong to do. Consider your asking someone to repay a debt that is already overdue when you could get by reasonably well without the money but she will have a considerably harder time. Cases like this have sometimes been offered as cases of a "right to do wrong," cases in which one has a moral entitlement to do what is nevertheless morally wrong. I think some cases of calling in a debt like this are indeed morally wrong, particularly when the effect on the person who owes would be very bad. But consider a case in which the effect on her wouldn't be *very bad*. I think we can think of cases where we would say that one *shouldn't* call the debt in, all things considered, *for moral reasons*, though it would not be morally wrong to do so. In such a case, calling in the debt is a morally permissible moral mistake, and it is a counterexample to principle (*).

I've now argued that there can be morally permissible moral mistakes. Here is a further terminological clarification:

> S's φing is a mistake
> = (def) S should not φ, all things considered
>
> S's φing is a moral mistake
> = (def) S should not φ, all things considered, and the reasons against φing that win out to make it the case that S should not φ are moral reasons
>
> S's φing is a morally permissible moral mistake
> = (def) S should not φ, all things considered, and the reasons against φing that win out to make it the case that S should not φ are moral reasons; and S's φing is not morally wrong[11]

Note that my discussion here does not refer to what one "morally should not do" (whatever that means), nor do I refer to "what one should not do, just considering moral reasons." Rather, I am talking about what one should not do, all things considered; that is, in light of all of one's reasons. Sometimes one should not perform an action, all things considered, and the particular reasons against it that win out against performing it are *moral reasons*; such an option is a *moral mistake*. The judgment *that one should not perform it* takes into account all of one's reasons, including non-moral reasons; we then focus on the reasons against doing it that settle that one should not do it; if these are moral reasons, but the action is not morally wrong, then the action is a *morally permissible moral mistake*.

Every morally wrong action is a *mistake*, but some mistakes are not morally wrong. For example, if I have a strong hand in poker, it is a mistake to fold my hand, but it is not morally wrong. Every morally wrong action is a *moral mistake*, but not all moral mistakes are morally wrong, as I have just argued: some moral mistakes are morally permissible. Suberogatory actions (if there are any) are moral mistakes that are morally permissible. And because some supererogatory acts *should* be performed, some failures to act supererogatorily are moral mistakes that are morally permissible. (Other failures to act supererogatorily are not mistakes.)

In the next section, I will offer a solution to the puzzle about accommodation with which we started.

Explaining Accommodation

Why do most vegetarians, even those who are vegetarian for moral reasons, accommodate meat eating in many ways? Perhaps they believe—perhaps only implicitly—that while everyone *should* be vegetarian (all things considered, in light of all their reasons), it is not morally wrong to buy and eat meat. This hypothesis would explain accommodation behavior. It is generally morally wrong to aid people in doing morally wrong things, but on this view accommodation of the buying and eating of meat is not doing that. On this view, buying and eating meat is a *morally permissible moral mistake*: it is something that one should not do, all things considered, for moral reasons, but it is not morally wrong. The appropriate way of behaving regarding morally permissible moral mistakes is quite different from the appropriate way of behaving regarding morally wrong actions. Consider a situation in which you thought someone *should*, all things considered, perform a particular supererogatory action; if she chose not to do so, it would seem morally unproblematic to support her in seeing that choice through. Even a suberogatory action, when it is within someone's rights, does not call for the same reactions that a morally wrong action does; for example, one might want to signal one's disapproval while nevertheless accommodating the agent's choice. A vegetarian who accommodates walks this line: she reveals and expresses her own view of how we should eat, while accommodating the meat-eating choices of others.

Let's consider two different cases of accommodation of others' behavior to bring out the ways that it may be morally wrong to accommodate morally wrong behavior, while it may not be morally wrong to accommodate morally permissible moral mistakes. Here are two background situations in which we will consider accommodation:

> Loan: Andrea loaned her coworker Betsy $100 a while ago. Right now, Andrea doesn't really need the money, but it would be very burdensome on Betsy to pay her back at this moment (as opposed to one month from now). Although Andrea knows all of this, she decides to ask Betsy to pay her back now.
> Sale: Carrie sold a painting for $500 to her coworker Dana recently, with the agreement that Dana would pay her today. Dana misremembered the price and left $600 in Carrie's office. Carrie decides to keep the extra $100 and not correct Dana's memory.

Let's suppose that Betsy's situation is not so dire that it is morally wrong for Andrea to demand repayment, but that all things considered, Andrea should not demand repayment right now: doing so is a morally permissible moral mistake. Suppose that the four characters in these two stories work together, and that you are another coworker at the same company. Suppose further that you are in a position to accommodate or thwart Andrea's and Carrie's actions in various ways.

First, suppose that Andrea asks you to say to Betsy, "Andrea would like you to pay her the money you owe her today." And suppose that Carrie asks you to say to Dana, "Carrie says thank you for paying her for the painting." Is it morally permissible for you to accommodate their activities in these ways? It is morally permissible for you to pass on Andrea's message. Although she shouldn't demand repayment, she is entitled to do so. But it is not morally permissible for you to pass on Carrie's message. Doing so falsely implicates that Dana did not overpay, and makes you complicit in Carrie's keeping of Dana's extra $100. This comparison illustrates that it may be morally permissible to help someone to commit a morally permissible moral mistake, while it may be morally wrong to help someone to do something morally wrong.

Second, suppose that you and Betsy are standing in the hall outside Andrea's empty office and you see the $100 that Betsy paid sitting on Andrea's desk. (Andrea was handed the money by Betsy earlier in the day.) Betsy says, "It's going to be hard to make ends meet this month now that I've repaid that debt." Next, suppose that you and Dana are standing in the hall outside Carrie's empty office, with the $600 on the desk, and Dana says, "It's going to be hard to make ends meet this month now that I've paid for the painting." Is it morally permissible for you to pick up the $100 from Andrea's desk and urge Betsy to take back her repayment of the debt—in effect, taking Andrea's money without Andrea's permission? No, it is not morally permissible for you to urge Betsy to take the money. Is it morally permissible for you to pick up $100 from Carrie's desk and urge Dana to take it, saying "You overpaid; you only owed $500." Yes, this is morally permissible; indeed, it is arguably morally required. This comparison shows that it may be morally wrong to thwart someone's commission of a morally permissible moral mistake (it is morally wrong to thwart Andrea's being repaid by urging Betsy to take her money back), while it may be morally permissible (even morally required) to thwart someone's doing something morally wrong (Carrie's keeping the extra $100).

The two cases we have been discussing differ in important ways. Is that a weakness of the discussion? It is not. Rather, the point is that the features of an action that make the action morally wrong will also tend to make it morally wrong to accommodate the action. And the features of an action that make it morally permissible will also tend to make accommodation of the action morally permissible, even if the agent shouldn't be engaging in the action.

Now let's compare two more cases:

> Eddie regularly buys and eats meat.
> Frankie runs an illegal dogfighting business.

Suppose that you know both Eddie and Frankie, that you socialize with them, and that you are in a position to help them with their projects or to thwart their projects in various ways. Suppose you are a vegetarian for moral reasons. As we've already discussed, there are many ways that vegetarians often accommodate meat eaters. You may allow Eddie's preferences to determine where you eat together; you may split the bill with him, subsidizing his meat purchases; and you may refrain from knocking his food off his plate or changing his order while he's in the bathroom. Is it morally wrong to behave in these accommodating ways? It is not, we might say, though it would be if animal suffering or animal lives depended on how you act. By contrast, suppose that you could accommodate Frankie's business in various ways, by driving his dogs from one location to another sometimes, by accepting payment on his behalf from some of his bettors, and by refraining from turning him in to the police. Is it morally wrong to engage in these accommodating behaviors? Yes, we might say, both because *he* is making a difference to whether these animals suffer, and because *you* are making a difference to whether these animals suffer. Again, these two cases differ in important ways. It is the facts in virtue of which running the dogfighting is wrong that make it morally wrong to accommodate it. And it is the facts in virtue of which eating meat is not morally wrong that will explain why accommodating it is morally permissible, even if eating meat is something that Eddie should not do, for moral reasons.

Here is my solution to the puzzle of accommodation:

> Those who are vegetarians for moral reasons may be implicitly committed to the following view: that the moral reasons against eating meat make it something one *should not* do, but do not make it morally wrong; that is, that eating meat is a morally permissible moral mistake. It is in general morally permissible to accommodate others' morally permissible moral mistakes, while it is not in general morally permissible to accommodate others' morally wrong actions.

I have furthermore suggested that although meat production—even so-called "humane farming"—is morally wrong, it is *plausible* that eating meat is a morally permissible moral mistake, and that it is morally permissible to accommodate it. So, the implicit belief I am suggesting that vegetarians may have is a plausible moral view.

Note that I am not making the stronger moral claim that it is always morally permissible to accommodate others' morally permissible moral mistakes.

Nor am I making the stronger moral claim that it is always morally wrong to accommodate others' morally wrong actions. There are cases in which agents have a moral "right to do wrong," and in which we may be morally *obligated* to accommodate their wrongful actions. Here are two examples. First, it is morally wrong to have an extramarital affair when one has agreed with one's spouse to have a monogamous marriage. Still, it may be morally wrong for a hotel clerk to refuse a hotel room to two people because he knows that they would be acting morally wrongly in this way. Second, suppose it is morally wrong to read lots of sexist princess stories to a three-year-old girl.[12] Still, it may be morally wrong for a bookstore clerk to refuse to sell ten such books to a parent of a girl. Note that these are special cases, in which the clerks have particular roles, and in which the clerks have particular powers. By contrast, if the parents told their friends that they want their daughter to receive particular (in fact sexist) princess books for her birthday, the friends would not be morally obligated to comply, and indeed might be morally obligated not to comply.

Objections and Clarification

In this section I will discuss some objections; this will enable me to clarify my arguments and claims.

> Objection: I framed the puzzle as *how could it be morally permissible to accommodate meat eating if one should not eat meat, and this is so for moral reasons?* I have argued that eating meat may be a morally permissible moral mistake and that it is often morally permissible to accommodate others' morally permissible moral mistakes. But the real puzzle is: if eating meat is a mistake (if one should not eat meat), how could *accommodation* not also be a mistake? While I have proposed that it is not *morally wrong* to accommodate meat eating, I have not yet addressed the question of whether it is a morally permissible moral mistake to accommodate meat eating.

As this objection points out, our puzzle is about *making sense of* the behavior of moral vegetarians—offering a story on which moral vegetarians are being rational, and indeed may be making the right choices, both in being vegetarian and in accommodating meat eating. I believe that my story can do this: it can explain not just how accommodation of meat eating may be *morally permissible* but also how it may be *the behavior one should engage in.* I am indeed offering the following claim: often, all things considered, one *should* accommodate others' morally permissible moral mistakes. I think this claim seems quite plausible, once we see that (as I have argued) it is often morally permissible to accommodate others' morally permissible moral mistakes. There are a great many reasons *to accommodate*: it is less psychologically taxing, it does less damage to one's friendships, and it is more respectful, for example. But these reasons are ill-suited to justify doing something that is otherwise *morally wrong*; they are well-suited to justify one choice among many morally permissible choices.[13] Note also that vegetarians accommodate to different degrees; what needs explanation is not the strong claim that all vegetarians should always accommodate meat eating in every way, but rather the weaker claim that sometimes accommodating meat eating is not a mistake.

> Objection: I argued that it is morally wrong to engage in meat production, whether on factory farms or on so-called "humane farms". Later in the chapter, I argued that it is often morally wrong to *accommodate* morally wrong behavior (as opposed to morally permissible moral mistakes). But

meat eating accommodates meat production. Wouldn't that make it morally wrong?[14]

There are many different ways that some behavior may be seen to *accommodate* some other behavior. One thing that is striking about the way that vegetarians accommodate meat eating is that they refrain from behavior that could *make a difference* to whether particular instances of meat eating occur. Vegetarians engage in what we might think of as *strong accommodation* (accommodation that makes a difference) as well as *weak accommodation* (accommodation that doesn't make a difference). My view is that there are moral reasons against both strong and weak accommodation of morally wrong behavior. Earlier, I examined the reasons that confront meat eaters. I argued that there is a compelling case to be made that there are no significant *difference-making* reasons against buying and eating meat, which means that if buying and eating meat is properly seen as *accommodation* of meat production, it is only *weak accommodation*. I developed a view on which there are weighty reasons against buying and eating meat—indeed, these reasons settle that one *should not* buy or eat meat—but eating meat is not morally wrong. My view is that either buying and eating meat is not a way of *accommodating* meat production, or if it is a way of accommodating meat production, it is a morally permissible form of accommodation (though still a moral mistake) because it is only weak accommodation.

> Objection: Is the view that eating meat is a morally permissible moral mistake just the view that, in each eating situation, the *morally best choice* is to refrain from eating meat? If so, that's not very significant. We already knew that animal pain mattered *somewhat* and we knew that it was *morally better* to refrain from having any gustatory pleasures derived from animal pain and the support of animal pain. What more is there to the view?

My proposal that eating meat is a morally permissible moral mistake is not the view that the morally *best* way to behave is to refrain from eating meat. In general, it is not true that a choice is a morally permissible moral mistake just in case refraining from that choice is the morally best option. Often there is an option that is the *morally best* option but is *not* an option that an agent *should take*, all things considered. For example, suppose that some dogfighting is going on and you could shorten tonight's episode of dogfighting (but not free the dogs) if you engaged in a physical confrontation. Knowing the players involved, you would probably be beaten up very severely, landing in the hospital for a long time. It may be that it would be the morally best thing to do to step in—you would be making a personal sacrifice to stand up against animal cruelty. But it also may be that, all things considered, you shouldn't do it.

The claim that the morally best thing to do is to refrain from buying or eating meat is weaker than the claim that it is a moral mistake to buy or eat meat.

Something can be the morally best way to behave without its being a mistake to fail to behave that way. The claim that eating meat is a morally permissible moral mistake is not just the claim that it's a morally better to refrain from buying and eating meat; it is the claim that, given all of one's reasons, one *should* refrain from eating meat.

> Objection: The solution you've offered to the puzzle is not the best solution.

This objection enables me to clarify the ambitions of this chapter and the scope of my claims. My goal is to offer *an* explanation of why moral vegetarians accommodate meat eating while making sense of this behavior. I have not discussed alternative explanations, and I will not do so at any length now. My goal is to put my solution on the table. Nevertheless, let me briefly discuss two competing explanations.

> Explanation 1: Moral vegetarians know they shouldn't accommodate but they lack the nerve to disrupt social norms by refusing to accommodate.

This explanation offers *weakness of will* as the diagnosis of accommodation behavior. This explanation does not offer a way to *solve* the puzzle because it merely offers a *psychological* explanation of accommodation behavior; it does not tell a story on which that behavior is reasonable.

> Explanation 2: Moral vegetarians are being pragmatic when they accommodate meat eating. They know they'll have more success in the long run if they don't come on too strong.

This explanation does not explain why it is *morally permissible* to accommodate meat eating. It is not in general morally permissible to help someone do some morally wrong things just because in the long term, this is likely to lead to less of that kind of morally wrong behavior. That there would be *better consequences* of doing so is not in general enough to justify helping someone act morally wrongly. Explanation 2 may be part of the full story of why vegetarians choose to accommodate, but only in combination with the story I have offered of why accommodation may be morally permissible.

Conclusion

Those who are vegetarians for moral reasons often accommodate others' buying and eating meat. This behavior is puzzling if these moral vegetarians are committed to the view that buying and eating meat is *morally wrong*. I have argued that we can make sense of the way that moral vegetarians accommodate if we see them as implicitly committed to the view that buying and eating meat is *morally permissible* but is a *moral mistake*: One should not buy or eat meat, because of the moral reasons against doing so, but doing so is not morally wrong.

Acknowledgements

For helpful feedback on this paper, I thank the editors of this volume, an anonymous referee, Mark Budolfson, Tyler Doggett, Peter Graham, Alex Guerrero, Adrienne Martin, Eliot Michaelson, and audiences at the Eastern APA and the University of Vermont. This paper was inspired by conversation with Tyler Doggett about his work on the accommodation practices of vegetarians; he convinced me there's an interesting puzzle here.

Notes

1. I will restrict my attention to people who are vegetarians because of their moral concern for *animals*. I will not discuss people who are vegetarians for moral reasons, but whose motivating reasons are restricted to concern for the *environment*.
2. The argument in this section appears at greater length in my "The Moral Significance of Animal Pain and Animal Death" in *The Oxford Handbook of Ethics and Animals*, ed. Tom L. Beauchamp and R. L. Frey (New York: Oxford University Press, 2011).
3. See Shelly Kagan, "Do I Make a Difference?," *Philosophy and Public Affairs* 39, no. 2 (2011): 105–141.
4. Mark Bryant Budolfson, "The Inefficacy Objection to Consequentialism and the Problem with the Expected Consequences Response" (forthcoming in *Philosophical Studies*).
5. In my "Is the Subjective 'Ought' Explanatorily Prior to the Objective 'Ought'? (What We Learn from Errands and Russian Roulette)" (manuscript), I argue that when we consider cases in which agents take small chances of violating deontological constraints, we see that whether the actions are permissible is not just a matter of the degree of risk and the degree of wrongness of violating the deontological constraint in question; rather, there are distinct moral principles that apply to different kinds of risk-taking. I argue that this shows that the subjective "ought" cannot be explained in terms of the objective "ought."
6. A further question is whether a person's adopting a life policy of not buying or eating meat makes a difference to how much meat production occurs. I will assume that it does not, and that the discussion in this section could be expanded to draw that conclusion. For arguments similar to Kagan's, but regarding life policies, see Peter Singer's "Utilitarianism and Vegetarianism," *Philosophy and Public Affairs* 9, no. 4 (1980): 325–337; and Alastair Norcross, "Puppies, Pigs, and People," *Philosophical Perspectives* 18 (2004): 229–245, pp. 232–233.
7. A consequentialist would reject these two claims. Cases such as the two I just mentioned show that consequentialism is false.
8. A special kind of case is one in which someone *chose* to undergo a burden *in order* to benefit you. In such a case, there may be no reason to refuse to accept the benefit on the grounds that it derives from someone's suffering.
9. Note that I am using the word "mistake" to apply to *actions* (or *failures to act*) rather than *thought processes*. When we say that someone has made a mistake, very often we mean that she has reasoned poorly. But we also sometimes refer to actions as mistakes. We say "it was a mistake to call that poker hand" or "don't make the mistake of paying the carpenter before she finishes the job." A person can perform an action

that is a mistake without making any mistake of reasoning, as when someone correctly realizes what she should do but then out of weakness of will fails to do it; one might truly say, "She made a mistake. How did it happen, you ask? She knew what she should do but she was weak-willed."

10. For interesting discussion of the suberogatory (also called "offence"), see Roderick M. Chisholm, "Supererogation and Offence: A Conceptual Scheme for Ethics," *Ratio* 5 (1963): 1–14; David Heyd, *Supererogation* (Cambridge: Cambridge University Press, 1982); Gregory Mellema, *Beyond the Call of Duty: Supererogation, Obligation, and Offence* (Albany: State University of New York Press, 1991); Julia Driver, "The Suberogatory," *Australasian Journal of Philosophy* 70, no. 3 (1992): 286–295; Hallie Liberto, "Denying the Suberogatory," *Philosophia* 40 (2011): 395–402; and Paul McNamara, "Supererogation, Inside and Out: Toward an Adequate Scheme for Common Sense Morality," in *Oxford Studies in Normative Ethics*, ed. Mark Timmons (Oxford: Oxford University Press, 2011), 202–235.

11. I introduce and discuss these concepts in greater detail in my "Morally Permissible Moral Mistakes" (forthcoming in *Ethics*); see also my "Morality Within the Realm of the Morally Permissible" (in *Oxford Studies in Normative Ethics*, ed. Mark Timmons [Oxford: Oxford University Press, 2015]) and my "Gamete Donation as a Laudable Moral Mistake" (manuscript).

12. This issue weighs on me, as a parent of a four-year-old girl who adores princess stories. Happily, not all princess stories are sexist.

13. Seana Shiffrin (in "Egalitarianism, Choice-Sensitivity, and Accommodation," in *Reason and Value: Themes from the Work of Joseph Raz*, ed. Philip Pettit [Oxford: Oxford University Press, 2004], 270–302) discusses the accommodation practices of vegetarians and offers some explanations of why these practices make sense. Tyler Doggett (in "Letting Others Do Wrong" [manuscript]) argues that Shiffrin's proposed explanations cannot account for why it would be morally permissible to accommodate morally wrong behavior. But her proposed explanations may do a better job at a different task: supplementing my account. Once we see accommodation as one of a number of *morally permissible* options, it is more plausible that the kinds of considerations Shiffrin offers can explain why one should accommodate in some cases.

14. Adrienne M. Martin's chapter in this volume, "Factory Farming and Consumer Complicity," argues that meat eaters of factory farmed meat are *accomplices* to meat production.

13
DOES LOCAVORISM KEEP IT TOO SIMPLE?

Anne Barnhill

I care deeply about food, and I care even more deeply about the environment. Indeed, I spent a couple of very earnest years riding the locavore bandwagon myself. My conversion to being an emotional and intellectual locavore was the only activist decision I'd made in my life. As my passion started to stir, I could be found haunting local farmers' markets around my hometown, Austin, Texas, bashing "big industrial" and "Frankenfood" at every opportunity, investigating like a Checkpoint Charlie the groceries that cross the threshold of my kitchen . . . I had found my cause: saving the environment through the way I ate. Empowerment! Turns out I wasn't much of an acolyte . . . Something about the "eat local" ethic, heady as it was, began to hit me as not only pragmatically unachievable but simplistically smug.[1]

James McWilliams has a problem with locavorism. It is, in his phrase, "simplistically smug"—a phrase that evokes a range of criticisms of locavorism made by McWilliams and others. The task of this chapter is to consider some of those criticisms. Locavorism is the practice of buying locally grown food. A first criticism is that buying *locally* is an overly simplistic approach to making the food system more environmentally sustainable: Buying locally will make little difference to the environmental impact of our food consumption, and might even be counterproductive. This is McWilliams's primary criticism of locavorism, and one that has many other critics of locavorism have made. A second criticism is that *buying* locally is an overly simplistic approach. The local food movement's endorsed mechanism of social change—that consumers choose to buy locally grown food—is unlikely to be effective and could blunt efforts at more radical change. A third criticism is that the local food movement, and more generally the alternative food movement, has an overly narrow set of priorities and largely ignores the needs of low-income people.

These three criticisms are all variations on a theme: Locavorism is an overly simplistic approach—or at least, an insufficiently comprehensive approach—given the complex problems of the food system. But McWilliams charges locavorism not only with being simplistic, but with being simplistically *smug*. To call someone smug is to make a moral criticism of her: that she is overconfident, overly pleased with herself, or self-righteous, and that this excessive self-satisfaction betrays a moral flaw. In the last section of this chapter, I try to unpack this moral criticism and consider whether the locavores McWilliams describes deserve it. I consider the related question of whether we should doubt the ethical sincerity of locavores whose locavorism is motivated not only by their ethical commitments but also by their social identities.

Is Buying *Locally* an Overly Simplistic Approach?

People who choose to eat locally grown food have a variety of motivations for doing so. Locavores may intend to reduce the environmental impact of the food system, to obtain food that's fresher and tastes better, to support local farmers and the local economy, to create a sense of local community by bringing consumers and farmers together, or to foster community empowerment and participatory democracy at the local level.[2]

Steven Schnell observes that "the term 'local' has become a stand-in for a host of other perceived virtues."[3] But based on interviews with community supported agriculture (CSA) members, Schnell concludes eating locally grown food should not be understood as motivated by one or a list of specific aims—an understanding that's too reductive—but rather is a way to have a fuller experience of *place*:[4]

> Food has become a key part of many individuals' place narratives, and has provided a key way for many to weave themselves into the broader narratives of the places they inhabit, in establishing a stronger sense of place. No longer is a tomato just a tomato, it is a tomato that came from this field, was grown in this particular way by this particular farmer. Such narratives contrast with mistrust of the abstractness and the anonymity of the globalized food system expressed by large numbers of my interviewees, and embed the individual in a web of meaning and place. In Casey's (2001) terms, local food has become a vital part of the "thickening" of place experience.[5]

For some participants, the local food movement, like the alternative food movement more generally, is "against global, big, conventional, environmentally degrading food systems."[6] Local food systems are embraced as the alternative to a global, industrial food system. Some adherents' rejection of the global and industrial food system, in addition, is part of a general rejection of globalization and neoliberalism.[7]

Scholars have argued that localizing food systems does not necessarily accomplish this agenda, and have questioned whether local food movements in their current form are successfully promoting localization and successfully promoting the ultimate aims of localizing food systems. The general criticism that local food movements are failing to meet their aims takes many forms. Scholars argue that local food movements may be falling short of being a "counterstrategy" to globalization and neoliberalism;[8] fostering a view of food as tied to a specific community and place, rather than just a product or commodity;[9] creating a food system that is regenerative;[10] and, most generally, creating a food system that better achieves social justice.[11] One specific criticism is that encouraging people to buy locally grown food is not an effective way to promote the localization of food systems (as described later), though it should be noted that buying and eating locally grown food is just one of many activities comprising local food movements (along with growing locally grown food in home gardens and community gardens, educating the public, supporting farmers, and political advocacy).[12]

Along with querying the efficacy of locavorism, local food movements, and localization, scholars have ethically critiqued them, arguing that local food movements are elitist, exclusionary, and have paid too little attention to the needs of low-income people. Thus the questions examined in this chapter—whether locavorism is overly *simplistic*, and whether locavores deserve moral criticism for embracing locavorism—are just one piece of a broader critical conversation about localism and local food movements.[13]

This section discusses arguably the most visible and influential critique of locavorism: The distance food has traveled is not a proxy for its environmental impact. But we should keep in mind, as Schnell argues, that this critique does not apply to locavorism as a whole, given the many motivations of locavores.[14] The "food miles" critique applies only to locavores who buy locally with the primary aim of reducing the environmental impact of their eating. More generally, the specific criticisms discussed in this chapter will not all apply to all locavores or to all submovements within the local food movement.[15]

A chorus of critics has argued that buying locally does not make a meaningful difference to the environmental impact of our diet, and is sometimes even counterproductive. Conventional agriculture is characterized by large farms that grow a single crop, the heavy use of synthetic inputs such as synthetic fertilizers and pesticides, the use of genetically modified crops, and a food distribution system that transports food long distances before it is consumed. This agricultural and food distribution system has a range of negative environmental effects both locally and globally, including the degradation of agricultural land, including soil erosion; runoff from fertilizer use that pollutes water and kills aquatic life; air pollution; the loss of biodiversity on agricultural land; and the loss of wilderness as land is brought into agriculture use. Agriculture is also a significant contributor to global warming, both because nitrogen-based fertilizers cause the emission of nitrous oxide (a greenhouse gas) and because a significant amount of energy is used in the production and distribution of food.[16] According to one estimate, the food system—including food production, manufacturing, distribution, preparation and disposal—accounts for 16 percent of the energy used in the United States.[17]

Concern with the environmental impact of agriculture is one motivation for locavorism. The thought goes that buying locally grown food will reduce the distance that our food travels, thereby reducing our food-related energy expenditure and our food-related contribution to global warming. But critics of locavorism argue that minimizing the distance food travels will, at best, only marginally reduce our food-related energy expenditure.[18] Only 11 percent of the greenhouse gas emissions created by the food system come from the transport of food, so food transport is not the best place to focus our energies in order to cut food-related contributions to global warming.[19] Additionally, critics argue, buying locally might actually *increase* the overall environmental impact associated with eating a particular food, depending on how the locally grown version is produced and transported.

The local transport of food can be less energy efficient than its long-distance transport. Less efficient means of transport are often used: Transporting food by truck or car uses more energy per mile than transporting food by rail or by sea. Local transport of food typically involves smaller quantities of food: for example, a small farmer who drives a pickup truck of food fifty miles to a farmer's market as compared to a long-haul trucker who drives a much larger load across the country. And consumers, in their quest to procure local food, might put in extra miles in their cars. As Singer and Mason write:

> Driving 20 miles in a big SUV to pick up eggs from a local farmer and then heading off in a different direction to get fresh local produce would almost certainly be less energy efficient than buying everything at a single supermarket, even if the food has traveled further to get there.[20]

Even if locally grown food travels fewer miles before being eating, more energy might have been used in its transport nonetheless.

Environmental locavorism can also backfire for another reason: Locally grown versions of particular foods can be produced in less environmentally sustainable ways. If the local climate has a shorter growing season, less water, or less fertile soil, then growing food locally can have more environmental impact than growing it elsewhere and transporting it.[21] A favorite example is buying tomatoes in winter: A British study showed that buying local tomatoes grown indoors produced three times as many carbon emissions as buying tomatoes grown outdoors in Spain and trucked to Britain.[22] Consumers might assume that locally grown food is produced in more environmentally sustainable ways than food shipped over longer distances—perhaps in the popular imagination, a local farm is a small farm that engages in sustainable agriculture—but this is not uniformly true.

Thus, critics argue, applying the simple rule "buy local" will not guarantee that you're significantly reducing your food-related environmental impact, or even reducing it at all. A food system in which food is consumed close to where it is grown will not necessarily use less energy and produce fewer greenhouse gas emissions, or have less overall environmental impact. If the goal is reducing the environmental impact associated with our food consumption, buying locally is too simplistic.

Rather than focusing on the distance food travels ("food miles"), a more meaningful measure of a food-related energy consumption is *life-cycle assessment*, which incorporates many aspects of the production, distribution, and consumption of food, including the use of fertilizer and other inputs; how the food is harvested, packaged, and stored; how the food is transported; and how the food is cooked.[23] As an alternative to buying locally, James McWilliams proposes a "hub-and-spoke" food system: Food is grown in those climates (hubs) where it can be grown most efficiently, using fewer inputs than conventional agriculture, and is transported (along the spokes) in energy-efficient ways.[24]

Critics make a persuasive case that a food system in which consumers eat locally grown food is not necessarily a more environmentally sustainable food system. Reducing the environmental impact of the food system will require much more complex and extensive changes. But have these critics made a trenchant criticism of the personal practice of buying locally grown food in order to reduce food-related environmental impact?[25] Even if the environmentally preferable food system is not one in which all food is locally distributed and consumed, but is a much more complex system, it could still be true that individuals concerned with the environmental impact of their diets should adopt the simple personal policy of eating locally grown food, given realistic limitations on their knowledge, attention, and motivation. A more complicated rule that requires effort to implement won't be implemented as often. Consumers do not always know how their food was produced or transported, nor could they always find out this information even if they were motivated to try. The best rule is likely to be a simple rule. Even so, there might be better simple rules than "buy local." Singer and Mason suggest "buy locally *and* seasonally," to exclude out-of-season local foods that are less likely to be produced in environmentally preferable ways (such as the hothouse tomato).[26]

Is *Buying* Locally an Overly Simplistic Approach?

We've been considering the criticism that buying *locally* is an overly simplistic approach to making the food system more environmentally sustainable. A complementary criticism is that *buying* locally is an overly simplistic approach to changing the food system. According to this criticism, the local food movement's endorsed mechanism of social change—that consumers buy locally grown food—is unlikely to be effective and could blunt efforts at more radical change.[27]

This criticism is levied against the local food movement and the alternative food movement more broadly, and even more generally against *ethical consumerism*, the practice of purchasing or not purchasing certain products with the aim of eliminating objectionable production practices. Critics argue that ethical consumerism is unlikely to succeed as a strategy for changing production practices, simply because many consumers will not choose products produced in ethically better ways.[28] Consumers lack reliable information about the products they consume, and have competing considerations, such as saving money, that determine their consumption choices.[29] A related point is that the local and organic food movements have embraced a means of social change—buying locally grown, organic food—that only relatively wealthy people can adopt.[30] Excluding the nonaffluent is objectionably elitist according to critics, while also limiting the number of adherents the movements can expect to have.

By advocating that people "vote with their pocketbooks," critics claims, ethical consumerism reinforces the idea that change should happen through the marketplace *rather than* through increased government regulation or improved policies.[31] As Jacobsen and Dulsrud write:

> The "new orthodoxy of the active consumer" comes part and parcel with the promotion of a rearrangement of responsibilities between the state and private markets in an evermore liberalistic world economy . . . The proponents of a more distant state are the obvious beneficiaries of the dissemination and stabilizing of the idea of a more responsible consumer role.[32]

In other words, by promulgating the idea that the consumer—and not the government—has the responsibility to make sure products are produced ethically, ethical consumerism undercuts efforts to change policy. In the specific case of locavorism, the criticism goes, buying locally is not an effective strategy for changing the food system given that it will not be widely adopted. Furthermore, by exhorting people to buy locally, the local food movement simply reinforces the idea that change should happen through the marketplace rather than through government action, which could blunt more effective means of change such as revamped agricultural policies. Some critics would add that by shoring up the idea that change should happen through the marketplace and the choices of consumers, rather than through improved policies or regulation, market-based solutions shore up neoliberalism.[33]

Are these criticisms fair? The concern that market-based solutions will undercut efforts to change policy should give activists pause. If encouraging people to buy locally thwarts policy change by reinforcing the idea that market-based solutions are the way to go, but only a minority of consumers will ever participate in these market-based solutions, then activists should question the wisdom of advocating "buy local." It stands to reason that locavorism will not be widely adopted so long as locally grown products are more expensive than the alternatives. So encouraging people to buy locally is not likely, in and of itself, to bring about a food system in which most food is grown locally. In other words, encouraging people to buy locally is not a comprehensive strategy for bringing about this alternative food system. But so what? Wearing a hat is not a comprehensive strategy for staying warm in the cold, but that's no argument against wearing a hat, along with taking other steps to stay warm. So long as activists recognize that ethical consumerism and market-based solutions are just one element of a more comprehensive reform of the food system, there is nothing inherently problematic about embracing and advocating them. That market-based solutions are noncomprehensive is not a good argument against them.[34]

It's also worth noting that criticisms of buying locally apply to locavorism as a *purchasing* practice. But there are other ways in which proponents of eating locally get local food—such as growing it in home gardens or community gardens. These approaches are not market based, and thus cannot be criticized as reinforcing the idea that change should happen through the marketplace. Nonetheless, the criticism could still be lodged that growing one's own food is not an effective strategy for changing the food system given that it will not be widely adopted, and that such efforts will be less effective means of change than broader institutional or policy reform.

Are the Goals of Locavorism Objectionably Narrow?

Along with questioning the effectiveness of locavorism as a strategy for making the food system more environmentally sustainable, food scholars and activists have criticized locavorism and the local food movement as overly focused on a narrow range of goals to the exclusion of other morally important goals.

Peter Singer and Jim Mason criticize one ethical motivation for locavorism, that it will strengthen the local economy:

> Is this [that it will strengthen the local economy] an ethical reason for buying locally? . . . If we have the choice of using our purchasing power in our local economy, or buying products imported, under fair terms of trade, from some of the world's poorer nations, is there any merit in keeping our money within our own community? . . . There are, of course, further questions to ask: Is exporting food really going to help the poor in developing countries, or would they do better to become more self-sufficient rather than growing commodities for export? . . . These questions all need to be investigated, and we will return to them in the following chapter. Until we do, we can't reach any conclusions about whether we should buy locally or from developing countries. Our point now is simply that "keep your dollars circulating in your own community" is not an ethical principle at all. To adhere to a principle of "buy locally," irrespective of the consequences for others, is a kind of community-based selfishness.[35]

Whether we ought to support local farmers, rather than farmers from other countries, depends upon a range of moral and empirical considerations. Adopting locavorism simply because it will strengthen the local economy—without considering that we might have moral duties to support farmers in distant places—is failing to appreciate the moral complexity of the situation and to recognize all the relevant moral facts, Singer and Mason argue.

A related criticism is that the local food movement, and more generally the alternative food movement within the United States, has paid insufficient attention to the needs of low-income people. Alison Hope Alkon and Julian Agyeman describe the alternative food movement thus:

> The food movement encourages eaters to turn away from the industrially produced and processed goods created from monocultures—what New York Times bestselling author Michael Pollan (2008) refers to as "edible food-like substances"—and instead to choose fresh, local, and often organic offerings supplied by local small farms . . . The purchase of local and organic food is cast as a "vote with your fork," to quote a common movement refrain. It is a vote for environmental sustainability . . . It is also a vote for small, family-owned farms, as opposed to their large, corporate counterparts, and for creating local communities filled with rich interpersonal interactions. . . . By transforming our food practices, the movement tells us, we can live healthier, more authentic lives while supporting positive social and environmental change. In this way, the food movement is responding to popular anxieties that modern life is alienating and antisocial, and an American mythology that locates the good life in romanticized small towns.[36]

So described, the alternative food movement is pro-environment, pro-community, anti-industrial food, and pro-family farm, and sees local, small-scale agriculture as a healthy and authentic alternative to industrial agriculture; it is typified by Michael Pollan, farmers' markets, and community supported agriculture.

While the alternative food movement might seem to embrace a range of values and goals, it has been criticized as being overly focused on the concerns of the middle class while largely ignoring the needs of low-income people.[37] For example, anti-hunger advocate Mark Winne argues that the organic food movement within the United States has not meaningfully addressed food insecurity, the inability to reliably afford enough food, a problem experienced by 15 percent of Americans each year.[38] Nor has it addressed the broader problem that low-income people, whether or not they are food insecure, have difficulty affording healthier foods like fruits, vegetables, and whole grains, which cost more per calorie than processed foods—not to mention that they cannot afford organic food, which is typically more expensive.[39] In Mark Winne's words, "the poor get diabetes; the rich get local and organic."[40] The same critique applies to locally grown food. In a study of food access among a lower income rural population, Jesse C. McEntee concluded that locally grown food is unaffordable for low-income people: "The large majority of respondents interviewed regarded contemporary local products as prohibitively expensive to purchase regularly. One homeless shelter resident described how the farmers' market prices were 'outrageous.'"[41]

Julie Guthman has criticized the alternative food movement in the same vein. Along with tasting better, organic food is also healthier for consumers, and therefore low-income consumers' inability to afford organic food is an issue of "inequitable access to safe, nutritious, and tasty food," according to Guthman.[42] She maintains that the organic food movement has done little to address this inequity and to address other inequalities.[43]

Partially in response to the perceived failures of the alternative food movement, the *food justice* movement explicitly encompasses a range of goals: improving food security in low-income communities; making sure healthy food is accessible in all communities; establishing fair working conditions for agricultural workers and food service workers; combating racism and classism within agriculture, the food industry, and within other foods movements; and achieving a more environmentally sustainable food system.[44] Food justice concerns, including food security concerns, *are* increasingly being incorporated into the "mainstream" alternative food movement.[45]

But the criticism remains that the alternative food movement has focused on a narrow range of goals and has by and large paid insufficient attention to racial and economic injustices in the food system, most notably that many low-income people cannot reliably afford enough food or healthy food.

Is this a legitimate criticism? If the alternative food movement has largely failed to address food insecurity, is it criticizable on that account?[46] Are specific organizations involved in the alternative food movement criticizable if they fail to address food insecurity in their communities? For a social movement to focus its energies on one set of morally important goals, and ignore a related set of morally important goals, is not necessarily problematic; it might be the only way that the movement can hope to make progress. Movement participants might be committed to the full range of goals, but believe that a unified solution is infeasible. For example, members of a community supported agriculture organization might see food insecurity as a morally urgent problem, but believe that it is most efficiently and systematically addressed by federal programs that give low-income people food assistance, whereas their activism is focused elsewhere, on the creation of alternative food distribution systems and alternative food marketplaces. They would not be criticizable for having the wrong moral priorities if they were strategically focusing their energies on one set of goals (though they would still be open to the criticism that their narrow focus is bad strategy). That a social movement's goals are noncomprehensive is not necessarily a cause for criticism; it matters why its goals are noncomprehensive.

The "why" in this case, according to some critics, is that the alternative food movement is homogeneous and exclusive, with mostly white and middle-class adherents.[47] As Alkon and Agyeman put it, the alternative food movement is a "monoculture."[48] The movement has only a narrow range of goals because its central narrative—and the moral priorities that this narrative establishes—resonates with its middle-class white participants, but is largely uninformed by the experience of low-income people and people of color—those who, in Alkon and Agyeman's words, "have been, and are currently, most deeply harmed by the food system."[49] The movement's narrative and language reflect the experience of white Americans. Julie Guthman argues, for example, that the movement consistently evokes an agrarian past—small farmers working the land—that is "far more easily romanticized by whites than others" given that nonwhites in the United States were systematically denied land ownership. Guthman argues that the alternative food movement uses idioms, such as valorizing "putting your hands in the soil," that reflect white experience: "For African-Americans, especially, putting your hands in the soil is more likely to invoke images of slave labor than nostalgia. Such rhetoric thus illustrates a lack of cultural competency that might be deemed an exclusionary practice."[50]

As another example of how the alternative food movement reflects the experience of white Americans, Alkon and Agyeman discuss Michael Pollan's exhortation not to "eat anything your great-grandmother wouldn't recognize as food." This exhortation assumes a particular cultural history that is not shared by everyone:

> Some [of our great-grandmothers] were enslaved, transported across the ocean, and forced to subsist on the overflow from the master's table. Others were forcibly sent to state-mandated boarding schools, in which they were taught to despise, and even forget, any foods they would previously have recognized. . . . Of course it is not these histories that Pollan intends to invoke when he urges readers to choose fruits and vegetables over processed foods. But because of his privileged positionality, Pollan fails to consider the effects of race on food access and the alternative meanings his words may hold for people of color in the United States. In this same way, whites in the food movement often simply do not see the subtle exclusivities that are woven into its narrative.[51]

The alternative movement's language and narrative reflect the experience of white Americans, according to Alkon and Agyeman, and this "dominant narrative . . . compelling as it may be to some, might drown out other stories. In these additional stories, food is not only linked to ecological sustainability, community, and health but also to racial, economic, and environmental justice."[52] In other words, the alternative food movement's priorities are noncomprehensive not because it is strategically focusing on certain morally important concerns rather than others, and not even because its adherents have judged certain concerns to be more important than others, but because its adherents simply fail to get beyond their own experience and appreciate the range of injustices in the food system.[53] If this diagnosis is correct, then the noncomprehensiveness of the alternative food movement's goals is deserving of moral criticism.[54] It is a kind of moral obtuseness enabled by occupying a privileged social position.

Are Locavores Overly Self-Satisfied?

In the previous sections, we've discussed three ways in which environmental locavorism, and the alternative food movement or ethical consumerism more generally, are criticized as overly simplistic or not sufficiently comprehensive: Buying *locally* will make little difference to the environmental impact of our food consumption, and might even be counterproductive; *buying* locally is unlikely to be an effective means of social change; and the alternative food movement has an overly narrow set of priorities and largely ignores the needs of low-income people.

But James McWilliams charges locavorism not only with being simplistic, but with being simplistically *smug*: "Something about the 'eat local' ethic, heady as it was, began to hit me as not only pragmatically unachievable but simplistically smug." To call someone smug is to make a moral criticism of her: that she is overconfident or overly pleased with herself, and that this overconfidence or self-satisfaction betrays a moral flaw of hers. Smugness is overconfidence, excessive pride, or self-satisfaction that is excessive or otherwise misplaced. Given that McWilliams considers locavorism to be a largely ineffective strategy for making the food system more environmentally sustainable, there's a straightforward sense in which environmental locavores are overconfident: It's overconfident to think we can solve a problem as complex as the environmental unsustainability of the food system with something as simple as buying local.

There's another sense in which locavores might be criticized as overly confident: They are confident in their own moral vision, when in fact this moral vision is limited. As discussed in the previous section, the alternative food movement is criticized as failing to appreciate the full range of problems with the food system, and failing in this way because it is comprised mostly of white, middle-class people who do not appreciate other perspectives on the food system besides their own. In other words, locavores are confident in their moral vision, but this confidence is misplaced because their moral vision is in fact quite limited.

I suspect that McWilliams has something more in mind when he charges locavorism with smugness. Consider this passage:

> It's hard to identify exactly when my skepticism [with locavorism] became committed doubt, but several random observations nudged me down the path of crankiness. Maybe it was watching one too many times the

pretentious woman with the hemp shopping bag declaring "This bag is not plastic!" make her way to market in an SUV the size of my house. Or maybe it was the baffling association between buying local food and dressing as it if were Haight-Ashbury circa 1968 that got me thinking that my sacred farmers' market was a stage set more for posturing than environmental activism.[55]

I'd like to suggest that there are two distinct criticisms of locavores in this passage—two distinct ways in which locavores' self-satisfaction is misplaced.[56] The first is a familiar criticism of activists: that they are unwarrantedly self-righteous. Some locavores, typified by the "pretentious" women driving an SUV, are self-righteous about engaging in locavorism and other environmentally friendly practices (such as using a hemp bag rather than a plastic bag) even while engaging in other, environmentally damaging actions (such as driving a large, energy-inefficient car). Their self-righteousness about their environmentally friendly conduct is misplaced because their overall pattern of behavior is not environmentally friendly.

McWilliams's second criticism, I'd like to suggest, is that some locavores—typified by those "posturing" at the farmers' market—take themselves to be acting solely from an ethical commitment to the environment, but are, in fact, primarily motivated by conformity with a social identity. The "baffling association between buying local food and dressing as it if were Haight-Ashbury circa 1968" makes sense if some locavores' embrace of locavorism is primarily motivated by seeing themselves as, or by wanting to be, a certain type of person—the type of person who buys locally and dresses as if it were Haight-Ashbury circa 1968. Environmentalism is a posture they adopt; what's really motivating them is their social identity—a specific kind of hipster/counterculture identity. If these hipster locavores are pleased with themselves for being ethically committed to the environment—and by extension, pleased with themselves for being virtuous—but their locavorism is not primarily motivated by an ethical commitment, then their self-satisfaction is misplaced. This misplaced self-satisfaction bespeaks something wrong with their moral character—if not smugness exactly, then self-serving inauthenticity. As I'm interpreting McWilliams, these hipster locavores are criticizable because they misunderstand and misrepresent themselves: They have a less significant ethical commitment to the environment than they purport to have.

But imagine a hipster who is also a locavore, and who makes no pretention that his locavorism is rooted solely in an ethical commitment to the environment. He sees his locavorism as motivated both by concern for the environment and by his identity as a hipster. Is he criticizable? Is there anything worrisome about his locavorism reflecting not only an ethical commitment but also a social identity? In the above passage, McWilliams speaks contemptuously of some hipster locavores and accuses them of posturing rather than having a genuine commitment to the environment. To my ear, this is a familiar accusation. We doubt the genuineness of ethical commitments when they are wrapped up in social identities; for example, we're skeptical of activists who dress and act alike. But should we be? If someone's locavorism expresses both an ethical commitment and a social identity, should we doubt the genuineness of the ethical commitment?

Let's say that someone's *personal identity* is her understanding of who she is or what kind of person she is. Our personal identities include seeing ourselves as people with certain personal characteristics—for example, seeing oneself as an athlete or an activist. Our identities also include racial or ethnic identities, gender identities, sexual identities, and class identities—for example, identifying as an African-American or identifying as of Italian descent, and identifying as a woman or as a transsexual man. Our identities also include seeing ourselves as members of groups, such as families, communities, organizations, and nations—for example, identifying as an American, a Mormon, and a Green Bay Packers fan.

Ethical commitments are constitutive of some identities: Having the identity consists entirely of having a specific ethical commitment, as with the identities "pro-life" and "pro-choice." In other cases, there are characteristic ethical commitments that go along with identities, though these ethical commitments are not constitutive of those identities. For example, being morally opposed to abortion is a characteristic ethical commitment of Catholicism, even though many or even most Catholics are not morally opposed to abortion. A characteristic ethical commitment of Tibetan Buddhism is showing compassion towards animals by refraining from killing them, though not all Tibetan Buddhists have this ethical commitment.

"Locavore" is an identity constituted by a food practice (buying locally grown food) and for which there are characteristic ethical commitments. To identify as a locavore is to see oneself as a certain kind of person, one who is committed to purchasing local food for certain characteristic ethical reasons. Another identity constituted by a food practice, and for which there are characteristic moral commitments, is *vegetarian*. To have the identity vegetarian is to see oneself as a person committed to not eating meat, and many (but not all) vegetarians have an *ethical* commitment not to eat meat.

Food practices are not definitive of most social identities, though they are central to many social identities. Groups engage in distinctive food practices—eating certain foods and avoiding others, buying particular food products, celebrating special occasions with particular dishes—and invest meaning in these food practices, seeing them as emblematic of the group. Food practices are a key way in which social identities are instilled, shored up, and expressed.[57] For example, part of identifying as Italian or Indian for many people is appreciating traditional Italian or Indian foods. Religions prescribe certain food practices, including eating special foods as part of rituals, eating special foods on holidays, and not eating certain foods; having a religious identity can include observing these food practices. Families have food traditions or food practices that help to create a shared identity as a family—for example, having Taco Night every week, or celebrating holidays by eating specific dishes.

In some cases, a group's characteristic food practices reflect their characteristic ethical commitments. For example, Tibetan Buddhists' vegetarianism reflects an ethical commitment to show compassion towards animals by refraining from killing them. Both the vegetarianism and the ethical commitment are characteristic of Tibetan Buddhism, though not all Tibetan Buddhists are vegetarian and not all have this ethical commitment. Imagine a particular Tibetan Buddhist who is a vegetarian and is ethically committed not to harm sentient creatures. We should not assume that her vegetarianism is motivated by an ethical commitment that stands free of her identity as a Tibetan Buddhist; she might have this ethical commitment only in virtue of identifying as a Tibetan Buddhist. But this does not mean her ethical commitment is not genuine, or is merely a posture. For her, being a Tibetan Buddhist involves certain ethical commitments, and thus being motivated by her identity as a Tibetan Buddhist involves being motivated by these ethical commitments. The identity *Tibetan Buddhist* does not displace ethical commitments in her motivational economy, but rather incorporates them.

This bring us back to the hipster locavores. Buying locally grown food is one of many characteristic activities that hipsters engage in, along with urban farming mainstays such as planting rooftop gardens, canning vegetables, and raising chickens in the backyard. Engaging in these kinds of activities, along with having characteristic aesthetic preferences and ethical commitments (such as a commitment to environmental sustainability), together constitute being a hipster and express hipster identity. One interpretation of the hipster's locavorism is that it is analogous to a Packers fan eating bratwurst: It is a food practice that reflects an identity but does not reflect an ethical commitment. But another interpretation is that the hipster's locavorism is analogous to the Tibetan Buddhists' vegetarianism: It expresses an identity *and* reflects an ethical commitment that is characteristic of this identity. The hipster's locavorism reflects his hipster identity and is motivated by it *and* the hipster's locavorism concomitantly genuinely reflects an ethical commitment characteristic of hipsters, namely a commitment to environmental sustainability.

Conclusions

Is buying *locally* an overly simplistic approach to making the food system more environmentally sustainable? Yes. Is it still a practice that individuals should adopt, if they wish to reduce the environmental impact of their food? Yes, though Singer and Mason's "buy locally and seasonally" is better. Is *buying* locally a limited approach to changing the food system? Yes. Is it still a good practice for activists to advocate? Perhaps, depending upon whether advocating a market-based solution undercuts public support for regulatory or policy changes. Are the goals of the alternative food movement too narrow? These goals address only some of the morally urgent problems with the food system. Is the alternative food movement, or its adherents, morally criticizable for not embracing other goals, such as reducing food insecurity? It depends upon why they fail to embrace these goals. They are morally criticizable if they simply fail to get beyond their own experience and appreciate the range of injustices in the food system. Lastly, should we doubt the ethical sincerity of someone whose locavorism reflect both her ethical commitments and her social identity? No.

By and large, locavorism is an overly simplistic approach to changing the food system. But the fact that one's approach to a problem is noncomprehensive does not necessarily warrant criticism. It's only when this noncomprehensiveness is counterproductive, or goes unrecognized, or has a blameworthy origin, that criticism is warranted.

Acknowledgements

Thank you to Terence Cuneo, Andrew Chignell, and Matt Halteman for insightful comments on an earlier version of this chapter. And thank you to Andy Egan, Tyler Doggett and Mark Budolfson for many conversations about all things food ethics.

Notes

1. James E. McWilliams, *Just Food: Where Locavores Get It Wrong and How We Can Truly Eat Responsibly* (New York: Back Bay, 2010), 10.
2. Laura B. DeLind, "Are Local Food and the Local Food Movement Taking Us Where We Want to Go? Or Are We Hitching Our Wagons to the Wrong Stars?," *Agriculture and Human Values* 28, no. 2 (June 2011): 273–283, doi:10.1007/s10460-010-9263-0; Steven M. Schnell, "Food Miles, Local Eating, and Community Supported Agriculture: Putting Local Food in Its Place," *Agriculture and Human Values* 30, no. 4 (December 2013): 615–628, doi:10.1007/s10460-013-9436-8; Ian Werkheiser and Samantha Noll, "From Food Justice to a Tool of the Status Quo: Three Sub-Movements within Local Food," *Journal of Agricultural and Environmental Ethics* 27, no. 2 (April 2014): 201–210, doi:10.1007/s10806-013-9459-6. For a critical discussion of some of these motivations, see Peter Singer and Jim Mason, *The Ethics of What We Eat: Why Our Food Choices Matter* (Emmaus, PA: Rodale, 2007), chap. 11, "Eating Locally"; Pierre Desrochers and Hiroko Shimizu, "Yes We Have No Bananas: A Critique of the 'Food Miles' Perspective," *Mercatus Policy Series*, no. 8 (2008), http://papers.ssrn.com/sol3/papers.cfm?abstract_id=1315986; McWilliams, *Just Food*, chap. 1, "Food Miles or Friendly Miles? Beyond the 'Farm to Fork' Paradigm of Production"; Dwight Furrow, "Locavorism and 'Food Miles,'" *Edible Arts*, July 12, 2012, http://foodandwineaesthetics.com/2012/07/12/locavorism-and-food-miles/.
3. Schnell, "Food Miles, Local Eating, and Community Supported Agriculture," 623.
4. For a compelling explanation of the connection between *place* and culture, and the importance attached to place/culture by advocates of localism, see Lisa Heldke, "Down-Home Global Cooking: A Third Option between Cosmopolitanism and Localism," in *The Philosophy of Food*, ed. David M. Kaplan (Berkeley: University of California Press, 2012), 33–51.

5. Schnell, "Food Miles, Local Eating, and Community Supported Agriculture," 625.
6. David Goodman, E. Melanie DuPuis, and Michael K. Goodman, *Alternative Food Networks: Knowledge, Practice, and Politics* (New York: Routledge, 2013), 12. As Goodman et al. observe:

> Localization has also been widely canvassed as a solution to the problems of global industrial agriculture. In the USA, the academic literature on alternative food networks emphasizes the strength of their embeddedness in local norms, such as the ethics of care, stewardship, and agrarian visions. (11)

7. Neoliberalism is here understood as a political economic system emphasizing free market capitalism and a minimal state. For a very brief synopsis of neoliberalism, see Julie Guthman, *Weighing In: Obesity, Food Justice, and the Limits of Capitalism* (Berkeley: University of California Press, 2011), 17, Alison Hope Alkon and Teresa Marie Mares, "Food Sovereignty in US Food Movements: Radical Visions and Neoliberal Constraints," *Agriculture and Human Values* 29, no. 3 (January 24, 2012): 348, doi:10.1007/s10460-012-9356-z. Guthman cites David Harvey, *A Brief History of Neoliberalism* (Oxford: Oxford University Press, 2007). Many scholars of food movements, food systems, food sovereignty, and food justice explicitly or implicitly critique neoliberalism. Julie Guthman and Melanie DuPuis, "Embodying Neoliberalism: Economy, Culture, and the Politics of Fat," *Environment and Planning D: Society and Space* 24, no. 3 (2006): 427–448, doi:10.1068/d3904; Julie Guthman, "Neoliberalism and the Making of Food Politics in California," *Rethinking Economy; Agro-Food Activism in California and the Politics of the Possible; Culture, Nature and Landscape in the Australian Region* 39, no. 3 (May 2008): 1171–1183, doi:10.1016/j.geoforum.2006.09.002; Abby Wilkerson, "'Obesity,' the Transnational Plate, and the Thin Contract," ed. Eduardo Mendieta, *Radical Philosophy Review* 13, no. 1 (2010): 43–67, doi:10.5840/radphilrev20101314; Goodman, DuPuis, and Goodman, *Alternative Food Networks*; Alkon and Mares, "Food Sovereignty in US Food Movements." Indeed, a recurrent criticism of alternative food systems is that they are not sufficiently opposed to neoliberalism. See Werkheiser and Noll, "From Food Justice to a Tool of the Status Quo," 206–207; Guthman, "Neoliberalism and the Making of Food Politics in California"; Alkon and Mares, "Food Sovereignty in US Food Movements."
8. Goodman, DuPuis, and Goodman, *Alternative Food Networks*, chap. 2; Werkheiser and Noll, "From Food Justice to a Tool of the Status Quo."
9. DeLind, "Are Local Food and the Local Food Movement Taking Us Where We Want to Go?"
10. Ibid.
11. Goodman, DuPuis, and Goodman, *Alternative Food Networks*, chap. 2.
12. Patricia Allen et al., "Shifting Plates in the Agrifood Landscape: The Tectonics of Alternative Agrifood Initiatives in California," *Journal of Rural Studies* 19, no. 1 (2003): 61–75. See, for example, the activities of the organization Just Food. http://justfood.org/about-us.
13. For a critical discussion of localism, see Heldke, "Down-Home Global Cooking: A Third Option between Cosmopolitanism and Localism."
14. Schnell, "Food Miles, Local Eating, and Community Supported Agriculture," 616.
15. Werkheiser and Noll (2014) helpfully identify three sub-movements within the local food movement. The sub-movement that has gotten the most mainstream attention and critique is the "individual-focused" sub-movement concerned with changing individuals' personal practices so that individuals eat locally grown food; locavorism, the practice of eating/buying locally grown food, is part of this sub-movement of the local food movement. This paper by and large concerns the individual-focused sub-movement of the local food movement. Werkheiser and Noll also identify two additional sub-movements of the local food movement: the "systems-focused" sub-movement focused on systems-level change, such as changing policies or creating

new organizations; and the "community-focused" sub-movement that sees food "as a collectivizing force, especially among marginalized groups, which can become seats for activism" (207) and focuses on building relationships "within and between communities" (208).

16. Organisation for Economic Co-operation and Development, *Environmental Performance of Agriculture in OECD Countries Since 1990* (2008), http://www.oecd.org/greengrowth/sustainable-agriculture/44254899.pdf; McWilliams, *Just Food*, chaps. 1 and 2; Robert Paarlberg, *Food Politics: What Everyone Needs to Know* (New York: Oxford University Press, 2010), chap. 10. For a very parsimonious description of the environmental problems with industrial agriculture and alternative agricultural practices, see National Geographic Society, "Sustainable Agriculture," http://environment.nationalgeographic.com/environment/habitats/sustainable-agriculture/.

17. Patrick Canning et al., *Energy Use in the U.S. Food System* (USDA Economic Research Service, 2010), http://www.ers.usda.gov/publications/err-economic-research-report/err94.aspx#.U4jY0cbiYR4.

18. Singer and Mason, *The Ethics of What We Eat*, chap. 11, "Eating Locally"; McWilliams, *Just Food*, chap. 1, "Food Miles or Friendly Miles? Beyond the 'Farm to Fork' Paradigm of Production"; Desrochers and Shimizu, "Yes We Have No Bananas." All of the objections to locavorism discussed in this section are made by Singer and Mason, Desrochers and Shimizu, and McWilliams.

19. Christopher L. Weber and H. Scott Matthews, "Food-Miles and the Relative Climate Impacts of Food Choices in the United States," *Environmental Science & Technology* 42, no. 10 (2008): 3508–3513. As quoted in Desrochers and Shimizu, "Yes We Have No Bananas" and Singer and Mason, *The Ethics of What We Eat*.

20. Singer and Mason, *The Ethics of What We Eat*, 148–149.

21. As Desrochers and Shimizu write:

> For one thing, producing food in the most suitable locations and delivering it over long distances is much greener than manufacturing dairy products or growing vegetables near final consumers where these operations requires large volumes of animal feed to make up for less productive pastureland, energy-guzzling heated greenhouses instead of natural heat, and massive amounts of water for irrigation rather than abundant rainfall.

Pierre Desrochers and Hiroko Shimizu, "The Locavore's Delusion," *The Fraser Forum*, August 2012, http://www.fraserinstitute.org/uploadedFiles/fraser-ca/Content/research-news/research/articles/locavores-delusion.pdf.

22. Alison Smith et al., *The Validity of Food Miles as an Indicator of Sustainable Development: Final Report*, July 2005. http://webarchive.nationalarchives.gov.uk/20130402151656/http://archive.defra.gov.uk/evidence/economics/foodfarm/reports/documents/foodmile.pdf. As discussed by Singer and Mason, *The Ethics of What We Eat*, 146–147; Desrochers and Shimizu, "Yes We Have No Bananas"; and McWilliams, *Just Food*, 26.

23. McWilliams, *Just Food*, 23–30; Desrochers and Shimizu, "Yes We Have No Bananas."

24. McWilliams, *Just Food*, 46–51.

25. Have these critics made a trenchant criticism of locavorism as a movement? Perhaps the critique of "food miles" is something of a red herring as a criticism of the locavorism movement. Sarah Laskow argues that adherents of locavorism do not necessarily understand locavorism to be the practice of buying food that is grown nearby (e.g., within a radius of one hundred miles), but rather the practice of buying food that is produced by small farms that use sustainable methods. "Local" is shorthand for "sustainably produced." Sarah Laskow, "Giving Local Food the Raspberry," *American Prospect*, July 10, 2012, http://prospect.org/article/giving-local-food-raspberry.

26. Singer and Mason, *The Ethics of What We Eat*, 150.

27. Delind (2011) critiques locavorism for promoting change through changes in personal consumption, rather than other means of social change. As Werkheiser and Noll (2014) characterize Delind's view,

> The many wide-ranging problems with the food system are seen as being addressable by your personal changes, rather than looking at these systems or working collectively. This can let us off the hook from the much harder work of actually addressing systematic problems while still letting us feel that we are one of the ones who care and are making a difference. (204)

28. Christian Coff, *The Taste for Ethics: An Ethic of Food Consumption* (Dordrecht: Springer, 2006); Eivind Jacobsen and Arne Dulsrud, "Will Consumers Save The World? The Framing of Political Consumerism," *Journal of Agricultural and Environmental Ethics* 20, no. 5 (August 7, 2007): 469–482, doi:10.1007/s10806-007-9043-z.

29. Coff, *The Taste for Ethics*; Jacobsen and Dulsrud, "Will Consumers Save the World?"

30. Alison Hope Alkon and Julian Agyeman, "Introduction: The Food Movement as Polyculture," in *Cultivating Food Justice: Race, Class, and Sustainability* (Cambridge, MA: MIT Press, 2011), 3.

31. Christian Coff also argues that the idea of ethical consumerism helps to shore up the existing capitalist order, and to promote consumption:

> When consumption is understood as one of the most efficient ways of making a difference, we are indeed tempted to see and understand ourselves as consumers. The articulation of the political consumer is a strategically very subtle display of power that never questions consumption in itself. Consumption becomes good *per se* as long as the ethical profile of the manufacturers is good." (Coff, *The Taste for Ethics*, 83)

32. Jacobsen and Dulsrud, "Will Consumers Save the World?" 479.

33. Alkon and Mares, "Food Sovereignty in US Food Movements." See also Werkheiser and Noll, "From Food Justice to a Tool of the Status Quo," 206.

34. But keep in mind that some advocates of local food systems object to market-based solutions because they object to the structure of the market—that is, they object to neoliberalism and minimally regulated global markets. To such critics, market-based solutions are problematic in part because they shore up neoliberalism, or at least do nothing to undermine it.

35. Singer and Mason, 140–141.

36. Alkon and Agyeman, "Introduction: The Food Movement as Polyculture," 1–2.

37. Patricia Allen, "Mining for Justice in the Food System: Perceptions, Practices, and Possibilities," *Agriculture and Human Values* 25, no. 2 (June 2008): 157–161, doi:10.1007/s10460-008-9120-6; Patricia Allen and Clare Hinrichs, "Buying into 'Buy Local': Engagements of United States Local Food Initiatives,'" in *Constructing Alternative Food Geographies: Representation and Practice*, 2007, 255–272 (Emerald Group Publishing Limited; Bingley, UK); Jesse McEntee, "Contemporary and Traditional Localism: A Conceptualisation of Rural Local Food," *Local Environment* 15, nos. 9–10 (2010): 785–803, doi:10.1080/13549839.2010.509390; Alkon and Agyeman, "Introduction"; Julie Guthman, "If They Only Knew: The Unbearable Whiteness of Alternative Food," in *Cultivating Food Justice: Race, Class, and Sustainability* (Cambridge, MA: MIT Press, 2011), 263–282; Alison Hope McEntee, "Realizing Rural Food Justice: Divergent Locals in the Northeastern United States," in *Cultivating Food Justice: Race, Class, and Sustainability* (Cambridge, MA: MIT Press, 2011), 239–259.

38. Mark Winne, *Closing the Food Gap: Resetting the Table in the Land of Plenty* (Boston: Beacon Press, 2009), chaps. 7–9. For more information on the frequency of food insecurity as measured by the USDA, see US Department of Agriculture Economic Research Service, "Frequency of Food Insecurity," http://ers.usda.gov/topics/food-nutrition-assistance/food-security-in-the-us/frequency-of-food-insecurity.aspx.

39. For a discussion of the price differential between categories of foods (e.g., sugary drinks, fruits and vegetables, fats), see Eric Finkelstein and Laurie Zuckerman, *The Fattening of America: How the Economy Makes Us Fat, If It Matters, and What to Do about It* (Hoboken, NJ: Wiley, 2008), 19–22.
40. Winne, *Closing the Food Gap*, 125.
41. McEntee, "Contemporary and Traditional Localism."
42. Julie Guthman, *Agrarian Dreams: The Paradox of Organic Farming in California* (Berkeley: University of California Press, 2004), 183.
43. Ibid.; Guthman, "Neoliberalism and the Making of Food Politics in California" and "If They Only Knew."
44. Robert Gottlieb and Anupama Joshi, *Food Justice* (Cambridge, MA: MIT Press, 2010); Alison Hope Alkon and Julian Agyeman, *Cultivating Food Justice: Race, Class, and Sustainability* (Cambridge, MA: MIT Press, 2011).
45. An example of incorporating food security concerns into local/alternative food efforts is having a CSA with a sliding scale, so that participating in the CSA is affordable for lower-income families. See, for example, http://foodshuttle.org/events/coordinating-sliding-scale-csa/andhttp://www.justfood.org/tipsheet/csa-nyc-toolkit/flexible-payment-options/sliding-scale.
46. According to Werkheiser and Noll, one sub-movement in the local food movement is the systems-focused sub-movement, which they understand to be "the intersection between the local food movement and the food security movement" (205). The criticism that the local food movement has paid insufficient attention to food security might apply to the individual-focused sub-movement, which is focused on changing individuals' practices, but this criticism would not apply to the systems-focused sub-movement.
47. Alkon and Agyeman, "Introduction"; Clare Hinrichs and Kathy S. Kremer, "Social Inclusion in a Midwest Local Food System Project," *Journal of Poverty* 6, no. 1 (January 2002): 65–90, doi:10.1300/J134v06n01_04; Guthman, "If They Only Knew."
48. Alkon and Agyeman, "Introduction," 2.
49. Ibid., 4.
50. Guthman, "If They Only Knew," 276.
51. Alkon and Agyeman, "Introduction," 3.
52. Ibid., 4.
53. Goodman et al. raise the related concern that localism can be too focused on promoting one conception of what counts as "good" food, while paying too little attention to democratic processes, leading to exclusionary movements that promote the normative views of one group. Their concern is that "a normative, values-based localism leads to an elitist, undemocratic politics of perfection marked by problematic conceptions of social justice and civic tolerance" (Goodman, DuPuis, and Goodman, *Alternative Food Networks*, 13.) Rather than a local food movement that aims to convert people to the "right" view—according to which the local is "a bulwark against anomic global capitalism"—Goodman et al. advocate for a food movement that is more participatory, reflexive and "open-ended" (ibid., 23–24).
54. Schnell forcefully pushes back against the critique that local food movements are exclusionary:

> This critique is a narrower version of a more general one made of local food projects by Winter (2003), among others, who have argued that local food movements are intrinsically exclusionary, and are examples of "defensive localism," characterized by elitism, reactionary politics, and xenophobia. Yet such arguments almost always dodge a key question: just because they theoretically could be exclusionary, are they actually? Despite these scholars' lack of concrete evidence, their assertions are quoted regularly by others as if they

have been proven to characterize all local food projects, the same sort of slippery logic that has typified much usage of food mile critiques. (618)

55. James McWilliams, *Just Food*, 11.
56. Schnell (2013) notes, and takes issue with, the ad hominem nature of McWilliams's critique:

> The stereotype of the wealthy but clueless locavore has become a part of our "common knowledge," bolstered by the work of some popular writers, but also, unfortunately, scholars as well.
> Indeed, such ad hominem attacks are not difficult to find in the scholarly literature. McWilliams (2009), whose book *Just Food* is in general a thoughtful and nuanced consideration of the complexity of issues surrounding agriculture and sustainability, opens his book with a monodimensional portrait of "locavores" obsessed with food miles above all other considerations. (619)

Schnell thinks that

> [McWilliams and other] critics of local food on both the left and the right have often erected straw men (and women), caricatures of those who seek out local food, treating them as Berkeley-dwelling dupes snookered by local food advertising campaigns and the siren songs of Michael Pollan and Alice Waters. (620)

57. E. N. Anderson, *Everyone Eats: Understanding Food and Culture* (New York: New York University Press, 2005); Paul Rozin and Michael Siegal, "Vegemite as a Marker of National Identity," *Gastronomica: The Journal of Food and Culture* 3, no. 4 (2003): 63–67; Amy E. Guptill, Denise A. Copelton, and Betsy Lucal, *Food & Society: Principles and Paradoxes* (Cambridge: Polity, 2013), chap. 3; Carole Counihan and Penny Van Esterik, *Food and Culture: A Reader* (New York: Routledge, 2013).

References

Alkon, Alison Hope, and Julian Agyeman. *Cultivating Food Justice: Race, Class, and Sustainability.* Cambridge, MA: MIT Press, 2011.
———. "Introduction: The Food Movement as Polyculture." In *Cultivating Food Justice: Race, Class, and Sustainability*, 1–20. Cambridge, MA: MIT Press, 2011.
Alkon, Alison Hope, and Teresa Marie Mares. "Food Sovereignty in US Food Movements: Radical Visions and Neoliberal Constraints." *Agriculture and Human Values* 29, no. 3 (January 24, 2012): 347–359. doi:10.1007/s10460-012-9356-z.
Allen, Patricia. "Mining for Justice in the Food System: Perceptions, Practices, and Possibilities." *Agriculture and Human Values* 25, no. 2 (June 2008): 157–161. doi:10.1007/s10460-008-9120-6.
Allen, Patricia, Margaret FitzSimmons, Michael Goodman, and Keith Warner. "Shifting Plates in the Agrifood Landscape: The Tectonics of Alternative Agrifood Initiatives in California." *Journal of Rural Studies* 19, no. 1 (2003): 61–75.
Allen, Patricia, and Clare Hinrichs. "Buying into 'Buy Local': Engagements of United States Local Food Initiatives.'" *Constructing Alternative Food Geographies: Representation and Practice* (2007): 255–272.
Anderson, E. N. *Everyone Eats: Understanding Food and Culture.* New York: New York University Press, 2005.
Canning, Patrick, Ainsley Charles, Sonya Huang, and Karen R. Polenske. *Energy Use in the U.S. Food System.* USDA Economic Research Service, 2010. http://www.ers.usda.gov/publications/err-economic-research-report/err94.aspx#.U4jY0cbiYR4.
Coff, Christian. *The Taste for Ethics: An Ethic of Food Consumption.* Dordrecht: Springer, 2006.

Counihan, Carole, and Penny Van Esterik. *Food and Culture: A Reader.* New York: Routledge, 2013.

DeLind, Laura B. "Are Local Food and the Local Food Movement Taking Us Where We Want to Go? Or Are We Hitching Our Wagons to the Wrong Stars?" *Agriculture and Human Values* 28, no. 2 (June 2011): 273–283. doi:10.1007/s10460-010-9263-0.

Desrochers, Pierre, and Hiroko Shimizu. "Yes We Have No Bananas: A Critique of the 'Food Miles' Perspective." *Mercatus Policy Series*, no. 8 (2008). http://papers.ssrn.com/sol3/papers.cfm?abstract_id=1315986.

———. "The Locavore's Delusion." *The Fraser Forum*, August 2012. http://www.fraserinstitute.org/uploadedFiles/fraser-ca/Content/research-news/research/articles/locavores-delusion.pdf.

Finkelstein, Eric, and Laurie Zuckerman. *The Fattening of America: How the Economy Makes Us Fat, If It Matters, and What to Do about It.* Hoboken, NJ: Wiley, 2008.

Furrow, Dwight. "Locavorism and 'Food Miles.'" *Edible Arts.* July 12, 2012. http://foodandwineaesthetics.com/2012/07/12/locavorism-and-food-miles/.

Goodman, David, E. Melanie DuPuis, and Michael K. Goodman. *Alternative Food Networks: Knowledge, Practice, and Politics.* New York: Routledge, 2013.

Gottlieb, Robert, and Anupama Joshi. *Food Justice.* Cambridge, MA: MIT Press, 2010.

Guptill, Amy E., Denise A. Copelton, and Betsy Lucal. *Food & Society: Principles and Paradoxes.* Cambridge: Polity, 2013.

Guthman, Julie. *Agrarian Dreams: The Paradox of Organic Farming in California.* Berkeley: University of California Press, 2004.

———. "Neoliberalism and the Making of Food Politics in California." *Rethinking Economy; Agro-Food Activism in California and the Politics of the Possible; Culture, Nature and Landscape in the Australian Region* 39, no. 3 (May 2008): 1171–1183. doi:10.1016/j.geoforum.2006.09.002.

———. "If They Only Knew: The Unbearable Whiteness of Alternative Food." In *Cultivating Food Justice: Race, Class, and Sustainability*, 263–282. Cambridge, MA: MIT Press, 2011.

———. *Weighing In: Obesity, Food Justice, and the Limits of Capitalism.* Berkeley: University of California Press, 2011.

Guthman, Julie, and Melanie DuPuis. "Embodying Neoliberalism: Economy, Culture, and the Politics of Fat." *Environment and Planning D: Society and Space* 24, no. 3 (2006): 427–448. doi:10.1068/d3904.

Harvey, David. *A Brief History of Neoliberalism.* Oxford: Oxford University Press, 2007.

Heldke, Lisa. "Down-Home Global Cooking: A Third Option between Cosmopolitanism and Localism." In *The Philosophy of Food*, edited by David M. Kaplan, 33–51. Berkeley: University of California Press, 2012.

Hinrichs, Clare, and Kathy S. Kremer. "Social Inclusion in a Midwest Local Food System Project." *Journal of Poverty* 6, no. 1 (January 2002): 65–90. doi:10.1300/J134v06n01_04.

Jacobsen, Eivind, and Arne Dulsrud. "Will Consumers Save the World? The Framing of Political Consumerism." *Journal of Agricultural and Environmental Ethics* 20, no. 5 (August 7, 2007): 469–482. doi:10.1007/s10806-007-9043-z.

Laskow, Sarah. "Giving Local Food the Raspberry." *American Prospect*, July 10, 2012. http://prospect.org/article/giving-local-food-raspberry.

McEntee, Alison Hope. "Realizing Rural Food Justice: Divergent Locals in the Northeastern United States." In *Cultivating Food Justice: Race, Class, and Sustainability*, 239–259. Cambridge, MA: MIT Press, 2011.

McEntee, Jesse. "Contemporary and Traditional Localism: A Conceptualisation of Rural Local Food." *Local Environment* 15, nos. 9–10 (2010): 785–803. doi:10.1080/13549839.2010.509390.

McWilliams, James E. *Just Food: Where Locavores Get It Wrong and How We Can Truly Eat Responsibly.* New York: Back Bay, 2010.

Organisation for Economic Co-operation and Development. *Environmental Performance of Agriculture in OECD Countries since 1990*, 2008. http://www.oecd.org/greengrowth/ sustainable-agriculture/44254899.pdf.

Paarlberg, Robert. *Food Politics: What Everyone Needs to Know*. New York: Oxford University Press, 2010.

Rozin, Paul, and Michael Siegal. "Vegemite as a Marker of National Identity." *Gastronomica: The Journal of Food and Culture* 3, no. 4 (2003): 63–67.

Schnell, Steven M. "Food Miles, Local Eating, and Community Supported Agriculture: Putting Local Food in Its Place." *Agriculture and Human Values* 30, no. 4 (December 2013): 615–628. doi:10.1007/s10460-013-9436-8.

Singer, Peter, and Jim Mason. *The Ethics of What We Eat: Why Our Food Choices Matter*. Emmaus, PA: Rodale, 2007.

Smith, Alison, Paul Watkiss, Geoff Tweddle, Alan McKinnon, Mike Browne, Alistair Hunt, Colin Treleven, Chris Nash, and Sam Cross. *The Validity of Food Miles as an Indicator of Sustainable Development: Final Report*, July 2005. http://webarchive.nation-alarchives.gov.uk/20130402151656/http://archive.defra.gov.uk/evidence/economics/foodfarm/reports/documents/foodmile.pdf.

US Department of Agriculture Economic Research Service. "Frequency of Food Insecurity." Last updated September 3, 2014. http://ers.usda.gov/topics/food-nutrition-assistance/food-security-in-the-us/frequency-of-food-insecurity.aspx.

Weber, Christopher L., and H. Scott Matthews. "Food-Miles and the Relative Climate Impacts of Food Choices in the United States." *Environmental Science & Technology* 42, no. 10 (2008): 3508–3513.

Werkheiser, Ian, and Samantha Noll. "From Food Justice to a Tool of the Status Quo: Three Sub-Movements within Local Food." *Journal of Agricultural and Environmental Ethics* 27, no. 2 (April 2014): 201–210. doi:10.1007/s10806-013-9459-6.

Wilkerson, Abby. "'Obesity,' the Transnational Plate, and the Thin Contract." *Radical Philosophy Review* 13, no. 1 (2010): 43–67. doi:10.5840/radphilrev20101314.

Winne, Mark. *Closing the Food Gap: Resetting the Table in the Land of Plenty*. Boston: Beacon Press, 2009.

14

WHAT'S WRONG WITH ARTIFICIAL INGREDIENTS?

David M. Kaplan

The *Wall Street Journal* reports that Frito-Lay will no longer use monosodium glutamate, FD&C Red 40, and more than thirty other artificial ingredients in any of its chips.[1] The company intends to make half of its snacks sold in the US with only natural ingredients. The *Guardian* reports that Nestlé has removed all artificial colors, flavors, and preservatives—eighty additives—from all of its confectionary products.[2] The company has already removed all artificial ingredients from its beverages; the Nestlé Crunch bar was the last to have its artificial flavorings replaced with natural ones. Kraft Foods is looking for a natural alternative to replace artificial colors Yellow 5 and 6 in its macaroni and cheese powders;[3] General Mills is looking for natural colorants for its baking products.[4] By producing more and more natural and organic products, the food industry is gradually responding to increasing public wariness about artificial ingredients. This is good news for consumers. We all know what it is like to struggle to pronounce the long, unfamiliar names on a label and wonder what exactly it is we are putting in our bodies. There seems to be something intuitively untoward, inappropriate, or wrong with eating too many artificial ingredients.

But what exactly is wrong with it? Granted, some artificial colors and preservatives should be avoided for health reasons but what about additives that pose no health risks such as ascorbyl palmitate and polysorbate 60—or more familiar ones, such as vitamin C and baking powder? Should they be avoided as well, and is it always better to choose foods with no artificial ingredients? Are there other reasons to avoid artificial ingredients that have nothing to do with health?

When we examine the common arguments for and against food additives we find a mélange of reasons. Some are moral and political, others appeal to the putative superiority of anything natural, and others appeal to religious concepts of the sacred and the sublime. We are just as likely to appeal to nutritional science as we are to our deepest held (but sometimes baseless) convictions about what we should eat. Like most of our food preferences, our reasons for choosing or avoiding artificial ingredients are often a jumbled mess.

This chapter discusses the moral arguments for and against artificial ingredients. The most common arguments in defense of them are consequentialist and deontological. The most common arguments against them are also consequentialist and deontological in addition to those that appeal to their effects on our relationships with nature and on the quality of life. After sorting through the merits and the shortcomings of each class of argument, I propose we focus our analysis. The class of food items and range of uses of foods with artificial ingredients is surprisingly large. That makes it hard to generalize. It is, therefore, also important to consider (1) which ingredients are in question; (2) how often something is consumed; (3) if it is consumed with knowledge; and (4) if the food manufacturer is one you should support. Answers to these questions should help us get a clearer picture on what we should produce, purchase, serve, and eat.

What Are Artificial Ingredients?

An *artificial ingredient* is anything added to food to maintain or improve freshness and safety, nutritional value, taste, texture, and appearance. They include sweeteners, thickeners, stabilizers, colors, nutrients, and preservatives. An artificial ingredient is one kind of *food additive*: a substance used in producing, processing, preparing, packaging, transporting, or holding food. A food additive is defined in Section 201(s) of the 1938 Food, Drug, and Cosmetic Act as "any substance the intended use of which results or may reasonably be expected to result, directly or indirectly, in its becoming a component or otherwise affecting the characteristic of any food."[5] This includes any substance used in producing, packing, processing, preparing, packaging, transporting, or holding food—including any source of radiation intended for any such use. A *color* additive is any dye, pigment, or substance used to offset color loss, to enhance natural colors, or just for fun (e.g., green ketchup).

The US Food and Drug Administration (FDA) maintains a list of every substance added to food in the United States, called (appropriately enough) "Everything Added to Food in the United States (EAFUS)."[6] EAFUS provides chemical, administrative, or toxicological information on more than three thousand substances. The list is daunting. Most of the ingredients are unrecognizable.

EAFUS is, however, not without its critics. The Center for Science in the Public Interest (CSPI) warns against some of the additives the FDA claims are safe.[7] CSPI recommends we avoid: acesulfame-potassium (artificial sweetener); artificial colorings Blue 2, Green 3, Red 3, Yellow 5, Yellow 6, Orange B, and 4-methylimidazole (caramel coloring); butylated hydroxyanisole (BHA, which protects fats from oxidation); olestra (aka Olean, a fat substitute), partially hydrogenated oil (trans fat); potassium bromate (flour improver, increases volume); propyl gallate (preservative); saccharin (artificial sweetener); and sodium nitrate (preservative, coloring, and flavoring).[8] The additives on the CSPI "caution" list includes three food colorings (Blue 1, Citrus Red 2, Red 40); aspartame (aka NutraSweet); brominated vegetable oil (an emulsifier used in soft drinks); butylated hydroxytoluene (BHT, an antioxidant/preservative); diacetyl (butter flavoring); heptyl paraben (beer preservative); mogrosides (artificial sweetener); rebiana (artificial sweetener); and transglutaminase (aka meat glue).[9] Who should we believe, the FDA or CSPI?

What Are the Arguments in Favor of Artificial Ingredients?

There are a number of reasons why artificial ingredients are good to put into food—mainly practical and technical issues food manufacturers and distributors have to contend with. For example, some foods need additives to prevent spoilage, some to allow smooth mixing of ingredients, and some to replace vitamins and minerals lost in processing. But food and food ingredients also raise ethical issues. Anything people do is (in principle) subject to moral evaluation including, of course, making and eating food. The most common moral defenses of producing and consuming artificial ingredients are either consequentialist (roughly, right or wrong because of consequences) or deontological (roughly, right or wrong but not simply because of consequences).

The consequentialist arguments claim that the benefits artificial ingredients provide outweigh whatever other harms they might pose. From a consequentialist perspective, food additives are:

- Useful. Additives can make food safer, fresher, healthier, better looking, and better tasting, hence preferable to anything less safe, less fresh, less nutritious, and so on. They provide useful functions. For example, they can add sweetness without adding calories; give reduced-fat foods the texture and mouthfeel we have come to expect; offset color loss due to storage conditions; and prevent crystallization in food products. Additives solve practical problems for food manufacturers and distributors.
- Convenient. Artificial ingredients provide our food with the properties most of us have grown accustomed to such as increased shelf life, fortification, and recognizable appearance. Few of us have diets of exclusively fresh foods. Foods with preservatives can be more readily available to consumers who cannot obtain fresh food. Food additives also benefit people on low-fat or low-calorie diets. Often weight-loss foods are fortified to help dieters eat nutritious meals without spending the time and energy to cook from scratch. The same is true for people on gluten-free, vegetarian, or vegan diets. Anyone on a special diet can easily find a range of food items at most grocery stores in the US. Typically, these gluten-free, soy-based, fake meat products have long lists of artificial ingredients. Additives make it easy to be gluten-free, vegetarian, or vegan.

- Harmless. Regulatory agencies, such as the FDA and UK Food Standards Agency study, monitor, and regulate all food additives to ensure their safety. A food manufacturer must seek FDA approval to make a new food or color additive, or even to use an already approved additive in a not yet approved manner. Manufacturers must provide evidence that a substance is safe. Since 1999, indirect additives must be approved, as well. The FDA relies on the best available science to ensure that there is a *reasonable* certainty of no harm. (Science is never *absolutely* certain, of course.) The not-for-profit, nonpartisan CSPI acknowledges that the vast majority of additives are completely safe to eat.[10] At best, artificial ingredients improve our food; at worst, they do no harm.
- Traditional. People have added ingredients to improve the quality (not just taste) of their foods for hundreds if not thousands of years. Salt, sulfites, gelatin, and MSG have been safely used for generations. So have mogrosides in China and stevia in South America, both sweeteners derived from plants. People have always added substances to alter their food.
- Beneficial. The extended shelf life of products allows people to eat in the absence of fresh food or preparation facilities. Products such as ready-to-eat-meals used in famine and disaster relief would be impossible without artificial ingredients. In addition to feeding people who otherwise would go hungry, food with additives can also be fortified to be more nutritious. For example, Plumpy'Nut, a nutrient-enriched peanut butter used to treat severe acute malnutrition, has made famine relief far more effective than it has ever been.[11] Enov Nutributter is a nutritional supplement intended to fortify the diets of children after they stop breastfeeding. It provides missing nutrients in children ages six to twenty-four months to aid in their motor and cognitive development. In addition, preservatives can slow spoilage and help control foodborne illnesses, including salmonella and botulism. And the wide availability of additive-rich vegetable proteins helps support vegetarian and vegan diets, which lowers the demand for animal products, reduces animal suffering, and helps to reduce the litany of environmental problems associated with confined animal feeding operations.
- Functionally equivalent. Chemical components are equivalent to their natural counterparts. Sucralose functions the same as sugar, sorbitan monostearate as egg yolks, and sodium erythorbate as citric acid. If there is no functional difference between the artificial and natural ingredient, then there is no cause for concern. Any argument against the effects of artificial ingredients should apply to their natural counterparts, which renders the artificial character of something moot.

The deontological arguments in defense of artificial ingredients maintain that individuals have the right to eat whatever they wish and producers have the right to produce whatever they wish, with this limitation: In exercising these rights, they must not impinge upon the rights of others not to be harmed, coerced, or deceived. In turn, governments have an obligation to protect the rights of consumers and producers to make, eat, and feed as they please. On a rights model, food additives are a matter of:

- Freedom. Individuals have the right to purchase, prepare, and consume foods with artificial ingredients. Even if someone chooses to produce or ingest a substance that is known to pose health risks (e.g., alcohol or tobacco), it is within our rights to choose freely. The right to food is a basic human right enshrined in Article 25 of the 1948 UN Declaration of Human Rights. It protects the fundamental right of all people to be free from hunger, free from malnutrition and food insecurity, to access either directly or by purchase sufficient food to live with dignity in accordance with the cultural traditions to which they belong. The right to adequate food means that (all else being equal) every man, woman, and child must have physical and economic access at all times to adequate food using a resource base appropriate for its procurement in ways consistent with human dignity. The state has the obligation to respect, protect, and fulfill each person's access to food. The UN Declaration of Human Rights was ratified by nearly two hundred countries, in principle guaranteeing individuals both freedom from want and freedom to choose what to make and what to eat.
- Justice. Governments have an obligation to protect the rights of producers and consumers to freely choose what to make and eat, respectively. If we have a right to produce and consume food with artificial ingredients then, minimally, governments should not interfere in the exercise of our freedoms. Maximally, governments should take active measures to ensure our food rights by, for example, assessing laws, institutions, and programs, strengthening the legal framework, and ensuring effective recourse for rights violations. Justice requires the protection of the rights of producers and consumers of food with artificial ingredients.
- Responsibility. Food banks typically are stocked with foods with long shelf lives. These items contain artificial ingredients. If they did not, they would spoil and it would be difficult to feed those in need. Foods used for emergency disaster, such as Meals, Ready-to-Eat (MRE) always contain artificial ingredients. MRE have a shelf life of three years; they are designed to withstand a parachute drop of fifteen hundred feet; and their ingredient lists are long and read like typical vending machine snack food. Disaster relief would not be nearly as effective if limited to fresh foods. The US National Guard, for example, distributed food to thousands of victims of Hurricanes Katrina, Ike, and Sandy; the US Air Force dropped fifty-five thousand pounds of food into Haiti after the 2010 earthquake; and the US Army distributed MRE to civilians in war-torn regions of Iraq and Afghanistan. Arguably, the duty to provide others with emergency food relief is tantamount to a duty to feed others junk food.

The arguments in defense of artificial ingredients are a bit more difficult if the FDA is wrong and some ingredients do indeed pose real health risks. If something is bad for your health, it is safe to say you probably should not eat it. This is especially true for people with food allergies or who, for whatever reasons, cannot eat foods with certain ingredients such as lactose, caffeine, or salt. But even the use of unsafe food additives is not hard to defend. A consequentialist will affirm that you can still lead a worthwhile life (presumably maximizing happiness for everyone) while eating a poor diet laden with additives. It might be unwise or shortsighted to eat unhealthy foods, but so are many other things people routinely do, like drive cars, own firearms, or refrain from exercise. So long as the (long term) benefits (for everyone) outweigh the health risks or other harms, a consequentialist can justify making, selling, or eating just about anything.

The deontological justification for eating unhealthy foods is even more straightforward. If someone has a right—whether guaranteed as a general right to freedom or a specific right to food—it deserves protection regardless of the consequences. Our right to make, sell, and eat what we choose is inviolable so long as the rights of others are not violated.

What Are the Arguments against Artificial Ingredients?

The common arguments against artificial food ingredients are more colorful. They come in four groups: arguments that appeal to consequences, rights, harmony with nature, and quality of life.

The consequentialist arguments claim that foods with artificial ingredients either pose risks or have some other adverse effects that outweigh safety, nutrition, taste, and appearance benefits they might have. A consequentialist might say that artificial ingredients are:

- Bad for your health. The consensus among nutritionists is that highly processed foods—the kinds of convenience foods that only exist because of artificial ingredients—should be avoided. These foods are high in saturated fats, sodium, and sugar and provide little nutritional value. Most of processed convenience foods contain additives, including several of those on the CSPI list of substances to avoid or cut back. These foods pose health risks unless consumed in moderation. Yet you can easily avoid eating foods with artificial ingredients simply by eliminating processed convenience foods from your diet. Your health will improve as your diet improves, and worsen as your diet worsens.
- Bad for children. Junk food, fast food, and convenience foods are heavily marketed to children. These foods erode the health of young children, who are incapable of making good decisions for themselves. Although the responsibility lies with the parents to ensure that their children eat properly, food

marketers have learned that a begging, pleading, whining child is the best way to influence an otherwise responsible parent. Even the best parents occasionally relent and succumb to their children's desires. The danger is from certain artificial colors and flavors that have been linked to cognitive and behavioral deficits in children, albeit not definitively. The UK Food Standards Agency recommends that parents eliminate food colorings from the diet of children with attention deficit hyperactivity disorder. The European Food Safety Authority (EFSA) maintains a list of food additives and colors that pose risks for infants and very young children.[12] Recently, the European Commission requested that all authorized food additives are to be systematically evaluated by the EFSA. There are legitimate concerns about the safety of many food ingredients, particularly for infants and children.[13]

- Bad for public policy. Most food additives are the creation of the food industry, which needs things like colorings to entice consumers and preservatives to increase sales of unhealthy foods. None of us actually needs these things. We can enjoy perfectly good diets without them. The more public policy (e.g., public school lunches, industry regulations, tax incentives, and subsidies) is geared toward the segments in the food industry that profit from processed foods, the worse our diet becomes. The basic ingredients in junk food—corn and sugar—cost next to nothing thanks to payoffs to large-scale agricultural corporations and food manufacturers. These government subsidies make junk food ingredients inexpensive hence widely available to consumers. The result? According to the Centers for Disease Control and Prevention, 33 percent of the US adult population over twenty and 48 percent of those under twenty are obese.[14]

- Bad for international policy. Nearly as many people in the world are overweight as they are malnourished. Although artificial ingredients are by no means the sole cause of the health related problems associated with a high-fat, high-sugar diet, they do play a key role. Without artificial flavors, colors, sweeteners, and preservatives, Western-style convenience foods would likely be consumed far less. The more international policies (e.g., trade regulations, financial backing, and multinational corporations) are geared toward enabling the sellers of nutrient-poor foods to profit, the worse the world's health becomes. According to the World Health Organization, 35 percent of adults are overweight; 11 percent are obese. Sixty-five percent of the world's population lives in countries where being overweight and obesity causes more death than being underweight.[15] The causes are urbanization, sedentary forms of work, and a diet of calorie-dense foods high in fat. Food additives make unhealthy foods available and thus enable unhealthy lifestyles.

The rights arguments against artificial ingredients are even stronger. Simply put, we have a right to liberty; that is to say, a right to pursue our aims freely. To do so, we must be safe, secure, educated, and healthy. A government has a duty to respect our right to liberty. A rights approach maintains that the use of artificial ingredients is:

- Disrespectful. A person who knowingly eats processed foods that have little nutritive value fails the Kantian duty of beneficence to oneself: the obligation to care for and better ourselves. A person who knowingly serves unhealthy processed foods to others fails the duty of beneficence to them. According to Kant, we have an obligation to at least sometimes help ourselves and help others and improve the quality of life. Processed foods—not counting the occasional disaster relief—are no help here. In addition, producers of foods with little or no nutritional value are similarly disrespectful of persons. While they may operate within the bounds of the law, exercising their property rights, they fail in their obligation to help to improve the quality of life—to further the ends of others, as Kant would put it.
- Irresponsible. Public policy should promote public goods like health and well-being rather than merely support the private accumulation of capital. Public officials have an obligation to secure justice for all. Laws should advance everyone's aims and desires, not just those of the food industry. When public officials fail to protect our right to health, safety, and freedom to pursue a worthwhile life, they fail to protect the lives of citizens. They are irresponsible. In addition, the food industry bears at least some responsibility for the health consequences its products cause. Like any manufacturer of a harmful product, a food producer contributes to the harms suffered by consumers. The extent of liability is debatable; that they bear some degree of moral culpability is not.
- Deceptive. The food industry relies on artificial flavorings to make their food as irresistible as possible. They marshal the expertise of food scientists to create cravings for flavors chemically designed to keep people eating. The goal is to sustain the "bliss point"—the point where we desire a food the most but never grow tired of it. Only the conscious effort of food scientists (and not a chef) can engineer flavors so that we only crave them and not feel that we have had enough. Working with psychologists and marketers, the food industry exploits our susceptibility to the combination of salt, sugar, and fat. Although we are, of course, not powerless in the face of such foods, we are nevertheless vulnerable to their flavor formulations. These foods are designed to overwhelm our ability to stop eating them. They are nearly addictive and, therefore, compromise our ability to think, choose, and act for ourselves—that is to say, our autonomy. Manufacturers of these foods are deceptive: They play on consumer ignorance of the effect of engineered flavor combinations. They disregard human agency and seek to influence our actions by hijacking our powers of decision. Food dyes are deceptive, as well. They are used to entice us by making foods appear better than they otherwise would without colorants.

Another set of arguments, distinct from deontological ones, appeals to an ideal wherein we live in harmony with our surroundings. Food, according to this ideal, should have natural, organic origins and be free from additives and excessive processing. Agriculture should also aspire to maintain harmony among farmers, communities, animals, and the environment. On this reading, foods with artificial ingredients are:

- Impure. Foods that contain artificial ingredients are not found in nature. When we eat them, we introduce unnatural elements into our bodies. Food additives are impurities that should be eliminated in the name of wholesome living. The more we eat natural foods and live in accordance with nature, the more healthy and balanced our lives will be. Impurities such as food additives are bad in themselves, not simply because of their consequences.
- Alienating. People, food, and the environment are all connected in the act of eating, provided we eat the right foods in the right way. Artificial foods, with artificial ingredients, produced by industrial agriculture and factories, disconnect us from the land and from each other. The closer we are to our food sources, the more in touch we are with a vital part of our health and our communities. The further we are from our food sources, the less knowledge we have about local agricultural life, the fewer shared experiences we have with our communities, and the less aware we are our how our lives are woven into the fabric of our surroundings. At the risk of oversimplifying: Connection is good, disconnection is bad. It is better to be connected to than cut off from our food producers, from our neighbors, and from nature.
- Disgusting. Artificial food ingredients are intuitively unappealing. The uncomfortable feeling we get reading a long list of chemical ingredients on a food label is telling: There has to be something wrong with eating unnatural foods. The very idea of ingesting these ingredients is repugnant. Good sense tells us to eat wholesome foods, not chemical cuisine. Given the choice, most of us would choose food grown in the ground or raised on a ranch rather than anything synthesized in a laboratory. We might not be able to articulate the reasons why we prefer natural to artificial foods beyond saying "yuck!"—but that does not mean our preferences are arbitrary or irrational. The expression summarizes the displeasure we experience when we know we are eating unnatural foods.

The arguments from quality of life maintain that we can do better than to eat food with artificial ingredients. Our food is qualitatively better without them, a cook is qualitatively better without using them, and our lives are qualitatively better when we eschew them. On this reading, foods with artificial additives are:

- Undesirable. Typically, we settle for foods with additives; we rarely seek them out. Given an informed choice, we would opt for something whole and natural rather than processed and packaged. There is little choice-worthy about artificial ingredients. They are less desirable than their natural counterparts, other than MRE and famine relief, of course. We can offer dozens of good reasons to seek out all-natural foods, but few reasons to seek out unnatural foods.

- Inappropriate. According to our long-standing customs and traditions, it is more appropriate to serve high-quality than low-quality food to guests. It is always better to try to be a good host who makes an effort than to be unwelcoming and indifferent to others. In general, something home cooked and well presented is more generous than something processed, packaged, and unhealthy. Although Doritos are fine for taking in a game with friends, for a formal event it is more hospitable to prepare something generally recognized as being good to eat and good to serve. Foods filled with artificial colors and flavors are simply inappropriate and out of place at a wedding, religious ceremony, or even a dinner party. These foods are neither the most suitable nor fitting items for a special occasion or any time when it is more generous to extend oneself for others.

- Unrefined. There is very little that is noble and fine about foods with artificial ingredients. The best foods have none at all. If we take our standards from what good cooks and good restaurants prepare, then there is nothing refined about foods with additives. If we take our standards from heritage and tradition, then only the foods that reflect time-honored practices are prized: farmed fruits and vegetables, cage-free livestock, traditional food preparation. Novel foods are invariably worse than traditional foods in this respect. They debase rather than elevate our food.

- Yucky. As a rule, the fewer artificial ingredients the better the food tastes (stale, rancid, and spoiled food notwithstanding). Outside of red dye in red velvet cake, baking powder in quick breads, and the concoctions of high-end molecular gastronomists, good tasting food rarely has any additives. Watch any cooking show on television: None of the chefs uses artificial ingredients. You would think that these experienced chefs would know how to enhance the taste of their food with additives. You would think that a motivated contestant in a cooking competition would try to gain any advantage possible to win. But instead of chemically modifying ingredients, we see how the best chefs seek out the highest quality ingredients and prepare them with skill and creativity. The experienced cooking show judges never suggest artificial ingredients to contestants to help make their dishes more delicious. Food critics and the general public can often agree on the difference between good and bad tasting food. As a general rule, foods with artificial ingredients taste worse than foods that have none.

- Cheating. Artificial ingredients are a shortcut. Their functional properties can be achieved with more planning and effort. It might be more difficult, for example, for producers and consumers to only eat foods with short shelf lives and no preservatives, but so be it. There is nothing praiseworthy about convenience. It might take more time and expense to make food appear better without artificial colorings, but so be it. The best food preparation does not have to take any shortcuts. In fact, it is often the effort—and even inconvenience—of good food that makes it praiseworthy. Think of the difficulty involved in making a soufflé, the patient layering of phyllo dough, or the detailed decoration on a nice wedding cake. Or imagine that an artificial ingredient could reproduce the taste of foods that take time to age or ferment, like cheese, cured meats, or pickled vegetables. Let's say that instead of months, any food that requires aging could be done in a matter of moments with the right additives. Would you consider this a time-saving innovation or cutting corners?

• Apostate. Food can be special. It can sanctify and elevate our lives above the mundane into the realm of the sacred. We have all had experiences where food becomes something greater than mere nourishment. Eating can be a transcendent experience. It might have been during a feast or special occasional; it might have come while savoring a uniquely delicious morsel; or it might have occurred to you while preparing an animal you have hunted and killed for food. Special meals often serve special occasions. There is, however, nothing glorious about artificial ingredients. They are rather profane. They not only make food worse, they almost defile it. Foods with artificial ingredients are tainted, corrupted, even stained.

What's Wrong with Artificial Ingredients?

We have examined arguments both for and against the use of artificial ingredients in food. Whether it is better not to use such ingredients, we have seen, will be relative to circumstance. If our discussion has been on the mark, the four most relevant considerations in arguments for or against artificial ingredients are: (1) which ingredients are in question; (2) how often something is consumed; (3) if it is consumed with knowledge; and (4) if the food manufacturer is one you should support.

Consider the FDA's main classes of common food ingredients: preservatives, sweeteners, color additives, flavors and spices, fat replacers, nutrients, emulsifiers, stabilizers and thickeners, pH control agents, leavening agents, anticaking agents, humectants, yeast nutrients, dough strengthener and conditioners, firming agents, enzyme preparations, and gases. Is it the case that all of these are problematic simply because they have chemical-sounding names, or are some ingredients more problematic than others? Some of the arguments that we've considered arguments against the use of artificial ingredients hinge on the man-made, artificial character of these ingredients, which inherently worsen food regardless of their function or consequences. Other arguments that we've explored hinge on the consequences of eating or using them. Presumably, if the bad consequences could be significantly lessened or removed, then there would be little reason to avoid these ingredients. Of this class of ingredients that are bad, some seem to be worse than others. Preservatives, food dyes, sweeteners, fat substitutes, and artificial flavors tend to be the ones that we have qualms about, either because they have health risks or are a part of deceptive schemes. Emulsifiers, thickeners, nutrients, anticaking agents, and the rest are less controversial.

Next, it is important to know how often artificial ingredients are consumed. If only on occasion, the implications are trivial. A little processed food here and there is most likely harmless, sometimes convenient, and maybe even delicious. Such food might taste bad, be inappropriate, or be served in poor taste, but these are all relatively minor offenses. If, on the other hand, their consumption is widespread and habitual, then there are more serious concerns about public health, national and international food policy, and broader cultural changes in cuisine. These are matters that affect entire populations not just individuals. When assessing either artificial ingredients, in general, or a particular food ingredient, it is important to be clear on how frequent and widespread the consumption. The health arguments against artificial ingredients are about the role they play in an unhealthy diet, not an unhealthy meal or snack. It is not difficult to demonstrate that a steady diet of artificial ingredients is bad for your health. But a meal or a snack that contains such ingredients? Unless one's health is already at risk, the reasons to avoid eating even the least nutritious processed food on occasion are far less compelling.

It is also morally relevant to know whether something is consumed with or without knowledge. If food ingredients are labeled and legal, then it is the consumer's responsibility to make informed food choices. If the best available science can establish long-term harms to the habitual consumption of legal food ingredients, then producers bear some responsibility as well. There are a number of ways manufacturers can be held responsible for their products: strict liability, taxes to offset health expenditures, or warning labels like those found on alcohol or tobacco products. Children, of course, need special protection since they are unable to make informed decisions about their well-being. Policy makers can rightfully govern school lunch programs, advertisers, and marketers if their products compromise the welfare of children.

Adults need special protection from ingredients whose effects we cannot reasonably be expected to understand. Although adults *should* know the effects of eating too much fat, sugar, and salt, we cannot be expected to know that certain combinations of these ingredients are addictive, as mounting evidence seems to indicate.[16] Nor can we be expected to know that certain artificial flavors are designed to entice us to eat more than we would a naturally occurring, nonsynthesized flavor. Addictive foods and ingredients should be labeled as such.

Finally, because artificial ingredients are produced by the food industry in large-scale industrial complexes, it is reasonable to questions whether it deserves your support or if it should be eschewed in favor of more ethical alternatives.

This is an industry that very aggressively creates a favorable sales environment for its products. It does so by lobbying political representatives to eliminate or not enforce unfavorable regulations; by co-opting nutrition experts by supporting favorable research; and by marketing and advertising, often to children who are unable to read ads critically.[17] Sometimes the food industry succeeds in producing and publicizing goods that people actually want and need; other times its means are less honest and serve to deceive people into thinking they want and need things they really do not. The success of the food industry is due less to consumer demand than to its own efforts, even force. The deck is stacked in their favor. Or to put it another way, foods made by mom-and-pop producers typically do not have artificial ingredients in them; foods made by multinational food companies do. That is reason enough to avoid their products on ethical grounds.

What's wrong with artificial ingredients? The foods that contain them are probably not good to eat too often but won't harm you if you eat them on occasion; they typically do little to improve the quality of the food but often serve useful functions. Hopefully, none us will find ourselves in such dire circumstances where these foods are by far the best available option.

* My father-in-law, Robert Schreiber, read an earlier draft of this chapter and offered helpful feedback—not by giving advice but by asking the right questions. He always read whatever I sent him.

Notes

1. Mike Esterl, "Can This Chip Be Saved? Frito-Lay Retools Snack Recipes to Include More Natural Ingredients." *Wall Street Journal*, March 24, 2011.
2. Caroline Davies, "Nestlé Removes All Artificial Ingredients from Entire Confectionery Range." *Guardian UK*, March 1, 2012.
3. Kraft Foods Collaboration Kitchen. http://www.kfcollaborationkitchen.com
4. General Mills Innovation Network (G-WIN). https://genmills.inno-360.com/
5. US Food and Drug Administration, "Federal Food, Drug, and Cosmetic Act (FD&C Act)." http://www.fda.gov/regulatoryinformation/legislation/federalfooddrugand cosmeticactfdcact/default.htm
6. US Food and Drug Administration, "Everything Added to Food in the United States (EAFUS)," November 2011. http://www.fda.gov/food/ingredientspackaging labeling/foodadditivesingredients/ucm115326.htm
7. Center for Science in the Public Interest, "Chemical Cuisine: Learn about Food Additives." http://www.cspinet.org/reports/chemcuisine.htm
8. According to CSPI, Green 3 is rarely used; Orange B hasn't been used in years; potassium bromate poses very small risks and is rarely used in the US (and banned worldwide); and the studies of propyl gallate on mice and rats "were peppered with suggestions but not proof" that it causes cancer.
9. According to CSPI, Blue 1 needs to be better tested; the amount of Citrus Red 2 typically consumed is so minute that the risks are minimal; brominated vegetable oil is rarely used and it is unclear if it poses risks; diacetyl is safe to eat but long-term exposure poses risks to manufacturers in factories, not consumers; the FDA has deemed rebiana and other processed stevia leaf products to be safe; and meat glue is safe when used properly.

10. Center for Science in the Public Interest, "Chemical Cuisine."

11. Andrew Rice, "The Peanut Solution," *New York Times Magazine*, September 2, 2010.

12. European Commission, "Food Safety: From the Farm to the Fork." http://ec.europa.
eu/food/fs/sc/oldcomm7/out06_en.html

13. With the exception of potassium bromate, the EFSA has approved all of the additives on CSPI's avoid list.

14. Centers for Disease Control and Prevention, "Obesity and Overweight." http://
www.cdc.gov/nchs/fastats/obesity-overweight.htm

15. World Health Organization, "Obesity and Overweight," January 2015. http://www.
who.int/mediacentre/factsheets/fs311/en/

16. Tara Parker-Pope, "Craving an Ice-Cream Fix," *New York Times, Well Column* (blog), September 20, 2012. http://well.blogs.nytimes.com/2012/09/20/craving-an-ice-cream-fix/

17. For evidence of precisely how the food industry creates a favorable sales environment through lobbying, marketing, and co-opted nutrition experts, see Marion Nestle, *Food Politics* (Berkeley: University of California Press, 2003), pp. 95–136, 175–218.

15
THE MORAL PROBLEM
OF PREDATION

Jeff McMahan

Predation as a Moral Issue

Viewed from a distance, the natural world may present a vista of sublime, majestic placidity. Yet beneath the foliage and concealed from the distant eye, a continuous massacre is occurring. Virtually everywhere that there is animal life, predators are stalking, chasing, capturing, killing, and devouring their prey. The means of killing are various: dismemberment, asphyxiation, disembowelment, poison, and so on. This normally invisible carnage provided part of the basis for the philosophical pessimism of Schopenhauer, who suggested that "one simple test of the claim that the pleasure in the world outweighs the pain . . . is to compare the feelings of an animal that is devouring another with those of the animal being devoured."[1]

The unceasing mass suffering of animals caused by predation is also an important though, at least until recently, largely neglected element in the traditional theological "problem of evil"—that is, the problem of reconciling the idea that there is a benevolent, omnipotent deity with the existence of suffering and other evils. Referring to "the odious scene of violence and tyranny which is exhibited by the rest of the animal kingdom," John Stuart Mill commented that

> if there are any marks at all of special design in creation, one of the things most evidently designed is that a large proportion of all animals should pass their existence in tormenting and devouring other animals. They have been lavishly fitted out with the instruments necessary for that purpose; their strongest instincts impel them to it, and many of them seem to have been constructed incapable of supporting themselves by any other food. If a tenth part of the pains which have been expended in finding benevolent adaptions in all nature, had been employed in collecting evidence to

blacken the character of the Creator, what scope for comment would not have been found in the entire existence of the lower animals, divided, with scarcely an exception, into devourers and devoured, and a prey to a thousand ills from which they are denied the faculties necessary for protecting themselves! If we are not obliged to believe the animal creation to be the work of a demon, it is because we need not suppose it to have been made by a Being of infinite power.[2]

The suffering of animals is particularly challenging to the task of theodicy because it is not amenable to the familiar palliative explanations of human suffering. Animals are assumed not to have free will and are thus incapable either of choosing evil or of deserving to suffer it. Neither are they assumed to have immortal souls; hence there can be no expectation that they will be compensated for their suffering in a celestial afterlife. Nor, finally, do they appear to be conspicuously elevated or ennobled by the final suffering they may endure in a predator's jaws. Theologians have had formidable difficulties attempting to explain to their human flocks why a loving deity permits them to suffer; but the labors of theodicy will not be completed even if theologians are finally able, in Milton's words, to "justify the ways of God to men," for their God must answer to animals as well.

There have certainly been important religious thinkers who have found fault with the arrangement whereby a large proportion of sensitive beings are able to survive only by feeding upon others, and some of these thinkers have entertained visions of a better order. The prophet Isaiah, for example, writing in the 8th century BCE, described some of the elements of an improved natural order, beginning with the abandonment of war by human beings and continuing with the conversion of predators to veganism:

> The wolf also shall dwell with the lamb, and the leopard shall lie down with the kid; and the calf and the young lion and the fatling together; and the little child shall lead them. And the cow and the bear shall feed; their young ones shall lie down together; and the lion shall eat straw like the ox.[3]

Isaiah does not mention whether the reformed, pacifist human beings would join the other animals in their veganism, but it is doubtful that he would have them fall below the moral standards set by wolves and lions. These are standards that most human beings, unlike other predators, could satisfy now with no sacrifice of health and little if any sacrifice of happiness; yet most persist in practicing forms of predation that are at once more refined and more dreadful than those of other predators. Instead of having to capture their prey and kill it with their hands and teeth, human predators tend to employ professionals to breed their prey in captivity, slaughter them, and prepare their bodies for consumption. And just as most human beings rarely observe acts of predation in the wild, so they do not witness the mass torment and killing that occurs in their mechanized farms and abattoirs, which is deliberately concealed, albeit with the collusion of those from whom it is concealed. A veil of propriety is maintained both to avoid putting people off their feed and to spare them the recognition that they too are predators, red in tooth even if not in claw (though curiously some do paint their vestigial claws the color of blood). Among our modes of sanitized predation, the one that is most common in developed societies—factory farming—inflicts a lifetime of misery and torment on its victims, in contrast to the relatively brief agonies endured by the victims of predation in the wild.

There are no even remotely credible arguments for the moral permissibility of factory farming. There is, in my view, only one argument for the permissibility of a practice of eating meat that has any plausibility, though it is restricted in scope. It supports the permissibility of eating meat only from animals that are caused to exist in order to be eaten, reared humanely to have lives that are worth living, killed painlessly, and then "replaced" by new animals that are caused to exist in a continuing cycle of production. I will not discuss this argument here, though I have done so elsewhere.[4] The problem with it is that one cannot know whether it is sound unless one can first determine whether and to what extent creating new individuals, whether human or nonhuman, can weigh against and compensate for killing existing individuals or allowing them to die. This question in turn cannot be answered with confidence unless the answer can be shown to have acceptable implications for a range of related but deeply intractable problems in "population ethics."[5]

In my view, it is only if this argument is sound, and even then only if meat is obtained exclusively from animals that have lived contented lives and been killed with little or no terror or pain, that there can be a permissible practice of eating meat, at least until meat produced in vitro becomes widely available. Unless these two conditions are met, we must fulfill our role in realizing Isaiah's vision not only by abandoning war (which also involves ceasing to act in ways that give others a just cause for war against us) but also by abandoning predation, with possible exceptions for the eating of animals that are arguably nonsentient, such as oysters and clams.

Ending Predation?

Granting, then, at least for the sake of argument, that morality requires that we eat straw like the ox, or at any rate the moral equivalent of straw, the question arises whether we also have a moral reason to protect animals from predation by nonhuman predators. This question is restricted in two important ways. First, the question is not whether there is a moral reason to intervene against all forms of predation, but only whether there is a reason to protect potential prey that are capable of suffering and of having a life worth living. Second, it is not, at least in the first instance, whether there is an *obligation* to prevent predation where possible, but only whether there is a moral *reason* to do so, and if so how strong that reason is. It may be, for example, that there is a strong moral reason but that it is outweighed by competing considerations, or cannot be effectively acted on, in present conditions—conditions that might, however, be susceptible to change.

There is some intuitive support for the idea that there is a moral reason to intervene against predation. If one were to happen upon a young animal that was about to be captured and slowly devoured alive, piece by piece, by a predator, one's impulse would be to frighten off the predator, if possible. One's sympathies are with the prey, not the predator. There is a video that can be viewed on the Internet that shows a small group of lions about to kill a baby water buffalo but are prevented by defensive action by a herd of adult water buffalos.[6] In watching this video, one's sympathies are with the buffalos, and one experiences relief and satisfaction when they succeed, even though one knows that the lions are neither immoral nor cruel and may go hungry for having been thwarted.

Yet despite their intuitive response in this case, most people's immediate reaction to the suggestion that there is reason to reduce or eliminate predation in the natural world is incredulity. Indeed, when the issue is raised in the philosophical literature, the usual response to this suggestion is to argue that if a moral theory implies that there is a moral reason to reduce or eliminate predation, that constitutes a reduction of the theory to absurdity—a reductio ad absurdum. It is a familiar objection to utilitarianism that it is excessively demanding in the sacrifices it requires individuals to make for the sake of other people. Recently Alison Hills has sought to strengthen this type of objection by arguing that when utilitarianism takes account, as it must, of the sheer magnitude of the suffering experienced by animals in the wild, it must imply that human beings have reasons, and in many cases duties, to intervene to mitigate it, including duties to reduce the incidence of predation. She assumes, however, that this implication counts strongly against the plausibility of the theory. "Utilitarians," she writes, "have severely underestimated both how demanding their theory is, and how counter-intuitive. The demandingness objection is much more damaging when we take animals seriously."[7]

Lori Gruen, a sensitive critic of human practices that are harmful or degrading to animals, also considers the claim "that those who argue that other animals deserve our ethical attention should be committed to ending predation." She recognizes that this claim is often cited "as a *reductio ad absurdum* [of] the idea that we have ethical obligations to animals."[8] But rather than challenging the assumption that the implication would be absurd, Gruen argues that none of what she considers to be the major moral theories, whether utilitarian, rights-based, or feminist, actually implies that we ought to intervene to reduce or eliminate predation. These theories therefore "avoid the *reductio* that critics have raised."[9] She suggests at one point that "perhaps a better way to go is to figure out how to minimize the pain prey experience when eaten by predators."[10] But this presupposes, mistakenly in my view, that the reason to protect potential prey is only to prevent their suffering and not to preserve their lives as well.[11] In the end she seeks to reconcile defenders of the well-being of animals to the abandonment of prey in the wild by suggesting that any efforts that might be made to help them would probably exacerbate rather than alleviate their predicament. "When we consider," she writes,

> the form human intervention often takes, and the havoc it wreaks, we may want to leave predators alone. . . . Perhaps we would do best to display more humility, to ask questions and explore options and to exercise restraint and perhaps even try to come to terms with tragedy, if need be.[12]

One reason why most defenders of animals are reluctant to acknowledge a moral reason to intervene against predation may be that they fear that embracing the conclusion of their opponents' reductio would diminish the credibility of their overall view in the minds of the majority. If so, their fear may well be justified. But unlike political action, moral philosophy is not a matter of strategic calculation, manipulation, and compromise. Its aim, as I conceive it, is to discover the truth about matters of morality. If we are ultimately to act in conformity with the reasons given by morality, we must know whether we do indeed have a moral reason to try to reduce the incidence of predation or perhaps even to eliminate it, if that becomes possible. The fact that the vast majority of people worldwide would now find it preposterous to suppose that we have such a reason provides little reason to suppose that they are right, just as the uniformity of opinion about the ethics of slavery among whites in the antebellum South provided little reason for supposing that it can be permissible to kidnap and enslave other people. Contemporary beliefs about the moral permissibility of harming animals and allowing them to be harmed are just as contaminated by self-interest, religious dogma, and prejudices masquerading as science as were the slave-owners' beliefs about slavery. Most commonsense intuitions about the question whether human beings ought, if possible, to eliminate or reduce the incidence of predation are therefore epistemically highly suspect. If the arguments in favor of intervention are better than the arguments against it, we can hope that they will eventually come to guide human action, in the same way that moral arguments against eating meat have, in only a few decades, increased the proportion of people who are vegetarians or vegans from negligible to substantial in those societies in which the arguments have been published and debated. In the meantime, there seems little reason to fear that people will be persuaded not to become vegetarian, or not to oppose factory farming, by becoming convinced that arguments that support vegetarianism and oppose factory farming also support the eventual elimination of predation. The moral case for vegetarianism has many dimensions that will remain compelling even if certain arguments for vegetarianism have implications that people are unwilling to accept. People can, for example, see that they bear greater responsibility for the suffering and premature deaths of animals that are killed specifically for human consumption than they bear for the suffering and deaths caused by predation.

The case in favor of intervening against predation is quite simple. It is that predation causes vast suffering among its innumerable victims, and to deprive those victims of the good experiences they might have had were they not killed. Suffering is intrinsically bad for those who experience it and there seems always to be a reason, though not necessarily a decisive one, to prevent it—a reason that applies to any moral agent who is capable of preventing it. (If suffering can be deserved, deserved suffering might constitute an exception, as its intrinsic badness for the victim might be outweighed by its impersonal goodness.[13]) There seems, indeed, to be a universally applicable reason not only to prevent the painful deaths of potential prey that exist now, but also to terminate the cycle in which new predators continuously replace the old, thereby ensuring an inexhaustible supply of sentient beings that can avoid suffering and death themselves only by inflicting suffering and death on others. The elimination of predation could therefore make the difference between an indefinitely extended future in which millions of animals die prematurely and in agony every day and an alternative future in which different animals would live longer and die in ways other than in terror and agony in the jaws of a predator.

Most people who read this chapter will recognize that we have a moral reason to avoid causing animals to suffer if we can do so without cost, and that this is because suffering is intrinsically bad for those that experience it. But if animal suffering is bad when we cause it, it should also be bad when it results from other causes, including the action of other animals. As Martha Nussbaum plausibly claims, "the death of a gazelle after painful torture is just as bad for the gazelle when torture is inflicted by a tiger as when it is done by a human being." This, she continues, suggests "that we have similar reasons to prevent it, if we can do so without doing greater harms."[14] Most of us believe, rightly in my view, that our moral reason not to cause suffering is in general stronger than our reason to prevent it from occurring—for example, to prevent someone or something else from causing it. If that is correct, our moral reason not to contribute to causing suffering by eating meat produced in factory farms is stronger than our reason to prevent comparable amounts of animal suffering caused by others, including predators. But that is compatible with our having a strong reason to prevent suffering in animals for which we would be in no way responsible when we can do so at little or no cost to ourselves.

The Counterproductivity Objection

There are two ways in which the incidence of predation could be significantly reduced, perhaps eventually to none. One is to bring about the gradual extinction of some or all predatory species, preferably through sterilization, and with the exception of the human species, which is capable of voluntarily ending its predatory behavior. The other, which is not yet technically possible, is to introduce germ-line (that is, heritable) genetic modifications into existing carnivorous species so that their progeny would gradually evolve into herbivores, in fulfill-ment of Isaiah's prophecy.

Both of these methods of eliminating or reducing the incidence of predation would obviously require substantial interventions in the natural world. Perhaps the commonest objection to the simple moral case I sketched for intervening against predation is that any such intervention would risk environmental catas-trophe, for the complexity of any major ecosystem so far surpasses our under-standing that an attempt to eliminate predation within it, however carefully planned and well intentioned, would have unpredictable ramifications through-out the system. The most obvious scenario is that the elimination or even sig-nificant reduction in predation would produce a Malthusian dystopia in which herbivore populations would expand beyond the ability of the environment to sustain them. Instead of being killed quickly by predators, herbivores would then die slowly, painfully, and in greater numbers from starvation and disease. Rather than diminishing the suffering and extending the lives of herbivores, the elimination of predation might increase their suffering overall and even dimin-ish their average longevity. We can call this the *Counterproductivity Objection*.

Given the state of our knowledge at present, this is a strong objection to almost any attempt to reduce predation *now*. But we should not be dismissive of Isa-iah's gifts as a prophet. Ecological science, like other sciences, is not stagnant. What may now seem forever impossible may yield to the advance of science in a surprisingly short time—as happened when Rutherford, the first scientist to split the atom, announced in 1933 that anyone who claimed that atomic fission could be a source of power was talking "moonshine." Unless we use Ruther-ford's discovery or others like it to destroy ourselves first, we will likely be able eventually to eliminate predation while preserving the stability and harmony of ecosystems. It should eventually become possible to gradually convert ecosystems that are now stabilized by predation into ones resembling island ecosystems that have flourished for significant periods without any animals with a developed capacity for consciousness being preyed upon by others. We should therefore begin to think now about whether we would have moral reason to exercise the ability to intervene against predation in an effective and discriminating way if we were to develop it. If we conclude that we would, that gives us reason now to try to hasten our acquisition of that ability.

One possible way to eliminate predation in an ecosystem without increasing the suffering of herbivores through overpopulation is to limit the expansion of herbivore populations by means other than predation. In some instances in which predation has been diminished unintentionally, human beings have then inter-vened to replace the original predators. In the United States, Britain, and vari-ous other developed countries, for example, the increasing incursion of human activities into hitherto stable ecosystems has diminished the number of animals that once preyed on deer, resulting in an increased number of deer that have then had difficulty finding sufficient food. Some suffer starvation or malnutrition while others survive by feeding in people's gardens, thereby becoming a nuisance to those whose who drove out the predators. Most human communities solve this problem by permitting or encouraging the hunting of the deer. Hunters then happily perform the service of culling the herds without having to be paid for it, as they enjoy both the killing and the eating of their prey.

But when they are successful, hunters, like other predators, deprive their prey of further life that could have been good. And they often cause great suffering as well, particularly when they wound an animal that is able to escape being killed. In principle there are better ways of controlling populations of herbivores whose exposure to predators has decreased. The most obvious of these is selective sterilization.[15] Scientists are already working to develop effective means of sterilization that do not require surgery. These are mainly intended for use in dogs and cats (in part to reduce the number of strays, which is the analogue for domesticated animals of overpopulation among wild animals), but some communities are seeking to use them to control local deer populations as well.[16] If we were ever to become serious about eliminating or reducing the incidence of predation, we could eventually develop a chemical means of sterilization that could be administered to herbivores in the wild in a discriminating and painless way. Presumably it will become possible at some point to regulate the size of herbivore populations through germ-line genetic modification as well.

The question whether predation is bad is relevant to present action in ways other than helping to guide or inform our research agendas. There are various predatory species that are now threatened with extinction. Many people advocate intervention to preserve those species and to restore their populations to some prior level. An example of such a species is the Siberian tiger. Human beings can decide now whether to allow (or cause) that species to disappear, to enable it to continue to exist in small numbers, or to try to restore the number of its members to a much higher level. Because the number of remaining Siberian tigers has been low for a considerable period, any ecological disruption occasioned by the great decline in their number has already occurred. If the several hundred that remain were all to disappear, the effect on the ecology of the region would presumably be negligible. But there might also be little ecological risk in facilitating the gradual reintroduction of a much larger population of Siberian tigers into the extensive region in which they once flourished, thereby greatly diminishing the probability that they will become extinct.

If this is right, human beings can choose between two ecologically sustainable options. One is to complete the elimination of predation by Siberian tigers in a large region, the other to increase the level of predation in that region by repopulating it with tigers. If the latter option would substantially increase terror, suffering, and premature death among other animals inhabiting the region, and maintain that increase indefinitely, then the view that there is a moral reason to prevent suffering and premature death among animals, however they might be caused, supports the option of allowing (or causing) the tigers to die out in the region—unless, perhaps, their role in the food web would simply be taken over by some other preexisting predatory species, in which case the extinction of the tigers would be a loss without any compensating gain in the reduction of suffering.

The Impersonal Value of Species

As the previous sentence concedes, there is generally a loss of value when a species becomes extinct. I accept that, and I also accept that there can be value in the continued existence of a species that is independent of or additional to the value for each member of the species of its own continued existence. The existence and survival of a species may, in other words, have *impersonal* value—that is, value in itself, independent of whether it is good or valuable *for* or *to* anyone. This may seem most obviously true of species, such as the Siberian tiger, whose members are beautiful, graceful, majestic, or otherwise aesthetically impressive—though the impersonal value of the species is entirely distinct from the aesthetic benefits that the existence of the species provides for us. That animal species have impersonal value is part of what Ronald Dworkin means when he observes that "we tend to treat distinct animal species (though not individual animals) as sacred. We think it very important, and worth a considerable economic expense, to protect endangered species from destruction."[17] Sacredness, as Dworkin understands it, is impersonal in that an entity can be sacred without being *good for* anyone. Yet it is unlike certain other forms of impersonal value in that it does not imply that it would be better for there to be more of whatever it is that is sacred. Thus, that a type of entity is sacred does not imply a moral reason to cause more entities of that type to exist. "Few people," Dworkin comments, "would think it important to engineer new bird species if that were possible. What we believe important is not that there be any particular number of species but that a species that now exists not be extinguished."[18]

This understanding of the impersonal value of species seems to imply that the loss involved in the extinction of a species cannot be wholly, or perhaps even partially, compensated for by the coming-into-existence of an entirely new species, whatever its properties might be. If that is right, it excludes one possible response to the claim that the extinction of, for example, the Siberian tiger would involve a significant loss in impersonal value—namely, that this loss could be made up for by the genetic engineering of a new, equally majestic herbivorous species.

But it is doubtful that this conception of the impersonal value of species is correct. Since animals first appeared, an indefinite number of species have become extinct and an indefinite number of new species have arisen. If the extinction of a species involves a loss of impersonal value that cannot be made up for by the appearance of a new species, it seems that the world must have got worse with every extinction, even when the extinction of one species has coincided with the appearance of more than one new species. It thus seems that, according to this understanding of the value of species, the world would have been better impersonally if none of the earliest species had become extinct, even if a consequence of that would have been that most of the newer species, perhaps including the human species, would never have existed.

This conception of the impersonal value of species also raises the question how the extinction of a species could involve a loss of impersonal value when the coming-into-existence of that species did not involve a gain in impersonal value. A parallel and perhaps more familiar question arises if we think, as Dworkin says we do, that individual human lives are sacred—that is, that the death of a person involves a loss of impersonal value, though the coming-into-existence of a person does not involve a gain in impersonal value. These beliefs, while common, seem to be in tension with one another.

Persons are, however, quite different from species. While individual persons do seem morally irreplaceable, in that the loss involved in the ceasing to exist of one cannot be counterbalanced or offset by the coming-into-existence of another, it seems that the loss in impersonal value from the extinction of one species could in principle be made up for by the coming-into-existence of another, even if the new species would not make up for the loss of the *instrumental* value of the previous species (that is, its value for other beings and its role in the ecosystem of which it was a part). Suppose, hypothetically, that some primate species would not have existed had some psychologically less developed species of reptile not become extinct. It is plausible to suppose that the replacement of the reptilian species by the primate species would not have been a net loss in impersonal value but an actual improvement in impersonal terms.

As this example suggests, the impersonal values of species can vary. Indeed, even those who are most convinced that species generally have impersonal value might accept that there are some species that lack it, so that their extinction would involve no loss of any kind—or even some species whose existence has *negative* impersonal value. Either of these might be true, for example, of HIV or the Ebola virus. But if one believes that even these species have impersonal value, so that the world would be *in one respect* worse if they were to become extinct, it seems clear that the impersonal loss would be vastly outweighed by the gain to human beings. This is important because it shows that we acknowledge that the impersonal value of a species may have to be traded off against other values.

One such value is the prevention of suffering. Although many philosophers are skeptical of the idea that species have impersonal value (some because they believe there is no such thing as impersonal value), almost no one denies that suffering is intrinsically bad (which is compatible with its being instrumentally good on occasion).[19] And not only is the intrinsic badness of suffering less open to doubt than the impersonal badness of the extinction of species, but also the *extent* to which suffering is bad is more susceptible of rough measurement than the extent to which the extinction of a species is bad. Imagine an animal species that has been slowly declining for more than a century and is now on the verge of extinction. Because the number of its remaining members is small, the effect of its extinction on the equilibrium of the ecosystem of which it is a part would be negligible. And suppose that its members are rather repellent, so that there would be no aesthetic loss in its disappearance. How impersonally valuable is the preservation of this species? How much ought human beings to sacrifice as a means of preventing its extinction? Such questions are notoriously difficult to answer. It is, moreover, quite difficult even to understand how to argue about them—for example, to know what considerations might plausibly be advanced in favor of one position or against another.

Imagine that the endangered species just described is a carnivorous species that preys only on human beings who live in the remote and undeveloped area in which the surviving members of this species are located. These isolated human beings seek to hunt down and kill all the remaining animals that prey on them. This is necessary for their safety and the safety of their children. No one else is proposing to preserve the species by keeping some of its members in captivity where they would threaten no one. The choice is therefore between eliminating the species and allowing its remaining members to continue to kill and eat human beings. Recall that this is a species that lacks any instrumental value. By hypothesis, the only reason to preserve it, apart from the interest its existing members have in continuing to live, is that it has impersonal value and contributes marginally to the diversity of species. It is difficult to believe that the impersonal value of the species could on its own outweigh the lives and well-being of the human beings who would otherwise be its victims.

It seems, then, that even granting that most or all species have impersonal value, this value may vary among species and may in some instances have relatively little weight in relation to other values such as the prevention of human suffering and the protection of human lives.

The Suffering of Animals

Given that the impersonal value of a species might not weigh heavily in our deliberations about its preservation if its extinction would have no disruptive ecological effects but its survival would cause significant harm to human beings, it seems that the impersonal value of the survival of certain carnivorous species could also be outweighed by the importance of preventing suffering and premature death among other animals. Yet, as I observed earlier, most people find it implausible to suppose that the harms that predators inflict on their animal prey constitute a significant moral reason for trying to eliminate or reduce the incidence of predation.

It is common for people to think that, while the suffering of animals matters, the continuation of the lives of individual animals generally does not, or does not matter much. It is this belief that motivates the action of many who avoid eating meat produced by factory farms but see no objection to eating the meat of animals that have been reared humanely and killed painlessly but at an early point in their natural life span. I believe this view is mistaken and that if the suffering of animals matters, that is because their well-being matters, in which case it must also matter whether they live or die, if death would deprive them of well-being they would otherwise have had. But I will not argue for this here.[20] I will put aside the loss that animal prey suffer in being killed by predators and focus entirely on the suffering they experience in being hunted and devoured.

The suffering that animals undergo while being caught and eaten may be intense, and the process by which they are killed may last for a quarter of an hour or more. Because the number of predators worldwide is enormous, and because, like us, many of them must eat with considerable frequency, the aggregate amount of suffering in the world at any time that is caused by predation is unimaginably vast. If human beings could eliminate even one carnivorous species while ensuring that its extinction would not have disruptive ecological effects, that alone could prevent a vast amount of suffering among animals that would otherwise have been prey for members of that species. As I argued earlier, the prevention of that suffering could outweigh the loss in impersonal value involved in the disappearance of the species. If the impersonal value of a species can be outweighed by human suffering, it seems it can also be outweighed by animal suffering.

Some might reject this inference on the ground that the suffering of animals does not matter, or matters much less than the comparable suffering of human beings. But it is unlikely that the idea that the suffering of animals does not matter at all can be reconciled with the idea that the suffering of human beings does matter. If we concede that the suffering of all human beings matters, that would seem to be because we recognize that it is in the nature of suffering that it is intrinsically bad for those who experience it and that it therefore matters that it should not occur. Thus, my recognition that the suffering of human beings matters is not the view that my suffering matters to me, while other people's suffering matters to them, or that theirs might matter to me *if* I cared about or were specially related to them. If that were my view, I should have the same view about the suffering of animals—namely, that it matters to them and that it might matter to me if the suffering animal were my pet. But my recognition is rather that the suffering of other human beings matters because it is in the nature of suffering that it ought not to be. As Nagel puts it, the "immediate attitude" of the sufferer is that "*this experience* ought not to go on, *whoever* is having it."[21] There is nothing in this thought about the species of the subject of the experience.

(The idea that the suffering of animals does not matter is also incompatible with at least one interpretation of the counterproductivity objection. That objection is that, without predators to control their numbers, herbivores would suffer even more than they do now, for their deaths from starvation or disease would involve substantially more suffering than a comparatively quick death inflicted by a predator. This would of course not be an objection if the suffering of prey did not matter.)

One might argue that the suffering of prey is offset by the pleasure that predators derive from eating them—a claim that Schopenhauer, in the passage quoted in my first paragraph, thought self-evidently false. But even if Schopenhauer were wrong, most acts of predation would still produce far more loss than gain, for each meal for a predator comes at the cost of depriving the prey of a great many meals it would have enjoyed, perhaps as much as the predator enjoys eating its prey. I know of no reason to suppose that carnivores as a rule get more pleasure from eating than herbivores do.

There is, perhaps, some reason for skepticism about whether animal prey actually do suffer, or suffer much, in being killed and eaten by predators. Some people, for example, speculate that when prey are caught, their brains release a flood of endogenously produced analgesics. Whether or to what extent this is true is an empirical question, for which there is some evidence on both sides. In human beings, great physical trauma sometimes induces unconsciousness, and there are also stories of soldiers fighting for their survival who later testify that they became aware of some grave physical injury only after the fighting had ceased. Yet there are also people who have survived being mauled by an animal who report having experienced agonizing pain and terror. Given these facts, it seems reasonable to suppose that there is some variation in the degree of suffering experienced by prey when they are being killed. While some may immediately become unconscious or numb, others may suffer excruciating pain. The higher the proportion of cases that involve numbness of unconsciousness, the less morally urgent the problem of predation is. But given the evolutionary function of pain, it seems likely that the killing of prey inflicts great suffering in a high proportion of cases. Thus, despite the possibility of numbness or unconsciousness, few of us would be indifferent between the prospect of dying without violence and dying by being torn asunder by a pack of wild dogs.

Even though it is implausible to suppose that the suffering of animals does not matter, there are various reasons why the suffering of an animal might matter *less* than the equivalent suffering of a person, or less than suffering caused in the same way in a person. One obvious reason is that suffering in a person may be accompanied by fear of its significance or anxiety about its continuation, whereas most animals seem to be immune to these higher-order thoughts. This does not, however, show that the same degree of suffering matters unequally in human beings and animals. It shows only that a certain degree of suffering may be increased or exacerbated in persons, though not in most animals, by self-conscious reflection upon it. This consideration also cuts both ways, for it is equally true that human suffering can be mitigated somewhat by an understanding of its cause, which can be reassuring if it indicates that the suffering is transient and without sinister significance. (One need not suppose that these different dimensions of suffering are crudely additive. It may be that self-conscious awareness of physical suffering yields a qualitatively different form of suffering that is much worse than mere physical suffering of the same degree. But, except at the high end of the spectrum of suffering, it seems that, for each degree of self-conscious awareness of suffering, there is some degree of merely physical suffering that is just as bad. The worst forms of physical suffering in persons tend to crowd out self-conscious reflection altogether.)

There are, however, two important respects in which a fixed degree of suffering can be worse in a person than in an animal. These are not ways in which equivalent suffering can be intrinsically worse in a person; rather they are ways in which suffering can be worse in a person because of its further effects on the victim. First, human suffering can be worse because of its opportunity costs. When suffering is distracting or debilitating, which it often or even typically is, it may prevent the sufferer from experiencing great happiness that he or she would otherwise have experienced, or from engaging in some valuable activity. This can be the case with animals only to a lesser extent, for their lower psychological capacities exclude them from many of the higher dimensions of well-being accessible to most human beings, and it is unlikely that an animal that is incapacitated by suffering would otherwise be engaged in an activity of substantial value.

Second, suffering can have damaging psychological effects throughout the subsequent life of a person. These effects may be especially pronounced when the suffering occurs early in life, but as our enhanced understanding of post-traumatic stress disorder has revealed, certain types of suffering can be highly damaging psychologically at any time in a person's life. Of course, similar phenomena can be observed in animals, as anyone who has known a dog that was mistreated as a puppy is aware. But the scope for damage is much greater in most human beings. In part this is simply because the lives of human beings continue much longer than those of most animals, so that the damaging effects within a human life are typically more protracted over time. But it is also because the greater psychological depth, complexity, and unity in most human beings make it possible for them to have lives that contain more, and arguably more important, dimensions of the good (such as significant accomplishment, personal relations based on mutual understanding, and so on) and are therefore more worth living than those of animals. In most cases, therefore, the psychological damage caused by suffering is worse in human beings because the life that is damaged matters more.

At least in most cases, however, what is primarily bad about suffering is the suffering itself, as it is occurring, not its opportunity costs or psychological ramifications throughout the sufferer's subsequent life. It is therefore important to consider whether the sheer intrinsic badness of suffering can matter less simply because the sufferer is an animal rather than a human being. Some think it cannot. Thus, Peter Singer maintains that

> pain and suffering are in themselves bad and should be prevented or minimized irrespective of the race, sex, or species of the being that suffers. How

bad a pain is depends on how intense it is and how long it lasts, but pains
of the same intensity and duration are equally bad, whether felt by humans
or animals.[22]

Yet it is possible that the suffering of one individual can matter less in an objective way than the equivalent suffering of another individual. It might be, for
example, that a certain amount of suffering matters less *morally* when it is experienced by an individual whose moral status is lower.

We can see how this might be possible by considering the common view
about suffering that is deserved. When a person experiences deserved suffering,
the suffering is as intrinsically bad *for him* as it would be if he did not deserve it.
But when the suffering is deserved, it may be *impersonally* good rather than bad
and others may have no reason to prevent it. So how suffering matters and how
much it matters may depend on certain facts about the sufferer. If what an individual deserves can affect the way in which that individual's suffering matters, it
may be that facts about the moral status of the sufferer could also affect the way
in which suffering matters.

Commonsense intuition suggests that moral status can be affect the extent
to which a death matters. Suppose that one can either save the life of a human
stranger who would then live only for another day or save the life of a stray
dog that would then live for another month. Assume for the sake of argument
that, because the person would lose so little good life in dying today rather than
tomorrow, the dog's loss in dying now would be greater. It might still matter
more to save the person—that is, one's moral reason to save the person might be
stronger—not because the person's continuing to live matters more to him or to
others but because the person's higher moral status makes his continuing to live
more important morally.

If it is true that the strength of our moral reason to save an individual's life
can vary with the individual's moral status, it may be that the strength of our
moral reason not to cause an individual to suffer, or to prevent that individual
from suffering, also varies with the individual's moral status. It seems that our
moral reason to prevent an individual from suffering is in general stronger than
our reason to enable that individual to enjoy further benefits. Yet to save an
individual's life is just to enable that individual to have further benefits. It seems,
therefore, that if the strength of our reason to enable an individual to have the
benefits of further life varies with the individual's moral status, the same should
be true of the strength of our reason to prevent that individual from suffering.

There is, however, a significant reason for doubting that the suffering of
animals matters less because their moral status is lower. It derives from the fact
that the lower moral status of animals cannot plausibly be explained by reference to their not being members of the human species. Their lower moral status
must be attributable instead to their lack of certain morally significant intrinsic
properties on which the higher moral status of persons supervenes, such as the

capacities for self-consciousness, rationality, and autonomy. But whatever the intrinsic properties are that distinguish persons morally from animals, there are some members of the human species that lack them. Consider, for example, an orphaned human infant with a genetic condition that both limits its potential for psychological development, so that it can never have psychological capacities beyond those of a day-old infant, and also makes it impossible for the infant to live for more than a few months after birth. It is arguable that this human infant lacks the properties that are the basis of the higher moral status of persons. Even though almost everyone has the intuitive conviction that this infant has a higher moral status than an animal with more highly developed psychological capacities, such as an intelligent and sociable dog, no one, to my knowledge, has given a plausible explanation of the basis of this higher status. Suppose, then, that the moral status of this infant is lower than that of a normal adult person. This would help to explain one claim that I think is true—namely, that our moral reason to save the life of a person who would live only another day would be stronger than our reason to save the life of the infant, even if the infant might live a few more months in complete comfort. Yet it is doubtful that the infant's *suffering* would matter less, so that, apart from the issue of opportunity costs, it would matter more to prevent the person from experiencing a certain degree of physical suffering than to prevent the infant from experiencing the same suffering. But if this cognitively impaired and inevitably short-lived infant would have a moral status no higher than that of an unusually intelligent and sociable dog, the equivalent suffering of the dog should also matter no less because of its lower moral status.

In this section I have argued that suffering is bad in itself and that there is a moral reason to prevent it in any beings that might experience it (with the possible exception of those who allegedly deserve it). I have conceded that in many cases our reason to prevent the suffering of a person may be stronger than our reason to prevent equivalent suffering in an animal—for example, because of opportunity costs, side effects, or special relations. I have considered the possibility that the suffering of animals matters less because of their lower moral status but have suggested that this has an implication that most would be reluctant to accept—namely, that the suffering of an orphaned human infant with psychological capacities and potential no higher than those of a higher nonhuman animal must matter less as well. The conclusion I draw is that there is a strong moral reason to prevent the suffering of animals in the wild when this is possible.

Playing God and the Principle of Nonintervention

In addition to the counterproductivity objection, the appeal to the impersonal value of species, and the claim that animal suffering does not matter, or matters much less, another reason for opposing intervention against predation is that it would be presumptuous for beings as imperfect and fallible as we are to attempt to regulate the natural world in accordance with our own notions of what is good and bad. Some people with religious commitments may object that any attempt to reduce or eliminate predation would be a usurpation of a prerogative that belongs to the deity alone.

This type of objection, which even now is sometimes also advanced against efforts to alleviate human suffering, is quite puzzling. Is the idea that it must be offensive to the deity if our action suggests that we can do a better job of running things than he can? This is reminiscent of the response by the central character in Saki's novel, *The Unbearable Bassington*, to a woman who expresses the wish that she could improve him:

> You're like a relative of mine up in Argyllshire, who spends his time producing improved breeds of sheep and pigs and chickens. So patronizing and irritating to the Almighty, I should think, to go about putting superior finishing touches to Creation.[23]

Yet while the God of the Old Testament is certainly portrayed as abnormally sensitive to criticism and neglect, it is nevertheless curious to suppose that the creator of the universe could be so insecure.

Nor can those who object to our "playing God" seriously suppose that we actually have the ability to thwart the designs of the deity. Indeed, it is one of the burdens of theodicy to explain why the deity does not consistently exercise the capacity to prevent our interference with his arrangements but instead stands by while people cause some terrible harm and only later intervenes by sending them to Hell. One might infer that a person can be guilty of playing God, usurping a divine prerogative that we expect the deity will not exercise, by preventing a crime rather than allowing it to be done and then punishing the offender. Yet theists generally assume that it can be permissible to prevent people from inflicting unjustified suffering on others—even by defensive force, if necessary. But if preventing people from inflicting unjustifiable suffering on others is among our legitimate prerogatives, it seems that merely preventing predators from coming into existence as a means of preventing animal suffering should be among them as well.

If, as many of us believe, there is no deity guiding events, our only options are allowing events to be determined by purposeless natural forces and guiding them ourselves as intelligently and beneficently as we can. The latter is significantly more likely than the former to result in better outcomes overall.

This seems an appropriate response not only to the objection to "playing God" but also to the closely related but more secular "principle of nonintervention" that has largely guided wildlife policy in the United States since the Wilderness Act was passed in 1964.[24] Since then, conservation biologists, ecologists, and environmentalists have generally sought to protect wilderness areas from all forms of encroachment or intervention by human beings. This is unsurprising given that most previous human interventions had been motivated by self-interest and were heedless of any consequences other than benefits the interveners sought

for themselves. And even when human interventions were more benignly motivated, they were sometimes ill-informed or incompetent. Insofar as the opposition to intervention has been a response to this history of damaging disruption, it
will cease to be appropriate once our science enables us to intervene with a high
probability of avoiding unforeseen effects—provided, of course, that our aims
are also morally justified.

It has been argued, however, that there is a more principled basis for nonintervention, which is that interferences with animals in the wild violate their
autonomy or self-determination. In the original edition of his landmark book,
The Case for Animal Rights, published in 1983, Tom Regan wrote:

> The total amount of suffering animals cause one another in the wild is not
> the concern of morally enlightened wildlife management. Being neither
> accountants nor managers of felicity in nature, wildlife managers should
> be principally concerned with *letting animals be*, keeping human predators
> out of their affairs, allowing these "other nations" to carve out their own
> destiny.[25]

A similar passage appears in the new preface to an updated edition of the book
published in 2004:

> Our ruling obligation with regard to wild animals is to *let them be*, an
> obligation grounded in a recognition of their general competence to get
> on with the business of living, a competence that we find among members
> of predator and prey species . . . As a general rule, they do not need help
> from us in the struggle for survival, and we do not fail to discharge our
> duty when we choose not to lend our assistance.[26]

Lori Gruen, who quotes the latter passage with approval, adds this reinforcing
summary: "Paternalism is appropriate in the case of children, but not so in the
case of individuals who are capable of exercising their freedom to live their lives
in their own ways."[27]

Despite my admiration for both these authors, I find their claims about the
autonomy and competence of animals inflated. When Regan says that "members
of predator and prey species . . . do not need help from us in the struggle for survival," he is at least obliquely invoking a familiar Darwinian notion that seems
to have no place in this discussion. It is true that predator and prey *species* will
continue to evolve through the competition for survival, but it is false that *individual* prey can do without our help in *their* struggles for survival. They would
do much better were we to protect them than they do now when we leave them
to deal with predators by themselves. The fact that predators tend to be well fed
when there are prey around, together with the fact that in some species only
about 1 percent of those born survive to adulthood, indicates that the "general

competence" of prey "to get on with the business of living" is less impressive than Regan's comment suggests.

The claims of Regan and Gruen are reminiscent of the claims of those, from John Stuart Mill to Michael Walzer, who have maintained a general opposition to ostensibly benevolent military interventions by arguing that they tend to violate the rights of self-determination of people in the states in which they are carried out.[28] The core of truth in this anti-interventionist position is that, when the internal balance of forces within a single political community has not already been skewed by prior external intervention, it is generally better for a dispute about the terms on which the members of this community will live together to be settled among themselves rather being imposed by others who will not share in the resulting common life. This is so even when the outcome is determined by the superior forces of one side rather than by agreement. For only in this way will the outcome be the product of a genuine process of *self*-determination.

The limitation of this argument, however, is that it fails to apply in situations in which there are two or more distinct communities, or collective "selves," living within the same political boundaries and one seeks to rule, expel, enslave, or exterminate another. When, as in Rwanda in 1994, one group is engaged in genocide, nonintervention is not a matter of "allowing these 'other nations' to carve out their own destiny." (Indeed, in Rwanda the members of one nation were allowed literally to carve up those of another.) Nor could intervening be plausibly described as acting paternalistically toward "individuals who are capable of exercising their freedom to live their lives in their own ways." But conditions in which the members of one human group systematically exploit and kill the members of another are the analogues in human affairs of predation among animals, though the analogy is imperfect because the situation of prey in the wild is generally even more hopeless in the absence of intervention. Prey are seldom able to defend themselves and there is certainly no prospect, as there is in conflicts involving human beings, that predators and prey will, on their own, eventually achieve a modus vivendi that will enable them to live together peacefully in the manner prophesied by Isaiah. All things considered, there seems to be no reason not to prevent the suffering or premature deaths of animal prey on the ground that this would involve a failure of respect for the competence or self-determination either of individual animals or of animal groups.

The "Values of Nature"

It is sometimes suggested that concern about the suffering of animals in the wild betrays a limited, parochial, or perhaps anthropocentric perspective on issues that are appropriately evaluated only from an ecological or environmental point of view. Several years ago I wrote a short piece for the online *Opinionator* column of the *New York Times* in which I argued for the moral desirability of controlling predation with the aim of reducing the suffering of animals.[29] The present chapter is, in effect, a rewritten, significantly expanded descendant of that little article. The online piece elicited quite a bit of commentary, the vast majority of which was highly and often indignantly critical. One comment was from Paul Falkowski, an eminent professor of ecology and evolution at my own university. He wrote that

> it is clear you have either never taken a course in ecology and evolution, or forgot the message. There is this strange thing called a food web—in which organisms are primary producers, eat primary producers, eat the eaters of primary producers—and so on. That is called life. It has NO ethical or moral values. Those are HUMAN values. A wolf or lion kills another animal—the pain and suffering are not ecological issues—the life of the wolf or lion is the issue. If the wolf or lion dies of starvation—then the prey potentially become over populated—like the deer in Princeton. Your values are not the values of nature.[30]

A prominent environmental philosopher, J. Baird Callicott, has made similar claims:

> Pain and pleasure seem to have nothing at all to do with good and evil if our appraisal is taken from the vantage point of ecological biology. . . . The doctrine that life is happier the freer it is from pain and that the happiest life conceivable is one in which there is continuous pleasure uninterrupted by pain is biologically preposterous.[31]

He adds that "if nature as a whole is good, then pain and death are also good."[32] Presumably, this is again "from the vantage point of ecological biology."

Both writers object that those who are concerned about the suffering of animals are wrong to assume that suffering is an ecological issue or that it matters from the perspective of ecological biology. But that complaint reflects an elementary confusion. While there are some philosophers who identify moral facts and properties with natural facts and properties, even they would agree that it would be a mistake to suppose that the question whether there is a moral reason to prevent the suffering of animals is a scientific question that could be answered by consulting theories of ecological biology.[33] Falkowski seems to think that I would do better if I were to put aside *my* values, which are perhaps merely personal or subjective, as well as what he calls human values, and instead consult the "values of nature." But I have no idea what he might mean by that curious phrase. Nor are there "human values" that contrast with nonhuman values.

Falkowski is of course right that whether we have a moral reason to prevent the suffering of animals is not an ecological issue. But that is because no moral issue is an ecological issue. Morality is nonetheless a part of reality. And while only science, including ecological science, can tell us what the consequences of our interventions in the natural world are likely to be, only morality can tell us whether those interventions are, all things considered, good or bad, justified or unjustified.

To suggest, as Callicott does, that the claim that suffering is bad for those who experience it is "biologically preposterous" makes no more sense than to say that it is mathematically preposterous. The claim that suffering is bad is neither biologically sensible nor biologically preposterous, for it is not a claim about biology at all. Nor does biology have anything at all to say about it. Suffering is of course a biological phenomenon and it occurs in the natural world. But the *badness* of suffering is not a biological phenomenon. It is nevertheless neither an illusion nor a projection; it too is a part of reality, just not a part that is accessible to the investigative tools of natural science.

Some ecologists have begun to challenge the venerable principle of nonintervention in nature by appealing to what they consider to be a higher value: the preservation of the "health" of ecosystems. They argue that we should regard a wilderness area as "a place where concern for ecosystem health is paramount, even if human action is required to maintain it."[34] In a recent op-ed column in the *New York Times*, three ecologists cite the example of a remote island in Lake Superior on which the number of wolves is dwindling, allowing for an ecologically disruptive surge in the moose population. The shrinkage of the wolf population is not the result of starvation but of genetic degeneration from inbreeding. In the past, the wolf population was replenished and diversified when wolves crossed to the island on temporary bridges of ice, but with global warming those bridges hardly ever form anymore. Without human intervention, wolves could disappear from the island. Arguing in favor of such intervention, the writers cite

> one of the most important findings in conservation science: that a healthy ecosystem depends critically on the presence of top predators . . . when large herbivores . . . are present. Without top predators, prey tend to become overabundant and decimate plants and trees that many species of birds, mammals, and insects depend on. Top predators maintain the diversity of rare plants that would otherwise be eaten, and rare insects that depend on those plants. The loss of top predators may disturb the nutrient cycling of entire ecosystems. In addition, predators improve the health of prey populations by weeding out the weakest individuals.[35]

The authors conclude by observing that if the health of the island's ecosystem is preserved through the reintroduction of a substantial population of predators, the island will remain a place "where we can witness beauty while reflecting on how to preserve it."[36]

According to these writers, we face a dilemma. While in general they support the principle of nonintervention, they claim that in this case it conflicts with the value of "ecosystem health." One of these guiding values must yield in this case, and they argue that it should be the principle of nonintervention. But the sufferings and premature deaths of the moose are not mentioned. They do not appear to be regarded as relevant considerations. Yet while it seems obvious that suffering and premature death are bad for those to whom they happen, it is much less clear that the "health" of an ecosystem has significant value independently of the well-being of its sentient inhabitants. Many philosophers, for example, are "welfarists" who believe that only the welfare of sentient beings matters.

Imagine a small island with an ideally healthy ecosystem. No one had ever been to this island until a person arrived and somehow loaded all the sentient beings, predators and prey alike, into his ark and transported them to another environment into which they were integrated without any compromise of the health of that environment's ecosystem. Suppose that no person will ever again go to the island. But the removal of the animals eventually fatally disrupted the processes of nutrient cycling on the island, and the health of the ecosystem began a decline that resulted eventually in its destruction, in that all but the most rudimentary forms life on the island disappeared. None of this was bad for any sentient being. The animals that were removed, along with their descendants, flourished in their new environment at least as well they would have on the island, and no person was or ever will be prevented by this one intervention from witnessing the beauty of a healthy ecosystem on the island.

Let us grant that the welfarists are wrong and that, even though what has happened to the island is not worse for any sentient being that will ever live, it is nevertheless impersonally bad, in that the island ceased to have a flourishing eco-system and became barren and lifeless instead. Even so, it does not seem terribly bad. It is a comparatively minor change for the worse. Suppose that shortly after the animals had been removed, a government learned what had been done. This government had a fixed set of resources that it could have used either to return the animals to the island, thereby preventing the destruction of its ecosystem, or to produce and distribute a medicine that would prevent thousands of patients from experiencing brief but intense suffering during minor surgical procedures. It decided to use the resources in the second way. It does not seem a mere human prejudice to suppose that this was the better choice.

Consider again the actual island in Lake Superior from which wolves may vanish. Some ecologists, as I mentioned, propose to transport wolves to the island, thereby ensuring that the cycle of predation continues, as a means of preserving the health of the island's ecosystem. Yet the cycle of predation they wish to preserve and prolong indefinitely is, for the prey, a cycle of fear, suffer-ing, and violent death. This is an essential element of what they call "health." In this actual case, as they point out, the alternative to reintroducing a substan-tial wolf population may be only to allow overpopulation among the moose, which would result in greater suffering as a result of premature but protracted deaths from starvation and disease. That is, the counterproductivity objection may apply to the option of *not* sustaining the cycle of predation. But suppose there were another alternative: intervention to control the size of the moose population through nonviolent means. It will eventually become possible, as I noted earlier, to use chemical means of sterilization to regulate the size of herbivore populations in the wild. If the counterproductivity problem could be solved in this way, by stabilizing the moose population and thus preserving the harmony of the ecosystem as a whole without increasing the wolf population, it seems that the only advantage of maintaining predation on the island would be that it might be less costly. But if the means of controlled sterilization were available, it is unlikely that the difference in cost could justify the perpetuation of avoidable suffering and premature death over indefinitely many generations of moose. If we were to take the suffering and premature deaths of animals more seriously than we do, it would probably not take long to develop effective chemical means of sterilization and techniques for administering them in a discriminating and precisely calibrated way to regulate the size of herbivore populations.

Conclusion

I have argued that the prevention of suffering in animals matters—arguably almost as much as the prevention of suffering in human beings does. Some people may concede this, and also concede the weakness of the objections to the reduction or elimination of predation I have reviewed, but nevertheless find it pointless to press the case for intervening against predation. This is not just because they anticipate that human beings will never become motivated to undertake so ambitious a project merely for the sake of animals, but also because they believe that there will always be more serious problems that will have a higher moral priority, such as the relief of poverty, the prevention of crime, the prevention of war, the mitigation of threats to human survival, and so on. Some argue that it would be wrong to devote our efforts and resources to the problem of predation when more important problems remain unresolved.

When this claim is pressed in public discussions, it is often made defensively and hypocritically by people who are not among those who are working seriously to address the moral problems cited. This is of course merely ad hominem and does not address the concern of those who make the claim without hypocrisy. There are, however, at least three responses to the genuine concern about moral priority.

Perhaps the most important of these is that the many problems that might be cited as more important than preventing the suffering that predation causes to animals are so vast and demanding that it is unlikely that any particular individual is morally required to devote significant time, effort, and resources to any one of them in particular. For any individual, making significant sacrifices to address any of these problems is likely to be supererogatory. When that is the case, it cannot be *wrong* to devote one's efforts to preventing the suffering of animals even when it would be *better* if one were to devote one's time and effort to a more important problem instead.[37]

Second, even if the extent to which the suffering of animals matters morally is discounted for the lower moral status of animals, the suffering of animals in the wild may still be one of the more important moral problems simply because the number of animals that suffer and die from predation is so vast. The number of animals in the world exceeds the number of human beings by many orders of magnitude.

Of course, predation is not the only cause of suffering or premature death in animals. Animals suffer and die from disease, parasites, malnutrition and starvation, dehydration, freezing, and so on. But this just means that we have moral reason to try to prevent animals from suffering and dying from these causes as well, when we can do so at reasonable cost and without neglecting other duties.

Finally, it may well be that any substantial efforts to mitigate the suffering of animals in the wild through the control of predation must await advancements in both our scientific and moral capacities. At present it does seem more important to concentrate on eliminating various major sources of human misery and premature death. We can, moreover, be more confident of our potential effectiveness in alleviating suffering and preventing premature death through, for example, the reduction and eventual elimination of human poverty than we can be in our ability to reduce the incidence of predation without causing unforeseen side effects. But even now there are cases, such as that of the island in Lake Superior, in which decisions must be made that will affect the level of predation in a certain area. In these cases, there is a strong moral reason to do what will diminish or eliminate predation rather than what will sustain or increase it.[38]

Notes

1. Arthur Schopenhauer, *Essays and Aphorisms* (London: Penguin, 1970), p. 42.
2. John Stuart Mill, *Three Essays on Religion* (London: Longmans, Green, Reader, and Dyer, 1875), pp. 58–59.
3. Isaiah 11:6–7.
4. Jeff McMahan, "Eating Animals the Nice Way," *Daedalus* (Winter 2008): 66–76, and "The Comparative Badness of Suffering and Death for Animals," in Tatjana Višak and Robert Garner, eds., *The Ethics of Killing Animals* (Oxford: Oxford University Press, forthcoming).
5. The seminal and still unsurpassed work in this area is Derek Parfit's *Reasons and Persons* (Oxford: Oxford University Press, 1986 reprint), pt. 4.
6. http://www.youtube.com/watch?v=LU8DDYz68kM. Last viewed December 7, 2013.
7. Alison Hills, "Utilitarianism, Contractualism, and Demandingness," *Philosophical Quarterly* 60 (2010): 225–242, p. 231.
8. Lori Gruen, *Ethics and Animals: An Introduction* (New York: Cambridge University Press, 2011), p. 179.
9. Ibid., p. 183.

10. Ibid., p. 181.
11. See McMahan, "The Comparative Badness of Suffering and Death for Animals."
12. Gruen, *Ethics and Animals*, pp. 184 and 187.
13. For a defense of the claim that there is a universally applicable reason to prevent suffering, no matter whose it is, see Thomas Nagel, *The View From Nowhere* (New York: Oxford University Press, 1986), pp. 156–162. I take no position here on whether anyone can deserve to suffer.
14. Martha C. Nussbaum, *Frontiers of Justice: Disability, Nationality, Species Membership* (Cambridge, MA: Belknap Press, 2006), p. 379. Nussbaum is among the few philosophers who have suggested that there is a moral reason to intervene against predation. The other two of whom I am aware are Eric Rakowski in *Equal Justice* (Oxford: Clarendon Press, 1991), pp. 363–367, and Tyler Cowen in "Policing Nature," *Environmental Ethics* (Summer 2003): 169–182. The latter can be found in manuscript form on his website at http://www.gmu.edu/centers/publicchoice/faculty%20pages/Tyler/police.pdf.
15. Compare Martha Nussbaum's claim that "any nonviolent method of population control (for example, by sterilization) is to be preferred to a violent method." Nussbaum, *Frontiers of Justice*, p. 380.
16. Douglas Quenqua, "New Strides in Spaying and Neutering," *New York Times*, December 2, 2013; Lisa W. Foderaro, "A Kinder, Gentler Way to Thin the Deer Herd," *New York Times*, July 6, 2013.
17. Ronald Dworkin, *Life's Dominion* (New York: Alfred A. Knopf, 1993), p. 75.
18. Ibid. Dworkin's claims are explicitly about what "we" believe or what "people" believe. They are not necessarily endorsements of the beliefs that he claims people have.
19. For a strong challenge to the concept of impersonal value, see Richard Kraut, *Against Absolute Goodness* (New York: Oxford University Press, 2011).
20. For elucidation and defense, see McMahan, "The Comparative Badness of Suffering and Death for Animals."
21. Nagel, *The View From Nowhere*, p. 161.
22. Peter Singer, *Animal Liberation*, rev. ed. (New York: Avon Books, 1990), p. 17.
23. Saki (H. H. Munro), *The Unbearable Bassington* (London: Bodley Head, 1929), p. 74.
24. John A. Vucetich, Michael P. Nelson, and Rolf O. Peterson, "Predator and Prey, a Delicate Dance," *New York Times*, May 9, 2013. There have, however, been some interventions that have been harmful to animals, such as the extermination of animals not considered to be native and the reintroduction of predators. See Jo-Ann Shelton, "Killing Animals that Don't Fit In: Moral Dimensions of Habitat Restoration," *Between the Species* 13/4 (2004): 1–21; and Oscar Horta, "The Ethics of the Ecology of Fear against the Nonspeciesist Paradigm: A Shift in the Aims of Intervention in Nature," *Between the Species* 13/10 (2010): 163–187.
25. Tom Regan, *The Case for Animal Rights* (London: Routledge and Kegan Paul, 1983), p. 357.
26. Tom Regan, *The Case for Animal Rights* (Berkeley: University of California Press, 2004), p. xxxvii.
27. Gruen, *Ethics and Animals*, p. 182.
28. John Stuart Mill, "A Few Words on Non-Intervention," *The Collected Works of John Stuart Mill*, vol. 21 (1825), accessible online at http://oll.libertyfund.org/?option=com_staticxt&staticfile=show.php%3Ftitle=255&chapter=21666&layout=html&Itemid=27; and Michael Walzer, *Just and Unjust Wars* (New York: Basic Books, 1977), chap. 6.
29. Jeff McMahan, "The Meat Eaters," *Opinionator* (blog), *New York Times*, September 19, 2010, accessible at http://opinionator.blogs.nytimes.com/2010/09/19/the-meat-eaters/#more-61873.
30. Ibid., comments section.

31. J. Baird Callicott, "Animal Liberation: A Triangular Affair," in Robert Elliott, ed., *Environmental Ethics* (New York: Oxford University Press, 1995): 29–59, pp. 52–53 and 54.

32. Ibid.

33. Prominent moral naturalists include Richard Boyd, Philippa Foot, and Peter Railton.

34. Vucetich, Nelson, and Peterson, "Predator and Prey."

35. Ibid.

36. Ibid.

37. For further argument, see Jeff McMahan, "Doing Good and Doing the Best," forthcoming in a book on philanthropy edited by Jonathan Dancy, John Deigh, and Paul Woodruff.

38. In preparing this substantially revised and expanded version of my original piece in the *Opinionator*, cited in note 29, I have greatly benefited from insightful written comments by Andrew Chignell, Terence Cuneo, Catia Faria, Matthew Halteman, Oscar Horta, and Ezekiel Paez.

INDEX

taste 107, 155; and artificial ingredients 263–4, 265; and justification for harm 98–9
tolerance, of meat eating 208–9; *see also* accommodation
transportation: and animal treatment 26; and sustainability 13, 177, 234–6
Twilight Zone Objection 36

unrestrained omnivorism 134
utilitarianism 271

value: impersonal 276–8; symbolic 24–34, 195–7
veganism 8–9, 154; and agrarianism 69–70; and complicity 80–5; and contextualism 50–1; and disadvantaged groups 47; and gender 39–45; and harm footprint 163–6, 168–70, 172–3, 175, 177; and health 45–6, 92–3, 97–8,

105–6; limits to 86–8; and moral malaises 130–1, 134–5, 137, 140, 142; and non-idealism 111–12, 120–1; objections to 100; and optimistic purchasing 195; and predation 269; wrongness of suffering 73–80
vegetarianism 6, 12–13, 14, 21, 182, 220, 244, 272; and accommodation 215, 223–29; and complicity 209; and health 45–6; and identity 244–5; and moral malaises 130–1, 134–5, 137, 140, 142; and non-idealism 109, 119; and right to life 22–3, 27, 29–30, 33–4, 36, 151–2

Warfield, Ted 24
weakness of will 121, 130, 209, 229; *see also* failure
Winne, Mark 16n, 239
World Health Organization 260
Wyckoff, Jason 41

Made in the USA
Monee, IL
08 January 2025

76439294R00171